In Search of Authenticity

D1206129

In Search of Authenticity

THE FORMATION OF
FOLKLORE STUDIES

Regina Bendix

THE UNIVERSITY OF WISCONSIN PRESS

The University of Wisconsin Press
2537 Daniels Street
Madison, Wisconsin 53718

3 Henrietta Street
London WC2E 8LU, England

1   2   3   4   5

Printed in the United States of America

Library of Congress Cataloging-in-Publication Data
Bendix, Regina.
In search of authenticity: the formation of folklore studies / Regina Bendix.
318 pp.   cm.
Includes bibliographical references and index.
ISBN 0-299-15540-4 (cloth: alk. paper).
ISBN 0-299-15544-7 (paper: alk. paper).
1. Folklore—United States—History.   2. Folklore—Philosophy.
3. Folklore—Germany—History.   4. Authenticity (Philosophy)   I. Title.
GR48.B45   1997
398'.0973—dc21   97-11607

To
Claire Leah and Helen Miriam

Contents

Contents

Acknowledgments

In the last weeks of writing up a big project I usually feel a certain amount of elation—the proverbial light at the end of the tunnel is in sight. With authenticity, things have been different. It is so painfully obvious that a study on authenticity cannot ever be finished, nor will it stop the violent acts committed in the name of some kind of authenticity—religious, ethnic, national—occurring daily on this planet and often legitimated by snippets from the intellectual history that I am presenting here. I dedicate this book to my daughters, Claire Leah and Helen Miriam, in the hope that they will grow up to appreciate the beauty and complexity of living and be spared the turmoils of seeking transcendent authenticities.

My husband, John Bendix, has participated in this venture before I ever started researching it. While I thank him, as ever, for his enthusiastic support, his intellectual generosity, and his help in editing my prose, I am most grateful for the unflagging optimism he has been able to muster even after a decade and a half of living with me. My late father-in-law, Reinhard Bendix, let me know that he felt I was "on to something" and initially pointed me to the right kinds of books and ideas to frame my study, and my mother-in-law, Jane Bendix, has sent me clippings on authenticity from her travels for years. My brother Rudolf Flückiger has regaled me with tongue-in-cheek letters on authenticity, treating every topic imaginable from literature to medicine, and finding humor in what for many people is such a deadly serious concern.

I am particularly grateful for the long-term encouragement I have received in this project as in many others from Alan Dundes. He as well as Roger Abrahams, Don Brenneis, James Dow, Barbara Kirshenblatt-Gimblett, and George Stocking have read and commented on the entire manuscript and given me their widely diverse insights and suggestions; I hope that the study reflects their generous assistance. Roger has also indulged my aversion to the telephone, and via letter, e-mail, and conversation he has provided me with the most extensive tutorial in American folkloristics and history that anyone could wish for. I have benefitted from comments on parts of this book by Richard Bauman, Michael Bell, Matti Bunzl, Paul Hanson, Doris Kaufmann, Yanna Lambrinidou, Joanne Mulcahy, Kirin Narayan, Martha Norkunas, Ron Radano, Greggory Schrempp, and Rosemary Lévy Zumwalt. Without the editorial assistance of Rosalie Robertson and her staff at the University of Wisconsin Press, as well as Bob Mirandon's copyediting, this book would have been longer and more cumbersome to read.

I have worked on authenticity in many places and incurred debts along the way. In 1989 I taught a seminar on the subject at UC Berkeley, and my students Austin Brewin, Sandy Cate, Karen Greene, Maria Massolo, Levent Soysal, and a helpful auditor, Peter Tokofsky, were an excellent sounding board for ideas on authenticity. A first talk on authenticity was delivered at the University of Wisconsin in Madison in 1991; three more in 1992, one at the University of Basel, another at the American Anthropological Association's meetings in San Francisco, and a third at the Institute for Advanced Study in Princeton; in 1995 yet another was presented at the History of the Human Sciences Workshop at the University of Chicago. Christine Burckhardt-Seebass arranged for an academic home during the year of research in Basel, where Rosemarie Anzengruber, Ernst Huber, Roland Inauen, Sibylle Obrecht, Nicholas Schaffner, and Beatrice Tobler shared conversations and ideas, coffee, library resources, and the Xerox machine. At the Institute for Advanced Studies in Princeton during 1992–93 Elliott Shore and his library staff, in particular Marcia Tucker and Faridah Kassim, outdistanced all the wonderful library support I had already enjoyed in Portland, Oregon, Berkeley, and Basel. At the Institute, I benefitted from conversations with Leora Ausländer, Albert and Sarah Hirschmann, Walter Jackson, Doris Kaufmann, Harold Mah, Shawn Marmon, Joan Scott, and George Stocking, as well as from the lively general discussion following presentation of my paper during the year's lecture series presided over by Clifford Geertz. Lucille Allson and Ruthie Foster smoothed the way on administrative and technical matters. Our whole family appreciated living and working in Princeton among academics from all kinds of disciplines; it is hard to imagine another environment where the kindergarten set's favorite new word is "googolplex." My daughter Claire's year would have been a dull one, indeed, if not for the presence of Max and Hanna Korevaar and their family's ever-open door.

In our new home, Philadelphia, finally, my colleagues and students have given me support and encouragement to finish up with the A-word.

Both Roger Abrahams and John Roberts asked me to speak to their classes on the subject. Dan Ben-Amos invited me to present a talk at a session of the University of Pennsylvania's culture studies seminar in 1994, and Yanna Lambrinidou has helped with research queries and manuscript preparation. During my first years of working at Penn, Janet Theophano has become the greatest source of both intellectual and personal support, and I thank her for being there in person and on e-mail, as I thank Lee Haring, Barbro Klein, Molly Lee, Sabina Magliocco, Margaret Mills, Joanne Mulcahy, Kirin Narayan, Martha Norkunas, Dorry Noyes, Bob St. George, Riki Saltzman, Mary Beth Stein, and Rosemary Zumwalt, who all in one way or another have been present to communicate about work and life.

Thanks also go to all those who have responded to my written and oral inquiries. Hermann Bausinger, Gottfried Korff, Konrad Köstlin, and Silke Göttsch all clarified matters regarding their own work. Burkhard Pöttler has been particularly helpful with materials relating to Austrian folklorists, as has Helmut Eberhard. Michael Bell very graciously shared source material and drafts of his work. Ron Radano's writings and his extensive comments on my early chapters were especially helpful, and Peter Seitel took the time to respond to an inquiry as well.

I have been very fortunate to receive financial support from numerous sources. The year in Basel was supported by a postdoctoral fellowship of the Schweizerische Geisteswissenschaftliche Gesellschaft. Subsequently, I received a John Simon Guggenheim Memorial Foundation Fellowship, and funds from the National Endowment for the Humanities supported my year as a fellow in the School of Social Sciences at the Institute for Advanced Study in Princeton. For the summer of 1994, finally, I received a Faculty Summer Research Stipend from the Trustees Council of Penn Women. My thanks go to all of these donors for supporting research and writing, living, and, most important to me, quality child care at a number of excellent Montessori preschool programs and at home where Flora Leah Jones has been nanny, teacher, helper, and playmate for all of us for a good part of the last few years.

In Search of Authenticity
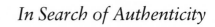

Introduction

There are certain terms that have a peculiar property. Ostensibly, they mark off specific concepts that lay claim to a rigorously objective validity. In practice, they label vague terrains of thought that shift or narrow or widen with the point of view of whoso makes use of them, embracing within their gamut of significances conceptions that not only do not harmonize but are in part contradictory.

—Edward Sapir (1951 [1924]:308)

[Authenticity] is a reflexive term; its nature is to be deceptive about its nature.

—Carl Dahlhaus (1967:57)

Born originals, how comes it to pass that we die copies?

—Edward Young (cited after Boni 1982:1)

As we approach the year 2000, the world is saturated by things and experiences advertising their authenticity. Dwellings are furnished with certified antiques and clothes made of genuine fabrics. We can dine in restaurants proclaiming the purest culinary heritage or eat canned goods labeled "authentic." Classical concerts distinguish themselves with original instrumentation, while rock idols struggle to maintain the legacy of raw sound and experience. As tourists, we can choose between a cruise to the last real headhunters, a stroll through the back alleys of famous places in search of the hidden authenticities of everyday life, and the opportunity to witness authentic belief experiences among parishioners in Harlem's churches. For all of our senses and all of our experiential cravings, we have created a market of identifiable authenticities.[1]

Recent decades have seen an interest, if not delight, in imitation as well. Museums—traditionally the locus for exhibiting the authentic—have mounted special exhibits of the fake.[2] Popular phenomena, such as Elvis look-alike contests and Karaoke singing, attest to a fascination with achieving the perfect copy, undermining the original in the very effort of striving to be just like it. By submitting to the same processes of repre-

3

sentation and commodification those things that were proclaimed to be opposites, the genuine and the spurious are converging, their identities separable only by their narratives (Baudrillard 1994:9). The movie *The Adventures of Priscilla, Queen of the Desert* (1994) shows drag queens in the Australian outback performing as and lip-synching the female lead singers of the Swedish band ABBA. In doing so, they realize Clifford Geertz's observation, "it is the copying that originates" (Geertz 1986:380).

Until recent years the commodification of the authentic so evident in present-day advertising remained outside the orbit of academic disciplines devoted to aspects of culture. Such disciplines originated at the same time as the Western world transformed itself from feudal to democratic, capitalistically driven states. The university was conceptualized as a place where the components of an ideal culture were researched and inculcated into the new economic and political power—the bourgeoisie (Readings 1996:62–88). Authenticity was a core ingredient of this idealistic project. In formulating the contours of this ideal culture, what lay outside its boundaries had to be inauthentic. At best, the inauthentic held the status of being unworthy of scholarly attention; at worst, it was decried as an agent spoiling or harming the carefully cultivated, noble ideal. The canons of the cultural disciplines, such as literary and language studies, music, art history, and ethnology, thus originated with a strong commitment to understand, restore, and maintain the genuine.

During the past few decades, however, these same fields have increasingly realized the problems inherent in their ideals. Art history has begun to scrutinize its canon and, in dialogue with other fields, is paying attention to the ideologies informing exhibition.[3] Music has come to question its systems of exclusion and authentification in music history and performance.[4] Linguistics remembers the commitment to original language in its foundational scholarship and considers the original's resonance in the current politics of language around the globe.[5] In anthropology, folklore, and history, discoveries of invented traditions, fraudulent tribes, and nationalistic imaginations undermined notions of cultural authenticity while fueling studies devoted to such politics of culture.

To reconcile this tension, scholars have begun to study their own cultures of inquiry, deconstructing the ways their disciplinary subject was constituted historically and examining the mechanisms and strategies through which authoritative knowledge is produced. Not least as a result of the problems gradually surrounding its central concept—culture—anthropology has developed an unusually varied historiography of its field. The project of deconstructing ethnography as idea and method, initiated by Rabinow (1977) and launched fully through the essays assembled in Clifford and Marcus (1986), has profoundly marked American cultural anthropology. George Stocking, through his own research and as editor of the *History of Anthropology*, has provided an unprecedented view into the ways of anthropological knowledge-making (e.g., Stocking 1968; Stocking, ed., 1983, 1985, 1986). The current growth of the history and sociology of science as a discipline of its own is indicative of knowledge-makers' need to develop a sense of the changing nature and legitimation of fields of learning.

This study contributes to such efforts, using folklore studies as one specific example within the burgeoning inquiries that contribute to the study of culture. Using a comparative approach, I examine this field as it evolved in German-speaking Europe and the United States. German *Volkskunde* is arguably the oldest version of folklore studies, while American folkloristics reached disciplinary coherence only in the middle of the twentieth century. Early American institutions of higher learning also modeled themselves to an extent on the German pattern. A number of important individuals within folklore and other fields built intellectual bridges to, or articulated clear departures from, Germanic intellectual practice in the formative stages of their fields. The differences and continuities regarding authenticity between the two cases are instructive, for despite different cultural and chronological contexts, the notion of authenticity legitimated folklore as a discipline in both countries.

Folklore's history and current predicament are revealing beyond disciplinary boundaries. Folklore's broad subject defies definition, but it has continually attracted attention from the entire spectrum of cultural disciplines that are implicated in the very interdisciplinary structure of the field.[6] Despite the field's heterogeneity, the effort to invoke disciplinary contours has been a constant—necessitated in part because clearly defined disciplines are institutionally privileged. This study details why and how facets of culture were isolated and reined in to constitute a disciplinary subject—a process that occurs in all fields claiming parts of culture as their core, from early anthropology and philology to the present plethora of area and ethnic studies. Authenticity, I argue, was variously used as an agent to define this subject, differentiate it from other cultural manifestations, develop methods of analysis, critique competing theories, or create new paradigms. Cultural scholarship and inquiry, furthermore, fueled societal interest in cultural fragments and cultural wholes, becoming one force in the "artifactualization" of facets of culture (Stewart 1991a). In doing so, scholarship prepared the way for the vibrant market and politics in commodified cultural authenticities, which, in turn, are becoming the new disciplinary subject. Dismantling the role of authenticity in this process explains the emergence during recent years of reflexivity in the scholarly habitus.

More than half a century ago Walter Benjamin characterized the contingent, elusive nature of authenticity through an analysis of art in the age of mechanical reproduction: "Precisely because authenticity cannot be reproduced, the arrival of certain techniques of reproduction . . . has provided the means to differentiate levels of authenticity" (1963:52, n. 3). Benjamin located art before mechanical reproduction in the realm of cult, irresistible to worshippers through its aura—the appearance of an inaccessible remoteness brought into material proximity. Reproduction reduces aura, and in turn such "secularization affords authenticity the place previously held by cult value" (1963:53, n. 8).

As secularization reduced the aura and cult status of art, so, too, did knowledge lose its divine status since knowledge was increasingly made by reason and empirical proof and was taught to ever-wider circles of learners. To maintain the linkage to divinity, authenticity in ever-changing guises became at once the goal and cement of cultural knowledge—the origin and essence of being human.

Yet until recent years the word authenticity and the role that the term has played largely escaped critical scrutiny, with the notable exception of Lionel Trilling's *Sincerity and Authenticity* (1972).[7] Fields such as ethnology and anthropology, philology, and disciplines devoted to national literatures and cultural histories emerged and evolved concurrently with political and economic interests in cultural, ethnic, and racial traits, occasioned by Western exploration, by the encounter with heretofore unknown peoples, and by the subsequent desire to colonize them. The rhetoric of authenticity permeated and at times intertwined disciplinary and political constructions. It is the recognition of this entanglement that has made reflexive scholarship of the present so excessively self-aware that disciplinary continuity today is either jeopardized or seems feasible only with ironic distance.

The histories presented in the following seven chapters will not liberate anyone from the burden of reflexivity. But by laying bare the intertwining of moral and practical dimensions in the uses of authenticity in German *Volkskunde* and American folkloristics, I intend to affirm the responsibility and accountability that scholarship entails. George Stocking observed that anthropology as a system of inquiry was "itself constrained— some might say systematically structured—by the ongoing and cumulative historical experience of encounters and comprehensions between Europeans and 'others.'" His history of anthropology thus encompasses the disciplinary accomplishments "against the backdrop of historical experience and cultural assumption that has provoked and constrained it, and which it in turn has conditioned" (1983:5–6). A focus on the longing for authenticity filtered through folklore's history demonstrates the contribution of scholarship to the "authored nature of society and of ourselves within it" (Köstlin 1995:274). Recognizing the mutual authoring of cultural and scholarly processes is not an absolution from continuing to contribute to such authoring. If this work assists in removing authenticity—in particular, its deceptive promises of transcendence—from the vocabulary of the emerging global script, its major purpose has been served.

The search for authenticity is fundamentally an emotional and moral quest. But this experiential dimension does not provide lasting satisfaction, and authenticity needs to be augmented with pragmatic and evaluative dimensions. Declaring something authentic legitimated the subject that was declared authentic, and the declaration in turn can legitimate the authenticator, though here such concerns as social standing, education, and the ability to promote one's views also play a role. Processes of authentication bring about material representations by elevating the authenticated into the category of the noteworthy. In the last decades of the twentieth century this process has accelerated exponentially, and so much has been declared authentic that the scarcity value is evaporating: once tomato sauce carries the label "authentic," the designation loses its special significance. The question of internalized authenticity—the authentic human experience, the exuberant search for the "soul of the people," as Herder called it—is a much more complex temptation, an attractive, troubling series of attempts to pinpoint the ineffable.

Folklore has long served as a vehicle in the search for the authentic, satisfying a longing for an escape from modernity. The ideal folk community, envisioned as pure and free from civilization's evils, was a metaphor for everything that was not modern. Equally relevant is folklore's linkage to politics, where authenticity bestows a legitimating sheen, with political change linked to modernity, affirmatively in revolutions, negatively in counterrevolutions. The most powerful modern political movement, nationalism, builds on the essentialist notions inherent in authenticity, and folklore in the guise of native cultural discovery and rediscovery has continually served nationalist movements since the Romantic era.

European nationalism was part of the effort to cast off monarchical government and establish democratic institutions. Yet the notion of national uniqueness harbors a conservative ethos of the past. Because of the insistence on national purity or authenticity inherent in the idea of a unique nation, the notion of authenticity ultimately undermines the liberating and humanitarian tendencies from which it grew. The universalist aspirations implicit in casting out the old order are contradicted by the particularist emphasis that each nation constructs to distinguish itself from all other nations. In emphasizing the authentic, the revolutionary can turn reactionary, a process all too vividly played out in global political movements of the late twentieth century.

The quest for authenticity is a peculiar longing, at once modern and antimodern. It is oriented toward the recovery of an essence whose loss has been realized only through modernity, and whose recovery is feasible only through methods and sentiments created in modernity. As such, it can be understood within the framework of reflexive modernization (Beck, Giddens, and Lash 1994). Coming to terms with the constructed and contingent, if not deceptive, nature of authenticity is the result of cognitive reflexivity; living in a capitalistically driven, mass-mediated world means to be surrounded by the mimetic products and enactments of aesthetic reflexivity (Lash 1994:135–43).[8] The continued craving for experiences of unmediated genuineness seeks to cut through what Rousseau called "the wound of reflection," a reaction to modernization's demythologization, detraditionalization, and disenchantment.

In the discipline of folklore the idea of authenticity pervades the central terms and the canon of the field. It has contributed a vocabulary that, as the following chapters will demonstrate, has been of amazing durability despite changing theoretical paradigms. The authenticating claim through its subject matter was also a means through which folklorists have staked institutional claims.

The transformation from felt or experienced authenticity to its textual or material representation harbors a basic paradox. Once a cultural good has been declared authentic, the demand for it rises, and it acquires a market value. Unlike an authentic van Gogh, folklore can be endlessly replicated and imitated—any member of the "folk" should be equipped with the skill and spirit to produce some lore. Individuals all over the globe have been sufficiently savvy to alienate themselves far enough from their traditions to market them.

Indeed, alienation itself is a notion alien to anyone not interested in thinking of cultural productions in the dichotomous terms that "authentic" and "spurious" imply. To scholars and ideologues engaged in commenting on culture, however, efforts to promote and market folklore invariably lead to a perceived loss of authenticity, because students of culture until recent years have considered ideological and market forces as outside agents that spoil folklore's authenticity. The transformations of the marketplace also weaken the stranglehold such students have as authenticators of cultural production.

Declaring a particular form of expressive culture as dead or dying limits the number of authentic items, but it promotes the search for not yet discovered and hence authentic folklore. In the mocking words of a German folklorist, it is best not to use the prefix "folk" at all, because as soon as something is presented as genuine folksong or genuine folk architecture, it loses its authenticity (Bausinger 1971:203). Baudrillard, speaking more polemically, argued that "in order for ethnology to live, its object must die, by dying, the object takes its revenge for being 'discovered' and with its death defies the science that wants to grasp it" (1994:7). The present study argues that it is not the object that must die—cultures do not die, at best they change, along with those who live in them and thus constitute them. What must change for cultural fields is how workers in those fields conceptualize the object. Removing authenticity and its allied vocabulary is one useful step toward conceptualizing the study of culture in the age of transculturation.

The notion of authenticity implies the existence of its opposite, the fake, and this dichotomous construct is at the heart of what makes authenticity problematic.[9] In religious discourse, identifying something as essential to a particular faith "serves to exclude other concepts, practices, even entire branches of [this religion] as inessential or even illegitimate" (J. Cohen 1988:136). Similarly, identifying some cultural expressions or artifacts as authentic, genuine, trustworthy, or legitimate simultaneously implies that other manifestations are fake, spurious, and even illegitimate. Disciplinary practice has "nostalgize[d] the homogeneous" (Kapchan 1993:307) and decried "bastard traditions," thus continually upholding the fallacy that cultural purity rather than hybridity are the norm. It is no wonder, then, that the idea of cultural authenticity has become such convenient fodder for supporting some positions in the political debates on race, ethnicity, gender, and multiculturalism.

Considering how much effort students of expressive culture have wasted with arbitrarily separating the wheat from the chaff, with delineating what is "bona fide" or "legitimate subject matter for the field," and with crusades against fakelore or folklorismus, it seems necessary to document just how empty and at times dangerous the quest for authenticity within and outside folklore ultimately has been.

Behind the assiduous documentation and defense of the authentic lies an unarticulated anxiety of losing the subject. Cultural scholarship in the late twentieth century is plagued by its own anxieties. The nature and place of higher learning is surreptitiously transforming. Modern universities were founded as a part of the project of nation-building. Their role was to teach and research knowledge that would link enlightened individuals in search of self-knowledge to their national cultures. "The German Idealists thought we could find ourselves as an ethnic culture" (Readings 1996:53), with humanistic scholarship at once interpreting and shaping a cultural canon for the national polity. In the late twentieth century the idea of homogeneous national culture confronts the reality of multicultural demographics—a reality acknowledged not least by movements within cultural scholarship. Postcolonial and feminist criticism coupled to deconstructionism have exposed the ideologies of disciplines and cultural canons and brought about a sense of lost authority and disciplinary fragmentation.

Simultaneously, "transnational capitalism has eroded the meaning of culture" (Readings 1996:119), both in the sense of civic (or "bourgeois" or "high") culture and in the sense of ethnographically documented diversity. Culture has become commodity, as has knowledge itself, and an increasingly corporate (rather than communitarian) university is supplanting the hollowed idea of a national or civic culture with the idea of "excellence." Once the language of production enters academia, Marx's dictum "All that is solid melts into air" applies to the institutional structures from which disciplines have drawn their legitimation. Cultural scholarship thus finds itself doubly challenged. Various reflexive moves bring with them the need to examine and understand disciplinary ideology, which is of necessity a divisive undertaking. At the same time, all knowledge-makers are cornered into convincing administrations of the excellence of their intellectual product.

In this unfolding demand to newly articulate the place and nature of cultural disciplines in terms of "excellence" within a market of knowledge, historiography plays an indispensable role. Historiography focuses on the role and goals of fields of learning, on individual researchers, on the discursive practices employed to achieve such goals, and on the interrelationship between learning and the larger web of social and political institutions. Turning knowledge-making itself into an area of investigation forces one to acknowledge the larger contexts empowering and disempowering certain kinds of learning at particular moments in time. Historiography thus forces us to understand what is experienced as momentary crisis on the backdrop of transformations that have been in the making for some time.

George Stocking locates the cause of such introspection in the "more general professional and social concerns centering on issues of knowledge and power" (1983:3). The Other—once the central preoccupation of variously named fields of cultural inquiry—has begun to challenge Western paradigms and their complicity in colonial domination. Postcolonial native ethnography, history, and linguistics have brought about an interest in unpacking phases of colonial encounters, the role of those encounters in shaping ideas of cultural self and other, and the imprint they left on disciplinary formations.[10] In the process Western structures of cultural inquiry have been increasingly subjected to reflexive examination. Fields concerned with culture thus face internal transformations of legitimacy and external reclassification from a source of empowerment to a transnational consumer good. Holistic, historiographic assessments of disciplinary ideology are vital in coming to terms with these transformations and in regaining a sense, if not of control, then at least of understanding the role of cultural knowledge on the eve of the twenty-first century.

I present this examination of some scholarly efforts to channel the longing for authenticity into a field of study as a case study. Folklore is a particularly poignant example for understanding the ideological currents in cultural scholarship. But what is demonstrated here for one field—which, not least because of its anachronistic name, has survived only in the margins of academia—is not an isolated example. Rather, it displays in microcosm problems inherent to many fields of inquiry.

The linkages between authenticity and folklore are many, covering the yearning for autonomy in the discipline, in politics, and in individual selfhood. It is with my personal linkage to the problem at hand that I begin, for my own "coming of age" as a folklorist coincided with the reflexive turn in social sciences and humanities that has critically examined the scholarly edifice. A discussion of the authenticity concept, its history, and the philosophical discourse surrounding it serves as the means to frame the historiography of folkloristic authenticities to follow.

There are deeply personal reasons for anyone to study and stay with folkloristics (Camp 1989)—a social commitment, an infatuation with some of expressive culture's beauty, or, conversely, amazement, shock, or outrage at the deep-seated hatred and ugliness packed into some forms of expressive culture. It is in such personal involvements with expressive culture that we may experience an immediate link to our object of study, and the present study lays bare how such commitments have shaped the course of the discipline.

At twenty, I began to study folklore out of an emotional attachment to what I perceived as authentic dances and music of the Balkans—a motivation and personal involvement that has led many into studying folklore. Participating in a folk dance group and listening to exotic music seemed to put me in touch with layers of myself that had been dormant. I was elated when I discovered that there was an academic discipline variously called *Volkskunde*, Folkloristics, or, in many European countries, European Ethnology, and hoped to expand my interests into a profession. The teaching assistant in *Volkskunde* at a Swiss university quickly disillusioned me: such things as I was interested in had little to do with serious European Ethnology; they were but the spurious by-products of sociopolitical processes in Eastern Europe and as such they were not really part of what the discipline studied.

Despite my best efforts to work within the boundaries of what were considered acceptable areas of research, my first fieldwork on a New Year's mumming custom led me to discover that this event, considered ancient if not pagan by natives and folklorists alike, at best began a few centuries ago and only took on its present form after World War II. I remember the discovery as both sobering and exciting. On the one hand, it undermined the generally held assumption of the festival's antiquity and pagan origin, but, on the other hand, it held the promise of interesting new directions for research. During one lengthy interview a primary schoolteacher told me with considerable pride how "degenerate" the festival had been when he began teaching in the area in the 1940s. After consulting with a lay folklorist as well as members of the national association for costume preservation, he embarked on a campaign to "clean up" the event and to "reintroduce" the pagan element in the celebration, using his students as promoters of a new costume type; he also advocated in the local newspaper the "authentic" way to celebrate the event. His campaign was so successful that the majority of the informants in the early 1980s believed the newest costume type to be the oldest (Bendix 1985:56–58). Although I had intended to study "the real thing," what was real or genuine to the performers obviously differed from the notions of authenticity held in my discipline where (re-) inventions were considered a form of tampering with "genuine" tradition.

In the process of doing the research for that study, I encountered the German literature on *Folklorismus,* catchily defined as "second-hand folklore." The serious problems with both folkloristic history and theoretical concepts raised in the *Folklorismus* discussions gave me the confidence to pursue rather than avoid or exclude what academic folklorists considered fake, spurious, or ideologically perverted, and I have not been able to let go of the question why people, whether scholars or lay people, were so intent on distinguishing (and promoting) "real folklore" from a spurious counterpart.

My own growing obsession fortunately coincided with the increased self-scrutiny within the discipline as well as the growing acceptability of interest in folklore and ideology, be this in the romantic or nationalist, communist or fascist guise. The 1980s saw a profusion of works exploring the invention of social behaviors and artifacts. Works such as Roy Wagner's *The Invention of Culture* (1981), and especially Eric Hobsbawm and Terence Ranger's *The Invention of Tradition* (1983), inspired anthropologists, folklorists, and historians to document the modern origins of what were once thought ancient practices. Charting processes of invention and reinvention, often cast in the framework of "the politics and poetics of culture," has become the rule rather than the exception.[11] It has been an unavoidable consequence of this line of inquiry that concepts central to the entire scholarly edifice would also undergo such deconstructionist treatment. Marginalized at first, "the politics of culture" is now at the center of research and theory, and authenticity has become one of the most frequently discussed terms.

The present study is a product of my own need to clarify the "authenticity problem," and its comparative focus on Germany and the United States developed in part from personal circumstances as well. I grew up in Switzerland and made the German-speaking areas of Europe my focus of research, but I received most of my academic training in the United States. Those two areas of study most familiar to me also display the interplay and tensions between European and New World cultures of inquiry.

After listening to my frustrations at reining in the relationship between authenticity and folkloristics, my colleague Ronald Inauen at the University of Basel only half-jokingly uttered the verdict, "The study of culture is the study of the inauthentic." After years of reading and thinking about what, if anything, could still be authentic, I saw authenticity at best as a quality of experience: the chills running down one's spine during musical performances, for instance, moments that may stir one to tears, laughter, elation—which on reflection crystallize into categories and in the process lose the immediacy that characterizes authenticity.

Cultural research, by virtue of being "the study of" but not the "experience of" behaviors, expressions, institutions, and practices, can then not help but present, in this existential sense, the inauthentic. Taking it a step further, authenticity as a criterion should not matter in attempts to appreciate and understand culture. It is hardly possible to get past the very emotional interests that may lead one into a field such as folklore, nor is it always satisfying to shed all romantic visions of oneself in touch with an Other, as such visions are part of the modern sensibility into which we are enculturated. However, some reflexive awareness of how this discipline has been constituted to seek the authentic should at least permit a challenge to the grip that this concept has on our life and work.

Authentic derives from the Greek "authentes," which carries the dual meaning of "one who acts with authority" and "made by one's own hand." Lionel Trilling's recollection of "the violent meanings which are explicit in the Greek ancestry of the word" deepens the meaning and contrasts it with the commodification that the term has undergone in a Western-driven marketplace: "*Authenteo:* to have full power over; also, to commit a murder. *Authentes:* not only a master and a doer, but also a perpetrator, a murderer, even a self-murderer, a suicide" (Trilling 1974: 131). Such etymological layers need not reverberate fully in the present usage of the term, although the violence caused in the name of, say, ethnic or religious authenticity are painful present-day realizations of such old Greek meanings.

Encyclopedias offer historically circumscribed meanings to the term, stemming from religious and legal usage and practice. Among the traceable meanings and contexts are authentic editions of liturgical songs as well as vouchers of authenticity required to prove the authenticity of saints' relics.[12] A seal could endow a document with authenticity, and a series of legal decrees by Frederic I were known as *Authenticae Fridericianae*. Explicating authentic scripture, however, leads one into vague terrain, for authentic scripture refers, in church legal practice, to the canonical writings and their normative and authoritarian claim to contain the revelation. Not surprising, the scholarly efforts on authenticity within biblical studies alone are legion.[13] The literary critics' usage, however, refers to the historical genuineness of a particular scripture. Current practice expands on meanings such as original, genuine, or unaltered. Trustworthy and guaranteed point to the legal dimension, whereas one of the Greek meanings, "made by one's own hand," can quickly be simplified into "handmade." One definition of authenticity, used in the realm of art and antiques, refers to the clear identifiability of maker or authorship and uniqueness of an artifact, relying on the "made by one's own hand" etymology.

Folklorists, in a peculiar reversal, for a long time located authenticity within the anonymity of entire social groups, or the "folk." Lack of identifiable authorship, multiple existence over time and space, variation of the items, and the social and economic circumstances of the "bearers of tradition" served, instead, as ways of testing folklore's authenticity. Once individual performers or makers of artifacts entered the discussion, the criterion of anonymity or nameless tradition began to unravel, and the problem of authenticity could have rendered itself obsolete. However, the vocabulary of authenticity that permeated disciplinary discourse escaped the paradigmatic changes. Original, genuine, natural, naive, noble and innocent, lively, sensuous, stirring—the string of adjectives could be continued.[14] Folklorists since the eighteenth century have used them to circumscribe the longed-for quality that they saw encapsulated at first in folklore texts and later in folklore performance.

In the following chapters this vocabulary will be continuously highlighted in order to point to the fact that the language used may be more lasting than the theories developed in trying to transcend this language. Over time, "authenticity" acquired a broad range of meanings, with old usages gaining new connotations as the term was applied by successive generations of scholars, not to speak of the meanings added in fields such as psychology and in the politicization of the Romantic nationalist legacy. Understanding authenticity means understanding the ideological fluctuations of language use and the changing goals of such language use over time and across contexts (Pörksen 1989). Linguists researching language ideology are pointing the way in studies of the ideology of linguistic discourse itself (Woolard and Schieffelin 1994:67–69). The challenge such inquiry poses toward those who proclaim the possibility of a value-neutral (hence more scientific and worthy) branch of linguistics is substantiated through historiographic research.[15] The present work similarly seeks to find a way around the "vague terrain of thought" mapped by the many concurrent meanings of authenticity in an exploration of the concept's use at different times and places.[16]

There are magisterial accounts of authenticity's emergence in the West that help to prepare the ground for an understanding of the fragmented, multivocal use of the term in the study to follow. "At a certain point in its history," Lionel Trilling wrote, "the moral life of Europe added to itself a new element, the state or quality of the self which we call sincerity" (1974: 2). The imperative of sincerity began "to vex men's minds" in the sixteenth century (p. 12), and the most poignant sources are, not surprisingly, to be found in theater—the domain that is constructed out of pretense and artifice, and hence "insincerity." Actors' ability to move one to tears or anger rousted suspicions in the audience. Drawing on Goffman, Trilling observes how the fascination with theater led to an awareness of role play in life and to the realization that role play compromises sincerity. Yet if the norms of behavior required insincerity, the question arose whether, underneath these demands of civilization, layers of uncorrupted selfhood could be found.

Rousseau's philosophy, formulated in the mid-eighteenth century, contained the most influential formulations of the shift from sincerity to authenticity. "From Rousseau we learned that what destroys our authenticity is society" (Trilling 1974:92). By contrast, Rousseau's ideal authentic person remains unaffected by opinion and lives in a paradisiacal state of innocence. Rousseau's work "was a program attempting to give dignity to [individuals], liberating [them] from the superstructure of society in order to give [them] back to society pure and uncontaminated" (Cocchiara 1981:116–117). This argument provided a philosophical program for the French revolutionaries who needed to legitimize the democratization of politics. Cleansed of the social superstructure, the original virtue of every human being would emerge, and in that stage all humans would be equal and worthy of liberty.[17] Rousseau's "savage" was the embodiment of authentic existence, and Rousseau found remnants of savages among the humble folk in the country who supposedly lived with their instincts and feelings intact and among whom "neither sentiment nor poetry (was) dead" (Cocchiara 1981:122).

The call for "authenticity" implied a critical stance against urban manners, artifice in language, behavior, and art, and against aristocratic excesses; it promised the restoration of a pure, unaffected state of being. Such nostalgic visions were clearly fueled by explorers' reports of encounters with "exotic" and "savage" peoples whose existence an enlightened age sought to link to itself.[18] Following the logic of their own philosophy, Rousseau, Herder, and their contemporaries assigned such purity and authenticity to the rural and pastoral way of life in their own countries. Upper-class literati in eighteenth-century Europe, however, did not desire to live like the folk in the manner that Thoreau or the communards later tried to. Herder's gift to his peers was to single out folk poetry as a locus of folkness, inspiring contemporaries and an entire social and literary movement to absorb and imitate the authentic aesthetic of the folk. Herder and the Sturm und Drang Romantics solidified the link between the search for personal, moral authenticity and its artistic expression and communication. To them, the verbal art of the peasantry became a means for humanity at large to get in touch with authenticity.

The "discovery" of the folk and the emergence of a field of study devoted to its culture is intertwined with the fascination for the exotic and the concept of "primitive culture" so formative for cultural anthropology. But while Adam Kuper argues that "the theory of primitive society is about something which does not and never has existed" (1988:8), the moral of my story is more diffuse. *Authenticity, unlike "primitive society," is generated not from the bounded classification of an Other, but from the probing comparison between self and Other, as well as between external and internal states of being.* Invocations of authenticity are admissions of vulnerability, filtering the self's longings into the shaping of the subject. This book deconstructs authenticity as a discursive formation, but such a project cannot simply invalidate the search for authenticity. This search arises out of a profound human longing, be it religious-spiritual or existential, and declaring the object of such longing nonexistent may violate the very core around which people build meaningful lives.

It is not the object, though, but the desire, the process of searching itself, that yields existential meaning. Pilgrimage, and its commodified form, travel, are loci of transcendence, communicated articulately in a slim travel diary chronicling "Travels on the Road." Its author, familiar with the feeling of disappointment on arriving at a longed-for destination, solved the problem by not arriving at all and seeking the authentic instead in the fleeting process of experiencing in passing (Schmidt 1992). Traveling is in many ways a key to the modern "sense of being,"[19] accompanying the transformation of Western societies since the Enlightenment and unfolding as a multidimensional activity of transculturation. Initially scorned as a field of study, tourism scholarship has elaborated articulately on human ways of searching for authenticity within the dynamic of self and Other.[20] "The issue of authenticity runs, like an obbligato, through tourism studies" (Hughes 1995:781), with interest trained on the marketing and consumption of reified versions of the concept. In contradistinction—perhaps because of their concentration on the self in isolation—existentialist philosophies' theorizing of modern selfhood remains locked in attempts to define authenticity rather than its uses.

The emergence of the authentic self is arguably the central outgrowth of modernity (Taylor 1989), the foundation on which political, social, and economic transformations rest. Striving for selfhood is intertwined with the attempt to locate or articulate a more authentic existence, and this effort necessitated philosophical articulations that probed the nature of individual existence in the age of mechanical reproduction. Modernity's pace brought forth an anguish, occasioned by the oppositional desires for progress and nostalgia for what is left behind in the invariable transformations caused by progress. Existentialist philosophies can be seen as a twentieth-century attempt to withstand the maelstrom.

Trilling (1974) traced the slow unfolding of the search for authenticity in the Western world since the seventeenth century. The twentieth century has come to endorse the raw and ugly as a truer version of authenticity than the simple and pure.[21] Norman Mailer's gloss, "We are a Faustian age determined to meet the Lord or the Devil before we are done, and the ineluctable ore of the authentic is our only key to the lock," is perhaps the quintessential version of the rawness of the twentieth-century authenticity quest (cited after Berman 1988:37). Mailer points to the paradoxical pairing of daring and angst engendered by the relentless probing of knowledge and power, the testing of selfhood and autonomy, which characterizes modernity.

Jean-Paul Sartre's version of existentialism updates seventeenth-century travails with role play, reacting against the artifice of the bourgeoisie rather than that of the aristocracy. Denouncing the conventions of respectability governing public behavior as "contaminated by hypocrisy and inauthenticity," he perceived his own struggle to be "civilized" as having "undermined his own inner sense of self" (Charmé 1991:6–7). Sartre sought redemption in nature—not in the natural purity envisioned by the Romantics, but rather in the physicality of the human body, and in the Otherness of the nonbourgeois.

Martin Heidegger preceded Sartre and was criticized by him.[22] His *Being and Time* (1962 [1927]) strove to be the ultimate formulation on the nature of being in the twentieth century. Heidegger calls the two basic possibilities of existence *Eigentlichkeit* and *Uneigentlichkeit*, translated as "authenticity" and "inauthenticity" (King 1964:59). He perceived individuals as caught in "everydayness" (*Alltäglichkeit*), preventing them from truly "owning" themselves, for the German *eigen* means "own."[23] To live a Heideggerian authentic existence and reach the "utmost illumination of which [one] is capable," one has to transcend the demands of "everydayness" (King 1964:58). Inventing the noun *Eigentlichkeit,* and bending the rules of German grammar and vocabulary so as to linguistically represent "being," Heidegger for some has become the inventor of authenticity in modern philosophical terms.[24]

Yet Heidegger's metaphysical lure provides a poor guide for the reflexive revision of the study of culture that has been under way for some years. The current rediscovery of Heidegger is disturbing, for even if one separates the work from the man—a member of the Nazi Party who in 1933 stated, "Not theses and ideas are the laws of your being! The Führer himself and he alone is Germany's reality and law today and in the future"[25]— Heidegger's writing is conditioned by and politically committed to the totalitarian time during which it was generated.

The logical critique of metaphysicians such as Heidegger rests on their use of language, that aspect which made Heidegger appear to be unique and mysterious. Rudolf Carnap in 1931 argued that Heidegger's philosophy relied on "pretend sentences" that suffered from "a scarcity of linguistic logic" (1931:229). To Carnap, metaphysicians attempted to express authenticity—which he termed "sentiment of living" (*Lebensgefühl*)— through the acts of thinking and writing which did not lend themselves to a task that to him needed to be experiential rather than reflexive.[26]

Writing after World War II, and thus fully aware of the dangers and power inherent in Heidegger's mystifying language, Theodor Adorno put forth a much stronger critique of existentialism. As the title *The Jargon of Authenticity* (1973) indicates, Adorno rejected existentialist thought through an analysis of language and style. The language of existentialists, epitomized in Heidegger's term *Eigentlichkeit,* becomes a dangerous weapon: "The sublime becomes the cover for something low. That is how potential victims are kept in line." Heidegger's work "acquired its aura" because it described "the directions of the dark drives of the intelligentsia before 1933—directions which he described as full of insight, and which he revealed to be solidly coercive" (Adorno 1973:xxi, 4–5). The "jargon," the lack of concreteness in the language, made it appear as if the existentialist vision of authenticity "belonged to the essence of man, as inalienable possibility" rather than being "abstracted from generated and transitory situations" (1973:59). To Adorno and others on the left like Georg Lukács, existentialism in the Heideggerian form is ultimately irresponsible; by reveling in "being," it reflects the existentialists' inability to cope with industrial societies. Withdrawing from society in the search for authentic being in a timeless realm, the individual flees interaction with society and history and his or her place within this relationship. Trilling's argument is similar when he regards the most dangerous manifestation of authenticity to be the exit from human community, "the great refusal of human connection" (1974:171).

Benefitting from the late-twentieth-century intellectual turn toward examining the social production and ideology of knowledge itself,[27] Bourdieu sees Carnap's critique as missing the point because it remains within the philosophical habitus. Bourdieu insists, instead, on a dual reading, reducing his assessment neither to the realm of "pure text," nor condemning it simply because of the known politics of its author. He engages with Heidegger's texts both within the political culture and the philosophical profession that brought them forth. In examining the "imposition of form that is effected by philosophical discourse," Bourdieu also seeks to go beyond Adorno and to "reveal the alchemical transformation which protects philosophical discourse from direct reduction to the class position of its producer" (Bourdieu 1991:3). Scrutinizing what Heidegger said and how he said it, Bourdieu also insists on examining Heidegger's "words which are in themselves vague and equivocal, and especially the value judgements or the emotional connotations which their ordinary usage entails" (1991:104). Bourdieu's conclusion renders Heidegger as deceptive as authenticity itself:

> It is perhaps because he never realized what he was saying that Heidegger was able to say what he did say without really having to say it. And it is perhaps for the same reason that he refused to the very end to discuss his Nazi involvement: to do it properly would have been to admit (to himself as well as to others) that his "essentialist thought" had never consciously formulated its essence. (1991:105)

A field such as folkloristics, with its emphasis on communal aesthetics, may seem to share few points of convergence with existentialist philosophy. Yet the "jargon of authenticity" and folkloristic vocabulary are related.[28] A very thin line separates the desire for individual authenticity and the calling to convince others of the correctness of a particular rendering or localization of the authentic. The most powerful and lasting example of this double legacy in folklore's disciplinary history is the (ethno-) nationalist project. Textualized expressive culture such as songs and tales can, with the aid of the rhetoric of authenticity, be transformed from an experience of individual transcendence to a symbol of the inevitability of national unity. In Heidegger's time, an ambiguous and vague vocabulary of existential authenticity could legitimate its collectivized corollary of cultural authenticity and serve in the unambiguous exclusion and annihilation of all who could not or would not belong.

This book makes no claim to chronicle or theorize authenticity in its entirety. As Barbara Kirshenblatt-Gimblett has noted, it is possible to argue that the concept of authenticity does not have a history.[29] The crucial questions to be answered are not "what is authenticity?" but "who needs authenticity and why?" and "how has authenticity been used?" There is no single answer to these questions, either in existential terms or within the confines of folkloristic history.[30] Instead, I have drawn together a variety of texts—essays, collections, letters, theoretical works—that allow me to map ways in which authenticity and its allied vocabulary was used in various stages of disciplinary formation.

Expanding on Roger Abrahams's invocation of phantoms in scholarship (1993), I argue that the idea of "authentic folklore," legitimated as a disciplinary subject through ever newly formulated shades of authenticity, has situated the field of folklore at the margins of both society and the academy. The radical, utopian, and antimodern lure of the authentic, all at times made folklore and some of the discipline's ideas sociopolitically attractive, propelling it into momentary and sometimes, in hindsight, regrettable fame. The greatest strength of folklore studies is the perennial finger they hold to the pulse of what human beings, through their expressive culture, crave or fear most deeply.

This book traces the scholarly paths that led from the "invention of authentic folklore," to the strategic use of changing shades of authenticity in building the discipline of folklore, to the current reevaluation of the way the disciplinary subject was constructed (Briggs 1993, Briggs and Shuman 1993, Kirshenblatt-Gimblett 1995a). The seven chapters chart the intertwined history of folklore scholarship and the use of authenticity in legitimating the subject in both German-speaking Europe and the United States.

Charles Briggs, among others, has begun to expose the "metadiscursive practices" employed to ascertain authority by those who draw the boundaries around what is "authentic folklore" (Briggs 1993). This study supports and expands such reflexivity through a historically more extended deconstruction. If I recount the story of Herder and folksong, of the Brothers Grimm and folktales, of fieldworkers and their exuberant discoveries, I do it not simply to repeat key moments, but to point to the role that the search for authenticity played in charting the course of a field of inquiry. But deconstructing how knowledge was constructed is not necessarily liberating. Folklore's "crisis" is not unique; across the academy there is a sense of loss of subject that deconstruction has brought with it.[31] Reflexivity is, however, a first step toward newly conceptualizing inquiry unhampered by concepts that are burdened by the very mode in which they are conceived.

The study is organized into three parts, arranged chronologically and comparatively. The first part discusses the emergence of the concept of authenticity. Chapter 1 discusses authenticity's impact on German intellectuals and the emotional involvement of scholar-authors with what they considered the locus of the authentic—the poetry of the folk. In Chapter 2 I deal with the attempt to turn the emotional, internalized involvement with authentic expressive culture into a field grounded in scientific rigor. Chapter 3 shows the contours of this development in the United States.

The second part is concerned with the institutionalization of folkloristics and the use of authenticity in claiming disciplinary status, respectively, in the German-speaking realm and in the United States (chapters 4 and 5). The third part, with a chapter on German *Volkskunde*'s challenge to the canon (chapter 6) and American folkloristics' engagement with the politics of culture (chapter 7), leads up to the problematization of authenticity in two countries in the face of an increasingly reflexive politics of culture.

Folklore, if institutionally marginalized, has always been profoundly interdisciplinary. Philologists and linguists, literature scholars, anthropologists and historians, and more recently scholars engaged in area and ethnic studies, all contribute to folklore, even if the number of scholars holding folklore positions is small. In terms of its base of practitioners and its institutional representation, such as it is, folkloristics is thus recognizably metadisciplinary. While the field's subject has been cast in continually changing authenticities, the field's practitioners have relished its escape from more typically positivist, disciplinarian purity of method and theory. Folklore is a small field that embarks on "a passion for the whole" (Köstlin 1995) and a daring that generates a longing of its own among intellectuals strapped into narrow specializations. Consequently, this story is about subjects and the approach to subjects—and much less about the disciplinary boxes into which those who approach subjects fit institutionally. In other words, this is a dual history of ideas and their consequences, not a history of the division of knowledge.

The book also does not aspire to the status of a treasure trove of primary evidence from every possible protagonist within the discourse. I have made an effort to contextualize the voices brought into relation with each other, but it is their contribution to the history of authenticity's use within folkloristics that is of interest here, not their individual and often considerable accomplishments. Passages of this history will be familiar to specialists within particular subject areas (such as historical linguists, mythologists, art historians, anthropologists, philosophers, literature scholars, and scholars in ethnic and area studies). Some will undoubtedly regret not seeing their area of expertise treated in the kind of depth in which they know it themselves. But some may feel moved to inquire after authenticity's role in the construction of their own disciplinary subject, and in the process they may come to appreciate the possibilities inherent in the age of reflexive modernization. They then may inch toward a more congenial symbiosis of disciplinary particularism and postdisciplinary knowledge-making.

A history of the constructions of authenticity within folklore studies, then, is also, hopefully, liberating. Such a history demonstrates that expressive culture is not about to disappear. Once we have overcome the dichotomy within our disciplinary thinking, "authenticity versus inauthenticity" can become an object of study itself. We can study the negotiation of authenticity once we have ceased to be a negotiating party, or once we admit to our participation in the negotiating process. This stance allows us to examine the meanings and the history of "authenticity" from a distance both within and beyond disciplinary discourse.

Part 1

The Instrumentalization
of Authenticity

"But you must give it, as it is, in the original language with modest explanation, without scolding or scorn, without beautifying or ennobling it; if possible with melody and everything that belongs to the life of the folk"

(Johann Gottfried Herder 1877–1913, IX, 533)

Modernity is a label for the transformations brought about through the decline of feudal estates and the emergence of bourgeois societies and nation-states. Change in all aspects of culture was the result of the slow process of the "structural transformation of the public sphere" (Habermas 1989). The new kind of public sphere that emerged, inhabited by an emergent bourgeoisie, was the result of multiple discourses. Within this transformation, the discourse on "authenticity" as a desirable state of being or acting was a significant element.

Discourse requires places that allow for the presentation of new ideas. Guilds, political and literary clubs, and societies with secrecy codes served as places to explore new, revolutionary ideas (Kosellek 1959:49–80). The publications of literary societies also served as a means to distribute thought, and in such circles people dared to articulate desires for political transformations and for democratic statehood based on the equality of human beings.

The notion of authenticity and its precursor, sincerity, was crucial in this program of sociopolitical transformation. Societies believed to be corrupted by the trappings of civilization had to find a way back to their authentic states in order to build a new kind of polity. Expressive culture was "discovered" as the poetic manifestation of authentic being, both in social classes and cultural Others, as well as in historical documents.

Preromantic and romantic philosophers, literary critics, and authors in eighteenth-century Germany tried to locate, feel, and ultimately appropriate the expressive culture of the "folk." Their endeavor curiously combined the modern mentality of the Enlightenment, which was essential for the process of democratization, and a fundamentally antimodern anxiety of loss. Chapter 1 outlines how folklore, perceived as the product of a particularly genuine social class—the peasantry—came to be seen as authentic and desirable in German-speaking Europe. Chapter 2 shows the transformation of the romantic script of authenticity—a desirable state of feeling—into a graspable, externalized entity, encoded in various forms of folklore that could be collected, printed, and disseminated. Authentic folklore was further instrumentalized through the scholarly need to participate in building sciences and public institutions for the teaching and furthering of such sciences. Chapter 3 turns to the nineteenth- and early twentieth-century United States. Here, philosophers and poets in their own search for transcendence revoiced the German discursive path, albeit under very different sociopolitical and temporal circumstances. What for Europe had been the folk was for a time the "common man" in the United States. Like the folk, the common man was constructed as living in the spirit of a spontaneous authenticity; emulating this spirit, in turn, could inspire a truly independent nation. Yet the European model as well as the longing for a European past intersected with this American blueprint. Through the competitive desire to build scholarly edifices equaling the European ones, similar processes of harnessing the essence of authenticity into scientific procedures ensued.

Chapter One

Poetry, History, and Democracy
Locating Authenticity

> "The Garden of Eden. It's what we are
> all trying to get back to."
> Astrophysicist-Jesuit observing
> the universe from Arizona
> —Jack Hitt (1994:39)

In pre-Enlightenment scholarship and philosophy the ultimate and unquestionable source of truth and authority had been God. Religion supplied the language of spiritual truth, and belief was the common, communal link to a fountain of authenticity. With the emergence of new charters in the seventeenth and eighteenth centuries came the search for different kinds of authenticity.[1] Although the language of religion, with its reliance on nature metaphors, suffused this search, the effort sought to locate authenticity elsewhere, particularly in secular realms.[2]

A central thinker in this transformation was Johann Gottfried Herder (1774–1839).[3] In his multiple roles as theologian, poet, and philosopher, he embodied the tensions and aspirations of his time. Addressing the questions felt to be most pressing in this era—from aesthetics to politics, from the origin of language to the history of humankind—he articulated a bundle of ideas concerning the *Volk* and located an authentic spirit within the folk's "natural poetry." Herder's voice has been accorded a prominent place in folklore's disciplinary history, but one might argue that his name has become vital at least in part because of disciplinary retrospection focused on individual father figures of the field.[4] This chapter, while offering a reading of Herder's role in circumscribing and locating authenticity, also unfolds a larger field of discourse to which Herder contributed his ideas.

In Western history, American Independence and the French Revolution

27

are the central events of the eighteenth century, each symbolizing a momentous political transformation. In German-speaking Europe, however, revolution was delayed as political arguments were absorbed and intertwined into other concerns, such as the discourse on the poetic. This discourse was intricately linked to the discovery of folk literature, and it also focused on authenticity as a new kind of truth. The poetic revolt contested Enlightenment assumptions, which held that neither poetry nor art, as products of fiction, could contain ultimate truths. Through both discussion of, and abandonment in, the poetic, German pre-Romantic and Romantic philosophers, literary critics, and authors tried to test and challenge the powers of such enlightened reason.[5] Eventually, Enlightenment truth gave way to acceptance of a possible *sensual* truth that was communicated in the poetic or artistic.

This chapter focuses on excerpts from this discourse on the poetic, examines the place of authenticity within it, and points to the role of the poetic in the emergent endeavor that located authenticity in folk expression.

With its emphasis on self-reflecting reason, the Enlightenment brought about two intertwined achievements—a break with tradition and an openness to the emergence of historical thought. As Nikolaus Wegman put it, "The process of the Enlightenment renders tradition alien. Separated from continuity with the present, tradition is changed into mere past." Tradition thus turns into historical knowledge; it no longer requires societal validation (1988:12).

Since the Enlightenment necessitated a different conceptualization of what human beings were, Gianbattista Vico's attempt to forge a new science of both philosophy and the history of mankind replaced the "concept of a static human nature . . . with a pattern of systematic change." Self-awareness led Vico (1668–1744) to historical insight; but it also led to cultural style, suggesting "such notions as *Zeitgeist* and *Volksgeist*" (Berlin 1976:140–41).[6]

The Enlightenment sped up changes in communicative modes, rendering previously unreflected spheres of life—the habitual, the unproblematic—into analytic categories appropriate for discourse. Yet in turning what was taken for granted into an object of discourse, the Enlightenment carried into modernity the problem of the paradisiacal tree of knowledge with its trope of "paradise lost" through the gain of knowledge. Once the unreflected becomes part of reflexive discourse, "a return to a restored world of tradition is impossible" (Wegmann 1988:14).

Such loss was painful to eighteenth-century thinkers, and it has remained painful ever since. Some critics embarked on a search for a realm of experience and expression free of the demand for enlightened reason and rational thought and practice. In the German-speaking realm, this quest took the form of a poetic—rather than political—revolt, which became known as *Empfindsamkeit* (responsiveness to sentiment)[7]—the search for feeling reified in the poetic and artistic. This search was not the radical countermovement it purported to be since the very ideas and images that it employed derive from the spectrum of discursive and reflexive modes that are facilitated by the "reason" from which one is trying to escape.[8]

WHAT SHOULD POETRY BE? FROM REASON TO SENTIMENT

One cornerstone of early thought on expressive culture is Johann Gottfried Herder's notion of *Naturpoesie* (natural poetry), later used synonymously with *Volkspoesie*. In its invocation of organic growth, *Naturpoesie* stood opposed to the artificiality of *Kunstpoesie* (artistic poetry). *Naturpoesie*'s linkage to a social group, the folk, emerged from intertwined arguments about language and the poetic.

The nature and the origin of language had to be understood if the goal of democratizing language was to be achieved. The question of what poetry should be and what it expressed was cause for heated debates. One needs to become familiar with how nature and poetry were linked in eighteenth-century thought to understand how central such debates were to the formation of the entire Romantic movement, for that background proved crucial to the emergence of folklore studies and the role of authenticity within them.

German literary authors in the early eighteenth century faced three major problems. First, the German-speaking area of Europe contained a profusion of dialects and lacked a common standard language. Latin often served as the literary language, and through the church it served as the educational language as well. Among the upper classes, French was "the only respectable medium of communication"; even Frederick the Great scorned his native German in preference to French as a language of discourse and writing (Ergang 1966:22). Second, French classicism, born of an Enlightenment recourse to antique models, dictated strongly regulated poetic works, thus constraining expression. Third, there was the apparent dearth of written poetry in German—"apparent" because it was only in the eighteenth century that a search for medieval manuscripts began that would prove the contrary. Works penned in New High German were so rare that authors of the eighteenth century such as Gotthold Ephraim Lessing (1729–81) and Friedrich Gottlieb Klopstock (1724–1803) became pioneers and models of new literary traditions.

In the framework of an Enlightenment philosophy based on a search for truth as the foundation for reason, literature, drama, and poetry had to be principled. "Poetry was conceived of as a genuinely sensual art, . . . and such sensuality could not then have the attributes of truth and reason" (Wetterer 1981:x). Enlightened poetry thus became method-based and reflected the civilizing or constraining of sentimental outpouring.

Yet numerous authors contended that poetic language appealed to beauty and other sensual perceptions and was not governed by reason. A philosophy of poetry that spoke to these contradictory impulses was necessary, and it would emerge from the literary war between the German Johann Christoph Gottsched (1700–1766) and the Swiss scholars Johann Jakob Bodmer (1698–1783) and Johann Jakob Breitinger (1701–76) (Bender 1973).

Gottsched, Bodmer, and Breitinger, like many intellectuals of their day, assumed the mantles of art critics, philosophers, historians, and poets. In these capacities they searched for ways to define the marvelous (*das Wunderbare*)—that aesthetic and spiritual quality which transforms mere language into the poetic. The marvelous—or what American discourse would call the sublime—was a term chosen to denote the indescribable element—that which was felt, which touched, moved, and stirred one sensually rather than rationally.[9] The term encompassed what eventually became known as authenticity.

Gottsched, by expounding on the principles of classically inspired poetry, attempted to incorporate the sensuousness of artistic production into a philosophy of art based on reason and function (Gottsched 1730). That poetry imitated the reason evident in nature (*Nachahmungspoetik*), for nature was conceived by the highest reason of God, and imitating nature was thus akin to imitating God (Wetterer 1981:86).[10] Gottsched assumed utility in every piece of poetry, from Homer to his own efforts; hence, writing poetry entailed lessons for those in need of moral betterment.

Many author-scholars disliked Gottsched's pedantic voice, and the Zurich scholars Bodmer and Breitinger initiated a literary battle with him over the nature of literature. While Bodmer prepared the way for both Romanticism and philology, Breitinger was more concerned with establishing a philosophical framework that would not subordinate poetry to the regularity of nature. Short-lived journals, initiated or inspired by the competing parties, served as vehicles for the debate (see Wilke 1978). Sup-

ported by fellow literati and wealthy benefactors, these journals constituted a building block in the transformation of the German public sphere.
The vigor of the debate illustrates just how important the question of the
poetic and originality was for the emergence of a new social order.

To the sensibilities of the early eighteenth century, imagination was, by
virtue of being human, potentially subject to vice.[11] Imagination's affinity
to vice made Gottsched insist that poetry imitate nature, for nature was
ruled by God (Wetterer 1981:83–84). Bodmer and Breitinger struggled
in separate treatises to recast this negative valuation of poetry (Bodmer
1740, Breitinger 1740).[12] Bodmer argued against strict imitation of reality, seeing the poetic act as a perfect combination of what a poet saw externally and experienced internally. Breitinger attempted to formulate a
philosophical definition that would remove the poetic from the realm of
untruth by distinguishing the truth of reason from the truth of imagination: "Something can appear untrue to reason which appears true to the
imagination. Conversely, reason can accept something as true which appears unbelievable to one's fantasy; and therefore it is certain, that the
untrue sometimes seems more probable than the true" (cited after Wetterer 1981:218). Breitinger claimed that, in its sensual aspects, poetry relied on the truth of imagination. Poetry was part of the marvelous, which
from the perspective of reason always gave off an appearance of the untrue (*der Schein des Falschen*). Once one recognized that there were two
human faculties for perceiving truth—that of reason and that of the
imagination—the appearance of falseness could be unveiled as but an
appearance.

Breitinger's approach was a radical enhancement of sensuousness since
it placed poetry in a realm of truth outside the reason-based notion of
truth. Postulating such alternate layers of truth later provided legitimacy
to the revolution in German poetry that would lead to Sturm und Drang.

Breitinger's ideas were part of the "poetic revolt" that stirred in England and elsewhere (Cocchiara 1981:131–50). Bodmer, his intellectual
partner, absorbed English literary events with fervor and organized a new
literary society in Switzerland whose goal was the publication of a journal
analogous to Addison and Steele's *Spectator*. It appeared as *Die Discourse
der Mahlern* (The Discourses of the Painters) from 1721 until 1723 (Brandes 1974:18–23).[13] Through articles in the *Spectator,* Bodmer had been
inspired to reflect on the concepts of fantasy, imagination, and how they
mattered in "art." Names such as "spectator" or "discourses of" indicate
a trend toward an externalized, reflexive perspective on what had formerly been internalized, habitual spheres of experience.

Bodmer at first was overwhelmed by English poetry, not just for its poetic qualities, but for its political significance, evident in his translation of Milton's *Paradise Lost,* which he considered a republican document and a screed against Charles I (Cocchiara 1981:157). This initial interest led Bodmer to engage himself on two fronts. One was the rendering of many foreign "classics" into German, among them Percy's *Reliques of Ancient English Poetry,* a work that would prove very important to later ballad scholarship as well as to more general questions of authenticity (see Stewart 1991a). The other front was the discovery of medieval German poetry—Parsifal, the Nibelungen epic, the *Minnesänger* (poets of courtly song)—and its rendering into an emergent new standard German. The politicized visions from abroad mixed with the "documents of an ancient poetry mirroring the German revolts" (Cocchiara 1981:157–58) and symbolized an empowerment of language and the poetic.

Medieval poetry was ammunition against Gottsched because it proved the existence of a native German poetic tradition. The manuscripts, salvaged from forgotten archives or from secondary use as book bindings, constituted "texts of true poetry . . . an escape from the rules dictated by Gottsched, but also [contained] an austere, solemn sense of life that imbued everything with the *simplicity* and *sincerity* of proverbs" (Cocchiara 1981:158; my italics).

In Bodmer an enlightened interest in history intersected with his own poetic experiments and his consuming awareness of the politics of language. Once he had recognized that what "he had found fascinating in Milton's language and that which Gottsched rejected also existed in Middle High German literature," he began to build a bridge "from Middle High German language to the Swiss language of his day" (Rohner 1984:96). His native language proved closer to medieval German than to the new German written language emerging from Gottsched's circle. This discovery for Bodmer held both political and artistic significance.

Gottsched favored the creation of one "correct" German language. He promoted the dialect of Saxony as a new literary medium, since the area lay geographically in the middle of the German-speaking realm, and the chance that northern and southern dialect speakers could adapt to it was great. Luther's Bible translation was in this dialect, and its widespread use suggested the linguistic choice that Gottsched promoted. The *Académie Française* seemed to Gottsched a strong example of the beneficial influence of language unification, which, in turn, could lead to national unity (Crüger 1965 [1884]:xxix–xxxvii).

Bodmer, discovering the "primeval power emanating from [medieval poetic] language" and perceiving the affinity of this poetry to his own language, feared and fought the loss that such standardization would bring (Rohner 1984:96). Another Swiss sensed precisely what was at stake when he wrote to Bodmer:

> As long as a Swiss may write in nothing other than the dialect of Meissen [in Saxony], he will never catch *the way of writing that the French call naïve*. To do that, one must write as one speaks; but how should he who has to learn Saxon much like one learns Latin be able to write naïvely? One writes Latin, one writes French, but who can involve *the tender and natural* within [those] languages? Only he who is raised [speaking] those languages. (Rohner 1984:69–70; my italics)

SELF, SOCIETY, AND SINCERITY

A discourse on authenticity was launched in this debate on the poetic, using the tropes of sensuality and nature, and affirming the importance of the affective dimension in literary production. Bodmer's circle thus foreshadowed and instilled the kind of consciousness of native language that proved of overwhelming importance in Romantic nationalism. Yet while Bodmer conducted literary politics by arguing for the legitimacy of Swiss (and any other dialectal) difference, his complex and industrious efforts also foreshadowed further searches for the authentic. His pioneering editorial work on medieval manuscripts points to the philological authentication that became so common in the era of the Grimms.

The social commentary that Bodmer and Breitinger authored in the 1720s for the "Discourses of the Painters" also reveal an acute critique of the lack of authenticity in the social mores of their day.[14] The targets of their critiques were the nobility's civilisatory mores. One can interpret Bodmer and Breitinger as voices of a budding bourgeoisie searching for an authentic culture to replace civilization's inauthenticities. The "Discourses" covered topics as diverse as women's political and intellectual rights, fashion, aesthetic philosophy, and calls for documenting history. In one of the first discourses, published in 1721, it was stated: "A person in his entire life never simply behaves as nature made him. . . . He hides his intention, the purpose and goals of his projects, his deeds, and his external actions. He knows how to pretend. . . . The world is one great exhibit space of masked people, and no one will know the other unless the mask is taken away from them" (1721, part I, discourse 2). A person acted with "authenticity and truth" only when he died, for "the last words of a person are brief, to the point and spoken from the innermost of the heart."

The search was for something beyond texts, history, and language. In using the term authenticity in conjunction with truth, Bodmer and Breitinger invoked an internalized, sincere sentiment, a stage of being that contains only the unadulterated, nonposturing self. The question that has been brewing since the eighteenth century (or very likely earlier than that) is whether we *have* such a true self.

The exotic within one's own cultures was sought as an antidote to the civilizatory malaise.[15] For some scholars and writers, native history was the avenue for excavating a better, more vigorous, and more sincere incarnation of one's own culture. Bodmer followed this path in his role as professor of patriotic history, as did the German Justus Möser (1720–94) and the Swiss Johannes von Müller (1752–1809) (Cocchiara 1981:159–67).[16] While these efforts at a restorative cultural history became important means to legitimate ethnic and national causes, the search for cultural authenticity through native, natural poetry proved of even greater consequence for both Romantic nationalism and folkloristics.

Early-eighteenth-century authors tried to reconcile apparently incompatible goals of the rational and emotional quest for truth. The attempted fusion made authenticity akin to truth. The French Revolution can be seen as a program for achieving the social and political authenticity yearned for in the moralistic critiques of social life, reflected as well in Bodmer and Breitinger's "Discourses."

The critique of one's own cultural habitus was inspired by the discovery and discussion of the cultural Other. "The experience with cultural variety and difference shed a new, unusual light on one's own culture" (Hartmann 1988:18)—a juxtaposition that preoccupied philosophers from Montaigne (1533–92) to Rousseau (1712–78).[17] In the eighteenth century the concern with the Other was also a concern with the progressive goals of civilizing and educating. In the search for suitable governmental policy, much research needed to be accomplished, and such pragmatically oriented effort already had established itself before the revolutionary period.[18] Intellectually more powerful was the development of a philosophy of authenticity lodged in human history, native language, and poetry, and it received its lasting impulses from Herder.

THE HERDERIAN SHIFT

The theologian Johann Gottfried Herder was, if not the first, then the most influential champion of expressive culture. The role he attributed to oral poetry in the history and philosophy of humankind, his efforts to collect and publish the folksongs of peoples, the cultural relativism he sought to formulate, and the exuberant and emotional vocabulary he chose to advance this cause inspired literary and scholarly romanticism. On the eve of an industrializing modernity, Herder's work solidified the modern invention of the "folk" category.[19]

The call for authenticity, articulated in moral-social journals as well as in Rousseau's work, implied a critical stance against urban manners; against artifice in language, behavior, and art; and against aristocratic excesses. The need to restore a pure, unaffected state of being required some tangible evidence, or, failing that, some gripping imagery. Among the choices of imagined, purer states of being were Rousseau's "savage" or the seemingly uncorrupted exotic Others, whose existence in faraway lands was becoming known.[20]

The Other as imagined in India was one powerful source for German intellectuals of the late eighteenth century. An interest in Hindu religion, successive translations of Indian drama and mythology, and a budding interest in pursuing Sanskrit studies provided fuel for both emotional and intellectual searches for loci of authenticity. Herder acted as a catalyst in pulling together disparate early Orientalist interests and contributed to the idealized image of India that inspired early Romantics in Germany from Novalis to the Brothers Schlegel.[21]

Yet Herder also inspired a search for the authentic close to home. In assigning authenticity to the pastoral way of life in one's own region, the least alien and thus perhaps most manageable choice gained the upper hand. That choice proved extremely powerful, and an entire social and literary movement—Sturm und Drang evolving into Romanticism—absorbed and imitated the seemingly authentic aesthetic of the folk, though upper-class literati at the time did not desire to live like the folk.[22] The literati were led by Herder to an appreciation of folk poetry as a genuine locus of folkness. In the debates over poetry and language, art and literary critics had only just begun to consider fables, myths, and oral stories in their medieval incarnations. Herder endowed such narratives of "the 'lower powers of the soul' with a positive valuation, and gathered them [into the category] folk poetry. . . . He regarded the turn to [folk poetry] . . . as essential for the development of a democratic culture with a globally oriented national literature" (Poltermann 1990:834).

Thomas de Zengotita (1989) has characterized Romantics like Herder as "Speakers of Being" who challenged the rational project that severed language as the instrument of thought and reason from language as the expression of innermost feeling.[23] In Herder's language philosophy (Herder 1978 [1770]) human sensuality could overcome the unavoidable self-alienating consciousness brought on by "the wound of reflection" (a Rousseauian term adopted by de Zengotita 1989:83). In this refutation the Romantic movement, as articulated by Herder, sought to achieve an *authentic totality* of political liberty, social individuality, and sensuous being. Oral poetry was central to recovering and experiencing such authenticity, and to Herder poetry was instrumental in demonstrating the creative beauty that united humanity, even as it affirmed national diversity.

Herder's vision entailed an enormous intellectual project that he could present only in fragments.[24] Folklore, or *Volkskunde,* was one intellectual trajectory that chose from the Herdian legacy "the voice of the folk," the oral expressions or *Naturpoesie* that had become the evidence, the representation, of what was Herder's political message.[25] Herder was the key figure in designating folk poetry as a distinct category (Bausinger 1980: 13–15), and that makes his vocabulary, experience, and vision of authenticity worthy of closer examination.

HERDER, LANGUAGE, AND THE VOCABULARY OF AUTHENTICITY

Herder's answer to the Berlin Royal Academy of Sciences' essay contest on the origin of language consisted of further questions: "Man, placed in the state of [self-] awareness [*Besonnenheit*] unique to him and . . . acting for the first time freely, has invented language. What is reflection? What is language?" (Herder 1978 [1770]:31). The only origin for Herder could lie in the peculiar, inventive nature of human beings, and if there had to be a divine origin for language, then it was because God had made human beings in such a way that they could not help but invent it.

In essence, Herder's language philosophy continued the poetic revolt, expanding the legitimation of sentiment within the domain of artistic language. In his conceptualization of self-awareness Herder distanced himself from the Enlightenment notion of reason separate from emotion. Herder's "reflection" was, at best temporarily, wrested from sentiment, feelings, or the soul. To him, it was impossible "to think without words. In the human soul such a state is impossible, as we have seen even in dreams and with the mad. As bold as it may sound, as true it is: a human being feels with reason and speaks while he thinks" (1987 [1770]:78). Herder sought language and poetry where "reason and the artificial language of society had [not] dethroned sentiment and the sounds of nature," and he looked for "the highest thunderclaps of eloquence, the most powerful blows of the art of poetry, and the magic moments of action, this language of nature," wondering what among "people pierces through hearts and turns souls upside down" (1987 [1770]:17). Native song and poetry were an answer to his search, showing humans' blissful use of their reflexive capability—blissful in that the sentient aspects of being and thinking were not at the corroded stage of Herder's contemporaries.[26] Poetic genius had to overcome the arbitrary differentiation of logic and affect in order to reach for the powers of expression hidden within (Heizmann 1981:80–84), which Herder situated in classical epics, biblical poetry, and folksong.

It is both ironic and logical that Herder developed his interests in the concrete representational powers of folk poetry in conjunction with *Ossian*, James Macpherson's projection of what might have been a Gaelic epic, but now more likely labeled "the Ossianic embarrassment" (Gauger 1987; see Shiach 1989:104–12). The search for authenticity by means of folk poetry in the British Isles had occurred earlier, corresponding to political transformations and cultural awakenings there. But in terms of Herder's philosophy and politics, the judgments on *Ossian*'s authenticity are of little consequence. *Ossian* was but an example of a greater principle that Herder acted on, and he was in the process of delineating notions of authenticity within which Macpherson's work might well have fit. In his earliest writings Herder had groped for ways to characterize "originality" and "perfection" in the poetic, with the assumption that the oldest, most original forms of poetry would also be the most perfect. In a student fragment of 1764 he argued that "the genius of the ode . . . is the most original, the seedling. . . . It is the God-like within nature" (cited after Heizmann 1981:30). Poetry such as *Ossian* appeared to speak with such originality.

Macpherson's project was perhaps the most extreme development in what Susan Stewart has called "the artifactualization of the ballad," a trend in Great Britain that set the course for "the commodification of literature" (1991b:105). *Ossian* was an early nationalistic exploitation of folk poetry, and in that regard it was but an extreme application of the construct of folk poetry (Dundes 1985). In his letters "About Ossian and the Songs of Ancient Peoples," originally published in 1773, Herder formulated a vocabulary of authenticity that set a tone of exuberant revelation which would reverberate in ever-new guise to the present.[27]

Herder begins with his expression of "enchantment about an epic original," and he continues to characterize Ossian as "a poet so full of *dignity and innocence in the emotions, and full of scenes of simplicity, agency, and beatitude* of human life" who would surely stir many hearts (Herder 1906 [1773]:1; my italics).[28] Herder's choice of nouns for this initial description constitutes a first semantic spectrum into which many later attempts to characterize authenticity would fit. His wording weds the simple and innocent to the noble or dignified—bestowing prestige and importance on the humble, and removing these characteristics from the social elites who traditionally had held them. Innocence and beatitude, which echo Herder's background in theology, invoke their opposites of guilt and contamination. His delight at discovering the fresh, unspoiled voice of Ossian rests on an unexpressed disappointment with the corruption within his own civilization.

Yet even in this initial delight, Herder's concern with a still higher degree of authenticity took shape. His correspondent apparently had doubted the genuineness of the English version of *Ossian* but was convinced of its authenticity upon reading the German translation. Herder, however, was pushed to further thought: "But you who have previously doubted so stubbornly the truthfulness and authenticity of the Scottish *Ossian*, hear me who had defended him now, not stubbornly doubt, but modestly suggest that *Ossian*, despite the industriousness and taste and elan and strength of the language, in this German translation might no longer be the true *Ossian*" (Herder 1906 [1773]: 1). In worrying about the losses incurred through translation, Herder thus linked authenticity and truth to original language—much in the way Bodmer's correspondent had been concerned about the ability of non-native speakers to capture the intimate aspects of a language.

Yet native language alone was not enough. Herder also sought to characterize the social and political human stage at which native language was expressed most vigorously. Herder combined the tropes of nature with what such tropes could mean in political terms:

> The more wild and freely acting a people is (for more the word [wild] does not mean), the more wild, that is, the more lively, free, sensuous and lyrically acting its songs must be . . . ! The farther from artificial, scientific ways of thought, speech and letters a people is, the less its songs are made for paper and for dead literate verses. . . . The essence, the purpose, the wondrous power of these songs are connected to this enchantment, this drive, to be a song of eternal heritage and joy for the people. (1906 [1773]: 5–6)

Emerging from civilizatory alienation and recovering freedom entailed, then, the recovery of a sensual poetics, unencumbered by the burden that Herder perceived in his own generation. "Beginning in youth, our souls today are shaped differently, after long generations of education. We hardly see and feel, we only think and worry; we don't write poetry about a living world, in the storm and flowing together of such things, such emotions; instead, we artificially come up with a theme, or a way to trest the theme" (1906 [1773]:14–15).

It is easy to see how Herder's message and vocabulary would sweep a generation of young poets into the Sturm und Drang movement. His argument opened the floodgates of emotions pent up behind Enlightenment rationalism. Yet his own project was far more concerned with social and political authenticity than with the exuberant engagement of his followers, who sought individual experience and authenticity.[29]

Herder's enthusiasm for epics and songs of the "old and wild peoples" was linked to the insights he had gained through his essay on the origin of language. Because original language to Herder emerged in the interplay of emotionality and reason, folk poetry proved a tremendous find, composed "in the immediate present" and containing many ingenious symbolic leaps (1906 [1773]:17).

Herder's letters on Ossian thus incorporated the ennobling, innocent variety of native authenticity, and wild and natural—coterminus with politically free—authenticity. At the same time, Herder's Ossian assessment also interacted with the discourse on the poetic, the marvelous, and the predicament of native language recounted above. In his critique of "new" German poets and his effort to push beyond their productions to a deeper, more original realm of poetry, he assisted the Romantic revolution in German literature with its intense interaction with folk poetry. Herder lamented the fact that the spread of "so-called culture" would drown the *treasure* of folk poetry, and it was the treasure metaphor, as much in its moral as in its capitalist meaning, that continued to inspire collection efforts. Herder wanted to begin the rescue, and he urged his correspondent to send him the kinds of songs he had himself encountered: "Folk songs, provincial songs, peasant songs which would be equal in liveliness and rhythm, naive manner and strength of language" (1906 [1773]:19).

The tentative thought to begin collection reached fruition in the publication of *Stimmen der Völker in Liedern* (1807 [1774]). In the short time since his observations on Ossian, Herder's hope of recovering authenticity in the folk of the present appeared dimmed. In the foreword of this collection, he differentiated between the noble folk who bore the noble tradition and the poor folk who peopled the streets of his own neighborhoods.

> The art of the master singers has maintained this manner [of making verse] truthfully, but ultimately spoiled it most untruthfully. About this

[art] and its noble origin, the so called *Minnesänger*, I don't want to speak here. They were folk singers and yet they were not, depending on how one looks at the matter. A folk singer does not have to be a member of the rabble or sing for the rabble, although the most noble of poetic art is not diminished by the fact that it can be heard from the mouth of the folk. *Volk* does not mean the rabble in the alleys; that group never sings or rhymes, it only screams and truncates. (1807 [1774]:69)

Although rarely expressed so crudely, this opinion was characteristic of Herder's class. The social distinction may have contributed more to the textual orientation taken by the quest for authenticity than has previously been acknowledged. The very real social gulf between an emerging urban proletariat and an emerging bourgeoisie made it appear impossible that the noble, "clean" fountain of authenticity would reside in the shabby, noisy living quarters of the folk. Herder's nature metaphors also reflected this social distinction: "The stream of centuries flowed dark and dreary for Germany. Here and there one voice from the folk, a song, a proverb, a rhyme was saved, but mostly [it is] muddy, and the waves rip it away immediately" (1807 [1774]:66).

The organic trope was characteristic of the post-Enlightenment conceptualization of history (White 1973:69–80). Herder's writings were particularly instrumental in this regard because he appeared to go beyond the metaphoric and sensed instead a reality that imbued the organic nature of verbal art. Herder's folksong project, then, was both a salvage and cleansing operation, and the promise of authenticity to be gained from participating in this project energized generations of scholars.

Yet what is bewildering about Herder's works is that he explored and advocated causes—quests for authenticity—that would be taken up by very different sociopolitical and individual interests. In his own search for a locus of authenticity he composed a body of writing that already contained shifting contours of the concept. Some of his writings fueled the intensely internal, individualistic probing of the soul and the self so characteristic of Sturm und Drang and early Romantic literature. But Herder's proposals on expressive culture also ran counter to the interest in individual authenticity, calling for a "reorientation away from 'the pathology of the head' to a 'physiology of the entire national body,' in which especially underrepresented and suppressed groups and classes should be included. . . . Folk poetry constituted an authentic expression of socially and ethnically different peoples: 'Their songs are the archive of the folk'" (Poltermann 1990:835, including citations from Herder 1877–1913, vol. 9, pp. 523, 532).

As Hugo Moser pointed out, Herder worked with the notion of a unified whole, which he variously labeled nation or tribe (*Stamm*), the nation associated with state, and the tribe with geographic territory (Moser
1956). *Volk* carried a social connotation. He postulated a whole people in
history, where everyone was suffused with myths and folk poetry. In the
course of history would occur a division of the people into a level of the
learned and a level of the folk, and the mythology would remain, in
the form of tales and folk songs and legends, among the folk where such
goods were taken care of and passed on. This passing on is what ennobles
the folk element (Moser 1956:134).

In his collection of folksongs, organized into ethnic categories, and
throughout his writings, Herder worked with national characterizations.
His intellectual investment in theology and philosophy intersected with
his German ethnicity and his long professional engagement in the German
border region of Riga—today's Latvian capital. The dramatic European
political transformations occurring during his lifetime, in turn, influenced
his position toward the idea of nation. Already as a young man he recognized differences in taste and patterns of thought among people, and he
spoke against ranking one as better than another, formulated in a fragment entitled, "Of the differences of taste and ways of thinking among
humans" (1877–1913, vol. 32, pp. 18–21). Also in his youth he drafted
a document on "what place the German nation should take among the
educated European peoples." He opened with the statement "National
pride is absurd, ridiculous and harmful. But love for one's nation is duty
for everyone" (1877–1913, vol. 32, p. 519).

Herder felt that groups had differing "spiritual centers" [*Volksgeist*],
but the differences were the best proof for an underlying universal com-
monality. His *The Spirit of Hebrew Poetry* (1833 [German original 1782])
is a particularly interesting document that speaks to this point. In an effort
to confront the anti-Semitic prejudices of his era he mustered his convictions about the beauty of any language to its native speaker: "To judge a
nation, does one not need to step in its time, its country, its circle of
thought and feeling" (Herder 1782:226; my translation). Yet these Herderian nuclei of cultural relativity were also linked to his learning on original language. As a theologian, he was bound to believe in the ultimate
antiquity of biblical language, and in the process of praising the beauty,
archaic nature, and vividness of action of Old Testament language he built
a case for understanding the New Testament, and with it Christianity, as
a beneficiary of the Hebrew heritage. Driven perhaps to summarize the best
of Enlightenment thought and to stand up against the worst of its ahistori-

cal and absolutist philosophy (Berlin 1976:147–52), his efforts were profoundly humanistic, universalist, and Christian (Moser 1956:139).

Herder's intellectual politics supported the rights of different nations to pursue their own political style—as celebrated or essentialized in the epic poetry so overwhelming to him. His insights were politically adapted, narrowed, and ultimately undermined by the Romantic nationalists. Intellectually, though, the insights that Herder expressed became the central pursuit of folkloristics.

However, in delimiting the boundaries of a discipline, Herder's anthropological philosophy of an embracing authenticity of the emotions, body, soul, and mind was compartmentalized and compromised. Exuberance was difficult to translate into scholarly research goals and methodologies. Much like their counterparts in other fields, students of expressive culture were incapable of maintaining in scholarly practice the holism and enthusiasm of Herderian anthropological philosophy. Scholars marginalized the emotional and political components believed to reside in expressive culture, at best voicing them in private correspondence, and emphasized instead versions of a more objective, instrumentalized authenticity suitable for scientific inquiry.

Herder's philosophical and literary legacy inspired countless philosophical, literary, and social experiments (Lohre 1902). In Germany his efforts in folksong collection were continued in the works of prominent poets; the nascent popular press also drew inspiration from him. A young Goethe collected songs and narratives, and his comments bespeak the mix of intensely emotional discovery and nagging differentiation in aesthetic value: "'I do not want to dwell on their excellence,' [Goethe] writes, 'nor on the difference in their value; but so far I have carried them like a treasure close to my heart; all the girls who want to find favor in front of my eyes, must learn and sing them.' It is remarkable how here, in the midst of bubbling enthusiasm, a 'difference in value' is being considered" (Lohre 1902:60).[30]

Herder's Ossian essay was a "baptismal document for the genre [of folksong]" (Lohre 1902:11), and the translation of English songs, the collection of native material, and the discourse on folksong in general were carried out in literary, moralistic, and even medical journals.[31] The pedagogically inclined saw in folksong a morally superior genre, useful to inculcate morally appropriate sentiment. Thus, in 1798 a certain Doctor Hoche gave a talk in which he presented folksong as the perfect means to "sing all human and bourgeois virtues into the folk, in particular patriotism" (Lohre 1902:22).[32]

Poets embraced folksong as an avenue to the inner self, exemplified by Gottfried August Bürger's "Pouring Out of the Heart about Folk Poetry" (*Herzensausguss über Volkspoesie*). Bürger was one of the first to compose German literary ballads that aimed for a genuine but "purified" and, hence, aesthetically legitimate emulation of folk style. Thematically, they dwelled on ghosts, the dead, and werewolves (Cocchiara 1981:174–75, 607; Lohre 1902:6)—experiences and fantasies that claimed a folklife authenticity. The theme of mysteriousness and the dark, unknowable sides of human nature and belief was central to the creation, particularly to the reception of the major collection of folk materials to emerge at the turn of the eighteenth to the nineteenth century, Achim von Arnim (1781–1831) and Clemens Brentano's (1778–1842) "The Boys' Magic Horn" (*Des Knaben Wunderhorn*, 1979 [1806]).

August Stephan Winkelmann wrote that "the simple and naive folksong is the beginning of poetry and the culmination of art" (Rölleke 1979:17). It was reputedly his "genial" idea to compile a volume of folksongs that would both repudiate Enlightenment folksong abuse and constitute the pinnacle of all earlier folksong collections. The "Magic Horn" is the best illustration of the importance of the idea of folksong to poetry and society. More than fifty authors and scholars sent texts; in addition, Arnim and Brentano consulted some 140 published works—anything from scholarly editions to anonymous journal contributions. The collection's content and style created the emotive atmosphere that the Romantics yearned for, and to suit this goal the two poets edited the texts to "regain the folksongs which had been variously worked over and contaminated in their 'pure' form" (Rölleke 1979:57).

The aesthetic mission of the "Magic Horn" and the keen interest in producing a volume that would become one of the books which a German bourgeois household could not do without lent the work a sense of social mission lacking in preceding efforts. One early collector had introduced a volume with the phrase "let us perambulate a little in the Garden of God," pointing to the originality and hence spiritual purity or authenticity of folksong (Gräter cited in Lohre 1902:103), but Arnim and Brentano wanted to demonstrate the creative potential of anonymous folksong and its ability to stir the heart. The work was dedicated to Goethe, whose youth ouevre was cited as inspiration for the collection of song. Defending their editorial work—which freely added or eliminated verses, and combined the anonymous with the authored—Arnim characterized the zeal that possessed them as a wondrous sensation, one that folded the past into the present, almost uncannily, but soothingly when expressed in the poetic (Arnim 1963 [1818]:264). In their decision to document only folksongs of their native language and land, their work clearly departed from the Herderian charter. "They believed that all the folk, the entire nation, could gain an awareness of its own nationality from such literature," and their goal, then, was ultimately both educational (Cocchiara 1981:207) and sentimental.

The "Magic Horn" constituted a victory in the long discourse on the poetic. Sentiment had outdistanced reason, and the seemingly "raw" and "natural" character of "folk poetry" replaced artificiality. The focus on the poetic and its authenticated locus in folksong contributed to the privileged position that such song took among the genres of expressive culture which would eventually shape the canon of folklore studies.

In the context of the dramatic political and social transformations of early nineteenth-century Germany, however, this emotional/experiential attempt to recover authenticity was soon joined by new, pragmatic demands. Chapter 2 recounts the emergence of the scholarly project to ascertain the authenticity of folkloric and literary materials on the backdrop of the equally praxis-oriented nationalist project's need for representations of the authentic. In the process, folktales emerged as a second generic favorite, which, like songs, permitted production and distribution of popular books for home and hearth. Folktale collections, spearheaded in Germany by the Brothers Grimm, continued to "enliven and exalt" cultural heritage by bringing it back, in restored and cleansed form, to the folk (Goethe cited by Arnim 1963 [1818]:262).

Chapter 2

From Experience to Representation
The Onset of a Scientific Search
for Authenticity[1]

He looked into the water and saw that it was made up of a thousand thousand thousand and one different currents, each one a different color, weaving in and out of one another like a liquid tapestry of breathtaking complexity; . . . these were the Streams of Story, . . . each colored strand represented and contained a single tale. Different parts of the Ocean contained different sorts of stories, and as all the stories that had ever been told and many that were still in the process of being invented could be found here, the Ocean of the Streams of Story was in fact the biggest library in the universe. And because the stories were held here in fluid form, they retained the ability to change, to become new versions of themselves, to join up with other stories and so become yet other stories; so that unlike a library of books, the Ocean of the Streams of Story was much more than a storeroom of yarns. It was not dead but alive.
—Salman Rushdie (1990:72)

Salman Rushdie's tale of Haroun Khalifa and his quest to rescue the Sea of Stories from the polluting poisons of a ruler intent on eliminating all that cannot be ruled stands as compelling testimony to the power and beauty of narrative. Rushdie locates the source of narrative inspiration on a separate moon made entirely of story waters, his hero in charge of restoring the purity and health of narratives. This moon, as a symbolic allusion to Romantic utopias, invokes both distance from the "real" and desire to attain and incorporate the utopian.

Rushdie's choice of organic metaphor indicates the longevity of the pure politics of Romanticism's trope of nature versus corrupting civilization. Folklorists have been familiar with this since the Romantic beginnings of their discipline, reflected in countless testimonies.

> When storms . . . have beaten the crops down into the ground, we find that near hedges and bushes . . . single stalks of wheat remain erect. When the sun shines again, they continue to grow isolated and unnoticed. . . . But late in the summer, when they are ripe and full, poor hands search for them, bundle them stalk by stalk, . . . carry them home and throughout the winter they are nourishment, perhaps the only seed for the future. (Grimm and Grimm 1976 [1819]:29)

The exuberant, highly emotional vocabulary of authenticity employed by the Romantics has received ample treatment. What I focus on here is rather the effort to render authenticity as a scientifically verifiable entity, a preoccupation of scholars in the early nineteenth century, in the era when a scientific mentality began to infiltrate the emotional vocabulary of Romanticism.

The scientific path was ostensibly chosen to lend credibility to a scholarly enterprise and to create distance from the emotionality and apparent imprecision of Romanticism. But "scientific methods" did not constitute a clear departure from Romantic longings. Systematic research agendas were instead a means of making operational and external what the Romantics had formulated in highly personal, experiential language.

Documenting these early efforts to ascertain authenticity by means of scientific methods is crucial for grasping folklore's disciplinary self-awareness. "Scientifically" oriented scholars up to the present have often distanced themselves from the Romantic nationalist legacy, yet the evidence shows that rationales for scholarly goals were entangled with latent sociopolitical fantasies. The craving for a communalist, authentic folk ideal increasingly shifted to private discourse, but it nonetheless continued to inform scientific goals. The scientific apparatus designed to define and verify authenticity legitimated academic endeavors, which were increasingly distant from sociopolitical concerns (Briggs 1993). But the apparent dichotomy was and is a mistaken one (Kirshenblatt-Gimblett 1988), for many debates of the 1980s and 1990s bear witness to the conflicts arising from sociopolitical and academic trajectories, each of which voiced its claim to guarantee "true" authenticity.

In a climate of scientism, the moral and emotional conceptualization of authenticity required material representation. Within this larger discourse among nineteenth century scholars, I will contrast the Brothers Jacob Grimm (1785–1863) and Wilhelm Grimm (1787–1859) with the philologically inspired literary criticism and reconstructionism of one of their friends and colleagues, Carl Lachmann (1793–1851).[2] I will delineate the emerging difference between an anonymous "folk" authenticity and individual, authorial authenticity. The two notions asserted themselves concurrently, and at the time they were not perceived as antagonistic. Their reverberations, however, have made themselves felt in countless disputes up to the present whenever competing visions of the locus of genuineness have been debated.[3]

In the contrast between locating authenticity in individual genius and in the folk as an anonymous community in an idealized past, one recognizes the bourgeois discomfort at identifying either with a heritage of high cultural, feudal, and individualistic authorship or a more democratic, but baser, folk heritage. Interwoven with this unease is the lingering question of spirituality and religion, for though emotional vigor was displaced by scientific probing, the search for origins and proof of authenticity could not lessen the civilizatory pain over the loss of God's ultimate authority (Berman 1988). The search for authenticity is ultimately a search for a *spiritual essence,* and scholars' differing paths toward integrating or excluding their religious beliefs in their consideration of authenticity remain a telling testimony to the hidden complexities of the "authenticity question."

EMERGING FROM ROMANTICISM

The Romantics reveled in their discovery of folk poetry, and their prose betrays their inebriate fervor. But were the songs and tales heard among the folk the "true" form of folk poetry? While the intellectual construct of "the folk" projected an image of purity and genuineness, the social reality of those from whom poetry was collected could hardly appear pure to an elite accustomed to disdaining the lower orders. Herder had stated in no uncertain terms that the folk were "not the rabble in the alleys: they never sing and compose but only scream and mutilate" (Herder 1807:69). Herder implied a differentiation between an idealized and rural "folk" and those new urban lower classes who were rapidly losing the "natural nobility" of their peasant forebears.[4] The transformation of feudal estates into the social and economic classes emerging with urbanization and industrialization is witnessed in unreflected experiences, such as Lachmann's report to Jacob Grimm about his exhilarating trip to Berlin: "You can't stand the folk of Berlin, and I perhaps even less. But one does not live anywhere as one does in Berlin, and one feels little of the folk" (Leitzmann 1927:372). Such lived judgments formed the basis of later articulations, distinguishing popular and mass culture from folk and elite.[5]

Authenticity came to be associated with materialized texts, while those harboring the texts remained largely anonymous and were increasingly projected into a more appealing past. This mental shift allowed a corresponding practical shift from mere Romantic longing to the scholarly search for authentic origins.

The "artifactualization" of expressive culture, as Susan Stewart has called it (1991b:105), entailed more than extracting texts while ignoring social and personal contexts. Rather, the process went hand in hand with favoring certain genres and contents over others deemed less wondrous or beautiful. Herder's generation favored folksong, as did Achim von Arnim and Clemens Brentano's *Wunderhorn* collection (1979 [1806]). But though the Grimms also collected folksong and contributed to the *Wunderhorn* (Denecke and Oberfeld 1989), they promoted the case of folktales with such tenacity that their voluminous scholarly work on legends, legal antiquities, heroic epics, and mythology has been forgotten by all but a narrow group of specialists. Yet it was through the study of genres other than the *Märchen* that the Grimms deepened their scholarly quest for original language and history.

Folksong and folktale had greater aesthetic appeal to the larger public than did the fragments of legal antiquities so dear to Jacob Grimm. But disembodied from their social context and gathered in books, the literate medium of communication, folksong and folktale turned increasingly into commodities. In rendering the oral and experiential into something material and readable, the early collectors assisted their social class in acquiring a "fragment of a larger whole . . . of the entire aura of the oral world—such a world's imagined presence, immediacy, organicism, and authenticity" (Stewart 1991b:104).

The commodification of folk genres sometimes facilitated nationalist thought, and the nationalist cause had a great impact on budding folkloristic theory and practice. Although Herder's enthusiasm for ethnically different folk poetries was fueled in part by a humanitarian and universalist orientation, such manifestations of ethnic difference could be (and continue to be) taken as symbolic evidence of political difference. Specific bodies of folk literature turned into vehicles to argue the case for political union or independence, starting with *Ossian* for the Celts, the Grimms' tales for a fragmented Germany (Dundes 1985), or the *Kalevala* epic for the Finns (Wilson 1976, Honko 1987). The connection rendered favored folk genres into icons of national identity—a latent legacy that has been among the first to be deconstructed in the historiography of the discipline in the West (Handler 1988, Herzfeld 1982, Linke 1990, Oinas 1978, Wilson 1976).[6] This well-known entanglement of nationalism and folklore forms at best a backdrop to the search for authenticity. My interest focuses on language as both an object of study and a rhetorical device.

The origin, evolution, and spread of language was of paramount importance to German intellectuals. Their preoccupation with expressive culture ultimately illuminated the aesthetics and politics of language more generally, for it was in the mystery of language that the essence of human existence and history was felt to lodge. How the Grimms and their contemporaries deployed language offers the clearest inroad into the discourse on authenticity. The emotional nature of the Romantic search for the origin of language, which in turn imbued the study of history, had thus far been addressed largely through philosophical conjecture.

The emergence of scientific and empirical modes of investigation demanded proof of authenticity. The Grimms and their circle in Germany are prime examples of the intertwining of Romantic ideology and scientific methodology. Their hearts belonged to the Romantics, but their findings were cast in the forms of scientific humanism.

AUTHENTICITY AND THE BROTHERS GRIMM

From the Soul of the Folk to Scholarly Collection

Herder had distinguished between "the rabble in the alleys" and the genuine folk, and the bourgeoisie convinced itself that "the folk" of their day were merely the carriers rather than the originators of an ennobling authentic poetry. The search for the original—hence, the most authentic—form became necessary. Assiduous scholarly ingenuity would try to recoup "the truth" from the rubble of history in an era when "scientific methodologies" permeated the natural sciences and influenced the humanities. What had been literary and social speculation now needed systematic research. The status issues rankled, however. "Finding half a dozen stars or producing an anatomy of a mosquito leg is approved of by everyone and results in medals," Carl Lachmann wrote in 1822. "But I can find a couple hundred fake aorists [Latin verse measures] and no one could care less" (Leitzmann 1972:373).

Lachmann's acerbic note alluded to the societal response to scientific travel journals such as those published by Alexander von Humboldt (1769–1859) on South America. Humboldt spoke as eloquently for a holistic, scientific study of earth and nature as his brother, Wilhelm von Humboldt

(1767–1835), spoke for the humanistic understanding of languages, literatures, and history.[7] The Brothers Humboldt as well as the Brothers August Wilhelm (1767–1845) and Friedrich von Schlegel (1772–1829), both influential in defining and disseminating Indo-Europeanist scholarship, all stand as paradigmatic examples of an era that shifted from generalist scholarship (*Universalgelehrtentum*) toward disciplinary specialization and subspecialization. All of them underwent periods of Romantic exuberance, but they also turned to forms of rigorous analysis. All four of them had the status and financial means to wield substantial influence on the unfolding intellectual landscape at institutions of higher learning. The authenticity problem is discussed here through the eyes of the Grimms and Lachmann, but it is to be understood that parallels can be found in the works and correspondences of the Humboldts, Schlegels, and the larger intellectual circles that they formed.[8]

The Grimm Brothers are the most widely researched figures in the history of folkloristics, and, given the tremendous impetus they gave not only to the study of folklore but to philology, literary scholarship, and the history of religion, such prominence is deserved.[9] Jacob and Wilhelm Grimm were also key players in the construction of the scholarly, pragmatic approach to the concept of authenticity.[10] Their works and correspondence illustrate a growing disenchantment with Romantic exuberance and an increasing concern with using systematic means to document a truer, hence more authentic past.

The initial publication of the *Kinder- und Hausmärchen* (*KHM*) in 1812 was influenced by *Des Knaben Wunderhorn* (Arnim and Brentano 1979 [1806]).[11] But even here, the Grimms confined themselves to what they perceived as genuine folk materials and kept records of their research, in contrast to the ebullient pastiche of texts in the immensely popular *Wunderhorn*. While there were earlier collections of tales in French and Italian as well as German, the preface and comparative notes in the *KHM* were a complete novelty in the publication of "simple folktales." The brothers' emphasis on generic distinctions led to Wilhelm's work on heroic legends and epic poems, Jacob's work on legal antiquities and mythology, and their joint work on legends. In short, they saw categories where their precursors and contemporaries preferred seeing a treasure with individual pieces whose glitter enhanced the value of the whole. The treasure metaphor has been frequently applied to folklore materials and constitutes a material parallel to the less materialistic nature metaphors.[12] In the Romantic spirit the metaphoric reference was to a social value—a treasure from the past to strengthen the culture of the present. But as scholars began to weigh the relative merit of oral, printed, and manuscript sources, literal notions of scarcity became more evident in the vocabulary.

The *KHM* appeared amid the turbulence of the Napoleonic Wars. Accepting French Revolutionary ideals intellectually was not the same as agreeing at the point of a bayonet. The settlements of the Congress of Vienna resulted in thirty-nine German states—thirty-five monarchies and four free cities. Old feudal orders had long begun to crumble, but now political developments caught up with economic and social transformations. The predictability of hierarchical social arrangements waned along with the Old Order. While the Romantic revolution had aspired to precisely such transformations, their actual occurrence made for more pessimistic assessments of the sociopolitical reality.[13]

The Grimms' tales became a central icon in the nationalization of a disparate German political realm and a moral guide for an emerging bourgeoisie. The Grimms may have hoped for such a development, but they certainly did not materially profit from it. Their introduction to the second edition of the *KHM* (1819) reflects the changing mentality of this decade, capturing the transition from the Herderian, Romantic search for the purifying voice of the folk to the nostalgic, pessimistic, and class-conscious view of the scholar who hopes to capture the remnants of unspoiled humanity. Rather than reveling in the natural beauty and abundance of folk poetry, there was now the anxiety of losing the last remnants of Eden's spoils, and religious imagery, although perhaps unintentional, shimmers through much of the Grimms' language.

With a few powerful images, the Grimms invoke nature metaphors and establish through them a vocabulary of authenticity. "The epic foundation of folk poetry resembles the many shades of green in all of nature, greens that satisfy and mollify without ever tiring" (1980 [1857]:31). Like children and like nature, folk artistry is unspoiled, and reading the tales promises to put the reader in touch with what seemed lost under layers of corrupting civilization. But unlike nature's abundance, folk poetry is characterized as a sparse good. Comparing folk customs and verbal art to single stalks of wheat that survive a great storm or drought, the Grimms state: "Of all that has flourished in earlier times, nothing remains, even the memory fades, except for the songs of the folk, a few books, legends and these *innocent* household tales. . . . Inside this poetry flows the same kind of purity which makes children appear so *wonderful* and *blessed*" (1980 [1857]:29–30; my emphases). Innocence, purity, and blessedness are terms delineating a morally and religiously suffused authenticity.

The scholar's task was to recover and restore such beauty. Jacob Grimm's enormous labor to restore Old High German and Middle High German vocabulary and grammar served to trace language back to find the earliest forms of Teutonic civilization. He brought similar principles to the study of mythology, and again the natural metaphors abound: "From the drying up waters [of mythology] one has to guess at the source, from the standing marshes the old stream['s flow]" (J. Grimm 1876 [vol. 2]:vi).

Jacob Grimm invoked the value of folk materials, carried away by his own language, without ever specifying why such value should be bestowed on them. "If those numerous written monuments have seemingly left individual bones and joints of the old mythology, we are nonetheless still touched by its unique breath from a mass of legends and customary practices ... with what fidelity they propagate themselves has only been recognized since their great value has been realized and one has begun ... to collect them" (1876 [vol. 2]:xi). Waters muddied and purified, nature trampled and restored to luscious greens, and even a skeleton revived to pulsate in flesh and blood were a part of the panoply of organic metaphors. Fields full of weeds, where little beauty was left unless restored by scholarly toil, was the organic trope for the present.[14]

The treasure of *Naturpoesie* had to be handled properly, that is, scientifically. Jacob stated:

> Folk legend needs to be read and broken by virgin hand. He [who] attacks her roughly will find only bent leaves and her fragrance withheld. In her, there is a find of rich unfolding and blossoming; even an incomplete deliverance of [such] natural jewelry suffices—which would be disturbed through foreign additions. He who would venture this would ... have to be inculcated into the innocence of folk poetry in its entirety (1876 [vol. 2]:xi).

Sage, or legend, is a feminine noun in German. But the imagery invoked here does not simply do justice to the grammatical gender but constitutes a familiar treatment of the feminine and the natural through the civilized male (Ortner 1974).

The Grimms' preface to the *KHM,* with practical observations on how they realized their goals in gathering the tales, was highly influential in delineating how authenticity in data would be ascertained by future generations. Historically worthy contributions could best be found in places where natural dialects had not been corrupted by standard language and where writing had not "dulled" tradition. The construction of a dichotomy between the "purity of dialects" and the spoiling effects of standard language is but one of the ironies or reversals in the history of the politics of authenticity. The German standard language was a hard-won political and literary asset after long periods when French was considered the superior language. The New High German that gained acceptance through exemplary works disenfranchised the speakers of dialect. The Grimms were concerned with textual authenticity, not the rights of dialect speakers, but the politics of language nonetheless bubbled under the surface. The very tools of their trade—writing and publishing in the new standard—were perceived as spoiling agents of the materials studied. Clearly, the privilege to speak and write in the politically powerful idiom was still to be kept from the bearers of tradition, who therefore, by implication, were also kept from social and political ascendance. With regard to the history of dialect scholarship, Hermann Bausinger has observed a scholarly "tri-furcation": patronizing Enlightenment, romanticizing conservatism, and emancipating democratization (1973:11). It appears that scholarly practices and dicta of the Grimms oddly combine elements of all three characteristics.

The Grimms' belief in an authentic tradition came out clearly in their description of one of their main informants, Frau Viehmann:

> She narrated in a measured way, *sure* and unbelievably lively, with quite some pleasure, first completely *spontaneously,* and then, if one wanted it, more slowly, so that is was possible . . . to transcribe her. In this way, much was maintained literally and its *truth* will be unmistakable. Those who believe in easy *falsification* of tradition, through sloppiness in memory, . . . should have heard how she always stuck with a narrative and was keen on its *correctness;* she never changed a thing in a repetition and corrected a mistake herself, as soon as she noticed it, in the midst of her speech's flow. (1980 [1857]:33; my emphases)

Authenticity to the Grimms was largely restricted to content, to motifs; they freely admit their own editorial work[15] and portray it as serving such authenticity. "Everyone who has done [similar editorial tasks] will know that this is no carefree, thoughtless endeavor; on the contrary, a kind of attentiveness and tact, gained over time, are necessary in order to distinguish the more *simple* and more *pure* from the *falsified*" (Grimm and Grimm 1980 [1857]:35; my emphases). Authenticity is thus recognizable in what the scholar claims to be an external simplicity of form. The Grimms are convinced of the "truth and reliability" of their judgment because of what they perceive as the purity of the folk. "Poetry can only be composed from that which the poet feels and experiences *truthfully* within his heart, whereby the *language will reveal the words to him half consciously and half unconsciously*" (Grimm and Grimm 1981 [1816], vol. 1: 4–5; my emphases).[16] The folk are in the fortunate position of not being consciously aware of their poetic power.

In such brief prefatory notes, authenticity has been divided into two parts. The texts are *externally* authentic, verified by the internal honesty of the people who transmit the texts. While the people's honesty cannot necessarily be preserved, the textual authenticity of the tales and poetry can be; in this regard the Grimms foreshadow the practical paradoxes of the search for authenticity. They offer a recipe to recover the lost treasure and stake a claim for the specialist to serve as mediator. The specialist extracts the material from the folk (who are doomed to submit to the corrupting influences of progress), restores it to its original beauty, and offers it for ingestion to those upper classes who need a fix of authenticity. While the Grimms saw the folk as blissfully unconscious of their poetic power, the brothers themselves grew unconscious of the class and ideological boundaries on which their judgment was based.[17]

Even in their early work the Grimms transformed the experiential nature of the Romantic search for authenticity.[18] The overwhelming "discovery" of the spirit of the folk was reined in, artifactualized, and compartmentalized into ever-evolving generic categories. The beauty of the first encounter paled and made room for the fervent search for the more highly original beauty in the past with the intention of restoring it. The Grimms were not alone in this effort, nor was there just one ideology and avenue toward original authenticity.

Diverging Paths in the Search for Origins

The Grimms' work was part of an evolving landscape of scholarly fields concerned with the history and origin of language and literature. While the intellectual enterprise was dominated by establishing and legitimizing scholarly domains and methodologies, the question of authenticity and its ultimate locus lingered. Modernity is associated with the rise of individualism in political and social life; hence, religious legitimation is weakened or lost (Berman 1972; Trilling 1974). However, placing the locus of authenticity within the individual self was too bold a move for many scholars. A spiritual or God-given explanation remained powerful and consoling to those unwilling to accept an ultimate sublime experience as man-made. An anonymous folk community, preferably of the past, could be an acceptable resolution of the divide between the secular self and the spiritual ultimate. The folk community also contributed to the semireligious tone of the Grimms' characterizations.

The Romantic nationalist inspiration for finding the origins of one's own culture was a common, underlying motivator in the nineteenth century, but it was not the only one. As in the eighteenth century, translations remained an important impetus for study, arguably laying the foundation for an emerging high cultural notion of (world) literature. Oriental works were of growing interest, and through their study and translation a different approach to the question of language origins arose.[19] From the desire to find a "true poetic art of translation" (Behler 1983:6), as propagated especially by August Wilhelm Schlegel (who himself translated from Sanskrit), grew an urge to understand the true development and relationship among human languages. How desired, even craved, was access to the original language of Oriental treasures emerges from Wilhelm von Humboldt's letter written on receiving an advance copy of Schlegel's reprinting of the *Bhagavad Gita.*

> I thank you for the great pleasure which reading even a fraction of this poem has brought me. A certain childlikeness still remains with me for such things, and I cannot deny that during the reading a true thankfulness to fate overcame me for granting me to read this poem in the original language. . . . I feel as if I had missed something truly essential if I had had to leave this earth without [this experience]. One cannot claim to have discovered new truths. . . . But one is seized by such a wonderful feeling of ancient, great and deep humanity that one believes to be sensing in one moment the spiritual development of all human races and their kinship with the reign of everything invisible. (Leitzmann 1908:158)

Conjectural, comparative Indo-European language research, the historical reconstruction of one's native language, and the use of conjecture with an historico-critical method to reveal the original spirit of literary masterpieces, all were enterprises that influenced each other. The context came in the vigorous debates of the flourishing landscape of scholarly and popular journals as well as extensive personal correspondence.[20] The Brothers Schlegel, for instance, published most of their insights in journals, some of which they launched and edited themselves (Behler 1983).

The linguist and Indo-Europeanist Franz Bopp (1791–1867) illustrates by his career the transformation from Romantic infatuation to scholarly argumentation. Bopp absorbed from his first teacher in Germany the spirit of mystic devotion to Oriental culture, literature, and mythology. In Paris, however, Bopp not only learned Sanskrit, but also encountered a linguistic course of study that separated language from literature. This division influenced his own stance. "If initially I was encouraged to work assiduously because of my love for oriental literatures, languages themselves eventually became a cause no less worthy and important, and I felt within me the desire to contribute to the foundation of a general and scientific study of languages to understand how language arrived at its current level" (cited after Sternemann 1984 : 12). Strongly influenced by models from the natural sciences, Bopp strove to find "genetic interconnections between Indo-European languages" (Sternemann 1984 : 8), and through his knowledge of comparative language he hoped to construct an accurate image of growth and decay. The organic metaphor thus stayed in the vocabulary, but the *metaphoric* dimension was increasingly displaced by a belief in the *actual* organic nature and growth of languages. Bopp was also influenced by Wilhelm von Humbolt who in an 1812 essay "had considered mankind as a giant plant whose branches embraced all the earth. The time had come, he said, to study the multiple relationships between nations and their influences, and he suggested that the difference between nations was to be found in language" (Cocchiara 1981 : 234).

Jacob Grimm, although also inspired by contemporary assumptions of Indo-European language interrelationships (Kamenetsky 1992 : 99), began to work on the history of language in order to better understand "the most original and natural testimony of the—German—people, the poetry that grew with its history and development" (Sternemann 1984 : 12). To him, language remained throughout his life the major vehicle to understand and reconstruct an authentic German (or other national) past.

It is not surprising that a national spirit affected the Grimm Brothers' work as they experienced the formation of a German nation-state out of a bewildering multitude of smaller kingdoms and dukedoms during the course of their lives. Their works contributed to the cultural institutions that were fundamental to the "nationalization of the masses" (Mosse 1975), as in the associations formed to preserve and practice regional or national folk cultural heritage in song, dance, or sport. In his 1831 curriculum vitae, Jacob Grimm stated: "If [my] studies may seem to many unproductive, . . . to me they were always an honorable, serious task which . . . nourishes love for our common fatherland" (1879 : 18). Thanking the compiler of a work on "German Christmas plays in Hungary" in 1859, Jacob expressed his pleasure at "the patriotic love of the [Germans in] Transylvania" and his conviction that "all hope was not lost if they still felt German in the midst of [more] favorably treated Hungarians and Slavs" (J. Grimm 1867 : 14–15). But it was scholarship that preoccupied both Grimms far more than nationalism, and when they took political action it was in the name of individual liberty and democratic constitutionalism rather than nationalism.[21]

Jacob Grimm's commitment to democratic political principles went hand in hand with a strong faith in Protestantism, which arguably influenced his views on folklore. In bringing his religion in accord with his science, he demonstrated that his central question was whether language was God-given or a human creation. If human, one could study its origin, but if God-given, one could not. His stance implicitly acknowledged a belief in the ultimate and unknowable authenticity of a superior being. Jacob's clearest formulations on science, origins, and religion appeared in a talk presented to the Academy of Sciences in Berlin in 1851 on "The Origin of Language" (1879:256–99). The same institution had honored Herder's essay on the topic eighty years earlier, and Grimm felt that the enormous developments in language research since Herder's day warranted a renewed consideration of the question.[22]

Grimm began with a comparison of natural sciences as opposed to humanistic ones. Despite surface similarities, language researchers in Grimm's perception differed from natural scientists who were concerned with "penetrating the secrets of natural life, that is, the laws of conception and continuation of animals, the seeds and growth of plants," but who were not concerned with the origin or creation of flora and fauna. While Grimm saw "an analogy between creation and procreation," he felt that the difference between them was as marked "as between a first and a second act" (1879:261). If language were considered God's creation, "its first origin would remain as hidden from our gaze as that of the first origin of an animal or a tree." If, however, language were a human invention,

> That is, not unmediatedly brought forth through divine power, but shaped through the freedom of man himself, one may measure it according to [man's] laws, through that which history delivers back through its first stem, one may walk back across . . . the abyss of millennia and in one's thoughts even land on the shores of its origin. The language researcher may therefore . . . go farther than the natural scientist, because he researches a human work, lodged in our history and our freedom (1879:261).

To strengthen his position, Grimm reasoned against the hypothesis of language as divine creation or revelation. He warned against constructing "Ur-languages" and "perfections of forms removed into a supposed paradise" (1879:283). The mature Jacob Grimm is thus removed from his own and his brother's early Romantic enthusiasm for folktales, which they had described in paradisiacal metaphor.

Although his ammunition for arguing the case for a socially constructed and historically grown linguistic ability was drawn from the newly researched laws of language, Grimm's answer ultimately deviates from Herder's only in its greater emphasis on human liberty. "The delusion of a divine origin of language has been fully eliminated. It would have been contrary to God's wisdom to restrain in advance that which is to have a free human history, as it would have been contrary to His justice to let devolve from its summit a divine language given to the first humans. That which is divine in language stems only from the divine essence that rests in our nature and soul" (1879:283–84).

Such clear statements were rare in the increasingly thick web of scholarly paths concerned with the specifics of language and literary history. Yet in an age when both serious and gentleman scholars avidly published a heady mix of painstaking linguistic reconstruction, bold articulations on ultimate language forms, and nationalistic applications of historical linguistics, Grimm felt a need to clarify the bounds within which humans could test the depth of origins.

Wilhelm Grimm, too, was concerned with the question of folk literature's ultimate origin. But he was more given to speculation, and in his major independent work, the *German Heroic Legend* (1889 [1829]), he explored the divine and mythological nature of legends—a subject he had discussed in extensive correspondence with Carl Lachmann since 1821. The bulk of his study amassed the known evidence about German heroic legends. Within his sketchy analytic efforts, Wilhelm grappled with issues of mythology as opposed to history, and with orality and literacy.

The importance he attributed to performance is evident from his closing sentence, a quotation from Roman historian Ammianus on the learned men among the Celts:

> Now the Bards sang to the sweet strains of the lyre the valorous deeds of famous men composed in heroic verse, but the Euhages, investigating the sublime, attempted to explain the secret laws of nature. The Druids, being loftier than the rest in intellect, and bound together in fraternal organization, as the authority of Pythagoras determined, were elevated by their investigation of obscure and profound subjects, and scorning all things human, pronounced the soul immortal. (W. Grimm 1889 [1829]:447)[23]

Wilhelm's consideration of historical and literary passages on bards, their social standing, and their assigned task indicate that he recognized the relationship between narrative truth and societal contexts; as with the *Märchen,* Wilhelm acknowledged variant versions as expressions of individual adaptations of traditional core elements. In a letter of 1821 he wrote: "I believe the earliest poetry is connected to the revelations of supernatural ideas made more or less cloudy" (Leitzmann 1927:793). He was interested in what happened to these "ideas" over time, and he wanted to pin down "the changes which the poetry experiences in the mouth of singers or through written recording" (1889 [1829]:421). He lamented that "we ought to know the actual meaning of 'singing' and 'saying' as it [was] used in connection with the performance of epic songs, in order for us to be better informed about the nature [of performance]" (p. 422):

> The written recording of poems must certainly have had a great influence. Both sources [written and oral] crossed each other and the impact on the purity of the legend could be either propitious or detrimental. Writing may capture tradition, but on the other hand it opens the door to a recording that might by chance be *defective* or *spoiled.* The dumb and solitary reading as it has now become possible lacks the impression of living song, and where the care for the maintenance of memory no longer applies, the power of memory is automatically diminished, which favors an incomplete knowledge of the legend. (1889 [1829]:427; my emphases)

Remarkable in foreshadowing concerns of the second half of the twentieth century, this passage points to Wilhelm's early awareness of contextualized "truths" or authenticities. He clearly sensed that heroic legends were neither mythological-divine nor fully historical, and he considered shifting attitudes toward narrative.

Both Grimms reflected on traditional (implicitly defined as oral) as opposed to the authored work of art (Kamenetsky 1992:63–64). The difference between individually authored poetry (or *Kunstpoesie*) and anonymous folk poetry, so central to the Herderian or Romantic outburst in favor of *Naturpoesie,*[24] went hand in hand with emerging notions of high cultural canons as opposed to popular or low cultural expressive forms.[25] Although folksong or folktales had been elevated to the status of sublime expressions of an authentic spirit, turning them into books made them high cultural possessions.

Throughout, the Grimms remained concerned with language and history as expressed in the folklore of their people as a whole. They searched for an authenticity lodged in the past that would nourish and educate their compatriots' present and future with the purity of a German spirit of the past. Yet among their scholarly friends and competitors there were others whose acquaintance with literary and linguistic history contributed instead to a favored status of the authored work. In the competing interests of anonymous *Naturpoesie*'s authenticity over that of *Kunstpoesie*, these scholars established canons to ascertain authorial authenticity.

In hindsight, the impact of print technology on scholarship is overwhelmingly obvious. Theoretically and methodologically, scholars were engaged in reconstructing languages, texts, and works of art. But pragmatically, this entailed deciphering handwritten, often singular manuscripts and hypothesizing on oral "originals" in order to ultimately produce for broad distribution printed works that contained a suggested authentic reading. Countless letters between the Grimms and Lachmann attest to the omnipresence of print, with printer's deadlines and with galleys shipped ahead for comment. Although not theorized in such terms by those who used them, print media as the major tool for sharing scholarly research clearly added further layers to the meaning of authenticity.

Carl Lachmann, Authenticity, and the Paradox of Literacy

In 1826 August Wilhelm Schlegel wrote this eulogy of the translator:

> One might praise the genuine translator who not only translates the content of a master work but also the noble form, who knows how to maintain the peculiar character, [for he is] a true herald of the genius. He spreads the fame and bestows the gifts [inherent in a work] beyond the boundaries of languages. He is a messenger from nation to nation, a communicator of mutual respect and admiration where otherwise indifference or even rejection took place. (cited after Behler 1983:7)

Schlegel did not write this passage with a particular person in mind (other than perhaps himself), but the Grimms' contemporary, Carl Lachmann, aspired to achieve precisely this kind of translation. In Lachmann, one may discern differentiations in what was meant by "genuine" or authentic during the early to mid-nineteenth century.

In the German context the eighteenth-century discovery of folk poetry was intertwined with efforts to establish German as a suitable language for literary writing. The sociopolitical tremors preceding the French Revolution produced in German areas a philosophical and literary revolution before political and constitutional movements toward national unity took hold. As in the scholarly systematization of language and folklore research, the enthusiastic pre-Romantic discovery of medieval German manuscripts gave way to a rigorous discipline of text-editing. If the effort to recover or demonstrate the existence of a *national* literature had been dominant in the pre-Romantic era, in the editing of medieval texts during the nineteenth century the patriotic element was joined by an increasing interest in the restoration of *individual* genius.

Carl Lachmann began as a classicist, and in his editions of Roman poets he established a method of evaluating manuscripts that differed from the prevalent approaches which were based largely on subjective criteria of aesthetic taste. Lachmann instead attempted to "objectively" construct a genealogy of handwritten manuscripts, and working backward through time he hoped to lay bare the oldest text; soon he included medieval German texts in his endeavors. Through this interest he began his lifelong correspondence, and at times his warm friendship, with the Brothers Grimm in 1820, despite their increasingly different orientation from his own toward the central tasks of a developing discipline.[26] Lachmann never fully formulated an account of his methodology,[27] but his correspondence indicates the emergence of a different concept of authenticity than that of the Grimms.

Authenticity as a criterion in scholarship already had been invoked in one of Jacob Grimm's first letters to Lachmann. In expressing his growing admiration for Lachmann's "precision and rigor," Grimm wrote, "What advantage you are able to extract from everything, especially in making a judgment concerning the genuineness of the single poems and of the dialects" (4.1.1820, in Leitzmann 1927:80). Jacob could draw on all available sources in his construction of a grammar of a historical German language, but Lachmann needed to make judgments on the age and authenticity of individual manuscripts in his quest to "peel out of the spoiling influence of a handwritten tradition the aesthetic meaning and artistic form of medieval poetry" (Leitzmann 1927:xiv).[28] In a letter from 1823, for instance, Lachmann details how he reached the conclusion that Wolfram's heroic poem *Parcival* must have been conceived in segments of thirty verses each. He compared manuscripts, observed the regular recurrence of capital letters, and relied on his knowledge of Wolfram as a poet "who, unlike all the others, used words sparingly" and who therefore might "not have been indifferent as to the length of his poem." This analysis allowed him to differentiate between "more and less truthful manuscripts," to judge one section "an addition, but obviously a genuine one," and to recommend the St. Gall manuscript "with one verse crossed off and those other ones added in as a Parcival lacking nothing in the way of integrity" (7.2. 1823, Leitzmann 1927:408–9).

The *material* authenticity of given manuscripts, distinct from the spiritual genuineness so central to the Romantics, emerges from both sides of the correspondence. Thus, Jacob Grimm in 1821 bemusedly discredited a review of his own German grammar, as the reviewer had used what he considered inauthentic evidence: "[I find] funniest that he introduces at the end the falsified or fake tablets which were, I believe, found in Goslar" (Leitzmann 1927:263).

The scholarly need to get hold of manuscripts in the first place was hampered by the entanglement of notions of material authenticity and monetary value held by collectors. Lachmann, the Grimms, and many others invested considerable time and resources traveling to libraries and archives to copy—or course, by hand!—as many manuscript versions of given texts as possible. Possession of such manuscripts itself became a means of materially partaking of authenticity, and friendships were made and broken over access to particularly important clues. Lachmann's difficult relationship with his wealthy Berlin friend Meusebach, an avid collector of original manuscripts, is just one case in point (Weigel 1989).

The collector's protectiveness clearly hampered scholarship, an obstacle that scholars found both annoying and amusing. Thus Jacob Grimm consoled Lachmann, who had been unable to borrow a manuscript from the library in Karlsruhe, by recalling "that when I once asked for a manuscript from Stuttgart, I received a formal reply from the state government (. . .): it was not possible, because a manuscript once used or copied lost part of its value!" (Leitzmann 1927:231–32). A bureaucratic and popular concept of genuineness, with judgments of its monetary value and causes for its depreciation, had taken hold and was applied to cultural products once deemed worthless. This change is also apparent when correspondents fret over the lack of value placed on authentic materials during past centuries—again in the words of Jacob Grimm: "Hofmann (an assiduous, good, still somewhat folkish library assistant in Bonn) has [discovered] and detached from a bookbinding the leaves of a splendid Otfried-manuscript. He now gets them printed authentically, with the accents; the shameful bookbinders of the fifteenth, sixteenth, and seventeenth century!" (Leitzmann 1927:275).

But the Grimms and Lachmann differed in their opinions on individual poets and on questions of grammar and reconstruction. Lachmann's goal was the discovery of the genuine text, and with that the genuine author, of a given work; the Grimms' goal was the genuine representation of an authentic cultural past. Thus, in an 1820 letter Lachmann praised a particular copy of a major Walther von der Vogelweide manuscript because "many of the songs are more genuine [in it]" (Leitzmann 1927:248). In

1822, when working on an edition of *Parcival,* he expressed his frustration: "I have finished the Heidelberg reading.[29] That which is really mistaken is mostly taken care of, in as much as we may hope for rescue from manuscripts at all. [It is] unbelievable how even Müller's printing errors mislead . . . : great doubts remain concerning the most genuine reading" (Leitzmann 1927:350). Jacob Grimm in 1823 praised the medieval poet Wolfram von Eschenbach (the presumed author of *Parcival*) for his use of "barbaric" words and names rather than metrically pleasing ones, which he attributes to Wolfram's "feeling for and fidelity to tradition" (Leitzmann 1927:384). But Lachmann expresses doubts about the idiosyncrasies of a given manuscript: "I have reached the point where in the [reconstruction] of *Parcival* I emphasize that which is idiosyncratic in a manuscript least. Your fragments confirm that especially [this] manuscript has the most idiosyncrasies and the least genuine text" (Leitzmann 1927: 393). Lachmann recognized the difference between their approaches, and in October 1825 he wrote: "The slavish dependence from a couple scribes makes for a dreadful feeling in doing critical editions. How I envy you your work, and yet I know how poorly I'd do it, and that I would never finish it" (Leitzmann 1927:463).

Still, the exchange between the Grimms and Lachmann was extremely fruitful for both sides. Lachmann's ultimate aim—the reconstruction of a pure text gained from the methodical comparison of extant manuscript—necessitated two things: a grammar and a metrical system of Middle High German, to both of which Jacob Grimm amply contributed.[30]

Lachmann came to hold the place of inventor of the text-critical method, which based itself on the following principles:

1. At the beginning of a known traditional text [such as *Parcival*], there must be one, and only one, archetype.

2. Each person copying the text may only use one single master copy, that is, all subsequent manuscripts have to refer back to a "mother-manuscript."

3. The kinship between the passed on manuscripts can be diagnosed without ambiguity.

4. The copyist must have intended a representation [of the original] true to the text. Between original and copy there may not be any discontinuities. (Weigel 1989:178)

Contrary to editorial practices that favored choosing one manuscript as the best on the basis of aesthetic criteria and publishing it with the least interference possible, the "genealogical" nature of Lachmann's "historical-critical" system allowed a "mechanical (i.e., "objective") means of eliminating those readings erroneously introduced into the author's text and reconstructing the lost original" (Hult 1988:79). Implied was the assumption that this editorial process was guided by fact rather than intuition. Nonetheless, both positive and negative assessments of Lachmann's stance praised his keen intuition that resulted in an aesthetically pleasing text.[31] Despite his almost pedantic insistence on the correctness of his scholarship, Lachmann's inspiration and drive, like the Grimms', stemmed from Romantic impulses, and his ultimate goal was to make available in as pure a form as possible the sublime poetry of a past age. "In Lachmann's editions one soul speaks to another. Through his text, says Lachmann in the preface to his *Iwein,* the reader gets the original authentically imprinted onto his own disposition" (Weigel 1989:228).

However, this purity was achieved at the cost of sacrificing much material that had already attained a certain currency for a reading public and scholars alike. Lachmann's *Nibelungen* edition, for instance, which has remained the standard one far into the twentieth century (Lachmann 1960 [1841]), hurt many sensibilities, including that of the Grimms. It carried a subtitle "according to the oldest tradition with indication of the spurious," and Lachmann's genealogical method resulted in omissions of substantial portions of what had been treated as the complete epic. Jacob Grimm, after reading the galley proofs, confessed his unease at seeing Lachmann work with an authenticity achieved by means of grammatical and metrical logic as opposed to "faithful adherence to a manuscript" (Leitzmann 1927:475–76). Even in Lachmann's obituary, Grimm could not refrain from noting that "a number of beautiful and moving stanzas one can hardly do without were dropped from Lachmann's twenty [*Nibelungen*] songs, and there is much in the *Iliad* that he denies that I would not want to take away" (Grimm 1879:157).

Lachmann's *Nibelungen* edition may have lasted far into the twentieth century, but in his own time his insistence on striving for a new and more rigorous editorial authentification cost him dearly. The *Nibelungen* saw several editions before and concurrent with Lachmann's, among them one by Lachmann's major competitor, Friedrich Heinrich von der Hagen (see Grunewald 1988). The rivalry between von der Hagen and Lachman could be considered almost a blueprint for one of the less pleasant aspects of academic politics. Ridiculed in letters and reviews by Lachmann for less careful and hence less truthful scholarship, von der Hagen, the first person to hold a German chair in 1812, received a chair in Berlin for which Lachmann had also applied.[32] Hardly remembered now, von der Hagen was motivated by the same ideological and scholarly currents as were the

Grimms, Lachmann, and scores of other now forgotten scholars; he, too, had embarked on a collection of folksong, and he, too, struggled with how to render what he found to preserve its authenticity while making it accessible (Grunewalt 1988:274).

Lachmann was not concerned with popular appeal, as is evidenced in his most embattled editorial project, an edition of the New Testament. On the surface this endeavor entailed a new challenge since suitable manuscripts were scarce and a variety of early medieval scripts had to be deciphered (Leitzmann 1927:525–33). But beyond the world of scholarship, Lachmann's edition "constituted a provocation," as it was the first to deviate from the *textus receptus* and to reconstruct the *Vulgata* text "as it had been used in East and West at the end of the 4th century" (Weigel 1989:162). In this bold—and to Christian authorities highly offensive— endeavor, one recognizes the explosive question of the ultimate locus of spiritual or divine authenticity.

Lachmann, an acerbic skeptic, plainly showed that the Bible was the work of human creativity. Although he claimed that his work was merely textual and external and that he would leave the "internal cleansing," the second step of this reconstruction, to theologians, he nonetheless recognized that "only that which you have never seen will last eternally" (cited after Weigel 1989:164). In other words, in the case of the *Vulgata* the authorial voice, or the soul that would speak to the reader of the reconstructed and cleansed work, would have had to be God's voice. Yet the Bible could at best be a very limited and flawed *representation* of the Holy Spirit. Lachmann must have accepted this insight for his many other editions as well.

The deconstructionist impulse has led to more critical assessments of Lachmann's impact on conceptualizations and standards of authenticity. The 1927 editor of the Grimm-Lachmann correspondence still characterized Lachmann's approach as akin to that of "an experienced restorer who frees a painting from that which has been painted over it—the business of cleaning and recovering original poetic form" (Leitzmann 1927:xvi). More recent analyses emphasize the psychological drive of a compulsive and moralistic man living during an age when the medieval reverence for textual content was replaced by the modern reverence for individual creativity and authorship. Only an age relying on the power of print could arrive at the worship of the "unique shape" of a work and the disdain for the "unconscious falsification through tradition" entailed in the oral and handwritten medium. Weigel argues that for early-nineteenth-century scholars the "absence of authors was a source of anxiety, because the fragmented, mixed and discontinuous texts lacked unity," and the scientific method is a means for controlling one's own anxiety (1989:178–79).

CONCLUSION

Anxiety may have motivated the establishment of early nineteenth-century methodologies applied to folklore materials in Germany. Since emotionality and exuberance so prevalent in the Romantic period can be anxiety-inducing to the rational mind, recourse to systematization may appear as a means to rein in what can be uncontrollable states of mind. Weigel goes as far as to state that "Carl Lachmann introduced to philology the detour. A meaningless apparatus is supposed to facilitate an undisturbed locating of the authentic origin. . . . Constitutive of scientific insight is the notion of hurdle, without hurdle there is no science, for science is contrary to everyday experience. Objective insight contains a world of corrected errors" (1989:153). Another recent critic similarly noted the strong editorial control that brought about a "pretended immediacy and transparency of the text," masking what was "really a highly artificial product" (Mueller-Vollmer 1986:40).

The idea of individualistic genuineness that Lachmann and those who followed him aspired to was influenced by the powers of print. Literacy was only the first step in capturing authorial genius, and handwriting was everything but perfect. Every copyist was likely to introduce errors that needed to be purged, and only print allowed for uniformity and perfection. Printed books facilitated the general spread of individual thought, and Lachmann's ideology of authenticity favored an individual creativity. In this regard, the printing press as "machine of the industrial age facilitate[d] its complimentary manifestation, modern narcissism" (Weigel 1989:228). Lachmann, himself fascinated with the uniqueness of first editions, was particularly pleased when a royal Berlin printer decided to commemorate the four hundredth anniversary of the printing press with a limited folio edition of Lachmann's version of the *Nibelungen* song that had taken on the character of a "monument of primeval authenticity" (Weigel 1989:217).

The Brothers Grimm, intrigued by the impurity and deviations of handwritten manuscripts, never sought an individual, authorial authenticity. Particularly in spreading the folktales, they used the print medium to salvage an oral treasure that they saw at risk. Yet Wilhelm Grimm clearly recognized and worried about the influence of writing on oral tradition, whereas Lachmann was bothered by the variability of a "hand-written literacy."

The Grimms' efforts were dedicated to uncovering and understanding an anonymous or collective authenticity, and the intricacies of historical circumstance remained to them intriguing rather than bothersome.[33] Carl Lachmann's efforts, by contrast, were dedicated to the removal of all interfering traces of time and history between the original work and the reader of his reconstructed text.

The Grimms' apparatus of notes to their household tales also places their work at the beginning of the nineteenth-century efforts to render humanistic study more scientific. The comparative nature of these notes represents a clear departure from the aesthetic, emotional, or even political gist in Romantic folklore collections. In discussions with Lachmann—for instance,in those concerning protagonists and narrative sequence in heroic legends—one recognizes the seeds of type and motif research (Leitzmann 1927:772). A century later, Johannes Bolte and Jiri Polívka published their five-volume comparative index to the Grimm tales (1913–31)—a reference work that further legitimized the Grimms' work as a scholarly rather than merely a Romantic quest. The so-called Finnish method as formulated by Julius and Kaarle Krohn represents a fusion of the origin quests by Indo-German and Germanic philology (Krohn 1971). The historico-critical comparison of texts is expanded into the historic-geographic method where linkages between tales in different cultural and historical settings are explained in genealogical and disembodied terms.

The concept of authenticity clearly played a central role in the development of scholarly disciplines devoted to German language, literature, history, and folklore. Against the backdrop of a nationalizing Europe that favored efforts to legitimize the history and uniqueness of native languages, purported "folk" materials constituted a major source for constructing both authentic language and literature. In an industrializing society with emergent new social classes, a literate, scholarly bourgeoisie increasingly shifted the authentic "folk" into a nobler past, or else it elaborated new notions of individual, authorial authenticity.

The rigorous scholarly apparatus created to prove such constructions allowed, with some struggle, for the establishment of chairs in Germanic studies. Neither folk materials nor authenticity could be contained within this particular niche, but this nineteenth-century German academic model continues to be invoked as a viable approach to ascertain authenticity. In the United States the model found a following within a nascent academic interest in the study of folklore.

Chapter Three

American Romanticism and the Emergence of American Folklore Studies

A simple label such as the "New World" signals a claim to a new origin, disenfranchising those native peoples for whom the Americas were the Old World. The Puritans themselves perceived their voyage as akin to the ancient Israelites. The wilderness surrounding them was sacred and pure, but ready to be conquered and tamed by those close to God who felt themselves to be sacred and pure. The theological and intellectual formulations of what constituted and legitimated the American essence, invoked and reformulated from the Pilgrim days to Independence and from then to the Civil War, drifted away precariously from social realities. Such early formulations contributed to the conflicts within social realities, which were not and are not racially homogeneous, but which were and are punctuated with ever-shifting multicultural configurations.

This chapter concentrates on American voices concerned with capturing the authentic in words or in art in the nineteenth century, first sketching aspects of the intellectual framework, and then turning to the several strands that developed to uncover a folk authenticity. Within this narrative the friendship of James Lowell and Francis Child stands as a New World parallel to that between the Grimms and Lachmann, oriented deeply toward authenticating the remnants of an unrecoverable past. Yet the confrontation with and appropriation of living black musics with which the chapter concludes point to the vastly different social and historical contexts within which these discourses on authenticity took place.

In literary or philosophical terms the nineteenth-century American discussion of authenticity emphasized the individual and his achievements in action and material representation. During the "American Renaissance" (Matthiessen 1941), the literary discourse and the Transcendentalist movement of the first part of the nineteenth century, the effort to formulate a distinctively individualistic American legacy free from European inspirations manifests itself strongly. The drive for an individualism unchecked by the confines of religious orthodoxy, expressed in everything from poetry to architecture, comes to the fore nowhere as clearly as in the writings of Ralph Waldo Emerson and others among the Transcendentalist circle from the 1830s into the 1850s. Within the modern formulations of selfhood laid out by Charles Taylor (1989), these American voices constituted the most intrepid departure relative to Europe from externally defined religious or, more generally, social sources of identity.

But the artistic, and more so the academic, realization of such intellectual aspirations leaned heavily on European (and often German) models. Many scholars involved in building American academic centers received their advanced training overseas. They brought back familiarity with German research agendas and theoretical paradigms, but they developed systems of thinking and educating suited to the New World context.[1] Even if the methodology employed by someone like Francis James Child (1825–1896) in the "legislation of originality and authenticity" (Stewart 1991b: 103) was akin to that of his German teachers, the discourse on authenticity and the corresponding audacious theories of origin postulated bore the imprint of the American context.

THE ROMANTIC LEGACY IN AMERICA

Between Religion, Democracy, and the Sublime

In assessments of the American "intellectual tradition" during the first half of the nineteenth century, Ralph Waldo Emerson's (1803–1882) name is usually the most prominent. Emerson's authorship of *Nature* (1836) could easily lead readers to assume a direct link with Rousseauian or Sturm und Drang poets' praises of nature. Similarly, Emerson's struggle with and abandonment of a career in theology invites comparison with the life of Herder, and Emerson's frequent journeys to England and the Continent point to his interest in European philosophy. But though Emerson expressed dissatisfaction with "the prevailing social reality" (Moran 1967: 479), his solutions differed dramatically from those proposed by the Germans. Emerson's engagement with the nature trope was very different from theirs. Whereas the vox populi (Boas 1969) for Herder and his followers became a means to regain poetic and cultural authenticity, Emerson sought the essence of the sublime within the individual self.

Herder's thoughts on national (folk) literatures may have left an im-

pression on Emerson. In "The Poet," Emerson included American equiva-
lents of "the folk"—Negroes and Indians—as important sources for an
American poetry (Bluestein 1972:18–20). Emerson's advocacy was, however, at best paternalistic, as when in 1838 he wrote to President Martin
Van Buren on behalf of the Cherokees: "In common with the great body
of American people, we have witnessed with sympathy the painful labors
of these red men to redeem their own race from the doom of eternal inferiority, and to borrow and domesticate in the tribe the arts and customs
of the Caucasian race" (cited after Black and Weidman 1976:272).[2] But
the young Emerson was far more concerned with laying to rest the troubling question of spiritual truth than with reflecting on the social sources
of a national literature, and he approached these issues in meditations on
language, on analytic as opposed to poetic creation, and on the sublime.[3]

As the son of a Unitarian minister, Emerson came naturally to choosing
the ministry. Yet his familiarity with European philosophy may have undermined his acceptance of received theological practice and encouraged
his interest in the transcendental (Mackenzie 1921:422). In addition, even
in his younger years Hindu scriptures, which became central to Transcendentalism, were a known and intriguing source of an alternate kind of
spirituality (Patri 1987), fractured through responses to the different European romantic images of India.[4]

For the anxiety that the loss of a strictly biblical faith could bring forth,
Emerson compensated with the basic assumption that "as a guide to solv-
ing the problems of life's meaning, there is 'really nothing external, so I
must spin my thread from my own bowels'" (Moran 1967:477). If no
longer attainable through the encounter with God's word, the sublime had
to dwell elsewhere, and Emerson placed it in the individual's self-conscious
power of perception and expression. "The sublime ... is not an attribute of
the art work but a psychological phenomenon in the witness who recovers
from a debilitating percept. . . . The exhilaration associated with the sublime comes about as we convert disorientation and meaninglessness into
evidence of our power over the things that cause these sensations" (Ellison
1984:7). This individual power sought its expression through a writing
free of influence, and Emerson's literary philosophy established the framework within which the likes of Melville and Whitman would struggle for
a poetic creation from the innermost, unfettered by the influences of earlier creations. "For Emerson, the best, the most consequential, literature
does not imitate, instruct, or delight—it galvanizes. Provocation, not edi-
fication is its concern" (Hodder 1989:106).

Emerson's dilemma stemmed from his suspicion that he was more analyst than creator, a dilemma he posed in asking, "Is not the sublime felt in an analysis as well as in a creation?" (cited after Ellison 1984:3). In his younger years he committed to his journal, "I am in all my theory, ethics and politics a poet" (quoted after Matthiessen 1941:23). Later he recognized that the analytic essay, not poetry, was his métier, and he found the sublime in it as well: "What draws us in others' works is our own alienated majesty" (quoted after Ellison 1984:6). The ability to find a response to what he read involved "the overcoming or demystification of cultural and social authority. Like the hermeneutical sublime, on these occasions it mark[ed] the pleasure of the ego's victory over influence" (Ellison 1984:8).[5]

Even though *Nature* is suffused with a "rhetoric of revelation" betraying Emerson's link to the ministerial tradition and the style and structure of sermons (Hodder 1989:4–19), the revelation that Emerson strove for was "self-expression, self-realization, self-fulfillment, discovering authenticity" (Taylor 1989:507). Emerson's *Nature* is not so much a eulogy of nature's many beauties as it is a sermon reveling in the individual's capability to perceive and, in the experience of perceiving, transcend nature and reach a spiritual state corresponding to the sublime.

Sociopolitically, Emerson's insistence on self-reliance was problematic. His sublime, cocoonlike and inward-turned, ignored the social reality of slavery—a collective practice that effectively barred a large minority from attaining such inner truth. In the German discussion on poetry and truth, concerns with social and political reality were a vital component. Eighteenth-century European literati were formulating new democratic values in opposition to decaying monarchical and feudal social arrangements; this effort, in turn, was shaped by a circumscribed, socially grounded sense of what was authentic (Berman 1972). American democracy formed in circumstances unfettered by old institutions and corresponding social practices, and the American notion of authenticity invoked in this context was correspondingly freer of class and historical constraints.

It is telling, however, that questions of race generated a discourse separate from the search for the sublime and authentic. The "black image in the white mind" was extraordinarily significant, whether mentioned, incorporated, or purposely excluded (Fredrickson 1971). In the European case, a native Other in the form of the folk had been embraced as an organic or familial link to a pure origin. In the United States, such organic linkage in national origin was challenged by the presence of Native American and black cultural Others. Yet those who generated the line of thought to be discussed opted for the most part to separate their intellectual search for authenticity from their—mostly abolitionist—social stance. Far into the nineteenth century the intellectual community of New England, and specifically of Cambridge, was deeply under the spell of Emersonian rhetoric, Transcendentalism, and the social utopias engendered by Transcendentalists.[6] The community's members, including Emerson, attempted to create a discourse on a native aesthetic that would emphasize the superiority of *individual* spirituality.

The Aesthetic of the Common Man

The folk uncorrupted by civilization, no matter how the concept was constructed, could not exist in a nation so recently settled by whites. Native Americans, far from the righteous religious background of many settlers, were portrayed ambiguously, not least because American immigrants, unlike European post-Enlightenment authors extolling the virtues of the exotic Other, lived in proximity to the unpredictable "savage." White views on the black race turned at first on moral questions and protoevolutionary racial comparisons, and only shortly before the Civil War were authenticity quests linked with considerations of race. Instead, the authentic, unspoiled man emerging in the American discourse bore the imprint of the white American experience.[7]

European Romantic concepts influenced American Romantics as well. Longfellow, for instance, borrowed the meter of the Finnish *Kalevala* for his *Hiawatha*, although the result "was destined in many quarters to provide only another set of literary artifices." Longfellow also attempted to compose "native ballads," and Whittier collected *New England Legends* in 1831, attempting to "*tap the sources* of [native] rural life" (Matthiessen 1941:34; my italics). The conjunction of nature metaphors with the tropes of treasure-hunting or the harvesting of natural resources clearly points to the similarity to the German case.

Given his intense preoccupation with language as a source of innermost revelation, Emerson remained dubious about imitating what was not even a Native American poetic aesthetic (see Abrams 1953). Emerson was apparently delighted "by the homespun veracity of [English folksongs'] plain style," and he approved of Luther's translating the Latin Bible into vernacular language (Matthiessen 1941:34). But the language that would cut through cumbersome conventions of literature was first and foremost living, spoken language.

Literate, college-educated man lacked, in Emerson's estimation, the gift of self-assured, idiomatic speech. He located authentic language in a different social class than his own, responding "instinctively to the 'vigorous Saxon' of men working in the fields or swapping stories in the barn, men wholly uneducated, but whose words had roots in their own experience" (Matthiessen 1941:35). Although such imagery appears parallel to the European intellectual fascination with the folk, Emerson's interpretation differed. The experiential connection between language and speaker that he praised led to his notion of "the common"—accessible to all who can rid themselves of affectation and artifice.

His 1837 address, "The American Scholar," captures his goals most clearly. "Our day of dependence, our long apprenticeship to the learning of other lands draws to a close," Emerson stated in his opening paragraph, and after summarizing what the true scholarly habitus ought to be, he extolled the virtue of the common:

> I embrace the common, I explore and sit at the feet of the familiar, the low. Give me insight into to-day, and you may have the antique and future worlds. What would we really know the meaning of? The meal in the firkin; the milk in the pan; the ballad in the street; the news of the boat; the glance of the eye; the form and the gait of the body;—show me the ultimate reason of these matters; show me the sublime presence of the highest spiritual cause lurking, as always it does lurk, in these suburbs and extremities of nature; let me see every trifle bristling with the polarity that ranges it instantly on an eternal law; and the shop, the plough, and the leger, referred to the like cause by which light undulates and poets sing;—and the world lies no longer a dull miscellany and lumber-room, but has form and order; there is no trifle; there is no puzzle; but one design unites and animates the farthest pinnacle and the lowest trench. (1971:52, 67–68)

Emerson's "common" engulfs more than did the European notion of the folk, as it includes a sensual absorption in the heterogeneous everyday world. The eulogy of the common was combined with the notion of the singularity of each human being, the importance of which he saw both as "a sign of our times" and constitutive of a "political movement" appropriate for such a time. Self-reliance to Emerson was the cure for all that was wrong in the world of American business: "If the single man plant himself indomitably on his instincts, and there abide, the huge world will come round to him" (Emerson 1971:69).[8] A betterment of the polity and the social collective was a logical outgrowth of individual purity.

Even clearer enunciations of the ideal American aesthetic came from Emerson's friend, the sculptor Horatio Greenough. Extensive stays in Europe and exposure to classic Greek and Roman sculpture and architecture left Greenough appreciative of having been able to touch clay and marble, but mostly he was filled with the need to develop his native capability, organically grown from the American context. Although he died before realizing his own aesthetic principles, he lectured and wrote fervently on what he perceived as America's artistic strength—the production of "functional beauty." Greenough was "almost unique in discerning . . . the beauty of objects that had sprung out of an adaptation of structure to the needs of common life—the New England farmhouse, the trotting-wagon, the clipper ship" (Matthiessen 1941:144–45).

Greenough argued against art for art's sake, and he did not "yearn for a revival of the conditions that had produced the great cathedrals," but rather he "looked directly around him for healthy roots from which American art could grow" (p. 146).[9] The functional art of Greenough's common man was intricately linked to the possibilities of democracy, a stance fueling his dislike of the neoclassic and imitative architecture that dominated the capital.

In Greenough, one sees the ideal democratic aesthetic organically emerging from a community of common men. Whenever efforts have been made to essentialize an American spirit, this fusion of a commonsense, plain aesthetic and a democratic disposition appear together as hallmarks of an American authentic spirit.[10]

The construct of the American "common man" markedly differs, then, from the German *Volk* construct. The *Volk* was rooted in an idealized past, encumbered by the complexities of historical influences, and it could be redeemed only by those who, by virtue of their learning and class, had gained insight into its aesthetic and social value. The American "common man," by contrast, lived authentically out of necessity. In acknowledging the common tasks of all Americans to build a new country and to negate class differences, literate men such as Thoreau felt themselves capable of enacting the lifestyle of the common man. A particular group or way of life was singled out from the larger social landscape in both American and German cases. The virtues of this group—whether common man or *Volk*—were praised, and it was contrasted to the decay threatening the social fabric of the nation.

Equally noteworthy is the American emphasis on the aesthetics of material culture. The European Romantics extolled the virtues of folk literature and had sought to experience authenticity spiritually in the celebration of verbal folk expression. Greenough, as well as James Fenimore Cooper[11] or Emerson, praised the shape of the plough, the craftsmanship of boatbuilders, and the aesthetic of native houses. Thoreau seized on these currents of the times in *Walden,* where he attempted to experience through his own body, rather than just his spirit, the simplicity of form and style grown in the American pioneer landscape.

More adamantly than Greenough, Thoreau rejected the materialism and focus on property of his fellow citizens. *Walden* is suffused with a rhetoric of authentic living, an existence devoid of the trappings of false identity. New clothes are but one sign of such civilizational alienation: "We don garment after garment, as if we grew like exogenous plants by addition without. Our outside and often thin and fanciful clothes are our epidermis of false skin, which partakes not of our life" (Thoreau 1985 [1854]:341).

Thoreau reveled in the physical exertion of building his cabin, stating that "no house should be painted except with the color of its builder's own blood and sweat" (Matthiessen 1941:153). More so than Emerson's *Nature,* Walden celebrated the wholeness of nature to which the trappings of man's civilization add but unnecessary burdens: "I would observe, by the way, that it costs me nothing for curtains, for I have no gazers to shut out but the sun and the moon, and I am willing that they should look in. . . . I find it still better economy to retreat behind some curtain which nature has provided than to add a single item to the details of housekeeping" (1985 [1854]:375).

Walden bears testimony to Thoreau's (undoubtedly beautified) effort to live and create independently and individually and to experience in such independence his true self. His increasing interest in Native Americans eventually moved his existential search outward, as he recognized in different Native American ways of life alternate understandings of nature. Although he did not live to write a book on American Indians, he took thousands of pages of notes on everything he found about them, and through this quasi ethnological interest he began to penetrate beyond the readymade white image of the stoic, savage Indian doomed to make way for a progressive white civilization (Troy 1990). Yet this interest was less a cultural mission than it was fueled by Thoreau's need to incorporate the wild wisdom of "the true heirs" of America into his own quest for authenticity.

Interestingly, this "native" and individualistic quest for authenticity, with its celebration of everyday aesthetics and a nature both spiritually revealed and bodily experienced, thus rejecting Old World influences, later proved influential in academic arenas. The emergent interest in the cultural Other that would grow into cultural anthropology seems to have benefited from this American romantic charter. But aside from flourishes of Emersonian rhetoric, the initial search for authenticity in American academe focused on literature, not material culture or whole cultures. This search was thoroughly influenced by, if not copied from, European examples. It was not the material culture and art of America's "common man" that became its focus, but rather the folk ballad, defined at first as a European tradition of the past. The "dialogue of dissent" that Rosemary Zumwalt (1988) chronicled may have been fueled by alternate visions of what kind of authenticity first needed to be academically legitimized: that of one's own dwindling ancestry, or that of the culturally Other threatened by the progress of one's own civilization.

The Quest for Authentic Ballads

Early American colleges emphasized Greek and Latin, and students were trained for Christian leadership and the ministry. But the study of English language and literature was also "an essential instrument of socialization" in polite society, and as political leadership became increasingly secularized it was clear that the college system, tailored after the English one, did not prepare its students for professional careers (Graff 1987: 19–20). Because Germany (rather than England, where foreign students were less easily accepted) was the place in which Americans did graduate study before graduate programs were established in the United States, German research interests inspired young American scholars, especially in language study (McMurtry 1985: 16).[12] The American exposure to German humanistic inquiry might even have been an aperture into "authentic" engagement:

> What was new to Americans . . . was not only the study of literary texts in their entirety (a practice not general in American colleges of the day), but a historical insight which we may now take for granted, but which offered fresh authenticity to both Germans and Americans. For Germans there were many social and institutional aids to fan that sense of authenticity into a commitment to a life of scholarship. But for Americans throughout the first three-quarters of the century, there were almost no such aids. Scholarship . . . implied a sense of vocation which demanded to be felt and made into a specifically American thing. (Diehl 1978:4)

The advanced philological scholarship practiced in Germany left a strong imprint on Francis James Child. In the work of Child and his followers, one rediscovers the interest in medieval literature, language reconstruction coupled with text editing, and folk poetry that so dominated the work of Bopp, the Grimms, and Lachmann (all of whom taught at Berlin).[13] Although Emerson's circle celebrated a distinctively American authenticity, and despite the influences of the American brand of Romanticism, the American trajectory in the quest for authenticity led back to an English or European past.

James Russell Lowell and the Authenticity of Poetry

Child's work echoed German models, but his interest in "popular" (meaning "from the people") poetry meant Romantic exuberance and scientific work emerged jointly, not successively. The Brothers Grimm had immersed themselves in the intricacies of historical accuracy, reducing their speculative, exuberant vocabulary. While Child modeled himself on the Grimms and the Danish ballad collector Svend Grundtvig, Child's students and contemporaries happily employed an exuberant vocabulary of authenticity and engaged in speculative hypotheses on origin.

The 305 English and Scottish ballads compiled and annotated by Child constitute monumental proof of the desire to recoup the genuine and to celebrate the authentic spirit of the folk in the English language (1965 [1884–98]). Yet Child published little in the way of theoretical or programmatic statements that would have attested to his belief in authentic balladry.[14] Fortunately, beyond the writings of Child's students George Lyman Kittredge, Francis Gummere (1855–1919), and Walter Morris Hart, there exists another source to examine the mentality that inspired this gargantuan opus: James Russell Lowell. Poet, ambassador, and intimate friend of Child for some four decades, Lowell both lectured on issues pertinent to the ballad and corresponded with Child (Howe and Cottrell 1952).[15]

In 1855 Lowell, although still relatively young, was a well-known poet and literary scholar. He was invited to deliver twelve lectures on English poetry at the Lowell Institute, which he gladly accepted, though he felt he had to do "an especially creditable job in order to justify having been appointed by a relative."[16] Lowell had never spoken in public before, but public interest was so great that every lecture had to be delivered twice (Duberman 1966:14).

As a student, Lowell had heard Emerson's "The American Scholar," and in 1848 his *The Biglow Papers* substantiated his conviction that "poets and peasants please us in the same way by translating words back again to their primal freshness." Lowell characterized Hosea Biglow as having "sour-faced humor" and a "wild, puckery, acidulous . . . flavor," writing in what he called "the Yankee-lingo" (cited in Matthiessen 1941: 37) and thus producing what his contemporaries regarded as a work of authentically American literature.

Lowell's twelve lectures on English poetry ranged from definitional statements to the works of individual authors; eventually, he discussed the function of the poet.[17] The American clergyman and author Edward Everett Hale assessed Lowell at the end of the nineteenth century: "It is no wonder that the lectures were so popular. They are of the best reading to this day, full of fun, full of the most serious thought as well. And you find in them at every page, I may say, seeds which he has planted elsewhere for other blossoms and fruit" (1899:114–15). Parts of the lectures were printed in newspapers far beyond New England, and many individuals cherished them sufficiently to paste them into scrapbooks, which became the basis of a limited edition in 1897 (Hale 1899:116). Lowell's rhetorical talents evidently were considerable, and his views on poetry stirred his audience.[18]

The fourth of his lectures, "The Ballads," communicates the American literary and cultural infatuation with the genre better than any of Child's statements. It could be argued that Lowell's fervent portrayal of balladry, its poets and aesthetics, roused the kind of public interest needed to sustain the long research process behind the Child Ballads. At the same time, Lowell's imagery illustrates the continuity between German Romantic folklore scholarship and the beginnings of American folklore interests. Lowell's infatuation with the authentic, natural voice he felt in the ballads, coupled with statements betraying alienation and disappointment with his own times, replicate the enthusiasm and simultaneous fear of loss that had stirred scholars such as the Grimms.

Lowell revoiced themes from Herder's political assessment of folk poetry when he praised poets as the ones "who first made Public Opinion a power in the state by condensing it in a song." He saw anonymous songs as a powerful weapon, "for what tyrant could procure the assassination of an epithet or throw a couplet into a dungeon" (Lowell 1897:D-2). Singers as safekeepers of the past offered legitimacy to rulers in their creation of epics, "the central inspiration of . . . nationality" (1897:D-6). Nationality, a notion German scholars had addressed only obliquely, takes a prominent place in Lowell's rhetoric as an element in poetic production. "Thus Virgil attempted to braid together the ravelled ends of Roman and Greek tradition into a national past, and it is not impossible that the minstrels of the Norman metrical romances were guided by a similar instinct" (1897:D-6).

Print, however, was a corrupting and endangerous invention, for print, "by weakening the faculty of memory, and transferring the address of language from the ear to the eye, has lessened the immediate power of the poet. A newspaper may be suppressed, an editor may be silenced, every copy of an obnoxious book may be destroyed, but in those old days when the minstrels were a power, a verse could wander safely from heart to heart, and from hamlet to hamlet as unassailable as music and memory" (1897:D-2). Sarcastic comments against newspapers and print are scattered throughout Lowell's lectures, forming an antiprogressive and negative counterpoint to a past alive with the spoken and sung language of the people. Thus he stated: "It is worth thinking of whether the press which we have a habit of calling such a fine institution be not weakening the fibre and *damaging the sincerity* of our English" (1897:D-22; my emphasis). The old Rousseauian "wound of reflection" seemed to reign in print, as editors were not moved by the passion of speech but by the task of creating an effect among their readers. Like his German predecessors, Lowell recognized the tensions created by the introduction of literacy. But unlike Carl Lachmann, who adored the power of print for its ability to fixate the authentic word authored by an individual, Lowell deplored print in all guises—never dwelling on the paradox that his own efforts, including considerable amounts of editorial work in early English literature, were facilitated by print.[19]

Balladry in Lowell's scheme emerged as "minstrelsy sank naturally enough [from the hall] to the cottage" where the poetic acquired its human touch (1897:D-10). In contrasting the artificial and overcivilized with the living, breathing language of balladry, Lowell reawakened the Herderian language of nature and revelation. While he considered ballads "as the first truly national poetry in our language," they also had "life and strength and wild blood in them which keeps them as fresh as ever." Ballad language needed to "touch simple men and women," which required that "words must cut deep-down to something real and living . . . to a human and not a class experience." Lowell's praise of "national ballad poetry" was not nationalistic rhetoric but an echo of Herder's cultural relativism: National poetry "is the common mother-earth of the universal sentiment that the foot of the past must touch, through which shall [steal] up to heart and brain that fine virtue which puts him in sympathy, not with his class but with his kind" (1897:D-10–11).

Like the German Romantics, Lowell himself was not free of class prejudice. Yet the condescension of an upper-class literate man toward the unlettered poets of a past underclass was rhetorically made praiseworthy. In the interest of naturalness it was fortunate that "the ballad-makers . . . were not encumbered with any useless information. They had not wit enough to lose their way" (1897:D-11). Similarly, it was so lucky for those old ballad-mongers that they had not any ideas" (1897:D-29), for if they did have them, the excess thought and labored language of the trained poet might have ruined the simplicity of "the language of passion" and stopped passion's ability to "consume the featherly substance of our artificiality" (1897:D-28).

What distinguished Lowell from the text-bound labors of Child was his keen interest in language, experience, and emotion. His observations built bridges back to eighteenth-century aesthetic criticism, but they also foreshadowed the preoccupation with spoken language and its connection to human nature in twentieth-century scholarship (Taylor 1985). He praised the "dialect of life," and he tried to distinguish "heart-words" from "brain-words." "Heart-words" came from the people, "brain-words" from the "governing class." "This mother-tongue is the language of life and talk, it is what we learn of our playmates and nurses. It may be a fancy, but I believe that words of this kind have a deeper meaning to us because they thrill a string which runs back through the whole of our being to something in us behind education and conscious memory" (1897:D-18).

Lowell admired "the freshness" in the "words of a back woods man . . . whose whole life and nature seemed to flow into his talk, [and] who gathered his illustrations, green and fragrant from the woods" (1897:D-20). In his use of nature metaphors, from allusions to greening forests to rushing streams, he echoed both the German Romantics and the British Romantic legacy, epitomized in a phrase such as "the whole wild spirit of the forest is imaginatively transfused into these few [ballad] verses" (1897:D-31). Lowell believed that "the nearer you come to the primitive, natural man, the more full of pith is the speech" (1897:D-20), and he yearned for living, spoken language, simply assuming that "a language is kept alive always among unlettered men, because they use it as if it belonged to them, and not to the dead people who have used it before" (1897:D-19). Lettered men, by contrast, appeared to have lost the ownership of language, treating language reverently and distantly.

The Romantics reveled in what they imagined to be the mysteries of a simpler past encoded in folk poetry, but Lowell praised the realism of ballads. There was no supernaturalism in the texts; death is death, and life is life. A ballad on murder and vengeance is authentic and stirring because it is "not more profoundly artistic than that eddying of the sorrow round the one fatal spot like a stream round a dead body that lies in it" (1897:D-40). The ballad poet was so absorbed in the terrible emotion "that the words came unconsciously" (1897:D-40–41)—an assessment parallel to the Grimms. Wordsworth, by comparison, who after a journey to Scotland attempted to retell a ballad, "had not in him even a suspicion of the dramatic imagination . . . and when he puts himself beside the older [folk] poet he seems not only tame but downright barn yard" (1897:D-41).

Despite his apparent awareness of folk poets' creativity and authenticity, rhetoric as well as class prejudice may have gotten the better of Lowell when he concluded his ballad lecture.

> Perhaps another charm of the ballads is that nobody made them. They seem to have come up like violets and we have only to thank God for them. And we imply a sort of fondness when we call these ballads *old*. It is an epithet we give endearingly and not as supposing decreptitude or senescence in them. Like all true poetry they are not only young themselves, but renewers of youth in us; they do not lose but accumulate strength and life. (1897:D-51)

The disregard for human creativity expressed in the phrase "nobody made them," and the assumption that ballad authenticity was free for the taking because "we have only to thank God for them" operated not only in the appropriation of such historical artifacts as ballads. The discovery or recognition and subsequent appropriation of black American musical expression for white consumption would run along similar, although more complex, routes.

Lowell's twelve lectures on English poetry "so astonished the town" that they earned him a place as professor of modern languages at Harvard; he did not even apply for the position, previously held by Longfellow (Duberman 1966:141). To prepare for the honor, he traveled to Dresden in the summer of 1855 to work on his German; he also improved his Spanish and Italian, the last a favorite language of play in his later correspondence with Child. If his lecture on the ballad is any indication, Lowell received the Harvard appointment not so much for his erudition—other candidates were more qualified—but for his ability to speak "authentically" himself, a gift arguably essential to convince an audience of the relevance of what is being said.[20] Lowell invoked images of a past linked in big strokes to what appeared pertinent in the here and now, and he "was too much of the showman to leave his audience breathing the rare air of theory any longer than necessary" (Bell 1995:147).

Francis James Child's Ballad Restoration

The lectures may have led Lowell's correspondence with Francis James Child to expand into an expression of loving friendship.[21] Their common interest in English medieval literature—both engaged in text-critical

editions—expanded into a common preoccupation with European balladry, references to which surface throughout more than thirty years of
correspondence.

Born the third child of eight in a Boston sailmaker's family in 1825,
Francis James Child owed to his public school teachers the opportunity
to attend Boston Latin, a prestigious secondary school, and go on to college. Graduating from Harvard College in 1846, he "immediately entered
the service of the college, in which he continued until the day of his death"
(Kittredge 1957: xxiv). From 1849 to 1851 he was granted a leave of absence, which he spent studying in Germany. The vigorous study of philology that had "passed from the stage of 'romantic' dilettantism into the condition of a well-organized and strenuous scientific discipline" left a deep
impression on him. The attention paid to the connections between "antiquity and medievalism," and between the Middle Ages and the present influenced the direction that his own research would take, and contact with
the Brothers Grimm (and presumably Carl Lachmann) certainly left its
traces. "[Child's] own contribution to learning, The English and Scottish
Popular Ballads, may even in a very real sense be regarded as the fruit of
these years in Germany. Throughout his life he kept a picture of William
and James [sic] Grimm on the mantel over his study fireplace" (1957: xxv).

Child's scholarly projects during the 1850s parallel the text-critical
work championed by Lachmann. His 1855 edition of Spenser's poetry relied on careful scrutiny of all the old copies to which he could get access,
and his revision was based on a careful comparison of these texts. Rather
than subjecting the Canterbury Tales to similar treatment, Child realized
that a need existed to recover Chaucer's grammar. In 1863 he published
this effort, which showed the influence of Jacob Grimm's grammatical reconstructions and reflected his own meticulous scholarship. Like his German models, Child conceived the path to authenticity as an arduous one
informed by scientific methods. It was this kind of devotion that he brought
to his major work, The English and Scottish Popular Ballads. Ideological
or emotional satisfaction remained at best secondary, unlike with Lowell,
and it hardly found expression even in Child's correspondence.[22]

Child's implicit definition of authenticity's locus is manifested in his
preference for handwritten manuscript sources. He distrusted oral versions, as he was convinced that English and Scottish ballads were sealed
or dried up forever (Zumwalt 1988:48; Hustvedt 1930:248). Charles Eliot Norton, another member of Child's circle, probably contributed to this
pessimistic stance; Norton also likely influenced Child's predilection for
English and Scottish material as the canon against which Continental ma-

terial was compared. In an 1869 letter to Lowell, Norton observed that
the rift between rich and poor in England had grown so great that "there
seems to be scarcely a passageway of communication between them, the
old traditions and customs die out, and even fun and cheerfulness dimin-
ish till little is left of them" (Norton and Howe 1913, vol. 1:314). Norton
built a bridge for Ruskin's work to be received by Americans. In a letter to
Ruskin in 1869 Norton echoes arguments on sincerity in social and poetic
terms.

> Why do I call Byron "insincere"? Because he seems to me a rhetorician
> more than a poet by nature; a man accustomed to make a display of
> his feelings, and dependent for his satisfaction of the effect produced on
> other people by the display. . . . I do not see evidence, in his descriptions
> of nature or of works of art, of the *sincere* vision of the poet, and in his
> passionate declamations concerning himself, his woes, his sleeplessness,
> etc. I often fancy that I catch the tone of *falseness*, at any rate, *the ring of
> thin metal.* I admire your phrase "his incontinence of emotion"; but this
> like all other incontinence soon leads to *a loss of purity in the emotion,*
> and drives the unhappy being to stimulants of a very fatal sort. Ex-
> treme self-consciousness and sincerity in a poet of undisciplined charac-
> ter seem to be almost incompatible; self-consciousness is apt to be ac-
> companied with more or less affectation—as often in Wordsworth; *Scott
> is unconscious, unaffected and sincere.* (Norton and Howe 1913 [vol. 1]:
> 249–50; my italics)

In 1878, Norton urged Lowell to put some pressure on Child to go to
print with the ballads; when the first part appeared, Norton proudly sent
a copy to Ruskin, describing it as "a masterpiece of pleasant scholarship
and character," and a "study of the favourite forms in which the poetic
imagination of the common people shaped themselves—the poetry of the
cradle and fireside" (Norton and Howe 1913 [vol. 2]: 147–48).

Lowell's interest and support also sustained Child through decades of
research, and when Lowell died in 1891, Child's sorrow expressed an
emotional reaction to ballads that he otherwise hid: "I can't say that I care
so much about [my work] without J. R. L., who has done much for me.
He would have been so much pleased to have it all nicely finished up. He
could take the fine points in a ballad. They seem stale. I go back to the fine
ones at times and sing them and cry over them like the old world" (Howe
and Cottrell 1952:83).

Child's efforts to compile all known genuine English and Scottish ballads so as to separate them from other poetry that came under the label
"ballad" but that to Child were "the products of a low kind of *art,* and

most . . . from a literary point of view, thoroughly despicable and worthless," would preoccupy his nonteaching hours until his death (1874:367).
The impression that Germanic scholarship had made on him came fully to
the fore in the care with which he assembled variant ballad texts and strove
to compare them with all known ballad poetry. In his erudition and determination to consult every available manuscript, the assured style with
which he pronounced judgments, and most of all in his reliance on internal textual criteria to verify ballad authenticity, he resembled Lachmann.

Child set in motion everything that he could think of to get his hands
on source materials. To a large degree, it was because of his insistence that
the heirs of Bishop Percy permitted the printing of the original manuscript
that Percy had used for his *Ancient Reliques*.[23] Once Child read the manuscript, he was disappointed—perhaps almost as a pretext to dig further:
"Poor stuff, most of it and in the main not new"; but he took comfort in
the fact that, unlike Percy's embellished publication, the source material
at least was "all genuine, bad or good" (Howe and Cottrell 1952:18).

Once his friend Lowell entered the diplomatic service, Child enlisted his
help. When Lowell was ambassador in London, he secured the assistance
of a certain Campbell of Islay. Child expressed his thanks, and added:
"[Campbell's] last word was that he had found a Scottish gentleman who
possessed a fine old house & *two manuscript vols. of ballads*! This Scot
would not let me know his name—did not wish to be persecuted by 'collectors': but would have a judge look over his MSS., and if they would suit
me, *perhaps* let me have what I wanted" (Howe and Cottrell 1952:51;
Child's emphases). While it was not Lowell's doing, once this ballad collection was in Lowell's hands, he sped them to Child via diplomatic pouch.
After his first perusal of the manuscript, Child responded that "the ballads
are not what they would have been two hundred years ago, but could not
possibly be dispensed with" (Howe and Cotrell 1952:55–56).

Child also yearned for comparative material, and he hoped that Lowell
would further the cause of ballad collection in general. When Lowell was
stationed in Madrid, Child wrote to his "dear Jamie":

> Can't you make somebody collect the ballads in other parts of Spain as
> they have been collected in Catalonia (and Portugal)? A word from an
> ambassador to a man like Gayangos (is he in Madrid?) and passed by G.
> to some enterprising young fellows in one province and another, might
> have good effect. The popular ballads that are collected now are of the
> universal sort, you know, and considerably more to my purpose. . . .
> There must be a great lot to be recovered in Spain—no country more
> likely to be rich in them. And they are well preserved, with beautiful bur-

dens, and all the popular charm—so different from Italy, where mostly ballads have lost their wild grace. (Howe and Cottrell 1952:41–42)

Lowell did not share Child's high hopes, as those he encountered in Spain were "singularly indifferent to such things, if not contemptuous of them" (Howe and Cottrell 1952: 46).

Child at times seemed overcome with the urge to himself "hunt the treasure"—so familiar a trope in the discourse on authenticity—if time and financial resources would only have allowed it. In 1879 he excitedly wrote about "a recent discovery of Odinic song in Shetland," and he dearly wished someone would go seek more:

> It seems to me that they must linger there. They spread like Norway rats, and there is plenty of Norway in the Orkneys & Shetland. . . . Only if I were on the spot . . . I could be continually prodding up the people. There *must* be ballads there:—how else have the people held out against poverty, cold & darkness? . . . Do I talk like a feller trying to get stock taken in copper-mines? . . . Surely there is a vein for the silver & a place of gold where they *find* it. . . . Were you careless and I richer, I would try to make you meet me there. The summer is pleasant—there is 3 months of afternoon—the people primitive. How I wish we could do it! (Howe and Cottrell 1952:44–45)

When students elected Lowell as rector of the University of St. Andrew in Scotland—an election later challenged—Child jokingly wrote: "Let thy first decree be that every ballad known to any lady, maidservant, fishwife, dairywoman or nurse be given up under penalties of misprision & praemunire to all that shall be art & part in the withholding of the same" (p. 57). One can guess that Child presumed or hoped for an oral continuity through women, a gender hypothesis perhaps once again the result of the influence of the Brothers Grimm, as they in their folktale collecting had relied on women. While Child in his 1874 entry for *Johnson's New World Encyclopedia* referred to the balladmaker as male, in discussing ballad preservation he talked of "noble ladies" in Denmark and Sweden who wrote ballads down to preserve them (see Bell 1988:293).

Child's pronouncements remained sparse, compared to his massive compilation and annotation, on what exactly constituted the genuine ballad. The encyclopedia piece did contain rather clear definitional and ideological criteria (Bell 1988). He defined ballad as "a narrative song, a short tale in lyric verse" whose most "fundamental characteristic" distinguishing it from the later "poetry of art" was "the absence of subjectivity and self-consciousness." This quality made ballads "extremely difficult to imitate by the highly-civilized modern man, and most of the attempts to reproduce this kind of poetry have been ridiculous failures" (Child 1874: 365). Child's critical assessments and "cleansing efforts" relied, then, on the "internal evidence" inherent to the authentic ballad and the recognition of editorial tinkering that reduced the genuine qualities.

Hart updated Child in 1895, and attempted to spell out these internal criteria:

> A ballad must tell a story, and that only partially; the transitions must be abrupt, although not incoherent; the introduction must be closely integrated with the story; there must be brevity; the action can seldom be carefully localized; description or exposition of the supernatural is omitted. The style must be artless, homely, without conceits or description of states of mind; it is marked by commonplaces . . . ; it must be impressive, fine, spirited, pathetic, tender, and finally, lyrical. The subject matter must be of popular origin, the foreign parallels should exist; it may be pseudo-historical, must deal with heroic sentiment . . . ; it must not be prosaic, over-refined, cynical, sophisticated, sentimental, moralizing; but a certain degree of probability is demanded for the plot, which must not be trite. (Hart, as summarized by James 1961 [1933]: 17)

This list may have derived from pronouncements Child made in his teaching. Some criteria could also be guessed from the different standards of inclusion that Child applied to the five-volume edition of *The English and Scottish Popular Ballads* he began to publish in 1883. In 1858 Child stated that "no genuine relic of olden minstrelsy, however *mutilated* or *debased* in its descent to our times, has been on that account excluded," but in 1882 he indicated that he had refrained from printing *"The English and Scottish Ballads* until this unrestricted title should be justified by my having at my command every *valuable* copy of every known ballad" (quoted after James 1961 [1933]: 13; my italics). A comparison of the ballads in different editions makes it clear that Child successively excluded many texts that he came to consider as lacking in ballad style, as overly edited, or as belonging to the romance genre.

As with the assiduous Lachmann, Child used criteria of genuineness that grew more exclusionary the more he worked with expanding amounts of material. What to one of Child's first critics, Thelma James, appeared as ultimately arbitrary criteria defined by nothing but Child's approval (1961 [1933]: 19) was to Child's devoted students—much as with Lachmann's admiring disciples—proof of Child's superior gifts. To Kittredge, Child possessed "a kind of instinct" that allowed him to "detect the slightest jar in the genuine ballad tone." Thoroughly convinced by the rhetoric of authenticity pervading ballad research, Kittredge's eulogy dwelled on how badly needed a scholar of Child's genius had been in ballad studies:

> Few persons understand the difficulties of ballad investigation. In no field of literature have the forger and the manipulator worked with greater vigor and success. . . . Mere learning will not guide an editor through these perplexities. What is needed is, in addition, a complete understanding of the "popular" genius, a sympathetic recognition of the traits that characterize oral literature wherever and in whatever degree they exist. This faculty, which even the folk have not retained, and which collectors living in ballad-singing and tale-telling times have often failed to acquire, was vouchsafed by nature herself to this sedentary scholar. (Kittredge 1957:xxx)

How immediately convincing Child's scholarly demonstration of "internal proof" was comes clearly from Lowell, only months after he read the first published part of the Child ballads: "I wrote to you the other day with a copy of du Maurier's ballad. I forgot to say (I think) that it is genuine & not a manufacture of Bromwichham. Indeed, so says the internal evidence" (Howe and Cottrell 1952:60). To his literate contemporaries, ever freshly scandalized by the Ossian "forgery" and the editorial tinkering in Percy's *Reliques,* the scholarly organization and arguments of Child's edition was convincing proof of the authenticity of the edition's contents.

Mute on the subject of his editorial methods, Child was more forthcoming on the question of origin. As in Germany, the social class of the supposed ballad poets posed a status problem to upper-class literates in the United States. By declaring authentic balladry an art form that could no longer be "imitate[d] by the highly-civilized modern man," Child, too, removed the origin far from the present. This made it possible for him to strive for a complete collection, as presumably no new ballads of the authentic type could be created. To further alleviate concerns of lower class versus upper class, Child presented a number of not necessarily congruent arguments. On the one hand, he wrote: "The primitive ballad then is popular, not in the sense of something arising from and suited to the lower orders of a people. As yet no sharp distinction of high and low exists, in respect to knowledge, desire, and tastes." This assessment he sharpened by stating:

> From what has been said, it may be seen or inferred that the popular ballad is not originally the product or the property of the lower orders of the people. Nothing, in fact, is more obvious than that many of the ballads of the now most refined nations had their origin in that class whose

arts and fortunes they depict—the upper class—though the growth of civilization has driven them from the memory of the highly-polished and instructed, and has left them as an exclusive possession to the uneducated. (Child 1874:365–67)

With creativity and origin suitably situated in the upper class, a class-transcending, aesthetic appreciation could safely be put forward.

> But whatever may be the estimation in which it may be held by particular classes or at particular epochs, it cannot lose its value. Being founded on what is permanent and universal in the heart of man, and now by printing put beyond the danger of perishing, it will survive the fluctuations of taste, and may from time to time, as it notoriously did in England and Germany a hundred years ago, recall a literature from false and artificial courses to nature and truth. (1874:365)

Yet even if his published pronouncements remained few, Child's belief in this purifying thrust inherent to ballad poetry must have permeated his everyday manner. Thus, Kittredge wrote that "constant association with the spirit of the folk did its part in maintaining, under the stress of unremitting study and research, that freshness and buoyancy of mind which was the wonder of all who met Professor Child for the first time" (1957:xxx).

Academic Speculations and Alternate Authenticities

Ballad scholarship was arguably the dominant pursuit of early American folkloristics, and once Child's textual reconstruction stood firm, arguments turned speculative, preoccupied with competing hypotheses of origin. Questions of race and, with it, alternate experiences and discoveries of the authentic remained marginal, explored on the separate trajectory conjoining social activism with musical experience.

In a splendid defense of Child as a theoretician, Michael Bell has characterized him as a Victorian Romantic, unable in the American context to adopt the Herderian, mythically removed folk legacy. Rather, he expresses the crisis of modernity—namely, the recognition of self-alienation. More sharply than in the German discussion, literacy featured in the American discourse as a source for the emergent, modern self-consciousness. Kittredge, Child's heir apparent, spelled out Child's assumptions on ballad origins relative to literacy: "When a nation learns to read, it begins to disregard its traditional tales; it feels a little ashamed of them; and finally it loses both the will and the power to remember and transmit them. What was once the possession of the folk as a whole, becomes the heritage of the illiterate only, and soon, unless it is gathered up by the antiquary, vanishes altogether" (Kittredge 1932:xii).

In his formulation of the Romantic dilemma—that self-reflection removes one from primal experience—Child placed the balladmaking folk within history. But he placed them in a medieval period where "the culture of the popular was produced by a singleness of faith, feeling and social class that was no longer possible" (Bell 1988:304), and this facilitated a ballad poetry of unalienated simplicity which modern poets aware of their individual creativity could no longer reproduce. Bell places less emphasis than I would on Child's differentiation of classes in medieval times. His encyclopedia article shows a deep concern with social distinction that Child, perhaps encumbered by his own class prejudices, needed to address.

Some of Child's contemporaries and students clearly processed his theory of folklore's origin and its demise and marginalization in modernity. Bell goes as far as to argue that William Wells Newell's encyclopedia definition of folklore in 1892 constituted a spelling out in bolder terms of Child's theoretical precepts (Bell 1988:306).

Other scholars, emerging from Child's tutelage, such as Francis Gummere, yearned for less historically grounded and more mystical origins. They proposed the theory of "communal origins" where an entire group, conceived as swept away from excessive self-reflection in the movement of dance, composed collectively. Such a theory, of course, echoed the disagreements on the ultimate locus of poetic authenticity in the German discourse: collectivists would see it in the anonymity of the "singing, dancing throng," whereas the historically minded would side with the genius of individual poetic inspiration.

The general American assessment of the communalist school in the "ballad wars" is that the inspiration came from the German Romantics, in particular from some statements by the Grimms (Wilgus 1959:10–12, 118). But the likes of Gummere were probably more potently inspired by the blossoming of evolutionary scholarship, by the growing body of ethnographic "data" from "primitives" around the world, and by the exuberant, speculative scholarship of the British solar mythologists (Dorson 1955; Dundes 1969). Gummere's summary essay, "The Ballad and Communal Poetry" (1961 [1897]), cites a debate on origins between Schlegel and a young Wilhelm Grimm, but it draws its main ammunition from elsewhere: "Material such as I have collected in proof of this assertion—all evidence in fact, drawn from the customs of savages and inferior races—is too cumbrous to be inserted here, and needs, in addition, so many allowances, balances, comments, as to deserve separate treatment. The reader may turn to the pages of Spencer's unfinished Descriptive Sociology and find plenty of raw material" (Gummere 1961 [1897]:263, n. 33). It was such evidence, and not the far more cautious deliberations of the German Romantics, that permitted Gummere's leap from Child's premodern, historically situated "people" to the "human throng, . . . the horde." It allowed Gummere to abandon himself into a clear description of presumed authenticity: "Add to these facts the lack of individuality, the homogeneous mental state of any primitive throng, the absence of deliberation and thought, the *immediate relation of emotion and expression,* the accompanying leap or step of the dance under *conditions of communal exhilaration*—surely the communal making of verse is no greater mystery than many another undoubted feat of primitive man" (Gummere 1961 [1897]:27; my emphases). Gummere's textual striving for an experiential authenticity was perhaps further influenced by the growing camp of German scholars interested in "folk psychology" who began to build academic disciplines in folklore and anthropology at the end of the nineteenth century. But it is also possible that communalists such as Gummere were indirectly drawing from reports about black American expressive culture.

Much like the Grimms and Lachmann, Child and Lowell preferred to dwell in the imaginary authentic worlds built by their intellectual endeavors.[24] Gummere worked with the vagueness of evolutionary hypotheses without touching on the perceived reality of black cultural performance. For this circle, even the diversity of white ancestries in the United States proved too much to cope with. The privileging of the ethnic heritage embodied in the Child ballads also represents an intellectual flight from the multicultural realities of post-Civil War New England.[25]

The mid-nineteenth century saw the blossoming of what George Fredrickson called "romantic racialism" in the North. The sources contributing to this shift in the perception of blacks in the white imagination were numerous, ranging from exposure to Herderian cultural relativism to abolitionism and Christian paternalism (1971:97–129).[26] But the encounter with black expressive culture, especially black music, also fed into another trajectory of the white Americans' search for the authentic.

In nineteenth-century aesthetic discourse, music conjoined the searches for the authentic and the national, still surpassing spoken folk expressions.

> Mediating between the rational world and a primordial creative wellspring, this "natural genius," whose knowledge transcended mere intellect, sidestepped the blocks of reason in order to reach intuitively toward a unified, collective unconscious. Whereas Beethoven had epitomized the

titanic artist . . . , folk artists demonstrated a comparable, and perhaps more naturally intuitive genius in acts of improvised, oral expression." (Radano 1996:518)

By seeking the essence of black music, American whites could confess to its emotional appeal and profess to their feelings of affinity. Beyond the spiritual linkage, they also could undertake to appropriate those aspects of black culture embodying such felt authenticity.[27] As in the German Romantics' expansion from a spiritual or emotional linkage with the *Volk* to an appropriation or imitation of those folk materials deemed authentic, American Romantic racialists moved from professing an affinity to black musical expression to attempts at capturing this music in Western notation and thus making it a commodity for white consumption.

Northerners had exposure to blacks before the Civil War, and they had been entertained by the ambiguous images of blackface minstrelsy since the 1830s.[28] The most powerful encounters, however, were the result of the Civil War, during and after which northern whites—military men such as Thomas Higginson, or teachers and social activists such as William Francis Allen—encountered black communities and were swept away by their music. Higginson, who had led a black regiment during the Civil War, projected his discovery to be akin to that of his admired Sir Walter Scott; he professed, too, to his "strange enjoyment . . . to be suddenly brought into the midst of a kindred world of unwritten songs, as simple and indigenous as the Border Minstrelsy, more uniformly plaintive, almost always more quaint, and often as essentially poetic" (1870, quoted after Radano, 1996, n. 19).[29]

Slave Songs of the United States saw its first publication in 1867 (Allen, Ware, and Garrison, 1992). In the introduction to this collection, Allen quotes a description of "the shout," a form of communal dancing associated with black church services that northern white observers in the South had clearly been impressed by:

The benches are pushed back to the wall when the formal meeting is over, and old and young, men and women, sprucely-dressed young men, grotesquely half-clad fieldhands—the women generally with gay handkerchiefs twisted about their heads and with short skirts—boys with tattered shirts and men's trousers, young girls bare-footed, all stand up in the middle of the floor, and when the "sperichil" is struck up, begin first walking and by-and-by shuffling round, one after the other, in a ring. The foot is hardly taken from the floor, and the progression is mainly due to a jerking, hitching motion, which agitates the entire shouter, and soon brings out streams of perspiration. Sometimes they dance silently, sometimes as they shuffle they sing the chorus of the spiritual, and sometimes the song itself is also sung by the dancers. . . . Song and dance are alike extremely energetic, and often, when the shout lasts into the middle of the night, the monotonous thud, thud of the feet prevents sleep within half a mile of the praise-house. (Allen, Ware, and Garrison 1992 [1867]: xiii–xiv)

Allen then speculated that "it is not unlikely that this remarkable religious ceremony is a relic of some native African dance, as the Romaika is of the classical Pyrrhic" (p. xiv). With one sentence, the speculative supposition of singing, dancing throngs in the white past is endowed with apparent bodily evidence in black American devotional practice.

Allen had traveled south with the Educational Commission for Freedmen. He related the extraordinariness of black music by pointing to its affective powers, drawing from the familiar vocabulary of authenticity:

The best that we can do, however, with paper and types, or even with voices, will convey but a *faint shadow of the original.* The voices of the colored people have a peculiar quality that *nothing can imitate;* and the intonation and delicate variations of even one singer cannot be reproduced on paper. And I despair of conveying any notion of the effect of a number singing together, especially in a complicated shout. (Allen, Ware, and Garrison 1992 [1867]: iv–v; my italics)

But convey Allen and others nonetheless did, even when they despaired of getting it all down on paper. Purportedly the effort served to salvage the music before it would be forgotten, for with the end of slavery the purity of suffering and the grandeur of spirit expressed in black spirituals would also vanish. As Allen put it, "The public had well-nigh forgotten these genuine slave songs, and with them the creative power from which they sprang" (p. i).

The statement is reminiscent of the model of salvaging and preserving among German collectors; indeed, Allen's stance and that of many individuals of similar mind may likely have been sparked by the European ideology of authenticity. But the social realities differed profoundly. Freed slaves were comparable to a vanishing or perhaps illusory pure peasant ancestry only inasmuch as American whites, like the European bourgeoisie, attempted to extract the "pure," and even sanctified expressions, from their creators. Abolitionist ideology endowed the spiritual with both religious and political significance, considering the affective power of shouts and voicings as evidence of how extreme human suffering transcends to a

purity and originality of expression. As Ron Radano put it, "black spirituals were not simply trivial expressions of 'primitive purity.'" Rather, the
music in its "soul-turning" quality was an object of desire, perhaps even
more intensively than German Romantics had craved peasant song, because by "appropriating the sonic light of nature from the darkness of
negro bodily insignificance, white Americans possessed the means by
which to construct a racially transcendent, national selfhood." Much as
European collectors had kept their distance from the often appalling economic circumstances of the "bearers of tradition," through the project
of collecting and documenting slave songs "whites could extract these
anonymous sounds of human transcendence from their real-life circumstances, thereby erasing blackness in the name of preservation" (Radano
1996:518–30).

Just as the European lower classes suffered economic transformations
in an industrializing Europe, freed slaves did not simply achieve equal status in American society. They created new artistic expressions, as did the
European proletariat. But those who had collected their musics with fervor in the years surrounding the Civil War withdrew into more academic
pursuits. Fighting for the humanitarian imperative to end slavery proved
an easier task than living with the resulting culture of supposed equality
of all Americans.

Romantic racialists may have disapproved of slavery, and they may have
craved the authenticity that they saw lodged in black Otherness. But many
of their convictions still bore the imprint of believing in the supremacy of
"Anglo-Saxon stock." At the time of his Lowell lectures, James Russell
Lowell was also known for his work as national editor in 1848 for the
Anti-Slavery Standard (Radano 1996: n. 18). In 1848 Lowell had been a
supporter of Irish nationalism. Forty years later, having served as an ambassador in England, he "decided that this very nationalism made Irish-
men impossible as Americans," and like many New Englanders he thus
had come to measure other ethnicities by the "native" Anglo-American
(Solomon 1972:55, 91).[30]

The communalist position eventually had to submit to both kinds of
"individualists": the literary elitists as well as the growing group of ethnographically seasoned folksong collectors in the United States. During
the years at the turn of the century the theoretical struggles on ultimate
origins were joined by equally fierce concerns over academic ownership
of the subject matter. This struggle over "authentic scholarship" and its
role in delineating the boundaries of the subject and of true insight are
the focus of the next two chapters. However, as with the German Roman-

tic ideology and the (pre-)nationalist rhetoric of authenticity fostered by nineteenth-century German scholars, the legacy of the American Romantics as well as of Child and his circle, their language and their concern with authenticity, lived on, legitimating searches for and constraints on authenticity in the politics of culture and conservation.

PART 2

The Role of Authenticity in Shaping Folkloristic Theory, Application, and Institutionalization

From the late nineteenth century to the middle of the twentieth century the Romantic, moral ideal of authenticity began to make way for a more scholarly documentation of the authentic and original. Efforts to prove the scientific nature of folklore studies in some cases pushed the individualistic and moralistic preoccupation with authentic experience and selfhood even further from academic consideration.

However, authenticity in its diversifying connotations hardly vanished from the scene. In the discovery of "truth" the quest for authenticity found its most externalized and instrumentalized shape. As the need lessened to find agreement between theological dicta and scholarly solutions, the question of the ultimate locus of authenticity was transformed by a variety of arguments over the correct theory to explain origins. Evolutionary and devolutionary orientations clashed with and mixed with psychological and sociological theories. The urgency to propose the correct theory moved to the forefront and displaced the once paramount quest for authenticity. Yet attempts to delimit the boundaries of what properly constituted folkloric subject matter continued to draw on authenticity's legitimating power.

Such dichotomizing was rendered even more pronounced in efforts to distinguish academic folkloristics from laymen's appropriations of the folk and their culture. Feudal monarchs and nobility had delighted in imitating peasant folks' dress and festivities (Abrahams 1993, Brednich 1988, Köstlin 1977a). Late nineteenth-century European bourgeois and working-class associations for the protection and revival of folk culture flourished as well, fueled by diverse sociopolitical agenda (see Braun

1965, Mosse 1975). Here, the ideology of authenticity led to policy and action, which academics felt ambiguous about, not least because they feared the spoiling influence of applied folklore work on the purity of their scholarly defined subject matter.

In the United States scholarly endeavors often depended on the generosity of learned (and less learned) philanthropists. Unlike in Europe, where social class was intrinsic both to the definition of the subject matter and to the contours of recruitment into academia, scholarship in the United States was in part the duty and privilege of "society" men and women. This elite was generated not by centuries of sociopolitical transformation, but by the peculiarities of a postcolonial situation. Influences and ideas from the old countries mixed with the needs of the new, and what was a slowly emerging phenomenon on the Continent could often be absorbed and rapidly implemented in the new nation.

Partly as a legacy of Jacob Grimm's work, and partly under the influence of Tylorian evolutionary anthropology, the second half of the nineteenth century saw a profusion of works dedicated to the comparative study of mythology, with the most notable works authored by Wilhelm Mannhardt (1831–80) in Germany (1905 [1875–77]) and Sir James George Frazer (1854–1941) in England (Frazer 1911–15; Cocchiara 1981:277–95, 375–429). Their works overshadowed the lesser quibbles of competing camps of solar mythology (Dorson 1955), and they influenced the emergence of the myth-ritual school (Ackermann 1991). The folkloristic quest for authenticity could fruitfully be documented through this mythological trajectory, based in part on localizing authenticity in religious practices. However, I am concerned here with the less well-understood institutional establishment of folkloristic inquiry. Unlike mythological theories, the arguments surrounding the institutional anchoring of the discipline had a less acknowledged but more powerful impact on the way the pursuit of an authentic subject matter continued.

One contrast between the German and the American case clearly emerges. While *Volkskunde* initially contained some of *Völkerkunde* or anthropology's research interests, institutionally the field remained separate, or, if anything, aligned itself with the study of cultural history or philology and literature, while *Völkerkunde* sought the proximity of the natural sciences. In the United States, folklore's intertwining with anthropology is more pronounced—institutionally in this early stage, and intellectually throughout. This may be attributable to Franz Boas's German intellectual heritage, specifically his commitment to the Humboldtian tradition (Bunzl 1996), which could be realized more creatively in the New World than in the less flexible German institutional structures.

Latent Authenticity Quests in Folklore Definitions and Theories in Turn-of-the-Century Germany

In the eighteenth century the literate and bourgeois could locate the authentic in the expressive culture of an Other, the peasantry or folk. They harbored a spiritual essence that the higher social classes had buried or lost in excessive civilization, and collecting this material and reciting or imitating it became a consuming passion. In some ways this passion is still with us.

But the scholarly need was to order, classify, and explain the rich treasure, not emotionally respond to it. This scientific impulse, qualitatively different and narrower than the exuberant, experiential quest for authenticity that marked Romanticism, began to exercise an influence on the notion of authenticity by increasingly rendering something felt into textual and material evidence.

The forging of disciplinary boundaries, begun in the nineteenth century, aided this more circumscribed concept. If folklore or any other field was to carve out its own intellectual and institutional territory, then its subject matter had to be reined in and differentiated from other emergent disciplines. The need to "essentialize" the discipline implicitly had an impact on what would be considered authentic folklore.

The Romantic assumption was that authenticity resided in expressive culture. Now the assumption gradually changed to "there is expressive culture that is authentic," and scientific methodologies were advocated. Both choice of subject and discipline were being legitimated, and the transformation can be followed in definitional statements within the landscape of newly created scholarly journals, as well as in keynote papers legitimating folklore as a science.

Concurrent with the academic discussion, social groups such as voluntary associations delineated their versions of what was "authentically folk" and "genuine heritage" in clubs devoted to facets of culture such as costume, music, custom, theater, or native sports. This chapter will address such sociopolitical initiatives only inasmuch as they intertwine with the academic discourse. The Nazification of German *Volkskunde* built on this sociopolitical base and perverted tentative theories into fascist and racist programs. German scholars have documented and theorized this process extensively during the past three decades.[1] If the present discussion touches on the fascist development only marginally, it is not to minimize its horrendous impact. My intent is to delineate how the allure of authenticity, coupled with a belief in scientific procedure could generate an intellectual playing field within which Nazi folkloristics was one possibility.[2] The central inclusion of authenticity into definitional practices is, I argue throughout this study, an invitation to exclusionary politics.

The following discussion purposely draws from German-speaking areas in general, for Austrian, German, and Swiss scholars, though ethnographically preoccupied with their own countries, all engaged in founding scholarly *Volkskunde* societies during the same decade.[3] They corresponded among institutes, referred to and debated each other's work intellectually, and for a time set up an umbrella organization whose purpose was to keep the regional and national associations in touch with one another. Definitional statements, then, grew out of this common discourse. For many scholars this international arena was a separate, quasi private realm far removed from the lay-oriented regional associations.[4]

DEFINITIONS OF THE FIELD AND ITS SUBJECT MATTER

"Scholars Versus Amateurs" or "Scholars and Amateurs"?

The generation of the Brothers Grimm was preoccupied with a plethora of scholarly tasks that laid the foundations for numerous and more narrowly specialized disciplines. Their interest in folk materials was interwoven with questions of linguistic and cultural history, Germanic literature, and ancient law. The Grimms' distinction between folktale and legend has awarded them a place in the history of folklore genre delineation, but they used generic distinctions largely to facilitate the integration of folkloristic data with their larger, if predisciplinary, concerns.[5]

Since the eighteenth century, journals were a crucial medium for the dissemination of new social, political, and scholarly ideas (Behler 1983,

Estermann 1978, Schenda 1977:287–99, Wilke 1978). Starting in the second half of the nineteenth century, journals increasingly differentiated between audiences. Yet folklore, linked to emergent nationalism and questions of heritage and preservation, appealed to the specialist as well as to the broader public. This inclusive legacy meant specialized folklore journals reflected the voices and goals of enthusiastic collectors and protectors as much as of those intent on making folklore a scientific discipline devoted to genuine research of genuine materials. I will examine editorial statements from a number of these publications for their continued use of the nature tropes associated with the Romantic discourse on authenticity as well as for their strategies to dichotomize between general interest and authentic scholarship.

Franz Pfeiffer, editor of the new journal *Germania,* proposed to go beyond the exclusivity of philological journals and to address "all of German life in all its expressions." Language, literature, and antiquities, with antiquities embracing "belief, law, custom, legend and life," all would receive treatment. Only political history was to be excluded, although if "the history was more ethnographic than political" it would be appropriate as well (1856:2). *Am Ur-Quell* ("at the Ur-source"), a monthly journal of *Volkskunde,* first appeared in 1890, the successor to *Am Urdsbrunnen* ("at the Ur-fountain"), begun in 1880. According to its editor, with its mixture of folklore collections and analyses, *Am Ur-Quell* had gained the respect of "the best disciplinary colleagues in Germany, Austria, Holland, Belgium, France, England and America." As publisher of "the organ for German *Volkskunde,*" the editor fully "joined the modern folkloristic movement" (Carstens 1890:1). The Romantic water metaphors were still in full flow, for as a leitmotiv the editor characterized folk culture as "the Ur-source [*Urquelle*—hence, the new name] of all knowledge about a people, but folk culture is also all people's fountain of youth which . . . rejuvenates them when decline threatens" (p. 3). Carstens used the untranslatable but ideologically loaded word *Volksthum* or "folk-dom," a term of nineteenth-century German folklore studies that was crucial to Nazi ideology. Elsewhere in this chapter I will use "folklife" for the noun and "folk-like" for the corresponding adjective, and by using these relatively "untainted" terms I want to indicate that for those authors the term *Volkst[h]um* was not problematic.

Karl Weinhold (1832–1901), a professor of German in Berlin, was distressed by such populist appeals, as is evident from a piece he published in the last volume of the *Zeitschrift für Völkerpsychologie und Sprachwissenschaft* (journal for people's psychology and linguistics)—a clearly interdisciplinary endeavor.[6] Weinhold railed against the pseudoscience practiced by "Gentlemen Folklorists," whom he saw as amateurs. By organizing international congresses, they gave themselves an air of scholarliness, but they lacked scientific training and failed miserably even in the basics of collection (1958 [1890]: 38). Having separated the genuine from the spurious scholar, Weinhold then provided a sketch of the analogous tasks that *Volkskunde* and anthropology performed, fields that differed in topics only geographically, with *Volkskunde* studying "the closer-by," anthropology "the farther away" (p. 39). To gain recognition, "*Volkskunde* [had] to be built on different pillars than [those provided by the] journals which so far represent [the field]" (p. 41).

Weinhold then founded the Berlin society of *Volkskunde,* and renamed the journal *Zeitschrift für Volkskunde.* In the first issue he continued his crusade against "folklore": "Folklore is but a segment of *Volkskunde.* . . . May this factual reason keep the German lovers of the foreign term [folklore] from its worthless and tasteless use. Of course, this tastelessness is outdone still by the use of the comical coinage 'folklorist'" (Weinhold 1891: 1). The appeal of language coinages is a matter of taste and context, and Weinhold would undoubtedly be distressed to find that *Volkskunde* in the post–World War II era was a word considered "worthless and tasteless" as well. However, his article did attempt to rein in "folklore" as at best covering the narrative aspects of folklife. He pleaded for "exact research and correct methods" if the field was to become a science and "escape the danger of dilettantism into which the folklorists easily divert it" (pp. 1–2). He outlined the discipline's subject matter to cover the four fields of anthropology, and he sketched a comparative methodology to be employed, but he pleaded for special emphasis of German materials. International discussion was welcome, but only as long as it was scholarly and adhered to the principle of "impartiality in all national questions" (p. 10).

Driven by an interest in professionalizing the discipline, Weinhold drew the boundary between scholarly and amateur research. "Real" scholars worked from a comprehensive research program, building extensive, logically constructed storehouses of knowledge. "Gentlemen folklorists," by contrast, entertained themselves on an international circuit that remained ultimately inconsequential, for it lacked the special knowledge, skill, and hence prestige awarded to the truly hard-working scholar. Implied was the claim that only the scholarly path could lead to true insights; the foundation was laid for a differentiation in both scholarship and subject matter of "genuine" versus "spurious." Weinhold's technique was startlingly similar to Richard Dorson's efforts in the 1950s in the United States to carve out scientific and institutional turf for folkloristics. Just as Weinhold derided "folklore," Dorson attacked "fakelore"—the terms can, in their different historical and linguistic contexts, be considered almost synonymous (see chapter 7).

However, lay participation in the folkloristic endeavor could not be stopped this easily. From the 1880s to the 1910s further national and regional folklore associations in the German-speaking realm were formed, and associations for protecting various aspects of folk culture were also formed or strengthened. Journal editors emphasized the scholarly nature of the enterprise, but amateur membership for various reasons could not be completely discouraged. Aside from financial considerations—for every association needs membership dues—educated amateur scholars such as teachers, pastors, and lawyers often aided "real" scholars in their collection efforts. Differentiating between genuine scholars and amateur specialists in an era when folklore degrees were at best a novelty, however, would have been as arbitrary as differentiating between genuine and spurious folklore.[7]

Throughout the nineteenth century, but especially in the decades leading up to World War I, protectionist and revival associations laid claim to the same domain as did the budding discipline. Growing from the same enthusiasm as the Romantic-bourgeois appropriation of certain folk materials, clubs for the preservation of song and dance, costume, or generally regional or national folk culture played a very large role in what has been called "the nationalization of the masses" (Mosse 1975). For the lower middle classes who engaged in such associational activities, they were a way to actively contribute to the building of new kinds of political communities.[8] Rudolf Braun has argued that associational activities served as a means to mediate the transformations wrought by industrialization and its concomitant social structural changes (1965).

Such associations issued their own journals, such as *The German Folksong*, which had as its goal "nothing more and nothing less than to revive the genuine German folksong which, as one hears so often, is about to die out" (Pommel 1899:1). This journal, as did so many others, formulated clear dichotomies within the revival realm that Weinhold scorned. Editor Pommel emphasized: "Folksong mean[t] the genuine, real song sprung forth among the folk themselves . . . not just simple songs that were created by artistic poets with higher education. . . . We are against falsifications of the genuine and against folksinger-songs that spoil soul and taste" (Pommel 1899:2).[9] To complicate matters further, many editors of scholarly folklore journals were themselves active in applied work, and the more scholarly among them wished at least to keep communication with preservationist organizations open.

Michael Haberlandt (1860–1940) announced the purpose of the new Austrian journal of folklore as comparative study that excluded physical and prehistoric anthropology (which Weinhold still included). Yet his formulation of what would be included invited general participation: "Within these boundaries, we welcome every folkloristic work, whether it be concerned with the inner or the outer aspects [of folklife], with life or art, language or custom, belief or superstition of the folk. We only ask for truthful and conscientious observation, modest, unadorned description, we only ask for objectivity and truth" (Haberlandt 1895:2). How such objectivity and truth would be ascertained remained unstated. Haberlandt also announced that the "dual, in part practical goal" of the association would serve both research purposes and the interests of museum exhibition. As a supporter of the endeavor, the association needed no further legitimation because it served both science and the fatherland (pp. 2–3).

Alois Riegl's astoundingly reflexive, programmatic statement followed Haberlandt's editorial. Riegl asserted that the association was not intent on studying "the folk in the political sense," nor the "third estate of feudalism, nor the fourth estate of the modern social order." He obviously sensed the ideological foundation of the field, which he saw as fueled by the stark contrast between harassed, modern, educated urbanites and the rural folk who remained largely uneducated and unmoved by urban progress. Riegl observed how urbanites "discovered" and craved the rural folk's peace of soul. "One could consider such a need a flight from the world," Riegl noted, but from that self-serving need, something bigger could grow:

> It is especially the educated, the urbanites, who find so embarrassing and unbearable the harshness and the base-egoistical sides of the modern fight for existence and who thus crave the spiritual contemplation of a golden age which they, like the poets of antiquity, correctly presume to exist in the childlike developmental stage of their people. . . . Here lies the reason for our present enthusiasm for all things folk . . . : one wants to create new ideals, after so many of the old ones have lost their warming strength. (Riegl 1895:5)

Riegl thus unabashedly articulated the social, therapeutic need on which the discipline was built—in terms that would resurface only in deconstructionist reflections (see chapter 6). He warned that while the folk could be protected from too quick exposure to modernization, there was no way to "artificially dam [the influx of modernity] despite best intentions" (p. 7).

A similar aim of stressing the scholarly while not rebuffing the amateur is evident in Eduard Hoffmann-Krayer's (1864–1936) remarks in the first issue of the Swiss journal of folklore. Like Weinhold, Hoffmann-Krayer outlined the discipline's subject matter, including the boundaries between *Volkskunde* and related disciplines.[10] He wanted to educate the "circles of amateurs" who in his experience "did not lack the necessity understanding for folkloristic subjects" and displayed a "greater interest in the folk" than one might presume. For them, he hoped to clarify the "vague image generally held of what *Volkskunde* comprised" (1897:2). He specifically invited the public, "in the hope that [the journal] will awaken interest in all regions in the character of the Swiss people and will find an echo in the farthest valleys of our fatherland" (1897:12).

As founder of the Swiss society of folklore, Hoffmann-Krayer was always concerned to deemphasize its scholarly aspects; folkloristic journals, he believed, had to remain "popular-scientific." When the official journal threatened to become too scholarly, he initiated *Schweizer Volkskunde,* a less pretentious sister of the *Schweizerisches Archiv für Volkskunde* (Bausinger 1966c:434–35). As editor, he saw his role as promoter of anything that would enlarge knowledge of the subject matter. To the compiler of a folksong collection concerned about matters of taste, he responded: "The obscene parts must be included in all cases; it is part of the character of the folk; one did not paint Liszt without his warts" (cited after Trümpy 1964:113).

Hoffmann-Krayer as a participant in German debates on what was "authentically folk" maintained more of an active, if not always uncritical, connection to applied aspects of folkloristics than many of his contemporaries, which is evident in his outline for the field:

> There is probably hardly another discipline that is as dependent on amateurism as is *Volkskunde,* and we [should not] underestimate the [amateurs'] valuable services for this science. . . . But [the amateur] should . . . not scare away with his arrogant behavior those who want to begin the true study of folklife. How many a researcher shies away from turning to an object which the amateur considers his monopoly?" (1946 [1902]:1)

During his time as a professor at the University of Basel, he developed the European branch of the university's ethnological museum. The need to decide on suitable objects and a logical and "educational" approach to exhibiting the materials forced him into a pragmatism both with regard to his theoretical perspective and in his involvement in protectionist endeavors (Burckhardt-Seebass 1988:49).[11] He actively participated in the founding of his native city's section of the Swiss *Heimatschutz*,[12] and he participated rather vigorously in efforts to stage folkloristic parades and displays, not just in Basel, but elsewhere in Switzerland. His actions reflected his "popular-scientific" inclinations; he seemed untroubled by the contradictions between amateur and scholar.

Hoffmann-Krayer's multiple identities are evident in his observations on folk culture on display. His critical assessment of the 1931 Swiss costume festival in Geneva is rife with a dichotomous vocabulary of authenticity:

> It is not enough to have swarms of young girls in attractive costumes march by, . . . the spectator wants to see *genuine* folk culture [*Volkstum*], not waitresses and casino-culture. Not every canton was able to convince. . . . The Ticinesi were *thoroughly genuine* with their *gripping and overflowing* temperament. . . . The people from Glarus were an especially *tasteful* costume group. . . . Bern visibly *suffers* from its costume culture designed for foreigners. . . . The Vaudois . . . put far too much emphasis on lovable show pieces (. . .) and *aside from the* genuine there were so many *new imitations* of costumes. . . . In the planning of such festivities one should pay better attention that *no spurious elements* (short dresses, high heels, modern hat ornaments) slip in. (1931:1–3, my emphases)

In his words we hear the scholar concerned with authentic representation, the theoretician aware of the pitfalls of revival, and the aesthete who makes judgments based on unreflected notions of taste.

When a woman complained about these harsh judgments, Hoffmann-Krayer replied most politely and apologetically by arguing that his scholarly side had felt called to make such critical observations. He had been particularly interested in the "newly created costumes" and wanted to point out what to the folklorist would be especially suitable creations, costumes "that naturally suited the peasant girl, and that are as if interwoven with her. I abhor everything that looks like a disguise." To further legitimize this scholarly concern, he pointed out that during an international costume parade the previous year, folklorists "had wrinkled their nose already when looking at our Appenzellers, and they were genuine!" (cited after Trümpy 1964:131).

Yet when Hoffmann-Krayer assessed a particular style of Bernese pottery, he first applauded the return to the "old, beautiful techniques" in contrast to the gaudy inventions made for the world exhibition, only then to muse: "But is this the right thing to do? The more realistically copied the old pieces are, the less artistic uniqueness has the copyist himself; yet it is only the elementary urge to create which brings forth . . . the truly beautiful" (cited after Bausinger 1966c:445).

Hoffmann-Krayer's "multivocality," assessed on his one hundredth birthday, was

> Not just a sign of stylistic insecurity in the judgment over individual data; these are above all hints that . . . problem[s] inherent in the newer development of folk culture had not been recognized yet—the question whether any of the yardsticks for the genuine and the original could still be used, or whether completely different measures would have to be developed. This problem is today more urgent and more pronounced—but the solution is no clearer. (Bausinger 1966c:444)

To Hermann Bausinger, Hoffmann-Krayer remains, despite his judgmental weaknesses, remarkable for identifying and being intrigued by the problems of folklore in modernity. To others, Hoffmann-Krayer's "commitment and simultaneous uninhibitedness . . . has a liberating air to it"— an "air" less easily embraced by reflexive scholars of the present for whom the intersection of "science, art and cultural politics" is far more problematic (Burckhardt-Seebass 1988:56).[13]

The young "science of *Volkskunde*" remained open toward the applied, sociopolitical legacy inscribed in its beginnings. Even if the Romantic nationalist vigor subsided in fin-de-siècle Europe, many organizations and institutions remained devoted to the display and promotion of emblematic aspects of folk culture. Museums and preservationist organizations looked to folklorists for both legitimation and guidance. Some folklorists, in turn, realized that their ability to satisfy the demands of such constituencies made their scholarly aspirations possible.[14]

EVOLUTION, PSYCHOLOGY, DEVOLUTION

Volkskunde as a Science

The disciplinary discourse about the subject of the field and how to study it occurred at the same time as the entanglement between scholars and amateurs. Starting with Wilhelm Heinrich Riehl's (1823–97) 1859 address, the title "*Volkskunde* as a Science" would be repeated by luminaries of the field over the next eighty years, signaling that German folklorists remained insecure in their conviction of whether they truly represented a science. There was a common concern with properly delimiting the authentic folk and their culture, even though many differences over the scope, methods, and purpose of the field existed. In the zeal to demonstrate the rigorousness of their field, one can recognize an implicit (and sometimes explicit) claim that genuine insight could come only from those who rigorously practiced a science of folklore.

Theory remained in the background, not because it was absent, but because, as is still true in German academic writing, authors rarely identify—either explicitly or overtly—their theoretical allegiance. Evolutionary, psychological, and devolutionary premises are recognizable in some arguments, but more germane is the question of whether scholars put the theoretical emphasis on origin or process—on the legacy of Romanticism or on the more pragmatically oriented statistical legacy of the eighteenth century (Sievers 1988:31).

Riehl's lecture had few immediate results, though he was well-known beyond Germany for his multivolume *Natural History of the Folk* (1855), whose exactness was a welcome alternative to British scientific theorizing (Lepenies 1988:199–200).[15] Riehl, who taught economics, statistics, and cultural history at the university of Munich, argued that "a branch of knowledge" only turns into a science "once it finds a center within itself, that is, once it appears free and independent" (1958 [1859]:23–24), and economics, chemistry, and physiology all had found such centers. *Volkskunde*, however, had to awaken from its medieval slumber and rid itself of the trappings of ancient travel writing. Its new center would be the nation.

> The more clearly a people reaches consciousness of itself as a nation, the higher it will climb not only in its general cultured behavior but also in its historical insight. . . . *Volkskunde* is unthinkable as a science as long as it has not found a middle way among its scattered researches in the idea of the nation. . . . [Only in the last one hundred years has *Volkskunde*] slowly found this center again, and simultaneously with that it has gained a plethora of ideas and materials, an independence and creative force. (p. 29)

Riehl also prescribed the nature of the true folklore scholar. "The genuine researcher of the folk travels, not only to describe that which is abroad, but rather to gain the right perspective for the situation in his homeland" (p. 30). The detour through the foreign, be this historical (as in the extensive labors of the Brothers Grimm) or contemporaneous and geographic, was to Riehl the necessary path toward the comparative perspective that made *Volkskunde* a science.[16]

The philologically trained Karl Weinhold in 1852–53 was probably the first academic to offer a seminar on *Volkskunde* (von Geramb 1958 [1924]:108; Eberhart 1992). He did his best to draw boundaries between academic and amateur folkloristics and to outline an ambitious scope for the "new science," but his own investigations remained in the bookish-historical tradition of the Grimms.[17] In the scientifically inclined second half of the nineteenth century, the legacy of the Grimms splintered because it was "so tightly interwoven with romantic views that it was alien to the [new] general mentality" (Spamer 1958 [1928]: 18).[18] The "honored" work of the Grimms nonetheless grew from "erroneous basic precepts," which, in turn, left a confusing record on which no unified science could be built. Instead, the Grimms had left the way open for all kinds of specu-lative mythological schools that were easily marginalized.

Riehl's methodological thoughts were taken up in part by *Völkerkunde* (anthropology), which under the influence of Adolf Bastian fused psy-chology and cultural geography into new theoretical frameworks. Bas-tian emphasized the study of the primitive to understand the "original, naturally caused and lawlike forms of thought developed in the human species," whereas folklore scholarship sought to answer these questions through the study of "cultured peoples" (Spamer 1959 [1928]:20). An-other new discipline, *Völkerpsychologie*, advanced by Wilhelm Wundt, became a temporary home for folkloristic interests and from it, through the efforts of Karl Weinhold, emerged the new German association for *Volkskunde* in 1891. But in the profusion of new disciplines and compet-ing styles of inquiry, the place and nature of *Volkskunde* was unclear, and scholars of different stature and interest felt called on to outline the true nature of folkloristics.

A typical justificatory statement came in an introductory *Volkskunde* text authored by Raimund Friedrich Kaindl, a historian working in the far-off "provinces" of the Bucovina (1903). While Kaindl had nothing new to offer "schooled folklorists," he still hoped to remove the "pitying shrug" that people with an interest in folklore research tended to confront (1903:41). Among the prejudicial labels that folk researchers encoun-tered, Kaindl lists "Social-Democrats of science," "subversive agents," "'amateurish' know-it-alls," "despisers of scholarly 'historical criticism,'" and "natural scientists who have the effrontery to look at the master of creation—man—the way one only looks at and describes the animal king-dom" (p. 44). Paraphrasing Bastian, Kaindl legitimated *Volkskunde* as an ethnological enterprise done in one's native region, and he justified it as a university discipline, a field with a cosmopolitan as well as a patriotic-national significance, and as a discipline with practical relevance. Folkloristic knowledge could be used in the administrative efforts to liberate the folk from its worst superstitions; conversely, much could be observed among peasants that overly civilized urbanites could learn from.

More telling in terms of the scientific "purification" of the authenticity quest was his offer of a manual for researchers detailing the traps that would be encountered in documenting the genuine in written and oral research. One could not rely on early collectors who "did not have the truth in mind, but rather the plentiful editions of their writings" (p. 76). Oral data could be equally treacherous; all too often, the unseasoned researcher "put words in the mouths" of informants, not taking into consideration the psychology of the fieldwork situation. Lay assistants needed to be checked periodically. "It is strongly advised to check suspicious material that was collected by not previously tested or careless correspondents. Sometimes it is enough to send, after some time has elapsed, one or another question back to the same correspondent; the careless correspondent will contradict himself . . . and one then knows how to judge his work" (p. 86). Kaindl thought it worthwhile on occasion to send books to particularly assiduous correspondents to broaden their range of questions, though that could ruin a more spontaneous questioning technique. Authenticity could best be verified by checking the correspondents' work against one's own fieldwork, perhaps even presenting some materials to "a trustworthy representative of that region." Kaindl mostly hoped to communicate the "difficulties with which the researcher fights. If he is himself gullible and careless, a veritable storm-tide of mistakes floods over his work" (p. 89).

Just how difficult the scientific, discipline-internal delineation of subject matter was manifests itself clearly in Hoffmann-Krayer's 1902 attempt to describe "*Volkskunde* as a Science" in dialogue with Adolf Strack, Adolf Dieterich, and Eugen Mogk. A major issue was to what extent *Volkskunde* could be rooted in the humanities. The natural science style of inquiry presupposed an analogy between natural and human "organisms," and the debate was over whether such argumentation and vocabulary, which was prevalent in the growing anthropological-ethnographic enterprise, should be or could be adopted or deemphasized for *Volkskunde*.

Hoffmann-Krayer was particularly intrigued by the permeable boundaries of ideal-typical cultural levels and the possibilities of cultural invention. It was correspondingly difficult for him to circumscribe a finite subject matter and exclusively folkloristic methodologies. The differentiation between ethnology and *Volkskunde* was easy, as they were concerned with similar questions pursued in different settings. The demarcation between *Volkskunde* and cultural history was more complex, as there were clearly areas of high culture that the historian was trained to tackle, and areas of folk culture that were in the domain of folklorists. Hoffmann-Krayer therefore stressed the need for specialization, though some objects and processes transgressed the boundaries: "A hay barn . . . belongs to the realm of folklife, and a modern palace is the product of a higher culture; but how is it with, for example, the urban chalet constructions? Here we have a case where [high] culture is strongly influenced by folklife" (Hoffmann-Krayer 1946 [1902]: 7). Hoffmann-Krayer made similar observations about the cross-fertilization of cultural levels' aesthetics in pottery design and decoration, and he raised the issue of the fluid transition between folksong and art song (*Volkspoesie* and *Kunstpoesie*); he also only half rhetorically posed the question of ownership: "Does Schubert's 'Linden Tree' melody belong to the composer or to an anonymous folk singer?"

The word conspicuously absent here is "genuine." Though Hoffmann-Krayer employs shades of an older vocabulary of authenticity elsewhere, here his usage points to an awareness of the processual nature of culture. The emotional longing for authenticity had disappeared years earlier from strictly scholarly folklore writing, but Hoffmann-Krayer, by questioning attempts to *essentialize* the subject matter at a time when others were eager to *finalize* such a project, inserted unsettling and—perhaps for that reason—repeatedly marginalized issues.

Hoffmann-Krayer's contemporaries (and even more his postwar critics) were far more exercised by his introduction of the terms *vulgus* and *populo*.[19] He wanted to differentiate two tasks that folklorists had faced thus far. The term *Volk* had two distinct semantic meanings, political-national (*populous*), and social-civilizational (*vulgus*). Folklorists more likely would be preoccupied with the social-civilizational, and while Hoffmann-Krayer intended *vulgus* to be an objective term, his definition was permeated by an upper-class or "high-cultured" distancing. This is the only place where he postulates the existence of an early authentic stage: "*Vulgus* [is] the low, primitively-thinking folk that is hardly permeated by individualities, in which the authentic, original folklife is reflected" (p. 2). *Populus* connoted the entirety of a population.

From Hoffmann-Krayer's perspective, the way that the discipline had been practiced had in effect included both *vulgus* and *populus*. Yet "questions of general significance" were just as important to him, and "general

Volkskunde" would preoccupy itself "with developmental factors [that were] valid everywhere, in short, the general agents that move the soul of the folk, whether this be among the Bantu or the peasants of lower Pomerania. [It] would have to consider not just how the folk's world views are shaped, but also how they are transmitted, changed and how they disappear" (p. 10).

The emphasis on *vulgus* and *populus* would exist within a general *Volkskunde*, which drew its conclusions from the regional or national data collections of a descent-based *Volkskunde*; the insights gleaned would enlighten the development of a particular regional or national folklore.

Adolf Strack's review took issue with every point that Hoffmann-Krayer made. Strack was most upset with the rejection of natural law theories in *Volkskunde*, as Hoffmann-Krayer asserted that every human was born with a measure of individuality: the collective spirit that *Volkskunde* wanted to understand sprang from an adaptive process. But the societal conventions in cultural levels varied, and

> The less educated a people, the weaker its individuality, and the more general, widespread (and also more primitive) its world views; the more educated a people, the more pronounced and independent its individuality and the more manifold and varied its world views. How monotonous are the huts of a Hottentott-kraal compared to the houses of a Swiss village, and how [monotonous] are those again compared to the buildings of a metropolis! (Hoffmann-Krayer 1946 [1902]:21)

Strack, however, felt strongly that individuality was not an issue in folk culture, and he even claimed that "every animal, every plant, every leaf owned a 'special individuality,'" but the effect of such individuality was imperceptible. "Where we can scientifically reach it, folklife shows us always the same uniformity and feeling of being tied: this is the form in which the mental life of the masses expresses itself. The ability and the need of the individual to express its peculiarity . . . is simply not present. The individual submits himself unconsciously and without reluctance to the masses in whose life he participates." Strack argued that "individual children, whose tastes later will be worlds apart," enjoyed the same games and rhymes not because they were assimilating their individual identities to each other, but rather because they were born with "an *original similarity*, from which only later a sharply defined individuality will emerge" (Strack 1958 [1902]:65; my emphasis).[20] Accusing the philologist of disregarding *Volkskunde*'s unique position between the natural sciences and the humanities—"the life of the folk and masses represents the transition from *purely natural life* to individual, conscious, intellectual life"—Strack endorsed an evolutionary stance. Human civilization progressed in clearly circumscribed steps, and it was for the folklorist to discover the laws that characterized the beliefs and actions of the transitional step in which the folk were caught.

Strack reflected the desire to apply natural scientific models of explanation to folklore, and by resorting to natural science language, the lingering ties to the vague, emotional, metaphoric vocabulary of authenticity could be cut. The evolutionary perspective allowed for a (seemingly unproblematic) demarcation of the "authentic" folk stage.

Hoffmann-Krayer vigorously denied the validity of this approach, and he sharpened his counterhypothesis that folk cultural manifestations, material or spiritual, were the result of individual invention, adapted and spread by ever larger groupings. In other words, an authentic origin could always be assumed to rest with individual insight. What was interesting to the folklorist was not this origin, but why particular inventions appealed to the larger whole. In emphasizing individual authorship, Hoffmann-Krayer stated: "The 'soul of the folk' reproduces, it does not produce" (Hoffmann-Krayer 1958 [1903]: 70). It was only in this realm of thinking that he could see "principles" of adaptation at work; to him there were no natural laws of folklore generation.

Hoffmann-Krayer also reacted to Strack's refusal to accept the covalence of *vulgus* and *populo* in folkloristic inquiry.[21] He may have sensed the danger inherent in Strack's essentializing efforts to restrict the domain of research to the peasantry within "descent groups." The German term uses was *Stamm* ("tribe" or "stem"), with adjectives like *stammeskundlich*, and it was drawn from historical linguistics; but the word *Stamm* also had strident nationalistic and eventually fascist potential. Given his assumptions of individual agency and his experience with the varied nature of Swiss folklife, Hoffmann-Krayer stated: "The 'specific' characteristic of a descent group or people, the study of which is the task of descent-based *Volkskunde,* consists to me of the sum of all local or regional or national peculiarities of a people" (1958 [1903]: 72). In the face of ample regional differences, he warned against the search for a "French" or a "German" folk essence.

Strack's renewed rebuttal attempted to push Hoffmann-Krayer's approach outside proper science. "As long as we think scientifically, it is a prerequisite to assume that all events are law-governed" (1958 [1903]: 74). But what he found most unsettling, and hence unsupportable, in

Hoffmann-Krayer's argument was once again a question of authenticity. To Strack, it was an "impossibility to prove that certain mentifacts were based on individual initiative" (p. 73)—an issue uninteresting to Hoffmann-Krayer to begin with. Strack defended, instead, the assumption of authenticity resting with a general stage of civilizational development. Because an individual origin could not be recovered, the concept of a "soul of the folk" had been postulated and accepted as a fully legitimate ultimate source.

In 1902 Struck founded the *Verband der Vereine für Volkskunde* (the association of *Volkskunde* associations) to provide an organizational center for this science, although some folklorists continued to regard the pursuit of an exclusive science as detrimental to folkloristic insight (e.g., Dieterich 1958 [1902]).

Eugen Mogk, dissatisfied with the poor progress achieved by the association considered disciplinary essence vital. Why did the membership resist discussing "where [essential] folkloristic material could be harvested best?" (Mogk 1958 [1907]:89). Mogk was even more concerned with circumscribing what exactly the essence was and which (past and present) classes could be considered its producers or carriers. He returned to the "soul of the folk," now bolstered with psychological insights.

> Why do we exclude the guild system from *Volkskunde*, even though youth and male societies (*Jünglings- und Männerbünde*), as well as the neighborhoods are included without question? Psychology gives us the answer: one [form] arose from the associative modes of thought of the soul of the folk, and continues to live through them, the other [form arose] from reflexive understanding. *Volkskunde* is only concerned with the products of the former. (p. 90)

Education that fostered rational thought was thus the "worst enemy" of folklore. Those groups that harbored the materials that best represented associative modes of thought were peasants, all "estates who have their occupation in nature," children and "women, who of the two sexes have a decidedly stronger tendency toward associative thinking and thus nurture folklore (superstition, folksong, etc.) better than the male gender" (p. 93).

With the potential collector thus alerted to the proper groups to work with, Mogk rephrased Hoffmann-Krayer to read, "The folk does not reproduce, it copies; the variations [in folklore] are not the result of reflective mental activity, but of a mental activity that is guided by sensations and emotions" (p. 94), thereby psychologizing rather than individualizing the creative process. It would take more than twenty years until

Hoffmann-Krayer wrote his final rebuttal in favor of individual creativity (1946).

Gesunkenes Kulturgut

Hoffmann-Krayer's last words on this debate were part of a response to a markedly different challenge, the one laid out in Hans Naumann's (1896–1951) *Grundzüge der Volkskunde* (1922). Whether spiteful or elitist, Naumann certainly harbored no secret desire to partake of the authenticity of a folk. His central notion was that creative genius was the purview of high culture, whence it trickled down to the mass. It was the antithesis of the amalgamation of reverence, scholarly interest, documentary fervor, and protectionist impulse characteristic of folkloristic endeavor of the day.

Naumann's thesis, developed first in a 1921 essay, derived from a simple evolutionist perspective based on a two-class theory. He perceived the major task of *Volkskunde*—which he saw as a bridge between ethnology and cultural history—to be the "clear dissection and neat separation" of every item of folklife in terms of its origin in one or another social stratum. "No matter how trivial a detail it may be, [ask whether] it is an item of primitive common good [*primitives Gemeinschaftsgut*] that has come from below, or of sunken [high] culture good [*gesunkenes Kulturgut*] that has come from above" (1921:1). "Primitive communal culture" (*primitive Gemeinschaftskultur*) Naumann characterized as devoid of individualism, whereas high culture had progressed to individualism and differentiation.[22] The emphasis on the lack of individuality had been present in Strack's arguments, but Naumann took his characterization considerably further.

> The life of the bearers of a primitive, that is non-individualistic culture, is a communal life, parallels for which one must seek without shyness in the animal kingdom, with ants, bees, monkeys and so forth. And one does not have to leave Europe to find a living primitive communal culture. For instance in the European East, among the Lithuanian peasants, the notion of primitive communal culture is overwhelmingly driven home. . . . When the Lithuanian peasants drive to market in the next village, they go, one behind another like ants. And [as with ants] the outsider cannot distinguish among them. In addition to identical beards, identical hairstyle, identical clothes, there are identical types of faces and similar build. (1921:5)[23]

In observing from a distance, Naumann's sketch of the authentic was perhaps the most dehumanizing ever proposed, reducing the folk to the level of unthinking insects. In 1921 Naumann proclaimed that "genuine *folkart* is communal art, no different from how swallows' nests, beehives, snail houses are products of genuine communal art" (1921:6; his italics). In 1922 he more radically emphasized the creative impotence of the primitive, arguing that the notion of even a creative "soul of the folk"—as Strack still maintained—was but an unfortunate remnant of Romantic scholarship. Naumann thus assumed evolutionary progress, but within a universal, constant differentiation into lower and higher orders of humans. "To believe that progress grows from the community is romanticism. Community pulls [cultural goods] down or at least levels [them]. . . . *Folk goods are made in the upper stratum*" (1922:5; his italics).[24]

The relationship between high culture and folklife was not a new question. In the discourse on folksong and art song (*Volkslied und Kunstlied*), this issue had been debated ever since *Ossian* burst on the European intellectual scene (see chapter 1). Eighteenth-century literati, most prominently Herder, praised the unaffected, even unreflected, naturalness of folk poetry. In the nineteenth century the notion of a communal folk soul engaged in poetic creation proved stronger than the counterargument that individual creativity always had to be the source, no matter whether posterity acknowledged it or not.[25] John Meier's (1864–1953) well-respected treatise on the subject had clearly sided with the argument for individual creativity. "The invention, or if you will, the first application of a poetic form can always be attributed to an individual" (1906 [1898]:13). Meier and Hoffmann-Krayer, both of whom taught at the University of Basel at that time, may well have reached this insight together.

But because it was nearly impossible to determine who among the folk authored a song—and not because Meier presumed creativity to be the prerogative of the upper classes—Meier advocated the comparative study of art and folksong. With art song, a written, authored text was available, even if the author, as with so many eighteenth- and nineteenth-century poets, had been inspired by a folksong.[26] Such texts permitted one to follow the folk adaptations of an art song, and a scholar could then determine the characteristics of folksong.

What distinguished folksong from art song in Meier's view was oral performance and reliance on memory. Print invariably brought variation, and these variations would point to poetic preferences of the folk taste. Pejorative terms such as *Zersingen* (lit. "to sing apart") had been used for this adaptive process since the early nineteenth century, and Meier himself used the phrase *Zerfasern* ("to fray"; 1906 [1898]:31). The process that rendered a song appealing was of interest, making an authored text (authored by an individual of any social class) anonymous and folk. John

Meier, though himself of quasi aristocratic background, was clearly not interested in making a case for the aesthetic superiority of art song.

Naumann's version of evolutionary theory, favoring the more "progressive" over the more "primitive," brought a different turn to this discourse. To Naumann, the creative individual could only be of upper-class background. Yet to Meier a productive back and forth existed between art song and folksong, with the aesthetics of folksong inspiring art song. Naumann only emphasized the devolution of upper-class cultural goods as they were appropriated by the folk.[27] His characterization of the folk mentality was so thoroughly drenched in negatives that any identification or empathy with such a group would have been surprising. The "mentality and character of the peasants" was not "bad, but primitive," and in his catalog of the "primitive ideal" are a phlegmatic attitude toward work, a passion for splendor in dress, immoderation in food and drink, and "squandermania" during festivities, "pigheadedness" and hard-heartedness, laziness, and mistrust. The character is premoral, the thought patterns prelogical, and the peasant's good relationship with animals derives not from love and empathy but from the fact that peasants themselves are still so much part of the animal kingdom (Naumann 1922:64–69).

In yet another assessment of *"Volkskunde* as a Science," the Austrian Viktor von Geramb (1884–1958) appraised Naumann's text as "the most important methodological innovation," which in its clarity of formulation "constitute[d] another step in the purification of scientific *Volkskunde*" (1958 [1924]:123). However, von Geramb's congratulatory words were immediately followed by concern that Naumann's categories might be misunderstood. Von Geramb thought it vital to include "the sunken cultural goods" in folkloristic study. He further resented Naumann's defamation of the Romantic heritage. "The whole of German culture and *Volkskunde* in particular owes so much to Romanticism . . . that it seems to me a duty to keep the terms romantic and Romanticism as honorary names . . ." (p. 124). Writing a folklore text implied to von Geramb reverence for the history of the field and for the subject under study. Scientific accuracy should not stand in the way of "writing a book of love" (p. 125). The secret of *Volkskunde* as a science to him was ultimately that it was an art, for it united "clear reason" with "warm love and worship" (p. 126).

Von Geramb, a young scholar at the time he wrote this essay, sailed a course that indulged the scholar's desire for feeling the authentic while nonetheless endorsing a protofascist "science" as Naumann proposed it— a posture that would bring him considerable political difficulty but leave him ultimately unscathed (see chapter 6).

Adolf Spamer, at the beginning of his career as a folklore professor in Berlin,[28] characterized Naumann's work as coherently and appealingly formulated, but it contained nothing new, theses that were "pre-shaped, pre-thought and pre-embattled" in two hundred years of research and philosophy centering on the idea of the folk (1924:68). Naumann's terminology and his cultural levels were obviously borrowed from Durkheim and Lévi-Bruhl. Spamer objected more to Naumann's simplifications in the interest of clarity—simplifications bordering on prejudice that hardly suited scholarly accuracy.

> Naumann's definitions would not need to contain any valuation, for his image of a lower and an upper class is nothing but a lastly [simple] metaphor [concerning the upward mobility of humans] . . . which is probably customary in most languages since antiquity. . . . For it is understood that in real life there is neither an upper nor a lower level of such diligently distilled purity. Rather, there is a crisscrossing of many mental and social levels, with vertical and diagonal linkages. (p. 89)

Spamer took further issue with Naumann's claim that on the basis of his two-level theory, the scientific duty of *Volkskunde* could be clearly circumscribed. Charting the trickling down of upper cultural goods was hardly a scientific goal. Cultural history would trace the reverse path, the progress of human ideas and ideals to ever greater heights. Without offering a clear disciplinary demarcation himself, Spamer considered the study of all social groups vital, and his goal was to work toward establishing "group spirituality" (*Gruppengeistigkeit*) from observing and analyzing material and spiritual artifacts (p. 106).

The romanticism against which Naumann had reacted, Spamer too perceived as dangerous, but he prescribed different methods against it:

> All the efforts of an enlarged or decreased aim of our science are just a testimony to the recognition of the practical meaning, even indispensability of *Volkskunde* for our present life and for the development of our own people. . . . It is no wonder that today the old Romanticism revives and that there are men again who like Görres sharply distinguish between *Pöbelhaftigkeit* (the nature of the rabble) and the holy spirit of the folk. They are going beyond the skepticism of a non-evaluating, observing science and feel themselves as missionaries of a purer and more rooted future. . . . But one should not forget that any science can only offer a diagnosis, not a therapy or a prophylaxis. . . . Applied *Volkskunde* may be a bitter necessity, but can never be a science. (pp. 98–99)

Sober research and abstaining from simplifying, essentializing claims was what Spamer postulated. Authenticity in his vision at best took the place of penultimate goal (1933a:260).

Hoffmann-Krayer waited eight years, but then he also delivered a pointed argument against Naumann's "two-level theory," maintaining that it was impossible to radically separate a "cultured" and a "primitive" level, and that there were creative and influential individuals at either level. Instead, Hoffmann-Krayer emphasized "individual agency" and "the theory of processes of assimilation" as the primary keys for explaining the spread of cultural practices (1946: 228). Furthermore, culture goods did not simply exist; they developed and changed historically. To prove his point, he presented examples of three types of assimilation processes, cutting across social tiers. A local baker invented a new bread for a baked goods exhibit, thus enacting Hoffmann-Krayer's first type, "invention by an individual." The second type, "transmission of existing folklore through an individual," was exemplified by the introduction of confetti in the Basel carnival, after a department store owner had seen it used in Paris, and it could be demonstrated with countless examples from changing rules in traditional sports to modifications of holiday practices initiated by enterprising individuals. Well ahead of his time, Hoffmann-Krayer also recognized in this category the "revival of disappeared folk customs" as an aspect of cultural transmission and change that deserved study, not scorn. And last, "change of existing folklore though an individual" could be shown in the documented history of any festival (pp. 228–31).

Finally, and perhaps most importantly, creative individuals could be found as much among the folk as among the elites, and a "mass" willing to follow someone's creative idea existed among an elite (willing to, for instance, follow the dictates of urban fashions) just as it did among the folk. Hoffmann-Krayer was still willing to stand behind his dictum, "The folk does not produce, it reproduces," as long as it was not misinterpreted along the lines of Naumann's notion of sunken cultural goods; instead, it centered on the twin assumptions of individual creativity and popular assimilation (p. 236).

For the latent preoccupation with authenticity, Hoffmann-Krayer's argument was doubly relevant. First, like Meyer, he located origin and hence authenticity with an individual, no matter what social class. He based his case on documentable evidence rather than on the "prejudicial gaze" (p. 225) in Naumann's theorizing that led to an essentializing vision, bypassing the intricacies of historical interrelationships. Second, the interest in the accidents of invention, transmission, and change logically undermined a craving for static, circumscribed genuineness, as the focus was on process. In refuting Naumann and Naumann-like arguments, Hoffmann-Krayer arrived at a position that it was nearly impossible to define or delimit who or what the folk are. While he argued for limitations on what folklorists could reasonably include in their studies, he repeatedly made it clear that a categorical differentiation of folk and non-folk materials was impossible (p. 236).[29]

Naumann's quasi Nietzschean favoring of a superior class could have made him an ideologue for the emerging Nazi powers, and, himself a member of the party, he apparently repeatedly tried to gain its ideological approval. But his disdain for the folk mentality stood in too sharp a contrast with the Nazi notion of a folk community arising from common blood ties, and Naumann's theory was branded as *too liberal* (Schmook 1991:82–83).

On the eve of World War II German *Volkskunde* had secured a considerable institutional and societal base. Like other disciplines engaged in circumscribing their subject and their contribution to knowledge and to society, folklorists had initiated scholarly societies, publications, and large-scale reference works[30] that were the infrastructural underpinnings of a respectable intellectual endeavor. Yet as this chapter has shown, there were discrepancies in opinion between those advocating folklore as a field of research: disagreements over methodology and over theoretical paradigms, and, more important yet, disagreements over the boundaries of the subject. Although terms such as "genuine" are mobilized far less frequently than a hundred years earlier, scholars' views of both folklore and "proper" scholarship were shaped by their concept of authenticity.

The prominence of a vocabulary of authenticity and an ideology of pure heritage in *Volkskunde*'s public profile—nurtured at the turn of the century more by public associational life than by scholars—led the discipline into Germany's political arena during the Nazi period. The discipline's infrastructure was open for invasion, and the lure of authenticity was sufficiently blinding for many folklorists not to see the politics of destruction.

Chapter Five

Defining a Field, Defining America

"The Zunis, in particular, were a sheer revelation to the somewhat waterproof East. . . . Never was a tour more skillfully managed. Perhaps never was another quite to curiously mixed between genuine scholarship and the arts of the showman."
—Charles Lummis (1900; cited in Hinsley 1989)

Reconstruction after the American Civil War was not only a matter of passing constitutional amendments or of rebuilding war-ravaged cities, but a matter of finding a new American identity. Escaping back into the English past was one possibility, though this luxury was probably most congenial to New England. The South was a more difficult heritage, with a far too recent fratricidal conflict to permit it to be a model for the United States. Instead, it was to the West, to the unexplored frontier, that politicians, adventurers, and academics looked.

In the span from Frank Hamilton Cushing to John and Alan Lomax one can see the powerful hold that the West had on the American ethnographic project as much as on the definition of professional fields of anthropology and folklore. The individuals involved were collectors, much as their predecessors had been, but they were also definers of the authentic within contexts that were new, both academically and in terms of the American project. Their motivations were not unified at all; one cannot speak of an "American school" of the authentic of the late nineteenth century. One also cannot speak of a fully formed American identity. Rather, there was a bewildering mixture of scholarly, social, political, and personal impulses and justifications for working with materials that professional folklorists would come to view as within their interest.

If New England society had been spellbound by James Russell Lowell's lectures on the origins and history of English poetry in the 1850s, then the white establishment emerging from the trauma of the Civil War added

119

to this escape into layers of the European past its romance with the Native American. White settlers steadily moved westward, mercilessly claiming the land from native populations. They were protected by U.S. army regiments who fought an enemy feared and hated, despised and looked down on, one collectively labeled "Indians" or "red men." Native Americans were forced into reservations, forced or coerced into adopting white people's cultures, or, most often, killed. Popular interest intensified just as this enemy no longer posed a real threat but was instead close to extinction. "Vanishing the Red Man" (de Caro 1986) became a nostalgic trope in legend and literature, which managed to put the blame for the demise of native cultures onto the natives themselves.

The government sent out soldiers, but it also supported expeditions to reconnoiter the lands and resources of the West. The task of the Bureau of American Ethnology was to document the physiological, cultural, and linguistic characteristics of the tribes as well as to furnish genuine artifacts for the newly founded Smithsonian National Museum. The "savages" took on features of noble, albeit doomed, moral character, and they were increasingly recognized to represent distinct, tribal contours—a process considerably aided by sketched and photographed visual images that reached the East Coast establishment. The thought was that those cultures had to be studied before they were lost forever, because their practices and beliefs might hold keys to the mysteries of the white civilization's own past.

Crisscrossing this unfolding web of policies of confinement, aesthetic curiosity, exhibition, and scientific appropriation were idiosyncratic and self-promoting individuals such as Frank Hamilton Cushing. In his sojourns among and writings about the Zuni, Cushing incorporated the individualistic adventure and transcendence exemplified by Thoreau. He provided one blueprint for the novel profession of ethnographer, who for the sake of science underwent hardship and was rewarded with acceptance by the innocent savages. A representative in the tradition of "speakers of being" (Zengotita 1989) as well as a "charismatic ethnographer" (Hinsley 1983), Cushing was also an entrepreneur who acted as culture broker between the natives and his own East Coast upper-class circles, to whom he appeared like "a revelation" (Hinsley 1989: 181).

After working as a curator at the American Museum in Washington, D.C., Cushing was chosen to be part of a bureau expedition to the Southwest. Contrary to the initial plan, Cushing remained with the Zuni when the research team moved on, a decision he would justify as intuitive, a connection and calling forged in dreams he had while working at the museum (Hinsley 1983). His long stay was hardly easy either on him or on the Zuni, who initially perceived his intrusion and incessant writing as a threat, and who, at least according to his own report, attempted to kill him (Georges and Jones 1980:5–8). His ability to navigate the cultural gulf that separated him from his hosts eventually gained him entry into the innermost mysteries of Zuni life.

With the help of a felicitous publicity team composed of a painter and a romantically inspired journalist, as well as a zeitgeist yearning for spiritual and exotic authenticities, the tour that Cushing and his genuine pueblo men staged in 1882 was enormously successful. Cushing's ability to give the impression that he had secret and sacred knowledge, allowed him to transfer "privileged information, spiritual energy, [and] historical viability" to circles of avid New England audiences, one of "the cleverest thing[s] that has ever been devised and carried out by a scientific student anywhere" (Lummis in Hinsley 1989:181, 183–84). Cushing in his role as Zuni initiate, together with his native friends, performed "restorations of behavior" (Schechner 1985). By seating his New England audiences in circles, whether indoors or out, he evoked the semblance of participation in rites around a faraway campfire, or better, in the mysterious darkness of *kiva* rituals.

By all accounts, Cushing truly felt deeply connected to the pueblo Indians, and his sensibility in recognizing "the importance of the mundane, in artifacts and activities, and their complex connection to the sacred" was at "variance with prevalent American attitudes" (Hinsley 1983:57). He was not a collector of vanishing remnants, but rather he thought Zuni history and religion alive, ready to be experienced in daily life, and he did so as a participant-observer. But as he proceeded in his study of language and narrative, arts and archaeology, all the while supplying the Bureau of American Ethnology with data, the Zuni he lived with were vanishing. Why else would Cushing in 1892 have written in his diary, "God help my poor doomed Zuni!" (Hinsley 1989:169)?

Folklore as a societal and scholarly interest was clamoring for attention in the face of this mélange of mystical, commercial, ethnographic, and colonizing impulses. It made a claim to participate in the fashioning of an American identity. There were the Harvard men with their sights firmly fastened on the purity of ballads and politics of the past. There were the growing number of ethnologists, collecting artifacts and texts from vanishing native tribes, attesting to the need to capture cultural treasures before they vanished. There were interested, educated elites and professionals who saw diverse efforts as compatible pastimes worthy of their support. The early membership of the American Folklore Society (AFS) included authors, politicians, administrators, philanthropists, physicians, army officers, lawyers, and clergymen (Dwyer-Shick 1979:13). But plenty of other organizations and institutions clamored for membership and support at the end of the nineteenth century, and success depended not only on the ability to characterize folklore as a central focus of the enterprise, as something intrinsically desirable and important, but also on the skill in maintaining the interest of a diverse membership.

In one of her contributions to the history of anthropology, Regna Darnell has argued that the content of "anthropological research, the institutions which supported it, and the social networks of practitioners" must be dealt with in the historiography of scholarship (1988:x). Four histories examining the turn-of-the-century attempts at consolidating American folklore studies have all sought to weave together these multiple demands (Bronner 1986, Dwyer-Shick 1979, McNeil 1980, Zumwalt 1988). What emerges from these works, as well as from a growing body of intellectual biographies and shorter articles on the period, is a bewildering mixture of social, scholarly, and personal impulses for working with folklore materials, as well as various explanations for why folklore, despite the often vigorous commitments on the part of individuals and groups, remained on weak institutional footing.[1] The very diversity was a major reason that folklore failed to gain a firmer foundation in academe until after World War II.

Americans were caught in the social and intellectual dilemma faced by any postcolonial society. They wanted to build cultural institutions—universities, museums, historical monuments—to provide continuity and to establish the leading place of their nation among all other nations. Using European models was an automatic way to proceed, its genesis emanating from Europhiles or recent European immigrants who were eager to fulfill in their new home the intellectual and institutional dreams that they had been unable to pursue in the places left behind. But in part the motivation lay in a competitive, academic, and high cultural spirit that sought to intellectually surpass the older European institutions. And Americans also faced the fundamentally different circumstances of their continent.

Accomplishing this task proved disorienting and divisive. Should folklore remain associated with vestiges of a European past, confined to disciplinary contours as they were being carved out in Germany, even though the division into *Volkskunde* dealing with folklore of one's own nationality and *Völkerkunde* looking at the cultures of former colonies was hardly applicable? How should other disciplinary boundaries, firmly established in Europe, between the study of language, culture, and religion be brought in line with American cultural circumstances? Should folklore be a science codifying and delimiting the authenticity of textual treasures of European descent, or should folklore regain the aura it had held for the generation of Herder—a key to hear the divergent, original voices of people all over the globe? These questions in hindsight appear to have informed much of the intellectual and institutional building around the turn of the century. Yet to those involved in the process, such larger structural issues must have been much more opaque. Clearly, there were important issues that were discussed and fought over, such as the battle against cultural evolutionist theories and allied racist ideology and policy, or the concern with the influence of technological transformations and mass cultural phenomena that appeared to weaken the fabric of society. Yet faced with the need to create something approximating normal science, seeking refuge in authenticity standards seemed one of the few "solid" means to establish authority over a landscape of shifting cultural productions.

Of the many interwoven stories of an emergent folkloristic enterprise, this chapter focuses on three elements, each of which incorporates authenticity arguments: the romantic or treasure-hunting authenticity vocabulary; the scientific authenticity legitimation; and the essentializing search for national or individual character. I will address first the founding of the American Folklore Society and its associated journal. This story illustrates a not entirely unintentional elitism that favored the study of authentic folklore as defined by scholars and that prevented the society both from profiting from the social momentum and vigor of cultural interventionist movements and from gaining broadly based support. Such support would have alleviated the marginal and financially precarious nature of the organization, and it would have helped to soften the recurrent schisms between academics and practitioners that plague the AFS to this day.

Historians of the field confirm that anthropological folkloristics dominated the AFS and its journal far into the twentieth century. The ways in which the anthropological project acquired an identity beyond museum collecting and generated research projects and methods, vocabularies, and a professional identity provide the second focus. Its practitioners were endowed with a certainty of knowing how to recognize or, if necessary, to recover the authentic. Last, I turn to efforts to recoup the authentic individualistic spirit of Emerson to fashion an American cultural identity expressed in a broad range of activities from folksong collecting and cultural intervention to theorizing on American culture.

The American Folklore Society: Real Science, Original Materials, and Vanishing Membership

In the founding of the American Folklore Society a number of goals and interests flowed together that compressed into a few decades developments in society and scholarship that had taken centuries to evolve in Europe. From scholar to army colonel and from curator to philanthropist, varied individuals had come to recognize folklore as a part of culture, whether in terms of antiquarian, evolutionary, medievalist, or anthropological interests. The positivist impetus to methodically separate spheres of learning made the professionalization of all intellectual activity an important stepping-stone toward legitimating disciplinary authority (Abrahams 1989b:617–18). A British Folk-lore Society had been founded in 1878, and thus a competitive impulse on the part of the Americans played a part as well. At the same time, the American variant of antimodernist alienation meant that some, rather than cheering the "taming" of the West, saw instead the demise of noble though primitive societies (Lears 1981). Rather than reveling in the achievements of industrial progress, they saw the "vulgarizing and deinvigorating tendencies accompanying 'progress'" (Abrahams 1989b:609). The social realities of a nation digging out from the physical and psychological destruction of the Civil War suggested the need for cultural repair.

William Wells Newell, active in various Reconstruction projects, wrote the initial circular suggesting the formation of a folklore society. Interested individuals gathered for a founding meeting at Harvard in 1888 and held their first annual meeting in Philadelphia in 1889. The aging and ailing Francis Child was persuaded to be the first president, and Newell himself acted as secretary-treasurer and first editor of the society's *Journal of American Folklore* (*JAF*).

Little is known of the motivations and sentiments that propelled the lesser-known among the 104 individuals into signing the petition to establish a "Folk-Lore Society in America" (Newell 1888a:3). At least one notable figure did not sign; that was Charles Elliott Norton, close friend of Child and the strongest representative of the British medievalist movement in the United States. Norton saw tremendous potential in turning the United States into the last stronghold of the great European tradition. In Child's ballad work Norton accurately saw a scholarly example of an American outdoing European research. Newell as well represented a challenge; though a former student of Child and part of Child's circle, he had set his interests on the United States, not Europe, and his intellectual allegiance was with Franz Boas, who himself perceived folklore as an element of the emergent anthropological project. Norton thus felt understandably threatened by these vigorous intellectual and curatorial designs at variance with his own.

In the anthropological perspective, museums should grow into treasuries of American art and archaeology. Married to a relative of Boas and helping him find contacts and resources to further his ethnographic projects, Frederick Ward Putnam directed Boston's Peabody Museum, which he hoped to turn into an American museum rather than a collection of European art. Within the social class that could support a folklore society, tensions already existed about the proper goals and intellectual orientation of the endeavor.

Among the wealthy circles of the Northeast were individuals with a strong social commitment to combat the societal decay that they associated with modern economies, with industrial mass production, and with the dislocation of ever-new immigrant groups into urban centers. In particular, the southern mountain areas appeared to be losing their cultural integrity as a result of urban migration and the loss of their agricultural base. New England society women, like Francis Child's daughter, were particularly committed to improve this situation. The War Department's sanitary commissions, to take one example, had begun projects of social intervention in the aftermath of the Civil War in urban centers of the Northeast. Newell served with such a commission in New York City, and undoubtedly he acquired his organizational skills from the women who ran the project. But the early twentieth century also saw new efforts, like the folk school movement (an intellectual import from Denmark) that tried to halt and redirect a society perceived as on the verge of breakdown. Folk schools drew from what were seen as traditional, wholesome ways of life, so as to restore community values in regions hardest-hit by urban flight.[2]

This momentum to prevent social decay employing a form of applied folklore was not harnessed into the new folklore society. The issues for the key founding figures, Newell and Boas, were more academic, and they resonate in the pages of the journal's first issues. The journal was to be "of a scientific character," and the adjective sent the signal that the moral, activist elements in folkloristically interested circles would remain outside the official published voice of the society.

Nevertheless, the primary publication goal was "for the collection of the fast-vanishing remains of Folk-Lore in America." Within this salvage collecting, Newell saw four major areas: English relics, American Negro folklore, lore of the native tribes, and other ethnic groups. He described them in terms of disappearing treasures in a language rife with assumptions of abundant authenticities lodged in the past and with laments over the inability of earlier generations to recognize the value of their own traditions. Among the "Relics of Old English Folk-Lore," he dwelled on ballads; he presumed the real thing had been "superseded by inferior rhymes," although he expressed a belief that "genuine ballads continued to be sung in the colonies" (Newell 1888a:3–4). Throughout the section treating his own culture's folklore, Newell used a vocabulary of threatened loss—"saved from oblivion," "gathered while there is time," "not to be allowed to perish"—but he also recognized that folklore transcended all social classes, informing the daily life and thought of children and adults, laborers and Boston Brahmins.[3]

In other areas the vocabulary of loss was coupled with different lenses of Othering. In the case of the American Negro, Newell saw "the origin of [their] stories" as a primary research interest, and he was certain that "a great mass" of folkloric materials could be gathered among "this people" (1888a:5). The traditions of native tribes seemed equally "promising and important," and because Indians were deserving of "opportunities for civilization," it was an urgent task to record tribal cultures in order to understand their contribution to "humanity as a whole." Natives were a treasure-hunter's dream, and for them Newell mobilized the romantic "riches of nature" vocabulary. "The harvest does not consist of scattered gleanings, the relics of a crop once plentiful, but, unhappily, allowed to perish ungarnered; on the contrary, it remains to be gathered, if not in the original abundance, still in ample measure" (1888a:5). An entirely different moral tone was mustered as well: "One race cannot with impunity erase the beliefs and legends of its predecessor. To destroy these is to deprive the imagination of its natural food; to neglect them is to incur the reproach of descendants, who will wonder at and lament the dulness and barbarism of their fathers" (1888a:6).[4] Clearly under Boas's influence, Newell expended his greatest efforts in conveying the need to work with the Indians. By contrast, the fourth emphasis—ethnic groups—merited only a single sentence. One may already recognize here the seed of dissatisfaction in the minds of those folklore scholars and enthusiasts interested in the English heritage rather than the American present. In Newell's journal editorship and in his private demeanor he clearly favored the anthropological direction.

A subsequent issue of the journal found Newell seeking to define the term folklore by delineating the primary subject matter as "oral tradition." This "vast region of human thought" was complementary to literature, except for those "primitive peoples" without literacy where the entire scope of oral traditions should be addressed. More than half of his note, however, refers to European periodicals as legitimation, pointing to their well-established nature; thus, by inference, Newell urged Americans to do their share of decent scholarship (Newell 1888b). Within a few years, though, Newell was sufficiently established to blast the theories and methods used by philological folklorists as fraught with speculation and generalization built on insufficient data. At a time when native tribal material was "perishing faster than it [was] recorded," engaging in idle speculation about origins was unscientific, if not immoral. "It is the fact of Navajo game itself, and not a theory about the source of the game, is the interesting point" (1890b:31). As much as he liked contemplating psychological connections between the state of mind of the Native American and the ancient European or Aryan, Newell stressed the wasted opportunities and the urgency of scientifically inspired collecting.

The journal wanted to offer "original material" that would facilitate scientific study. How desirable and superior the scientist posture must have been is reflected in Otis Mason's 1891 contribution. Comparing folklore "specimens" to the minerals or chemicals studied by the natural scientist, Mason claimed:

> The folk-specimen has this advantage, that no bungling or malicious analyst can destroy it by dissolving it into its elements. The archaeologist who rummages a mound, the paleontologist who removes a fossil from its associations, the anatomist of a rare animal who destroys the connections of parts, all have closed the door of research. The folk-cabinet is like the piles of enumerators' atlases in the Census Office. The material is ever at hand to be considered. (Mason 1891:100)

Collection for Mason was thus of the utmost importance. Aware of the impact of subjective influences—he referred to them as "the personal equation," thus alluding to a major scientific question of his day—Mason advocated that the modern collector should "carefully study out his own personal equation, and save the reader the trouble by eliminating it himself" (1891:101). Objectivity was introduced into the requirements of scientific folklore collecting and presenting.[5] Other already well-established fields could even become means to delineate the boundaries of folklore.

As an example, in a classification of folklore materials for the budding
collector, Fanny Bergen included animal and plant lore, and as a guide-
post for what should be considered "popular names of animals and of
plants" she stressed "especially those not mentioned in works on Zoology
and Botany" (Bergen 1891). The editor thus saw the journal as a repository for genuine folk materials, and ever-new efforts were made to circumscribe how such originality could be improved on.

The *JAF*'s second volume began with an effort to broaden the understanding of folklore from the realm of men of science to the general public.
The tropes of treasure were once again pressed into service: "It may be ore
scarcely impressed by the die; but among the treasures, silver and gold
are not wanting" (Newell 1889:1). Yet if this language was to enhance
Newell's appeal to the American public to give money to support the society's mining efforts, an exclusionary phrase such as "the only truly scientific habit of mind is that wide and generous spirit of modern research"
was surely off-putting, as it implicitly claimed folkloristic competence only
for the scholar.

Newell was not really addressing the American general public across
all classes and regions, but rather the small, elite public who already sub-
scribed to the journal. Writing of "our newer communities' [in the Western states]" resistance to take any interest in the native peoples, he turned
his fellow Americans into an Other as well, differentiated by experience,
class, and intellect. "It is only yesterday that [the settlers of the Western
frontier] regarded [the native races] as wild beasts, whose extirpation was
necessary for their safety. They are justly proud of their progress. . . . They
do not understand that the time will come, and that soon, when their descendants will regard the Indian with interest and respect" (1889:2).

Presumptions of Genuine Scholarship: Rebuffing the "Amateur"

"The study of folklore in America has taken an encouraging upswing during the past sixteen years," the German immigrant folklorist Karl Knortz
wrote in 1905. "Organizations known as 'folklore societies' have been
formed in most cities, and have become exceptionally vigorous. They have
unusually vast and rich material at their disposal and have the opportunity
to expand their studies to representatives of all nationalities on earth"
(Knortz 1988 [1905]:14). Yet little historical research thus far documents
(or celebrates) the vigorous collecting activities of these local folklore societies.[6] With the exception of Bronner's sociopolitical focus (1986), the
history of folkloristics has been written primarily in terms of the field's
ability to establish a place for itself in academia. Within such legitimating

efforts, groups of local enthusiasts represented at best a source of welcome support, at worst bothersome groups of nonscholars who detracted from the image of the proper, even genuine, scholar.[7] Concern with scholarly propriety contributed to the postures taken by those individuals trying to legitimate folkloristic inquiry academically, whether as literary folklorists from Harvard, or anthropological folklorists trained by Boas.

Although often linked with language and literature departments, German *Volkskunde* was able to establish itself institutionally as an independent academic entity at the same time that it negotiated contacts with amateur or hobby folklore societies and cooperated with new cultural institutions such as museums at the local and state levels. In the United States, by contrast, folklore became an academic domain claimed by both anthropological and literary scholars, reaching an uneasy and incomplete institutional disciplinary independence only after World War II (Zumwalt 1988); folkloristics is still divided today over the disciplinary nature of the subject, and it is distanced from the public practitioners engaged in folklore.

The three founders of the AFS, Boas, Child, and Newell, were "consciously engaged in a project of cultural intervention. They saw the founding of the AFS as a moral as well as an intellectual, scientific and scholarly enterprise" (Abrahams 1989b:612). Such exclusive commitment contributed to a failure to cooperate with one of the early local folklore societies. The Chicago Folklore Society was established in 1892 under the retired naval officer Fletcher Bassett, who had planned and organized an International Folklore Congress to be held in the department of literature of the 1893 World's Fair Auxiliary of the Columbian Exposition (McNeil 1980:452). Bassett clearly was deeply committed to the study of folklore, which he saw as a holistic enterprise deserving of disciplinary status. He situated it squarely between literature and science, seeing in it a means to gain insight into the past "not just as a remnant or a survival, but as a body of history and literature" (Zumwalt 1988:23–24).

To the AFS, however, the association of folklore with a literary congress posed a threat to its scientific credibility. Newell, writing in the *JAF,* cautioned not only against the "extravagant and pretensions and loose theorizing" that prevailed in studies of popular traditions outside anthropology, but he argued that folklore was a label for a subject matter, not for a separate discipline. It best remained studied within anthropology, under the "strict scientific directions" and the "modest method of all truly scientific research" (cited in Zumwalt 1988:26). The AFS did not cooperate with Bassett but instead participated in the anthropology division of the exposition. While Newell's folklorists' hope for a scholarly exchange of ideas did not materialize, Bassett's International Folklore Congress, by contrast, was highly successful. Its twelve sessions of scholarly papers were supplemented by a visit to Bill Cody's "Wild West" show; an accompanying folksong concert proved so popular that two halls had to be opened to accommodate the audience (Zumwalt 1988:28).

But it was just such combinations of scholarly meeting with popular entertainment that confirmed Newell and Boas in their disapproval. The events in Chicago validated the *JAF* policy to "minimize the effect of the amateur folklorists" and increase the rigor of scholarly standards. The editorship of the *JAF* remained firmly in the hands of anthropologist gatekeepers, keeping what they thought to be the amateurish and unscholarly out of its pages (Zumwalt 1988:29–31). Newell put a sheen of moral obligation on the division between scholar and amateur, pleading for "measures [to] be taken for systematizing and completing collection" by sending trained individuals to carry out fieldwork among the tribes. The task of providing "means for the publication of these researches" was to be left to the generosity of local (i.e., amateur) societies and private individuals (Newell 1888a:6).

The exclusionary publication policies of the national society hardly strengthened its membership. When Newell resigned his editorship, he noted that the journal barely paid for itself. Secretary-treasurer Alfred Tozzer informed Boas in 1908 that the affairs of the society and journal were far from rosy; membership largely comprised academic anthropologists, and financial needs were great. Boas shortly thereafter assumed the editorship, but after a decade he too tired of it. Tozzer pleaded with him not to resign: "You *must not do this*. The Society would die" (Zumwalt 1988:33–35).

The Chicago Folklore Society died along with its founder, Bassett, in 1893. However, the AFS recognized the need for local folklore societies both to increase the spread of its intellectual and societal goals and, more pragmatically, to enlarge its coffers. Publication, research, and the collection of primary materials required extensive funds. At the first annual council meeting in 1888, a policy was adopted to encourage AFS members to found local branches, and the *JAF* repeatedly reported on this effort. Members like Alfred Kroeber were entrusted with founding such groups, and between 1889 and 1940 a minimum of thirty-eight local societies were begun. Not all of them maintained ties with the national society, however, and most of them folded within a few years for lack of new members (Dwyer-Shick 1979:70–81).

Local societies did not bring greater vigor and respectability to the national organization, as association membership was voluntary, guided by both interest and needs for sociability. Local societies were formed in accordance with the needs of local members, not with the scientific program of the national society—a society whose program could hardly resonate with those collecting and celebrating local folklore for their own ends. Less Romantic nationalist than regionalist in sentiment, local societies created an awareness of folklore as a treasure trove of local history and character. The residents of newly formed American states had to find vestiges of authenticity in their recently settled places and in the ethnicities of other settlers. Thus, the quest to salvage the pure culture of vanishing Native Americans was hardly at the forefront of their enterprise.

For many such constituencies the *JAF* did not represent their interests, and other than branch societies with prominent AFS members, as in Boston and Cambridge, affiliation with the national society was not considered profitable. The AFS's attempt to grow into a strong national organization through forming branch societies failed, not least because the hierarchical model did not suit the broadly based network that a successful organization would have needed (Dwyer-Shick 1979:178).

Ultimately, the ascetic as well as elitist posture of academe, combined with an insistent association with anthropology, prevented the AFS from becoming as strong an association as many other national societies formed at the same time. Willing to forgo riches in the interest of genuine scholarship (or perhaps relying too exclusively on the goodwill of wealthy benefactors), and serving the restoration or, at the least, the salvaging of authentic folklore materials before their demise, the AFS failed to attract and maintain the large constituency of Americans who were interested in contributing to the understanding of folklore's place in the formation and maintenance of American culture. When Ralph Steele Boggs in 1940 lamented that "unfortunately, this development of scientific folklore in its own right is still in its infancy, and is restricted largely to the research activities of a limited group of mature scholars," he assessed a situation that the folklore society had brought upon itself (Boggs 1940:93).

SCHOLARLY AUTHORITY AND SCIENTIFIC AUTHENTICITIES:
THE ANTHROPOLOGICAL PROJECT

Mathematics can proclaim a finding right or wrong; that powerful dichotomy legitimates its claims to scholarly knowledge and authority. Discerning what is and what is not authentic material is an analogous claim, and this effort to determine the authentic played an important part in delineating the "study of man"—the broad domain of the study of society, language, arts, physiology, and archaeology from which the anthropological endeavor drew. With this move, the insecurity over what made up the content of a discipline could be overcome, and, imperceptibly, professional authority and identity could grow. Ironically, Boas, who favored the rigorous study of man, including folklore, built his career on an alliance of scientific fervor and aesthetic (as well as real) appropriation for institutions of mass education—museums.

Collecting: From Artifacts to Cultures

Daniel Garrison Brinton, considered with Powell and Putnam among American anthropology's founding figures, was known as "the fearless critic of Philadelphia," not least because of his exacting standards regarding authenticity. For reasons of health he conducted little fieldwork himself, but he was a great advocate of using "primary documents" and later of field training because "original research" was held as a crucial element in the emergent anthropological enterprise. His plan of instruction at the University of Pennsylvania included tests for "archaeological frauds," and he made a habit of not accepting "otherwise unquestioned ethnological truths" (Darnell 1988:21). Brinton's encounter with the Taensa language is particularly revealing, as his initial judgment and subsequent changing of his position point to a personal transformation (comparable to Carl Lachmann) from more romantic, perhaps gullible student to scientifically astute critic. "The Taensa language . . . was invented, apparently as a joke, by two French seminarians. In his 1883 discussion of aboriginal American literature, Brinton quoted an entire song, citing the 'striking and to me strangely so' songs of the Taensa to illustrate the potential heights of poetic expression attainable to primitive men" (Darnell 1988:25–26). Brinton even characterized some of these songs as "Ossianic in style," an especially poignant view given the imitative character of both works. Brinton was suitably incensed when he reexamined the material a few years later, haughtily pointing out "that scholars had failed to question the superficially authentic appearance" of the material, but he avoided drawing attention to the fact that he, too, had been taken in (Darnell 1988:26). In other cases, Brinton sought to establish authority through delineating criteria for authentication—using cultural and linguistic evidence, noting how colonial encounters might have influenced an oral corpus rendered into writing, and listing factors that added or detracted from a collector's ethnographic integrity.

In Brinton one can see a set of authenticity standards solidifying; competence in determining authenticity simultaneously became a part of the scholar's tool kit. What is also noteworthy is the close similarity in the scholarly posture of this anthropologist and an approach that one would expect from an art critic or collector. Rendering lived cultures into objects of study relied on techniques similar to those used in appropriating artifacts of the past for the canons of art.

The delineating of authenticity is the overt link between art and scholarship. In historical terms the close association between an emergent anthropology and the growth of natural history museums, with their collecting expeditions, explains a good deal of this similarity. Socially collecting art or curiosities was one of the leisure pursuits of the higher social classes, and Brinton himself belonged to numismatic, historical, and antiquarian societies. All such societies collected, appraised, and classified artifacts and were typical for an era when the upper classes sought identity in the accumulation and home display of artifacts (Lee 1991, Orvell 1989:40).

The history of collections is "central to an understanding of how those social groups that invented anthropology and modern art have appropriated exotic things, facts, and meanings" (Clifford 1988:220–21). Appropriation in both art and culture entailed assigning a value, generated through authentication systems that were dictated in part by a commitment to connoisseurship, in part by scientific ideologies, both suffused by elements of moral and aesthetic appreciation (Price 1989). Despite the growing divergence over time between art appreciation and scientific culture study, the differentiations in authenticity criteria have continued to reciprocally influence both.

Boas experienced the link between collecting art and collecting culture more consciously than Brinton, and his lasting influence on American anthropology was much greater (Stocking 1974:1). At twenty-five, Boas had an opportunity to carry out research among the Eskimo in Baffin Land, an experience that shaped his strong belief in the necessity of fieldwork. It also provided him with an insight, captured in a key phrase in the diary he kept during that expedition for the benefit of his fiancée: "The value of a person lies in his *Herzenbildung*"—it is the education of the heart or inner character, the mental or psychological outlook that defines a person" (Cole 1983). This insight would serve as blueprint for his later revoicing of Herderian, antievolutionary arguments for the "genius of a people." [8]

To make a living, however, the anthropologist-to-be remained associated with museums and hence with the collecting and exhibiting of cultural artifacts. On returning from Baffin Land, Boas received an assistantship at the new ethnological museum in Berlin where Adolf Bastian tried to build a first-class collection of cultural artifacts. Bastian also entertained visiting groups of natives, brought to the Continent by enterprising exhibitors, and in this museum setting Boas encountered a group of Bella Coola from the Canadian Northwest Coast (Cole 1985: 55–73, 102–40). His work with them, through an interpreter, added to his determination to build a career in the United States and to find ways to continue his research on Arctic and Subarctic peoples.

Launching this career proved less easy than Boas had hoped, and to initiate it he had to borrow money from a relative for an expedition to the Pacific Northwest. There, he forged a more sophisticated combination of the art/culture liaison than previous collectors or "artifact harvesters" had been able to muster, bringing to his collecting "the sensitivity of a seasoned fieldworker and the discriminating taste of an experienced ethnographer and museum man" (Cole 1985: 106). When Boas returned to New York, he hoped to make a good enough impression on ethnological circles to procure himself a position, as well as sell his collection with sufficient profit to cover the debts incurred during the expedition. He did not succeed in either objective, and it would take from the mid-1880s until 1896 before he was offered a more permanent position at the American Museum of Natural History in New York.

In a decade's worth of contract work as a collector, as curator at the World's Columbian Exposition in Chicago in 1893, as an independent researcher, and as a columnist, Boas developed a critical stance toward the principles governing the study and exhibition of so-called primitive cultures. More than likely, his critique grew out of his Baffin Island experiences. It was a culture that to him, despite physical hardships, had more happiness to it, as he noted on December 23, 1883, having shared in his hosts' meal of raw seal liver: "I often ask myself what advantages our 'good society' possesses over that of the 'savages' and find, the more I see of their customs, that we have no right to look down upon them. . . . We 'highly educated people' are much worse, relatively speaking. The fear of tradition and old customs is deeply implanted in mankind, and in the same way as it regulates life here, it halts all progress for us" (cited in Cole 1983: 33). Boas experienced the Baffin Islanders as a "whole," with his letter-diary continually explaining details of dress, housing, and travel, shedding light on how individual elements made up a cultural logic as sound as that of his own society. On the backdrop of this experience, he objected to the practice of ethnological collections in American museums to fragment cultural traits and exhibit them along evolutionary principles, like artifacts from many different cultures shown together and arranged along a presumed line of chronological development, from the "savage" drums to those used by present-day orchestras. Boas was incensed at this collection since he felt that "it told nothing about the character of the music of each, the very thing that was, after all, 'the only object worth studying'" (Cole 1985:115). Boas's own vision for museum display was to represent the individual character of a given culture, preferably creating a statuary of "live groups" engaged in typical activities. This would show the artifacts collected within a representation of the authentic cultural context—an idea that was also inspired by his apprenticeship under Bastian.

Statues made to look like real human beings, and groups of statues representing the enactment of daily life frozen as in a still photograph—the desire to communicate cultural authenticity could not be more plain. Such displays remain an increasingly sophisticated practice in museum and zoo exhibits even today. The intent is to startle a visitor for a brief time and to transmit the impression of actually being in another time and another place.[9]

Boas's belief in the validity of such representation must be one reason he agreed to oversee the anthropology section of the World's Columbian Exposition in Chicago in 1893. There, "native living groups in their own habitations" were to be displayed, "demonstrating their crafts, customs and ceremonies" (Cole 1985:126). Yet allowing a largely white public to glimpse the exotic Other was, at this point, far from the ingenious, semi-participatory techniques employed by Frank H. Cushing some ten years earlier. Viewing natives was one aspect of genre thoroughly commodified by zoo and circus entrepreneurs like Carl Hagenbeck; Boas's worries in coordinating the Kwakiutl troupe for this six-month display led him to swear "never again to play circus impressario" (p. 133).

Vanishing Tribes, Recovering Languages, Training Scholars

In his work as a museum anthropologist, Boas thus furthered a holism in display that expressed his growing belief in the need to study and understand cultures as complete entities rather than as fragments of evolutionary steps. When he broke with the American Museum in 1905 and began teaching full-time at Columbia University, he put all of his intellectual and teaching efforts into the project of documenting cultural wholes before they were lost forever.

Boas urged his early students to study Native American languages. He did so in the belief that knowledge could be recovered through language, but also because he made an assumption about what kind of researcher was needed to do the recovering correctly. This approach required an abstract assumption about linguistic authenticity and practical concerns for authoritative, authenticating fieldwork to converge. Boas's intellectual as well as ideological linkage to Herder is pronounced here, for, like Herder, he felt that the genius or voice of a people spoke most eloquently through their verbal art. Unlike Herder, however, Boas had no political commitment to support the aspirations of social groups for national autonomy, though he did support various legislative acts that favored indigenous cultural integrity. In his view, American Indians were not on a path to political independence but would be integrated into Western civilization. Boas was outspoken in his fight against racism, having physically fought anti-Semites during his German student days (Liss 1996:168–69). But sociopolitically he strove for racial and ethnic tolerance within one governmental state rather than political separation. His commitment was to science; he did not speculate philosophically on the origin of language.

However, Boas's interest in language combined appreciation of aesthetic Otherness with the search for a tool to disprove evolutionary culture theories. The radically different nature of Native American languages contained virtual proof of cultural polygenesis.[10] Yet to gather this proof, speed came foremost because Native American tribes not only were dying out but were quickly being diluted and culturally altered through contact with white civilization.

It is in Boas's pronouncements in his correspondence on where and from whom the most genuine data could still be procured that the vocabulary of authenticity—mostly metaphors of loss—appears most strongly.[11] Although a larger, scientific thesis, now commonly referred to as cultural relativity, informed the effort, the tropes common to salvage operations in search of the real thing were once again part of assumptions of authenticity.

In 1903 Boas wrote to Daniel Gilman of his efforts to convince the Carnegie Institute of Technology's trustees that "one of the most important undertakings in anthropology [was] the investigation of vanishing tribes whose customs and languages will disappear within a very short time."[12] W. J. McGee wrote on September 18 of the same year that he had been intent "to continue the work in accordance with your plan—i.e. collecting as rapidly as practicable the vanishing vocabularies of the remaining tribes."[13] John Swanton reported that there were only "three or four old men who still speak the Mohegan language and that when they are gone the language will be extinct."[14] The urgency of the salvage enterprise undoubtedly inspired Boas's teaching. Probably he made little direct use of the term authenticity, and he showed none of the enthusiastic romantic mood and little reflexive awareness of the self-gratifying experiences of the fieldworker immersed among the Other. Rather, his was a rush, not for gold, but for science. Margaret Mead recalls how Boas and his research assistant Ruth Benedict convinced her to commit to a graduate career in anthropology rather than psychology because "anthropology had to be done *now*. Other things could wait" (Mead cited in Handler 1990a:259).

By the 1940s Boas's worst fears had materialized. C. G. Abbot wrote: "All metaphors, symbolism and imagery has [*sic*] vanished from their [the Mohegans'] present conversation. The stories of the past are either forgotten or mutilated when not mixed with what they hear from Whites."[15] Another correspondent laments: "These people are the supposed 'Croatans' who call themselves Indians but are very much mixed up. . . . They want to be Indians so much; but can't produce a single bit of folklore or tradition, or a word of Indian speech."[16] For decades this image remained a constant for Boas and his assistants. Rhoda Metraux, reflecting on Ruth Benedict's work, concluded that "her field work, carried out among peoples with a broken culture, was based mainly on work with informants—on long, gruelling hours of recording text and comment as they welled up in the memories of old men and old women speaking about another time, about a lost world" (Metraux 1959:v). Margaret Mead described anthropology as "the science which has been devoted to catching the essence of a culture just as it was changing forever into something new and strange" (Mead 1952:11).

The training of as many competent scholars as possible was the best means to salvage authentic language samples before they vanished from spoken circulation. "You know, of course," Boas wrote, "how much energy we have spent in trying to train men to study American languages, and to record as many of them as possible before they become extinct!"[17] Yet even the training of fieldworkers and native informants could affect the authenticity of the data collected. "The intelligent interpreter . . . imbibes too readily the views of the investigator, and . . . his information, for this reason, is strongly biased, because he [the interpreter] is not so well able to withstand the influence of formative theories as the trained investigator ought to be" (Boas 1966 [1911]:55). Boas undoubtedly spoke from experience. In his introduction to *Tsimshian Mythology*, collected and recorded by the native informant Henry Tate, Boas speculated that on the basis of similar materials he had collected himself it was likely that Tate had omitted "those traits of the myths of his people that seem inappropriate to us." It was to be assumed that "the tales do not quite express the old type of Tsimshian tradition" (Boas 1916:31).

Whether Boas recognized the native informants' ability to furnish data without filtering them through his interpreter's lens in the case of his major interpreter and native assistant, George Hunt, remains unclear. Many collectors, anthropologists, and archaeologists from Europe and the United States worked through Hunt, and Jeanne Cannizzo's assertion that Hunt basically invented or created a version of Kwakiutl culture for Western scientific absorption seems at least plausible (1983). Given his programmatic statements, one would think that Boas was highly sensitized to the nuance needed to capture native materials. He repeatedly argued that originality was of the utmost importance in transcending the lexicon and getting to the essence or genius of a culture:

> The native language . . . is quite indispensable when we try to investigate the deeper problems of ethnology. . . . No translation can possibly be considered as an adequate substitute for the original [poetry]. The form of rhythm, the treatment of the language, the adjustment of text to music, the imagery, the use of metaphors, and all the numerous problems involved in any thorough investigation of the style of poetry, can be interpreted only by the investigator who has equal command of the ethnographical traits of the tribe and of their language. . . . the oratory of the Indians, . . . is not adequately known, because only a very few speeches have been handed down in the original. Here, also, an accurate investigation of the method of composition and of the devices used to reach oratorical effect, requires the preservation of speeches as rendered in the original language. (Boas 1966 [1911]:58)

In this manner Boas aspired to use ethnological publications to broadcast the voice of Native American peoples as immediately as possible, and his specific concerns foreshadow a program that ethnolinguists some fifty years later still considered urgent and crucial. Boas's assumption was that in narrative a people reveals most about its mental states and worldview; narrative, therefore, was the best key for recognizing the true genius of a people (e.g., Boas 1973 [1932]:viii). However, George Hunt recalled that Boas asked him to *tell* rather than *sing* various examples of verbal art, presumably because taking down the spoken word was easier (Cannizzo 1983:54).

The transformation of cultural authenticity notions that emerged in doing Boas-style research was profound. Edward Sapir's attempts to recover eleven treaty belts for the Six Nations Iroquois Reserve in Ontario are telling, as was Sapir and Boas's joint effort to avert a Canadian law prohibiting the Northwest Coast potlatch ceremonies (Darnell 1990:56–60). The belts belonged to the living context of the Iroquois League, and the potlatch ceremony was part of the Indian system of paying debts; there-fore, any law against it threatened cultural autonomy. Whereas Boas had started his career buying artifacts and even collecting bones and skulls retrieved by methods that later sensibilities considered to be robbing graves, the new ethic was to preserve cultural integrity, including effects on it caused by the political involvement of academics.

The circular progression in this drama of sought-and-bought authen-ticities is staggering. It begins with the seeking, finding, and purchasing of artifacts, thus alerting native populations to the "value" of their cultural productions in a transcultural marketplace. Then the scope expands to the study of mentifacts such as language in the interest of demonstrating the diverse cultural essences on the planet and refuting academic theses of cultural evolution. In the process, scholars gain the insight that true au-thenticity resides in cultural wholes. But at that point, acculturation and massive extinction of the natives has reduced the possibilities for "whole-ness"—which is at best attainable in representations, such as the treaty belts, that the natives, in turn, recognize as artifacts that can symbolize their status as a distinct group and endow them with the right to political autonomy.

Claiming Intellectual Terrain: Scientific Authenticity

Franz Boas's voluminous professional correspondence testifies to the in-tensive networking needed for struggling fields of inquiry to find accep-tance. Procuring resources for student research and funds for publica-tion seem to outnumber all other exchanges. Yet throughout the appeals and the increasing sureness of professional identity, assumptions of cul-tural authenticity can be found, along with the certainty that the scholar/scientist was uniquely qualified to recognize and record it.

Young scholars with particular gifts, such as Edward Sapir's ability with languages, helped Boas and others to make a case for why the study of disappearing languages was of utmost importance. Alfred Kroeber, af-ter encountering the "totally wild" Ishi, could bring in Sapir to carry out "salvage linguistics" with this last member of the Yahi tribe in California. The difficulty of the task was compounded by Ishi's worsening tuberculo-sis: in the name of science, as complete an understanding as possible of the Yahi language and mythology was demanded, but as Kroeber later rued, the pressure of scientific needs may have sped Ishi's death (Darnell 1990: 79–82).

Kroeber's early research was dominated by work with folkloristic data. He proceeded with a certain amount of unreflected efficiency, and he later referred to his work as an attempt to depict "cultural wholes." Despite "the dissimilarities in working contexts [from one Indian group to the next], the bulk of Kroeber's early work was salvage ethnography frequently dependent on the single technique of interviewing usually aged informants" (Thoresen 1973:43). Boasian cultural relativism, with its reliance on oral narrative as the repository of a people's genius, invigorated young scholars like Kroeber to do their share of a vast task.

Elsie Clews Parsons became a Boas ally, friend, and financial and moral supporter after her efforts to bring about social change were rebuffed within her own circles. Aside from liberally supporting the fieldwork of others, she was a prolific collector of oral traditions. Adventuresome by nature, Parsons conducted fieldwork in more locales than did any of her contemporaries. Her own glosses on research as being "informing and full of the romantic," or leading her to "islands and other places more or less romantic," point to experiential needs in the familiar tradition of travelers *cum* fieldworkers (Zumwalt 1992:239, 206). But her standards of collecting and transcribing were exacting and demanded a new kind of methodological accuracy. She wanted to gather as much material as possible and get it published comprehensively and accurately (including variants), always adhering to native ways of speaking. She expected these standards to be met by others, and she wrote to one collector, "Your rendering is almost too good. I am not charging you with the felony of 'dressing up,' only with the misdemeanor of rendering the narratives' inadequate English too indulgently" (cited in Zumwalt 1992:196). She was intent on recording the spoken word as it was heard instead of transforming it into standard English, and she even lamented that some informants had been corrupted by literacy to the point of their criticizing the grammar of their own dialect. As early as 1916, she experimented with phonographic recording. While she thus strove for standards of purity in rendering the code, she also fought to break the prudishness of collectors who included only morally "clean" materials (Zumwalt 1992:200–201).

While Parsons's insistence was scientifically driven in some of her publications on the Southwest, her comprehensiveness proved troublesome, for she wanted ethnography to be as complete and accurate as the researcher could manage. Yet her subjects read her writings, despite her efforts to keep works on Taos Pueblo and Jemez within scholarly circles, and they felt betrayed by having their religious secrets made public. Some of her informants suffered serious repercussions because of her works, but Parsons remained "adamant that the true record would yield good results" (Zumwalt 1992:247–57). The need for full and authentic ethnography in the interest of science ultimately outweighed her sincere regrets at the harm it caused among those she studied.

The impact of civilization on pueblo life fueled Parsons's commitment to contribute to the ethnographic record before it was too late. The intermingling of civilizations had left the sacred calendar intact in most places, "unaffected by American automobilists or other American progressives," with the exception of Oraibi pueblo where exposure to white ways already had led to a bitter split in 1904. The conservatives who withdrew "carried altar paraphernalia [with them], without which certain ceremonies were not authentic, thus impairing the calendaric integrity of Oraibi." Fortunately, to her, the pueblo had been studied earlier, so there was a record of the older, authentic calendaric practices (Parsons 1925:5).

Martha Beckwith, a Boas student and later the holder of the first folklore chair created in the United States—at Vassar—provides another example of how intertwined scholarly authority and cultural authenticity had become by the 1920s. The president of Vassar recalled Beckwith's behavior at a performance of Hawaiian hula, advertised as genuine, that both of them attended. Beckwith, the president related, said, "This is unscholarly, I must protest," and thereupon got up and addressed the audience: "'In the interest of truth,' she said, 'I must denounce this performance. It has nothing about it that in any way represents the true hula, except the skirt, and even that is artificial. You are being taken in'" (cited after Bronner 1992:12). Scientific standards and professional prestige granted a sense of authority, if not superiority, to scholars, provoking some to publicly comment on commodified cultural productions.

By the 1930s the professional identity of cultural researchers had solidified to such an extent that mechanisms of authenticating were second nature, as Margaret Mead's letter of February 9, 1932, from Alistoa, Wiwiak, New Guinea, to her former teacher and mentor Boas shows:

Dear Papa Franz,
We have not written to you about this place because we have been so essentially undecided about it. It's a delightful place to live, nicest field I've ever been in—good food, cool, no anopheles, and a friendly, unobstreperous people. But they have so little culture. They are principally sensationalists. The children suck their thumbs, and the adults fuss about their food. Possibly we haven't explored the field of sensations sufficiently in our own culture to know how to make it a rich field of comparison, but anyway this culture doesn't seem promising. . . . It's the kind of culture beginners shouldn't do because if they reported how sloppy it was, no one would believe them.[18]

Few twentieth-century anthropologists would dare utter such categorical pronouncements on a tribe. Yet Mead's trust in her scientific authority to recognize a "good" or "rich" culture and to distinguish it from one less worthy of an ethnographer's attention did not grow in a vacuum. She spoke from the security of a professional identity (although she was not securely employed at the time), an identity that had been built and taught in large part by Franz Boas.

For many scholars outside the Columbia University anthropology circle Boas had acquired the aura of an authority on cultural authenticity. He received letters such as one from Willard Johnson of Des Moines, on February 25, 1932, in which Johnson related that he had studied the Mesquakie Indian religion in Iowa but found himself disturbed: "I wish, if possible, to present some of the detailed mythology and beliefs. You know, of course, that with the present attitude of the Indians that this is almost impossible. They have commercialized any investigation among them, so that they will not now tell much real fact."[19] Johnson mostly wished to request permission to cite materials printed in *JAF*, yet even here he inquired whether an earlier collector's materials were "authoritative" and asked, "Where was he trained?" Thus, the authenticity of cultural material was now ascertained through multiple checks: the innocence of Indian informants concerning the value and desirability of their cultural productions, as well as the integrity and authoritativeness of the researcher who collected the material, which in turn was legitimated by the scholarly rigors of a given training program.

COLLECTION, PERFORMANCE, CRITIQUE:
TOWARD GENUINE CULTURE

The affairs and publications of the AFS may have been dominated throughout the first part of the twentieth century by the concerns of anthropology. But folkloristic interests of the literary-historical type, as well as local and national collection and intervention efforts informed by a blend of Romantic, medievalist, revivalist, and nationalist enthusiasm found realization in university settings, within state societies, and in private and public efforts.

Collecting Song: Imagining the American Experience

In the history of American folklore, both for scholars and people in general, song has held a special place. The ballad in particular has preoccupied collectors and theorists over centuries, with Francis Child's collection taking on the status of a monument of authentication for both past and future ballad finds. Drawing on Susan Stewart (1991a), Roger Abrahams attributes the attraction of this particular song genre to its "antiqued effect," which survives precariously in "the face of the forces of modernity," thanks to the simple folk who continue to sing them. The antiqued effect can be attributed to the storytelling technique of ballads, for they often are fragmentary and their narratives are rendered in "a kind of incompleteness, inviting the hearer to the mystery of their actions" (Abrahams n.d.: 79). The appeal of ballads to authenticity cravings is, however, also auditory. Abrahams points to a "sense of roundedness and of squaring off," created by the arrangement of beats and pulses (p. 80).

That ballads are sung and not told is relevant since musical performance exerts a different kind of affective power than does the spoken word. While earlier scholars dwelt primarily on ballad texts, differentiating the "genuine ballad" from "corrupted" products of later eras, it is arguably the musical element that for more than a century has made American ballads (and folksong in general) the most avidly collected and most readily revived form of folklore. Storytelling contents shift dramatically with changing socioeconomic circumstances. Orally told tales suffer in their appeal with the advent of literacy and other mediated forms of transmission, and tellers prefer shorter, often more conversational forms.[20] Material forms of folklore—crafts and folk arts—maintain their attractiveness but usually not their economic viability. Folksong, however, is a cultural resource that different constituencies have time and again considered worthy of revival, in a mixture of social commitment, nostalgia for a better past, hope for a cleansed future, and a desire to experience personal authenticity in performance.

In the later nineteenth century, some European classical composers had taken on the task of creating works expressing the spirit of their peoples. The use of folk melodies was a frequent strategy, one that has continued into the twentieth century. Some Americans had a similar desire that converged with salvage ethnography among Native Americans as well as the exploration of the black musical heritage (McNeil 1980:467). In 1892 the Czech nationalist composer Antonín Dvořák was invited to head the National Conservatory of Music in New York with the express purpose of inspiring Americans to create national music. Dvořák saw great promise in such endeavors, and he proclaimed that "in the Negro melodies of America I discover all that is needed for a great and noble school of music" (McNeil 1980:501–2). Some attempts to use Native American musics in classical compositions were made at the turn of the century, but black musical styles would be more readily incorporated into the growing spectrum of American musics.

Collecting and theorizing about folksong was a powerful interest in the early twentieth century. The anxiety over loss influenced the collection of song, and the hope to find an antidote to modern alienation was richly rewarded with the folksong found among blacks and whites in many regions and occupations.

Some scholars collected songs as data for the ongoing discussion on ballad origins—an enterprise that took up the better part of D. K. Wilgus's weighty tome on Anglo-American folksong scholarship (1959). Wilgus appropriately calls one of the warring parties in the ballad controversy's twentieth-century installment "The Emersonians" because they bolstered their arguments with materials found in the "natural" flow of life of the common folk. The proponents of the communal origin theory ultimately had to concede that those who argued for individual origin and subsequent communal re-creation probably had more evidence for their views. Child's generation considered the "genuine ballad" a creation of the past and its history complete. Younger scholars collected songs, including ballads, in the United States and eventually refused to classify them as spurious, even if they did not conform to arbitrary ballad criteria. The idea of a "singing dancing throng" collectively composing had arisen in part as a result of upper-class prejudice; it had seemed unfathomable that members of the folk should have the individual creative ability to compose. But as American collectors encountered singers proud of their repertoire, the notion of folk performers serving simply as imperfect vessels for authentic tradition crumbled.[21]

Phillips Barry, one of the strongest antagonists to the communal theory, wrote in 1912: "in the last analysis, it seems that much of our 'ballad problem' has been of our own making" (Barry 1939:58). Based on his fieldwork in Maine, he concluded:

> The folk-singer is the most passionate of individualists, as every field collector knows. The song he sings is not his own by right of authorship, but his version of the song is to him the only correct one. Every other version is wrong. . . . At the same time the folk-singer is equally sure that he sings a song learned from tradition exactly as his predecessors sang it. . . . There is in the folk-singer the latent creative artist, who will recreate what he has learned; there are the tricks which memory will play. (1939:86)

Barry thus argued for individual creation, while he simultaneously acknowledged the performers' desire to be part of an unbroken chain of transmission. That desire we may now attribute in part to the influence of two centuries of intellectual objectification of tradition, from Romanticism to the sense of individuality in the greater American community. Barry sought to clarify the point[22] by differentiating between art song and folksong:

> A folk song has *texts*, but no *text*, *tunes* but no *tune*. The interpreter of a [Stephen] Foster song has no right to deviate in the slightest degree from the author-composer's autograph. The interpreter of a folk song, however, . . . is something more than an interpreter: he is, together with every other folk singer who sings the song in question—past, present or future,—co-author with the author of the text, and co-composer of the air. (1961)

For Barry, Foster's tunes had an "authentic text and air," meaning that they could be attributed to a single author. Nonetheless, the individual performance of folksongs would make them equally authentic, even if a given folksinger lacked name recognition in the class hierarchy of acknowledged cultural production.

In ballad theory, printed broadside sheets and other literate versions of song had been characterized as agents spoiling the authenticity of oral tradition. Not immune to the tropes of loss, Barry turned this preoccupation upside down, lamenting the loss of "much good textual material, not to speak of the precious traditional music," because scholars had dreaded the impact of print. He postulated that printed versions could be seen as reinforcing rather than contaminating tradition. To him, printed evidence was a better record than the "restored antiques" and "fake-overs" that those insisting on the purity of orality had created (1939:85).

Barry was not about to break through distinctions that his class and taste provided him, concentrating his efforts on Anglo immigrants in the Maine woods. He was skeptical about the possibility of finding an "actual native folk music in American tradition," and he assumed that "[American folk music's] best hopes lie in the increasing use of folk themes and folk motifs by the composers who shall found the school of American music" (1939:110).

Of the same background but of different theoretical persuasion was Robert Winslow Gordon, also a student of George Lyman Kittredge at Harvard. Ill at east among the mountain folk from whom he collected songs, he favored a communalist position that associated the treasures of folklore with a more distant ancestry pure in its lifestyle. He amassed a great collection of folksongs, which became the nucleus of the Archive of

American Folk Song, founded in 1928 and initially headed by Gordon himself. He proclaimed folksongs to be full of the virtues of a native son like himself: they had "staying power, moral worth, and [the] steady upright values of the pioneers" (Kodish 1986:233). Gordon spent a great deal of time on the road, collecting for a work that never came to fruition, but that he in his journalistic endeavors was able to convincingly present as "a way of welding the nation together" (Abrahams n.d.: 203). He preferred to associate, not with the people he collected from—common mountain folk or Georgia blacks, but with "those people he imagined to be more like himself; the culture brokers of a community, those who were already self-conscious about folk culture, . . . those who had suffered some degree of estrangement" (Abrahams n.d.: 203).

Gordon's biographer sees authenticity as a notion that haunted Gordon. In his fieldwork, his correspondence with readers of his column in *Adventure* magazine, and in his dissertation, Gordon was preoccupied with circumscribing authentic song and authentic collecting and publishing. He rejected popular art forms other than song as "inauthentically American," and when he reached an impasse in his thinking, he resorted to conventions that allowed him to "separate conceptually the authentic from the spurious, the native from the strange." To Gordon, the passion for delineating the difference between the authentic and the spurious drove him to ever greater estrangement and isolation both from a community of peers and from the times he was a part of: "Nothing was pure in his day and age" (Kodish 1986:234–36).[23]

Many collectors were unhampered by such qualms, and "folksong collection in the United States probably owes as much to the pure enthusiasts as to any other group" (Wilgus 1959:156). That Wilgus does not disparage this notion reflects that in the realm of folksong the amateur/scholar divide was far less grim than in other areas.[24] Songs could be proof of the genius of a region, of an occupational or ethnic group, and, by extension, of the American people at large. Few individuals were as influential in bridging the scholar/amateur divide as John Lomax, who forged the link between his own rural background—which he mythologized and adumbrated to emphasize his own folk status—and the Harvard elite.

Lomax's collection of cowboy songs found little interest among his Texan teachers. He had tentatively titled it, in analogy to Sir Walter Scott's *Minstrelsy of the Scottish Border,* "Cowboy Songs from the Texas-Mexican Border."[25] To his Harvard professors Barrett Wendell and Kittredge, Lomax's song collection represented the exciting possibility of "living" folksong in the United States. The young Lomax, who had been

given a fellowship, "represented an almost alien breed—a real frontiers-
man who came from the same stock that Teddy Roosevelt had drawn up
for his Rough Riders and who Buffalo Bill Cody had persuaded to display
themselves in his 'Wild West' shows. Now here was someone who could
justly call himself both a dirt farmer and a cowboy" (Abrahams n.d.: 200).

Lomax dedicated his life to finding, recording, and publishing the songs
of the American people, and during a good portion of this adventure his
son Alan accompanied and assisted him. The Lomaxes collected ballads
and work songs, and, most importantly, they brought to national attention black singers and their repertoires. John Lomax's background furnished him with an intuition for finding what his era was looking for;
in addition, his connections to academic and society circles made possible the grants and positions to finance his fieldwork and equipment. In
Lomax one can recognize the ability of the literary camp of early folkloristics to mobilize resources and facilitate projects that aided its intellectual
aspirations, even though the AFS under anthropological dominance gave
far less attention to these endeavors.

An unmistakable romance permeates Lomax's work and person, which
essentializes not only his findings, but his ability to connect with the folk.
Lomax's first collection, *Cowboy Songs and Other Frontier Ballads,* appears to have been a work generated in equal parts from his own child-
hood repertoire, from sheaves of printed "ballets" he had owned as a
young man, from finds in books and magazines, from correspondents,
and from fieldwork recordings (Wilgus 1959:157–64). Greater access to
recording equipment and exposure to documentation standards promoted
at Harvard led Lomax to embrace a style of publication that focused on
particular singers such as Leadbelly (Huddie Ledbetter).

Unlike Gordon, Lomax reveled in his ability to forge linkages, and he
repeatedly discovered the real think in the process. His recollections of his
ballad-hunting days teem with instances of "genuine" encounters. These
encounters are alluded to in his characterization of those whom he sought
out, people who stand in silent opposition to a (presumably inauthentic)
modern crowd. "A ballad collector meets many people, the real people,
the plain people, devoid of tinsel and glamour, some base, a few suspicious and surly, many beautifully kind" (Lomax 1947:ix). Lomax's an-
ecdotes are full of delightful, humorous detail.

> At Terrell, Texas, thirty miles from Dallas, Alan and I made our first
> recording. A Negro washerwoman, as she rested from her work, sang a
> baptizing song. . . . Though her voice was high-pitched, it had a liquid

softness that made the effect beautiful and haunting. Alan blinked his
eyes as he bent over the machine. Long afterward he told me that from
that moment he felt no further doubts about enjoying ballad collecting.
(Lomax 1947:11)

Grown men overcome by uncontrollable emotion: this is one manifestation of authentic experience. Alan Lomax opens his own account with
the words, "There is an impulsive and romantic streak in my nature that I
find difficult to control when I go song hunting" (1993:3). The tales spun
by the son replicate much of what his father had succumbed to:

> We found the blind singer's wife. . . . She wore a gypsy costume, richly
> brocaded. . . . While I chatted with her, the old man disappeared into the
> tent. In a few minutes he came out. . . . Before me stood a young, hand-
> some, dark-eyed man, alert and athletic. He made no explanation. He
> was a perfect and fascinating faker. . . . [The gypsy woman] scorned the
> clumsy horn fastened to my recording machine, and I caught few of the
> tunes. I remember that she sang me the first blues that I ever heard, mov-
> ing me almost to tears. . . . Many many many another song she sang that
> unhappily are gone with the Texas wind. . . . After the refrain she would
> give the night-herding yodel of the cowboy, born of the vast melancholy
> of the plains. . . . As the gypsy woman, swayed by the beauty of her notes,
> yodeled on, the leaves of the overhanging cottonwood trees fluttered
> noiselessly, the katydids in the branches stopped their song and seemed
> to listen. In all our world there was no other song save that beautiful
> voice imploring all little dogies to "lay still, little dogies, lay still." (Lo-
> max 1947:43–45)

The familiar vocabulary of authenticity, rich with images of nature, carries John Lomax away from his brief recognition of where his discovered
genuine treasure blossoms. The proximity of the fake and the authentic,
even their complementarity, are, however, telling. The gypsy woman's
"fascinating faker" companion frames and enhances Lomax's perception of auditory authenticity. The sighted blind man plays into the cultural stereotype of the deceptive gypsy, constituting another undercurrent
of what is real and what is not. Lomax was aware that he had entered
the backstage domain of professional inauthenticity, and he thus experienced, paradoxically, authenticity among those making a living by staging
authenticity.

There were others, such as Frank C. Brown, who collected folklore and
folksong with no less fervor than Lomax. Yet Brown's relationship to his
finds was entirely different. In Brown's vision it was the value of authenticity's semantic domain which ranked foremost in that he treated individ-

ual "items" as trophies to be owned. Unlike the extrovert ballad hunter Lomax who shared his finds with the world, Brown guarded his collections like a personal treasure, voicing its value and the hardship endured in collecting it only in personal correspondence. Under the guise of needing to render the work into "an entire monument," he effectively stalled publication for decades; only after his death did the collection see print (White 1952).

Philipps Barry's attraction to Maine lumbermen, Robert Gordon's longing to put together "a great and definitive gathering of all of American folksong, modeled after but surpassing the work of Francis James Child" (Kodish 1986:233), and John Lomax's prolific celebration of recording and documenting those individuals whose songs represented the socio-economically marginal, were all expressions of finding uniquely American culture. For all three of them, quests for authenticity were driving motors—the individual performer, the American native son, the representative genius of different groups.

Projects such as these permeated folklore scholarship as well as the popular media of magazines and early commercial recordings. Unlike in Germany, the focus was on the "stuff" itself, not on ways to institutionalize the study or collection of the "stuff." Beyond creating the Archive of American Folk Song, little effort was made to establish lasting institutional frameworks for study and collection. The theoretical debate over collective versus individual origins of folksong parallels the German debate over the origins of folklore in general. Perhaps as a consequence, the systematic introduction of folklore chairs or research institutes with folkloristic forms was far less successful in the United States than in Germany. In the United States, where reliance on private money was common, private benefactors were among the main sponsors of cultural interventionist programs that arose during the early twentieth century and were inspired by folksong.

Cultural Critique and Intervention

> Some of the women [missionaries] I have met are very nice and broad-minded, but I don't think any of them realize that the people they are here to improve are in many respects far more cultivated than their would-be instructors, even if they cannot read or write. . . . For my part, I would leave them as they are and not meddle. They are happy, contented, and live simply and healthily, and I am not sure that any of us can introduce them to anything better than this.
> —Cecil Sharp (1916; cited in Whisnant 1983:123)

When the political integrity of [a Native American] tribe is destroyed by
contact with the whites and the old cultural values cease to have the atmosphere needed for their continued vitality, the Indian finds himself in
a state of bewildered vacuity. Even if he succeeds . . . in what his well-
wishers consider great progress towards enlightenment, he is apt to re-
tain an uneasy sense of loss of some vague and great good. . . . What is
sad about the passing of the Indian is not the depletion of his numbers
by disease nor even the contempt that is too often meted out to him in
his life on the reservation, it is the fading away of genuine cultures, built
though they were of the materials of a low order of sophistication.
                              —Edward Sapir (1951 [1924]:318)

Against the protestations of later generations of folklorists who wished to
see the academic study of folklore sharply separated from any applied or
public ministrations, the early decades of the AFS demonstrate the intermeshing of academic with public and personal concerns. The desire to
"preserve it before it's gone" was also a form of cultural intervention,
whether in salvage ethnography or folksong collecting. Even collection, as
in the Pacific Northwest, carries repercussions. Alerting a native population to the loss of its authentic treasures invariably initiates the generating
of new authentic cultural productions for both internal and external
consumption.

Thinking and acting on the "state of culture" was very much on the
minds of the social elites who spearheaded simultaneous projects to create
academically rigorous disciplines, preserve a record of cultures in decline,
and collect evidence of an American culture on the rise. Boas's ethnological project also had sociopolitical agendas. His effort to combat racism
and the theory of cultural evolution that he recognized as a pseudoscien-
tific support for racist arguments. He published several versions of his
thinking with the intention of convincing a broad readership of the faulty
logic of racism (Boas 1940). Boas's student Ruth Benedict on the eve of
U.S. entry into World War II published her own version of this argument
to counter renewed waves of xenophobia and racism (Benedict 1940).

Edward Sapir, another Boas student, chose another route in trying to
verbalize where an improved American cultural spirit might be found. His
essay "Culture: Genuine and Spurious" was written in the intellectual
spirit of the time which sensed that a "renaissance of the entire Western
world was overdue" (Darnell 1990:168). Sapir wrote his essay for a
wide readership, and he was clearly influenced by his experiments with
poetry, a creative outlet shared with Ruth Benedict and about which they
corresponded.[26] Poetry allowed Sapir to realize a personal sincerity—a
sincerity echoing the eighteenth-century European cultural critics—that

transcended the professional frame of ethnography. Sapir characterizes the "cultured person" who places emphasis "upon manner, a certain preciousness of conduct which takes on different colors according to the nature of the personality that has assimilated the 'cultured' ideal"—an effort that in Sapir's view easily degenerated into "snobbishness" and "radical aloofness." In addition, "The ghosts of the past, preferably the remote past, haunt the cultured man at every step. He is uncannily responsive to their slightest touch; he shrinks from the employment of his individuality as a creative agency" (1911 [1924]:309–310). Considering this particular "cultured ideal" as "a vesture and an air"—at heart a spurious pretense—Sapir sought to formulate how a genuine culture might arise from individual capability to grasp and realize the spiritual essence of a particular heritage.

Sapir wanted to find a way out of the "bewildered vacuity" felt by the Indian who had lost the harmonious wholeness of tribal life, and he wanted to overcome the alienation of the "cultured person." By daring to explore "the depths of our consciousness and dragging to the light what sincere bits of reflected experience we can find," it would be possible to build a "genuine culture—better yet, series of linked autonomous cultures. . . . And New York and Chicago and San Francisco will live each in its own cultural strength, . . . each serenely oblivious to its rivals because growing in a soil of genuine cultural values" (1951 [1924]:333). An internationalized world did not also have to be a world of "spiritual hybrid[s]" (p. 315).

Sapir's essay remains enigmatic, not least because of what Richard Handler (1989) characterized as antiromantic Romanticism. Sapir himself favored the pose of restraint, yet his essay on genuine and spurious culture is suffused with the romantic hope for societal improvement through the search, discovery, and voicing of the innermost in culture.[27]

Others, however, felt that cultural critique required concrete action. They were generally more intrigued with the legacy of Anglo-Saxon culture, some to the point of voicing their xenophobic critique of the United States in the early twentieth century as undermined by the influx of "low ethnic stock" from Europe (Whisnant 1983:3). The cultural interventionist projects started in the first decade of the twentieth century in the southern mountains rested on the assumption that people could not be entrusted simply with searching out their own genuine culture and extracting viable values from it.

The missionizing women encountered in the Appalachians by the British folksong collector Cecil Sharp, accompanied by the young Maud Karpeles, were often East Coast socialites eager to find meaningful ways to realize their professional skills in a world that had liberalized sufficiently to grant them an education, but not rewarding work. Thus, the movement to found settlement and folk schools in hopes of stemming the cultural decay caused by industrial expansion on the East Coast had complex roots (Whisnant 1983).

Those women from upper-class backgrounds who attempted to live in the mountains and to build model environments tried to preserve or re-teach the best and most wholesome aspects of mountain culture, with the idea that less-desirable features would be cleansed away. Song and music as well as craft and dance were considered evidence of an archaic European heritage that had been preserved unspoiled. In their daily work among mountain folk these women had compiled collections of songs and tales, and to them the arrival of Sharp and Karpeles from 1916 until 1918 was a godsend. The British collectors gathered some 1,600 tunes in the Appalachians, and to the missionizing women they represented academic patrons to whom they could pass on their findings. While these women were confident in their social commitment, for the most part they seem to have presumed the world of proper scholarship outside their reach.[28]

Sharp was delighted to find a place teeming with what he assumed were living survivals of a British past.[29] Karpeles recalls, using dichotomous vocabulary, that "throughout our stay in the mountains we never heard a bad tune, except occasionally when we were staying at a missionary settlement"; she and Sharp evidently did not look favorably on the cultural interventionists who welcomed their arrival. Karpeles describes their own work in the language of salvage: "Alas, the ideal state of affairs that Cecil Sharp and I found in 1916–18 has not persisted. The country has been built, and the serpent in the guise of radio and records has penetrated this Garden of Eden" (Karpeles 1973:96–98).

Fighting off the serpent may have been one rationale for putting the purest of folk music on stage in cultural displays such as the White Top Folk Festival.[30] The festival's principal promoter, Annabel Morris Buchanan, nevertheless used the language of scientific rigor in her "requisites" that the folk festival do more good than harm and that it not degenerate into a "pseudo-folk-festival." The standards of quality, classification (in terms of what materials are suitable), and strategies of presentation pointed the way: "The charm of native performance lies in its simplicity and sincerity" (Buchanan 1937:32). "A folk festival should encourage only the highest type of native material," she wrote, setting a high moral tone herself. Buchanan's public efforts may seem to stand at a considerable distance from the cultural critique and hypothetical program of an

Edward Sapir, but the two are united both in their assumptions of the curative powers of authenticity, and in their belief that such authenticity, although differently defined, could invigorate or save cultures in decline.

It took folklore studies fifty years from the founding of the AFS to create independent academic programs; as Tristram Coffin has acidly observed, the most prestigious universities kept their heads turned. It took until the 1970s for the discipline to recognize the connection between the field of study and the politics of culture. The posture of academic innocence kept the field from accepting and examining the cultural repercussions of what the "harmless" aspects of studying culture—namely, collecting— could do.

> The work of a "mere" ballad collector has inescapably political di-
> mensions. It involves presuppositions and judgments about the relative
> worth of disparate cultural systems; the selection of certain cultural items
> in preference to others—frequently in accordance with an unspoken
> theory of culture; the education (not to say manipulation or indoctri-
> nation) of a public regarding the worth (or worthlessness) of unfamil-
> iar cultural forms or expressions; and the feeding back of approval-
> disapproval into the "subject" culture so as to affect the collective image
> and self-images (and therefore the survival potential) of its members.
> (Whisnant 1983:125–26)

When the study of folklore finally did make a case for itself in academia, it did so by differentiating itself vigorously from the interventionist
model. Individuals such as Richard Dorson sought refuge from the legacies of earlier folklore practitioners and from the ideological dimensions
inscribed in the very word folklore behind an unreflected mantle of scientific theory and method. The confusing mélange of scholarly and societal
aspirations, entangled in projects with turn-of-the-century expressive culture, is probably the best explanation for the sparse success of institution-
alizing the discipline during that period. The marginality of the field institutionally, however, sharply contrasts with the deep attraction of folklore
across society, an attraction not least to be explained by the connections
of folklore to diverging searches for authenticity. Ultimately, it may be the
poorly verbalized spectrum of authenticity cravings, from the treasured to
the spiritual, from the purifying to the existential, that have allowed for
the subject's maverick status.

PART 3
Questioning the Canon

Introspection, a closer examination of programmatic terminology, and the eventual deconstruction of disciplinary canons are not unique to folkloristics. The "archaeology of knowledge," as Michel Foucault termed it, was hardly a lonely endeavor on this French philosopher's part. Rather, an increasing "blurring" of disciplinary boundaries between the social sciences and humanities (Geertz 1983) brought forth a simultaneous turn toward establishing which, if any, "genuine" disciplinary cores might remain. The currently popular "discipline" of history and the sociology of science can be understood as efforts to intellectually center the decentering of disciplinary subjects and canons that occurred over recent decades.

For an institutionally weak field such as folkloristics, any deconstructive activity is threatening, yet simultaneously vital, since only the continued adjustment of the disciplinary subject will warrant its institutional continuation. Folkloristics ostensibly focused on the poetics and politics of a vanishing social class, the folk, and this concern has forced practitioners from the very beginning of this discipline to continually address and redress the notion of who the folk/*Volk* are. The discipline's survival is in part a testimony to the extraordinary flexibility of its subject and the will toward introspection and adjustment on the part of some of its practitioners. The latest wave of introspection, however, brought about a greater challenge to the continuity of folkloristics, as it went beyond scrutinizing the subject matter's boundaries and moving toward a critique of how the canon itself was formed.

Disciplinary canons come about in part merely through a field's institutionalization and the accumulation of materials awaiting analysis. By the early twentieth century, folkloristics had brought forth a number of approaches toward the study of expressive culture. An interest in origin, differentiation of expressive culture into many different genres, experimentation with structural modes of analysis, and, increasingly, the cultural ecology of folklore were paradigms that folklorists inhabited (Bau-

155

singer [1968], Ben-Amos [1976], and Abrahams [1976]; also see Bendix [1995]). Yet it was collections of folklore and folklife—salvaged from history or ethnographically recorded, published, and archived—that demonstrated the weight of the discipline, and the way in which these collections were put together encapsulated canonical assumptions of the field. Folklorists had begun such enterprises, and their stature within the discipline legitimated the materials as authentic. Only in the decades since World War II did the ideologies of those canon-builders come under ever-closer scrutiny. With this scrutiny, authenticity as a criterion and authentication as a tool emerge as the discipline's questionable legacies. Yet authenticity is not easy to part with, and the differential ways in which German and American folklorists have chosen to acknowledge this fact is the subject of chapters 6 and 7.

In both German and American cases, folklorists questioned fundamentals. The German discourse faced the problem of the genuine versus spurious dichotomy, blatantly made into dogma during National Socialism, but also economically omnipresent through the commodifying forces of the market, a process initially labeled "folklorism." In the United States the continued concern with defining folklore led to the questioning of core concepts such as tradition. The American shift from a static to a processual definition of expressive culture eventually implicated absolute notions of authenticity as well, and only here did the connection to the notion of "fakelore" begin to be unraveled.

The revision of disciplinary canons occurred in the context of the ongoing sociopolitical climate. Postwar Germany was preoccupied with rebuilding society, regarding the new beginning as an opportunity to begin at the "zero hour" (*Stunde Null*), and the divided nation attempted to treat the National Socialist period as if it could be actively ended. This effort was simulated by scholars engaged in "salvaging" projects that appeared untainted by the political perversions of 1933 to 1945.

American scholars were engaged in a different kind of rebuilding. Since the turn of the century, an interest in establishing and celebrating an American history and culture distinct from European intellectual dominance had taken hold, not least influenced by the American role in World War I. Struggling to earn a living during the economic depression of the 1930s, students of culture and the arts, including folklorists, were enlisted in New Deal projects designed to capture the history and spirit of the nation. After World War II, carrying the victor's burden entailed latent or overt participation in the spirit of the Cold War against the perceived communist threat. Hence, the notion of "fakelore" was employed as a bulwark against the evils of commercial contamination of pure folklore, but eventually it was used as a means to decry the influence of political agents on cultural purity as well.

The 1960s brought vigorous challenges to intellectual paradigms that had been taken for granted, but the contours of change differed for the Germans and Americans. Germany experienced the severe critiques of the academic status quo emanating from the Frankfurt School. Theodor Adorno's writings on philosophy as well as social and artistic phenomena had challenged the dominant Heideggerian philosophy (see Heidegger 1962, Adorno 1973); Adorno also had opened up spheres of hitherto scorned mass culture for intellectual scrutiny, though his opening came from a perspective that did not necessarily appreciate such mass cultural production, preparing the way for politically inspired social analysis that was especially appropriate for postwar German research (Adorno 1973, 1991). His successor, Jürgen Habermas, expanded on this groundwork. Habermas's work on the interrelationship between scholarship and the public sphere (1989 [1962]) and, even more, his treatise on the relationship between knowledge and human interest (1971) were cornerstones on which challenges to the ideology of objective inquiry were built. Laying bare the interrelationship between any scholar's intellectual and sociopolitical interests and the kind of knowledge that was generated out of this matrix, Habermas could demonstrate how the nineteenth-century positivist paradigm had suppressed the fundamental epistemological insights of Kantian philosophy. Kant had acknowledged the influence of reflective judgment on the construction of "reliable knowledge," but subsequently the production of science was increasingly severed from this philosophical restraint on its absolute values (Habermas 1971:3–5). At that point, the positivist paradigm with its belief in science free of "human interest" took hold.

Although *Volkskunde* hardly had the standing of a hard science, scientific standards had been eagerly proclaimed. The Frankfurt School's critique of the ideology of value-free knowledge production found receptive readers among younger folklorists unwilling to erase the Nazi impact on scholarship. Unraveling the political abuse of *Volkskunde* in Nazi Germany led to the "critique of the canon" in *Volkskunde* in the 1970s and, for some schools, to the complete abandoning of almost every form (such as the canon of *Volkspoesie*—folk narrative and song) that *Volkskunde* had been investigating. Coupled with the increasing effort to tackle rather than exclude the phenomenon called *Folklorismus*, a vision of the discipline has begun to emerge that devoted a considerable portion of its energy to documenting and understanding the impact of its own precepts on German culture.

In the United States the deconstructive efforts born in the 1960s were less violent as well as less explicit. Here, the political upheaval of the civil rights movement encouraged folklorists to consciously drop the latent preponderance of an old, European notion of "folk" and instead to endorse a far more anthropological concept of a folk comprising any human group, with an emphasis on the underprivileged. The critique of the canon in the United States took far fewer historical and deconstructive turns; instead, it was fostered by an exuberant search for and celebration of the artistry hidden in groups that had thus far been overlooked or treated only marginally—residents of urban ghettos, practitioners and participants in black culture, and members of urban ethnic groups. In foregrounding a major new area of investigation—ethnic folklore—the politics of the civil rights movement also implicitly sponsored a new belief in searching out an authentic set of forms and practices that might be used to celebrate cultural differences. The legislation emerging from this movement, such as the Folklife Preservation Act, formalized and to an extent reified such earlier notions of authenticity. Similarly, the theoretical movement labeled "the performance revolution," despite methodological innovations, also harbored latent cravings for breaking through to the authentic core of folklore processes.

Only the 1980s and 1990s have seen a turn to an interest in the politics and commodification of culture and the recognition that the dichotomy between politically manipulated and hence spurious folklore or "fakelore" and genuine folklore cannot simply be documented in places other than the United States. Undermining or deconstructing the dichotomy, however, also entailed a renewed look at what was now termed "commodity culture" and how that cultural form is interwoven with scholarship.

Chapter Six

Departures and Revisions
Toward a *Volkskunde* Without Canon

When Hermann Bausinger's *Folk Culture in a World of Technology* (1990) was reprinted after twenty-five years, Bausinger's new preface pointed out that the book had contributed to overcoming conservative notions of the folk in German discourse (Bausinger 1986 [1961]).[1] Conceived in part as a "polemical treatise," the book challenged the notion of folk culture as an isolated part within a cultural whole untouched by modernity. Rather, "the modern, the 'technological' world had already penetrated traditional folk culture considerably . . . [and] folk culture was a construct that had perhaps only come into existence as an anti-modernist counterimage" (Bausinger 1986:3).

How difficult this deconstructive project was and still is can be gleaned from three decades of initially sparse but steadily intensifying discourse over the central tenets of *Volkskunde*, the name of the discipline, and the notion of folk culture. "Sparse" may be too harsh a term for the seminal conferences, collections, and disputes that were conducted from the mid-sixties to the mid-seventies (see Dow and Lixfeld 1986). I choose it rather to emphasize the enormous amounts of "normal science" (Kuhn 1970) that continued to be produced despite apparent paradigmatic changes. Even a casual look at the book review section and the list of new publications in Germany's most prestigious folklore journal, the *Zeitschrift für Volkskunde,* as well as the smaller regional journals, show many researchers continuing to document the expressive culture of a folk defined as predominantly agricultural, albeit one that was confined historically and regionally. The new, reflexive canon is thus by no means a mainstream phenomenon, as numerous articles—even in Brednich's 1988 overview of the field—illustrate. Yet where deconstruction set in, the politics of authenticity formed a latent background in discussions of the discipline's formation, institutionalization, and perpetuation.

159

This chapter first addresses the extension and application of older layers of folkloristic authenticity vocabulary during the Nazi era; it then
turns to postwar attempts to return to prewar scholarship and projects as
if nothing had intervened. The deconstruction of the general canon of
Volkskunde that followed this postwar attempt, beginning in the 1960s,
has continued to the present.

THE SPECTER OF NATIONAL SOCIALISM

It is hard to come to terms with a period in one's cultural history that
caused massive death and destruction and that met with outspoken universal disapproval and military defeat. Decades passed before a critical
assessment of scholarship under National Socialism took place. The 1986
conference "*Volkskunde* and National Socialism" in Munich represented
the first major effort on the part of the German Folklore Society to discuss
"that dark era of German history from 1933 to 1945" (Gerndt 1986:8).[2]
By turning historical self-reflection into a respectable field of inquiry, the
conference brought closure to an era of *Vergangenheitsbewältigung*, the
attempt to come to terms with the Nazi past (Stein 1987).[3]

Since 1945, evidence has emerged that many German folklorists collaborated with the Nazis. The most extensively documented case is the cultural ministry run by Albert Rosenberg that conducted "research" based
on racial dogmas (Bollmus 1970, 1987).[4] Collaboration was not exclusive
to folklorists, of course, but because of its theoretical constructs, terminology, and applied aspects, "*Volkskunde* was not a peripheral matter" (Bausinger 1987:132). This congruence with Nazi ideology eventually had to
be acknowledged and acted on by postwar scholars (Emmerich 1971).

The attempts by postwar scholars to fit the Nazi era into the history of
their discipline have been characterized as stages of emplotment (Stein
1987). Immediate postwar efforts to distinguish between a politicized and
bastardized version of the field and "serious *Volkskunde*" formed the narrative, which was constructed by scholars who emerged from the era unscathed. A next generation clarified "the common ideological ground
between Volkskunde and National Socialism" (Stein 1987:170). This emplotment, in turn, prepared the ground for younger scholars to overhaul
the discipline's canon and attempt to "change . . . the postwar institutional
structure in light of that history" (p. 180).

Christa Kamenetsky's critique of Nazi distortions of folktales, fitting
loosely between the first and second stages of this history, indicates how
difficult it was to sever past senses of authenticity from Nazi uses; Kame-

netsky herself remains confident about the untainted nature of the pre-Nazi tales and regrets their loss:

> Ironically, the new folktale interpretation achieved the very opposite of what it officially set out to do. While transforming the folktale into a stale product of Socialist Realism, it *severed it from its genuine connection with the living folk tradition,* thus *stifling its growth* and creative development. Finally, the folktale was *no longer a true reflection* of the *common peasant folk,* but only a medium for the Nazi ideology, and a mouthpiece of racial propaganda. (1977:178; my italics indicate her vocabulary of authenticity)

To what extent does language indicate or even seduce its users to a particular ideology? In the case of National Socialism this question has led to extensive study.[5] *Volkskunde* worked with a terminology that was in part congruent with concepts and vocabulary at the core of Nazi ideology, starting with the very term *Volk* and its compounds, such as *Volkstum* (folkness), or terms such as *Erbe* (heritage). The postwar issue hinged on the question, "to what extent can we continue to use this vocabulary without being accused of continuing its legacy?" Efforts to reconstruct terminological usage during the 1933–45 era and distinguish who was merely within the "tradition of scholarly language" and who actively promoted the Nazi agenda have been difficult if not vengeful or painful.[6]

The unresolved debate between Linda Dégh (1980) and Christa Kamenetsky (1980) on whether a particular folktale researcher supported Nazi views intentionally or inadvertently illustrates that vocabulary as much as individuals is under scrutiny. Kamenetsky pointed to Julius Schwietering's language use, which to her indicated his complicity. Dégh defended his pioneering community studies approach, arguing that he used a term such as *Volkssoziologie* because Riehl had already used it. Schwietering's terminological practice in the early 1930s had to be understood within the context of scholarship alone, not within the broader sociopolitical framework in which the scholar found himself embroiled (Dégh 1980:331–34). Perhaps inspired by the belief that scholarship can or even must be outside political discourse, Dégh left out the more pressing question of why this vocabulary was so appealing to National Socialism. Dégh suggested that attempts to change *Volkskunde*'s name and terminology should be abandoned because "a modern generation of researchers, recuperating from tragic memories, might not need such symbolic-formalistic self-chastisement anymore" (1980:334). Yet by making this argument, she misses the point that remaining attached to name and terminology carries the implication of accepting the past legacy. Herein lies the German dilemma of being caught between accepting the complicity of practitioners in the field with a now despised ideology and self-flagellation for their having so readily allowed scholarship to be corrupted.

The first major attempt to show the connection between *Volkskunde* and National Socialism was made by sociologist Heinz Maus in "On the Situation of German *Volkskunde*." Maus pointed out in his essay that the discipline's Romantic heritage made it prone to the kind of propagandistic abuse which it experienced during the Nazi period, and that folklorists' interest in questions of origin and their preoccupation with vanishing customs ignored the questions of the present (Stein 1987:159–60). The failure of folklorists during the immediate postwar years to seriously entertain Maus's arguments indicates not just postwar trauma and denial, but also the fear of mid-career folklorists that they would need to retool for substantially different research questions and abandon the views concerning folklore that had made the field attractive to them in the first place. This fate, after all, had befallen their former colleagues in the new German Democratic Republic. Clearly, the politically inspired retooling those folklorists underwent was actively denounced in the West, where, instead, lengthy research enterprises such as the *Atlas der Volkskunde* (Zender 1959–64) or the handbook of the folktale (begun by Mackensen 1930/ 33–1934/40) were considered worthwhile projects to return to. The busy work entailed in an enormous reference work such as the *Atlas* could easily help a scholar "forget" the kinds of goals with which the very same projects had been associated. Wilhelm Pessler, one of the founders of the *Atlas,* wrote in the preface to a general handbook of German folklore: "May German *Volkskunde* thus succeed to make accessible to all *Volksgenossen* (national comrades) the essence of Germanness and to make them open their hearts to their brothers in order for them to exclaim with us, united in their fight for Germany's resurrection: 'I believe in the German *Volksgemeinschaft* (people's community) and I believe in German immortality'" (cited after Jeggle 1988:60).[7]

Before turning to the awakening of German folklorists to the ideological proclivity of their central canon, I wish to illustrate the folkloristic vocabulary developed before World War II and the slippery paths on which scholars walked. I have purposely limited the evidence to works by scholars who have not been among the main targets of the movement to deconstruct the Nazi past. Rather, I present some individuals who stayed in the discipline or who were forced to the margins, where they expressed their difficulties with the political realities of National Socialism once those realities became manifest.[8] Much as the romantic vocabulary of authenticity ignited both scholarly enthusiasm for folklore research and political fervor for nation-building, the National Socialist extension of this vocabulary, with metaphors drawn from the realm of nature and allusions to cultural origins in a purer racial past, evoked an exuberant response from others beyond the masses who joined the new political party. Among scholars, too, this new "language of authenticity" found an echo as well as a following. Many scholars remained oblivious to how quickly such enthusiasm could be perverted into legislative efforts to promote racial "purity."

The Vocabulary of Authenticity During the Third Reich

National Socialism's central fascinations were faith in the leader, the surrender of the individual to the community, a belief in a master race and a corresponding obsession with racial purity, and defense of *Blut und Boden* (blood and earth). This list points to potential linkages with folkloristic theories. A preoccupation with cleansing folk materials from the debris of the ages, coupled with latent assumptions of the superiority of Indo-Germanic origins held many scholars captive. The tension between individual and community had been a touchstone in folkloristic debates since the turn of the century; Hans Naumann's popular notion of a communal folk spirit lacking individuality fit perfectly with Nazi ideology.

The desire for racial purity is linked to searches for the authentic; akin to strategic implementations of this craving for authenticity, Nazi ideology presented racial purity as the means to heal the wounds of the suffering German state. Hitler painted the ethnic heterogeneity of Germany as a major reason for the country's economic and political weakness, and he promised to restore a German realm based on a cleansed, and hence strong, German people. Racial or ethnic purity was, on the surface, the principal argument brought against Jews, but the urge for Germans to prove the authenticity of their own beliefs may have been an even greater motivational force than their wanting of "ethnic" purity.

The desire for purity of race also belonged, of course, to the Romantic nationalists. It is a long path, however, from the abstract idea of statehood based on shared language and ethnicity to a deadly policy of exterminating those who do not share the same ethnicity. This path was prepared in large part by language put to skillfully rhetorical use in oratory and writing destined to reach large audiences. The notion of "purity," racial or otherwise, obviously belongs to the vocabulary of authenticity, as do ideas of "pollutants" that endanger racial cleanliness. With the idea of restoring racial purity, Hitler aimed for a kind of "biological authenticity." In the unidimensional fashion in which his ideology drew from headlines of evolutionary theories and late nineteenth-century philosophy, he hoped that his policies of "racial cleansing" could restore an Aryan race. Folklore studies by the 1920s had stepped beyond a predominantly philological orientation and had begun to toy with social-psychological and evolutionary models, as had studies in other fields. Scholars used terms such as "race" and "tribe" (*Stamm*) and began using racial arguments to explain cultural difference, dabbling in questions of national character and cultural psychology and eventually sliding into asserting the racial superiority of Nordic tribes (Trümpy 1987:172–73).

An interest in evolutionary ideas was characteristic of Western social sciences, and although wiser minds warned against this way of thinking, a "racial argument" offered a facile explanation for many complex phenomena (Trümpy 1987:171).[9] Assertions that "folk character" was based on race rather than psychology began to mount in folklore texts and became politicized with the Nazi takeover in 1933.

Folklorist Herbert Freudenthal delivered not only an analysis of Hitler's *Mein Kampf* as a manifesto for a political *Volkskunde* (1934), but he advanced a program for the racial basis of such study (1935). Freudenthal pronounced that "becoming a *Volk*" entailed the "rejection of the biologically foreign" (1935:20)—thus supporting Nazi policies. By 1940 the ideology of racial authenticity had become entrenched, and the search for a great Aryan race translated into the old dichotomous distinctions of the politics of authenticity. Thus, a 1940 German dissertation began with the assertion that *Volkskunde* scholars "in the Third Reich [have pronounced] as a goal . . . the distinction between 'German' and 'Un-German'" (cited in Trümpy 1987:174).

One cornerstone of Nazi language, "race," was readily combined with the concept that most suited National Socialist ideologues, the *Volk*. *Volk* was defined as traditional, unchanged, communal, Germanic peasant culture. Terms like *Volksseele, Volscharakter,* or *Volkstum* and any number of additional compounds acquired a political meaning. The National Socialist adjective *völkisch*, in turn, found increased usage in scholarly works—perhaps naïvely—conceived as without political intent.

If post-Romantic Germanic scholarship had tried to restore epics and epic songs, National Socialist practitioners sought to make such texts work for the new ideology. Just as Wagner's operas had made epics come to life on stage, the Nazi invocation of Germanic folkness sought a revival of what some perceived as the genuinely Germanic spirit. Joseph Dünninger's *Volkstum und geschichtliche Welt* (Folkness and the Historical World, 1937) went to great pains to make this linkage obvious, and his reading of Nordic mythology assisted such rhetoric: "The power for the historic is inborn to the ancient Germans. Odin is the embodiment of this force that the ancient Germans have within them since the beginning (*Ursprung*), a power which is religious in origin. Herein lies the other side of the Germanic world view: the warlike-heroic, religio-political world!" (Dünninger 1937:44). The counterpart to this warlike aspect was the supposedly peaceful peasant world. In his predilection for an authenticity vocabulary connected to origins, Dünninger calls "the peaceful peasant world and the warlike world of male bonds" the "two *Ur*-principles from which everything Germanic grew" (1937:44).

Dünninger's work revived organic metaphors in his description of folklore and history clashing like the "realm of wood" with the "realm of stone." The laws of folkness differed from the laws of a polluting modernity, for they were "of eternal duration, timeless, self-fulfilling in the natural cycle of the year, unwavering in their innermost, [and] shaped and predestined since the *Ur*-beginning" (1937:22). The world of stone, associated in part with rational, enlightened, and progressive thought, had led to a "corroding" of folkness. But remnants were available to attempt a reconstruction of wholesome unity and drive away the agents of individuality that suppressed the community so central to Nazi ideology.

Dünninger's vision is rather thin on theory, and he struggles to show the linkage between history, which he describes as an account of constant change, and the never-changing folk. His writing is rich in the vocabulary of authenticity. Aside from a frequent use of "*ur-*" words—*Ursprung* (origin) or *urtümlich* (primeval)—the text is suffused with terms such as "unity" or "organic" and expressions like "the pure, untouched world of the folk" (1937:29). Through his language, Dünninger consistently points to an authentic essence.[10]

The "*ur-*" syllable invoking ancient and hence unspoiled beginnings appealed to many. The Austrian Victor von Geramb advocated a search for "new" terms to fit a new vision of what characterized folkness. As a conservative German nationalist, von Geramb, relying on Riehl's example, practiced *Volkskunde* as a science with both an educational and a political mission.[11] Von Geramb's language coincided with party rhetoric, though he privately expressed qualms and later anger about National Socialist interference in his professional freedom (Eberhart 1992:688, 695–96). In von Geramb's "last great essay before the catastrophe" (Lutz 1958:202) he lengthily debated the more evolutionary or, rather, devolutionary (Dundes

1969) *Volkskunde* of his day. Though he abstained from the term "race," he did believe in an inherited folk character, and he searched for a nobler term than "primitive" (Naumann's label) for folkloric manifestations.

> The "romantic" conception of *Volkskunde*—in its deepest and noblest sense—as it reigned until the 1920s, is gaining the upper hand again. Connected to this is the yearning and searching for a word which, both in its linguistic form and content, does more justice to the simple attitude and creativity of inherited folk goods as well as the "idea of the nation" of the Romantics and of Riehl, than does the foreign word "primitive." (von Geramb 1937:11)

Borrowing from Georg Koch (1935), von Geramb suggests the term *Urverbundenheit* (*Ur*-connectedness), which he defines as "those originally given (*urgegebenen*) total impressions of intuitive, logical perception which belong to the nature of primitive peoples, but also to the *vulgus in populo*, the mother ground (*Mutterboden*) of our Western civilizations as well as of the child from the very beginning" (p. 27). Von Geramb preempted potential accusations that his program was a return to a discredited Romanticism by endorsing "that which Romanticism really was," a "listening to the heartbeat of our people," and "a spiritual flight home to the foundations of primary *Ur*-connectedness." He wanted to make apparent the difference between ethnology, or *Völkerkunde* (devoted to the study of primitives) and *Volkskunde* (history and ethnology of one's own people). But his exuberant descriptions and his addition to the vocabulary of authenticity of yet another "*ur*-" word clearly point to his strong emotional endorsement of a political agenda centered on the folk.

Freudenthal, Dünninger, and von Geramb emerged from World War II with relatively unscathed reputations; they had productive careers in *Volkskunde*, honored by their students and respected within their institutions. Their political lives were less obviously entangled in the party than those of some more prominent scholars, and the party in turn treated them less gently than it had treated some scholars who collaborated more. The exuberance and emotional appeal of a search for authenticity among such scholars, who engaged in what they might later consider a youthful aberration, need not necessarily have led to such a sinister outcome as the National Socialist one.

National Socialist ideology was a conglomeration of decontextualized ideas culled from Romanticism to the 1930s (Kamenetsky 1972b). In reinterpreting Herder's works—to take a philosopher particularly relevant to folklore studies—Nazism misrepresented his humanitarianism in the most absurd fashion.[12] The few examples offered above illustrate how folklorists could fall for or even contribute to the Nazi rhetoric, because its terminology was so close to that of their own discipline.[13] The goals of National Socialism and its brand of *Volkskunde*—cleansing of the Germanic race and restoration of the spiritual unity and purity of a folk—are perhaps the most extreme example of a dream of authenticity translated into politics, legal action, and ultimately physical destruction.

THE *VOLK* DISAGGREGATED

Some German folklorists of the time disliked this vocabulary, and recognizing the inherent danger of Nazi infiltration of the discipline, they fought against it and died because of it.[14] Many folklorists felt threatened and worried about their personal security as much as about their professional integrity (Bollmus 1970:9). Their dilemma arose "from the dangerously apolitical perspective" that informed "many German folklorists' perception of themselves" (Emmerich 1971:112).

The actions of scholars who chose to cooperate must be explained in both political and psychological terms. To them, folklore studies were (and in many corners of the world continue to be) a politically conservative enterprise. Despite an often oppositional tone, movements that try to strengthen a state by restoring "originality" in language, culture, and religion are inherently reactionary. Co-opted folklorists in the Nazi period may have considered the rise of folklore terminology to the top of the political landscape as beneficial to the field. Nor can personal ambition be neglected as contributing to their collaboration. National Socialist folklorists were neither the first nor the last academics to ignore questions of ethics and morality in order to see their status and income improved.[15]

As a result, the notion of "genuineness" and its linkage to the folk took on a particularly distressing ring to some postwar folklorists. The *Volkstumsideologie* (ideology of folkness), as Wolfgang Emmerich called it, with its popular appeal was to some scholars a latent source of trouble for their field. Since the Romantic beginnings of *Volkskunde*, its terminology had always been open to polemic distortions and was latently motivating scholars themselves.

Hans Moser, who would found the historical school of *Volkskunde* in Munich, was one of the first to emphasize that *Volkskunde* would continue to find itself in a jeopardized position unless the field acknowledged its potential sociopolitical use (1988 [1954]:106–19). But his suggestion to abandon the mythological, speculative, and popularly appealing notions of a lasting *Volk* received little initial notice (Gerndt 1988:10–11). It took another decade for Gerhard Heilfurth, another prominent survivor of the war, to criticize the term *Volk* as "glittering and complex, packed with content and always open to nuances in meaning. It is nonetheless concise and compelling, almost a magic formula of fascinating power which since the French Revolution has been used in all domains of public relations, opinion making and propaganda" (1988 [1962]:179–80). Heilfurth cast the Nazi chapter as one among many:

> Ideological movements placed the *Volk* into an absolute realm, as a highest quality, a finite condition to which one could refer as though it were a highest authority. The older among us have experienced these reality-destroying, ideological extremes sufficiently! In its valuation and promotion, the word was strained in manifold ways, sometimes as rousing slogan, whereby the national, the collective, or the elemental were emphasized, [and sometimes] . . . for war, competition, revolution, class struggle, mass movement, founding of an association, large-scale operation, voting, or just for consumption (if you think of terms such as "folk-bathtub," . . . or "*Volkswagen*"). (1988 [1962]: 180–81)

Heilfurth perceived the "thick, entangled web" of "nationalisms, socialisms and democratisms" (p. 181) that constituted the semantic domain of folkloristic terminology, and he advocated, as did Bausinger, a vision of the discipline that would grow with rather than exclude the dynamic between expressive culture and technological-industrial transformation. Yet in suggesting a commitment to a "*Volkskunde* beyond ideology," Heilfurth maintained a belief in objective scholarship that could transcend the massive misuse done to the term *Volk* and rectify public opinion about the discipline by cutting through the masses of "subscientific literature" produced by amateurs (p. 184).

Bausinger wrote a far more critical essay than Heilfurth's on the connections between *Volkskunde*'s terminological practice and its ideologically charged character, and his student Wolfgang Emmerich subsequently expanded on the argument (Bausinger 1965, Emmerich 1971). The three points of convergence between folklore vocabulary and party ideology were "the *myth of the origin*, the *longing for meaning* . . . and the *concept of race as a scientific principle*" (Jeggle 1988:61; his italics). The racial argument was a strategy to answer the unanswerable first two issues. The myth of origin, however, was intrinsically linked to *Volkskunde*'s beginnings, and it formed part of an ever-reformulated ideology of folkness, fueling regressive dreams of a Germanic and pre-Christian continuity arising from different historical needs.[16] Attempts to bypass any specificity of historical insight were not just a mainstay of fascist reasoning (Jeggle 1988:62) but a recurring element in characterizations of the folk.[17]

It was the concept of the folk, then, that kept encouraging the hope for an attainable authenticity. Thus, this central concept ultimately needed to be analyzed, either to be healed or discarded. Bausinger's plea for a consideration of *Folk Culture in a World of Technology* was, in retrospect, a first effort toward this goal (1986 [1961], trans. 1990).

Bausinger's study began with Bertold Brecht who had urged that *Volk* (folk or people) be replaced with *Bevölkerung* (population), a change that would "already refuse to support many lies" (cited in Bausinger 1986 [1961]:7). The sober description "population" lacks the connotations of unity, ethnic homogeneity, national aspiration, and mythic descent that have grown to be part of the semantic domain of *Volk*. But terminological introspection immediately invited critique. Leopold Schmidt, the major figure in postwar Austrian folkloristics, in an early review maintained that a book starting with a spiteful quotation from Brecht did not really deserve to be reviewed, because "*Volkskunde* had nothing in common with Brecht" (in Bausinger 1986:4).[18]

Bausinger challenged the notion that folk culture was a thing of the past, whose demise had been brought about by technology: "Technology and modern expressions of society were practically absent in *Volkskunde*, . . . excluded by definition because folk culture was understood as pre-technological, pre-industrial, and pre-modern. [Folk culture's existence in] the present [was assumed to continue], even if only as strong relics or in shielded islands" (1986:4). Bausinger purposely chose nature metaphors to drive home the point that becoming accustomed to innovations is far more "natural" than adhering to arcane, labor-intensive work methods and tools. Trains and automobiles become topics of folksongs, technological inventions like large freezer units shared by entire villages could be a locus of community in an isolating age, and automobiles and tractors became integrated in agrarian festivals and belief. "The social circumstances" surrounding technological inventions showed that they did not spell the end of folk culture: rather, changes "brought on by technology . . . permeate folk culture in a natural fashion" (1986:4).

Modernity and industrialization had brought to everyday life an expansion of horizons in all areas—geographic, temporal, and social—even when such expansions occurred more rapidly than could be intellectually grasped. In considering Romantic exuberance and sentiment, and challenged again by people searching for a "pure folk culture" freed from sentimental overlay, Bausinger foreshadowed the entire discourse about, and deconstruction of, the *Volk* concept.[19]

The broadside attacks on the *Volk* concept were formulated at the *Volkskunde* department in the University of Tübingen. Led by Bausinger, his students stormed the seemingly unyielding bastions of the field with appeals at conferences and mimeographed circulars.[20] The revolutionary climate, in keeping with the late 1960s, eventually resulted in the *Falkenstein* debates of 1970, a place that German folklorists associate with the most pronounced paradigm change in their field since World War II.[21] Germany during that period instituted a general university reform that entailed the reorganization of entire divisions. Involved in that process, some folklorists felt the need to take a stance to avoid the arbitrary assigning of their field to either humanities or social sciences as well as to signal to academic authorities that *Volkskunde* was no longer what it used to be.

Two volumes of essays compiled by Tübingen associates fueled these debates; even their titles indicate the large-scale changes that were brewing. *Populus Revisus* (Bausinger et al. 1966) avoided the compromised term *Volk* by using Latin,[22] and *Abschied vom Volksleben* (Geiger et al. 1970) literally means "taking leave from folklife." Both volumes extensively revised the canon. The *notion* of the *Volk,* curiously, and the issue of whether an entity of that sort really existed, remained a separate issue that was debated only much later, influenced by the debate over folklorism. One reason for these separate considerations of the *Volk* concept was that it necessitated a historical retrospective which would methodologically counter the desire of the "revolutionaries" to devise a folkloristics capable of addressing issues of the present.

"One comes across the entity folk culture only in the modern age," wrote Konrad Köstlin, one of Bausinger's intellectual allies (1977a: 216). While he did not argue that the concept was an invention, as others have,[23] to him it was an image of a "cultural reality" finite in its existence in time and space, "a type of culture which can be . . . temporally described reasonably well for the time span between 1600 and 1850" (Köstlin 1977a: 218). The "cannon" that folklorists had chosen for study existed for this relatively short period, and Köstlin maintained that the historical, economic, and political context of that era—particularly the growth of the territorial state and the development of mercantilism—shaped this folk culture. The growth of central administrations in small and controllable territories furthered an increased emphasis on the specifics of local culture; hence, the growth of "regional culture," often labeled "folk culture," went hand and hand with such administrative efforts. Mercantilism, with its emphasis on enlarging the state's coffers, also furthered what Köstlin termed "dogmatized folk culture." To boost the economy, efforts to increase the population (by prohibiting emigration or lowering the legal age for marriage) were made on the assumption that "the more people, the better the economy" (1977a:223).

To Köstlin, tying people to an increasingly regionally defined territory contributed to a kind of "feudal identity" on the level of classes other than feudal lords. As such, folk culture became objectified and useful to the state, and the new fields of statistics and *Kammeralwissenschaften* (state administration) as forerunners of *Volkskunde* were testimony to this development (Linke 1990). Köstlin goes on: "If folk culture, in the manner that scholarship has regarded it and museums have collected it, is of feudal origins, then one can also locate its final phase in the nineteenth century. Costume wearers published a set of corporate rules [regarding correct apparel]. We don't know whether [such rules] ever existed in the clearness that the costumes are supposed to make us believe" (1977a:227). As economic and political reality changed, a grotesquely intensified variant emerged that Köstlin attributed to a general insecurity: "Never were old traditions as respected, . . . never was the petit-bourgeois and peasant world as devoted to the self-reflection of its own social status and estate as through colorful customs." As their own existence was increasingly questioned, the petit bourgeois and peasantry celebrated themselves and "glorified their present by resorting to a past that they believed in" (p. 227).[24]

Köstlin lodges the emergence of the folk concept in a "narrowing of horizons"—purposely playing with Bausinger's earlier notion of "broadened horizons" for a later era (Bausinger 1986 [1961])—"which alone could turn the population into a *Volk* (Köstlin 1977a:228). "Through this definition, the characteristic 'genuine' would have to be replaced with 'feudal' and both feudal and genuine could be discontinued, if one would understand *Volk* as a historical category, conceivable only between 1600 and 1850. *Volk* would then be a historical category for a population which tries to master life through a horizon made narrow in a narrowed, given cultural frame" (1977a:230).

Ina-Maria Greverus, who integrated folklore within the larger framework of cultural anthropology at her institute in Frankfurt, explained the rise of the *Volk* concept and the fascination with it as "the discovery" of phenomena: "'Folk cultures' were the discovery of a nationally engaged bourgeoisie and of folklorists," much as "mass culture was the discovery of psychologists and culture critics" (Greverus 1978:157). In a few strokes Greverus culls those theories and methods that rendered *Volk* into a category of longing and action.

> For the German humanists, the *Germania* of Tacitus in which a [set of old German virtues] . . . was established by a foreigner, was a revelation and stimulus in their search for "proof." Such proof was mostly sought in the linguistic traditions of the "*Volk*." . . . The humanist attention to the *Volk* foreshadows the later creed of romantic nationalism which regarded *Volk* as an organism, a grown community, something originally and culturally connected, which had been separated only through the development of an estate society and its passing into a society made up of social classes and which had to be recovered in the nation state. . . . The primary fixation on verbal evidence made the passage of the various *Volkskunden* into the appropriate national philologies possible. (1978:160)

Yet once "folk culture" was shown to be a construct, both societally and intellectually, and once its ideological handicaps had begun to be spelled out (Bausinger 1965, Emmerich 1971), the question remained who or what exactly were folklorists trying to study. For Greverus, the solution lay in a socially engaged anthropological route, where the cultures and subcultures of the present were appropriate objects of study, and where attention to disciplinary history and its intermeshing with social choices would always remain a stimulus in both theory and practice.[25]

Some German scholars took Peter Burke's notion of popular culture to be the equivalent of folk culture,[26] while others saw it merely as "new involvement with an old term" (Köstlin 1984). Yet others were intrigued with the French social historian Robert Muchembled's theses of a medieval folk counterculture.[27] In the midst of this search for a focus on alternate subjects, Köstlin specifically warned that the new historical work on folk culture could easily tempt folklorists to "discover" the true locus of folklore's spirit in workers' counterculture, a shift evident in some workers' folklore scholarship. Workers could all too easily turn into the new peasants of folkloristics, and, to Köstlin, the "discovery" of workers' culture performed a similar function as the discovery of peasants as "the exotic at home" did for earlier generations of scholars. Giving separate consideration to any group would move it, too, into the narrowing, ossifying circle "outside of the normalcy of unquestioned 'matter of course' -ness'" (Köstlin 1984:27). The turn to workers' culture represented a threat to the progress achieved by revising the canon. "Longed-for virtues, dreamed ones, covered-over ones" reappeared, located in a different social group but documented and discussed by scholars with the same kind of moral vigor as before (Köstlin 1984:30).

The historically constructed nature of the *Volk* concept is generally accepted[28]—witness Wolfgang Kaschuba's effort to summarize discourse and object (1988).[29] The rise of the history of everyday life, championed particularly by historian Richard van Dülmen,[30] has brought a rapprochement between social history and German folkloristics. Bausinger, invited to address the annual assembly of German historians in 1984, seized the opportunity to describe *Volkskunde* as a field that "in many ways is the cultural history of the lower classes," distancing himself from the misconception of *Volkskunde* as a field devoted to hunting down the last genuine treasures of the folk. Bausinger also questioned the "justification of presuming a separate system of folk culture," and he hoped to interest historians in the dissolution of idealized conceptions of folk culture (Bausinger 1985:173–74).[31]

DEPARTURE FROM THE CANON

Taking leave from the *Volk*—from the study of people and artifacts conceived as rustic, preindustrial, or marginalized remnants—was the first step toward formulating a revised canon. A working meeting on methods and insights in the study of present-day culture resulted in *Populus Revisus* (Bausinger 1966a). Aside from Bausinger's and Brückner's remarks on folklorism, the volume revealed more of a shift in focus than an examination or revision of the methods and theses presented, however. Customs and what happens to them in the course of industrialization, and topics such as voluntary associations, urban folklore, and migrant workers became fields of study.

However, both the volume *Kontinuität?* (Bausinger and Brückner 1969), the *Festschrift* for Hans Moser, and Bausinger's essay "Critique of Tradition" (1969b) challenged central tenets of *Volkskunde*. In his essay, Bausinger argued that the supposed crisis of the field was not new. Rather, the nineteenth-century development of the discipline itself had been a response to perceived social ills, to the "disorganization, mobilization and change of society. Much as early sociology can be called a progressive doctrine of salvation, *Volkskunde* can be called a conservative doctrine of salvation" (1969b:232). By singling out cultural objectifications or "goods" as the focus of study, scholars had created a disciplinary tradition of "tradition," which provided separate research trajectories for individual goods. This precluded an understanding of the increasingly plural and complex interconnections of such cultural objectifications (1969b:237).

This methodological choice, combined with the zeal entailed in a doctrine of salvation, contained a further embarrassment: "The missionary aspect—either presented in terms of general moral teachings, a socially conceived natural history or nationalistic orientation—was connected to an attitude of enjoyment, of aesthetic distance" (Bausinger 1969b:237). Elements of voyeurism appear, to Bausinger, encoded in nineteenth-century aesthetic vocabulary yearning for vitality, strength, and health. This aestheticization on the part of select connoisseurs set *Volkskunde* on the path of constructing both an image of tradition and a vocabulary of authenticity that set the entire discipline on a course destined to salvage and celebrate the artificially decontextualized. Unless the ideology inherent in the construction of such a canon was laid bare, Bausinger feared that the field would slip into triviality.[32]

The ideological critique erupted in article collections and conferences by the late 1960s. Probing for the deeper meaning of "continuity" was "a provocation [to find] . . . a far flung goal: a comprehensive theory of tradition" (Bausinger 1969c:30).[33] While such comprehensiveness remains elusive, this provocation—in hindsight perfectly justifiable—appeared in the volume *Abschied vom Volksleben*.[34] "It is oppressive how little consciousness there is in *Volkskunde* about the misery of its own history," wrote one contributor. There was an overwhelming emphasis on "collecting and preserving," coupled with an unacknowledged service—in vocabulary and ideas—to conservative politics in scholarly enterprises from the Grimms to atlas-making (Schöck 1970:93). Using a canon of collectibles as the "theory" that informed the field was confounded by the "disciplinary reverence for the traditional which led in almost grotesque fashion to the preservation [of this canon]. *Volkskunde* became in many ways a static science, its picture of reality exactly reflecting [the discipline's] own constitution" (Schöck 1970:100).

Critics could easily denounce the efforts of disciplinary revolutionaries as being informed by "leftist" ideologies. But in an academic landscape such as Germany's, where party politics is rarely divorced from the divisions between different schools of thought, such accusations were more beside the point than wrong. Utz Jeggle, Dieter Kramer, or Martin Scharfe recognized the political entanglement of their discipline precisely because of their own ideological awareness. Unstated values informed research, and to point to the vocabulary of authenticity meant an unsentimental approach to the subject matter.

Values had always informed studies of expressive culture. Jeggle's discussion of Max Weber's "value-free" social science was an attempt to bring into view an old struggle in sociology and to make evident how

Volkskunde had dodged even discussing it. Jeggle wanted a paradigm that would accept an educative role, focusing on "the suffering of the outcasts, the Protestant who does not celebrate carnival, the village idiot who is laughed at. . . . Researchers of peasant housing could show that the old people in the half-timbered houses[35] on the country side often live like the dogs, and could reflect on how their situation could be improved" (Jeggle 1970:35). Jeggle was inspired by Dieter Kramer's much-embattled address, "Who Benefits from Folklore?" (1986a). Kramer sent out a Habermassian call for an "emancipatory application of the social sciences," with the idealistic goal of employing folklore and other social sciences to "humanize our social world in order to emancipate people from social dependence and manipulation" (Kramer 1986a:49, 51). Implicit in such calls was a recognition that scholarly declarations of certain goods as genuine parts of folk culture were essentially irrelevant since they ignored the social web in which such goods were embedded.

Martin Scharfe's "Critique of the Canon" was more explicitly concerned with the latent influence of authenticity criteria (1970, trans. Dow and Lixfeld 1986:54–61). To illustrate how much a genre-oriented or "goods"-oriented canon infiltrated even works seemingly new and non-ideological in the postwar years, Scharfe looked at the vocabulary in Richard Weiss's "*Volkskunde* of Switzerland" (1978 [1946]).[36] Weiss's functionalist perspective was a pragmatic paradigm far from the mythologizing search for origins, and he included urbanism, media, and invented tradition in his overview. Yet Weiss's approach was anything but ideology-free. Using the backdrop of community, Weiss invoked the dichotomies so typical of the vocabulary of authenticity: "Civilization-culture, compulsion-relation, artificial-natural, mass-community, organized-organic, undermine-build, confusing-clear, impersonal-personal, ill-healthy, changeable-lasting, ecstatic-vital, etc." (Scharfe 1970:81).[37] By illustrating how frames of perception continued to inform substantially changed folkloristic paradigms, Scharfe brought to bear on the present Emmerich's paradigm (1971) of folkloristic history.

Abschied vom Volksleben, which contained the most scholarly forms of protest against the canon, formed the basis of argument at the *Falkenstein* meetings (Brückner 1971).[38] Students felt that the papers presented in 1969 had not been taken seriously, and by publishing *Abschied vom Volksleben* as quickly as possible they hoped to force the issues to the center of debate. In addition, open letters and memoranda, constituting a veritable paper war, circulated through all *Volkskunde* departments. In tones that came close to straining professional courtesy, everything about *Falkenstein* became an issue before the meeting ever happened: who would be invited to speak, who would control the proceedings, and what should be the focus of discussion?

This truly explosive meeting led to an acknowledgment of the discipline's loaded name and to changes or expansions of the name at many institutions. *Falkenstein* also explicitly rejected "the remnants of romantic images of the unmediated [hence authentic] natural person" (Brückner 1971:20). No new canon emerged, although at least one textbook attempted to produce one (Bausinger, Jeggle, Korff, and Scharfe 1978).[39] Earlier and more successfully, Bausinger had integrated the new perspectives on *Volkskunde*'s history as well as new foci of research both in his introduction to folk literature (1968) and in his standard introduction to the field (1971). Wolfgang Brückner's post-*Falkenstein* assessment reflects the calming return to "normal science" under new auspices: "The critique of the canon was necessary, but the canon cannot be done away with. What is needed is its constant relativising" (1976:3).

Bausinger had discussed "the tendencies toward the genuine" as the genuine was formalized. In his critique of the genuine versus spurious dichotomy he formulated a need for a "critique of ideology as a prerequisite in the historiography of the discipline" (1969b:234). Almost twenty years later, Bausinger asserted that the controversies surrounding folklorism— and hence authenticity—would, in the eyes of historians of *Volkskunde,* clearly be recognized as a major field of discourse enforcing paradigmatic change (1988:326).

"FOLKLORE" AND "FOLKLORISMUS"

The renovation of the canon received its greatest impetus through the concurrent discourse over *Folklorismus.* In hindsight, folklorists were awakening to issues of economic commodification and political manipulation of expressive culture. Hans Moser's catchy definition of folklorism as "secondhand folklore" captures the alienation from the "real thing" implied in the term. Indeed, the discourse on folklorism was ultimately a discourse on authenticity, forcing debaters to recognize the constructed nature of folk cultural authenticity itself.

Folklorism appeared initially as an insurmountable challenge because no theoretical framework existed to account for it. Unless one simply excluded folklorism as a legitimate subject, the term and the diverse phenomena it stood for had to lead to an extensive renovation in both folkloristic theory and practice. While the former has largely been achieved, the latter remains a hurdle.

Hans Moser launched the concept of folklorism[40] with two essays in which he proposed descriptive definitions and sketched an outline of the dimension that folklorism research would have to take (1962, 1964).[41] The name itself derived from the English term "folklore," a word long ago rejected as a new name for the discipline, precisely because its popular connotations detracted from the serious aura the discipline wished to project (Weinhold 1890, Bendix 1988:5–6). Moser proposed calling the evidence of the use of folklore *Folklorismus*.

> It is a term of great breadth which draws on two strands: the increased cultural levelling which leads to a growing interest in things "folk" and the practice of satisfying, strengthening or awakening this interest. Through various tactics, the audience is offered an impressive mixture of genuine and falsified materials from folk culture, particularly in cultural enclaves where life still seems to breathe originality, strength and color. (Moser 1962:179–80)

Moser intended the term to be an objective, nonjudgemental characterization (Moser 1964:44), but the value-laden nature of phrases like "genuine and falsified materials" and breathing "originality, strength and color" question the very possibility of objectivity. Rather, the term added a new dimension to the dichotomies so prevalent in the vocabulary of authenticity, and Moser grasped the issues with rare astuteness. He sensed that there were distinct forms or realms of folklorism, and he opted for an array of examples, hoping that others would assist in more precisely defining the concept (1962:180). In his own first attempt to define, he isolated three forms of folklorism (1962:190):

1. Performance of traditionally and functionally determined elements of folk culture outside that culture's local or class community.

2. Playful imitations of folk motifs in another social stratum.

3. The purposeful invention and creation of "folklike" elements outside any tradition.

Moser also pointed to political differences. In the West he saw the dominance of folklorism brought about through the expansion of industrial markets. In Eastern Europe and Russia he perceived a cultural-political mission, and in Third World nations he saw "a reaction to radical progress which did away with folk religion and custom, but opened the way to posthumous folkloristic conservation" (Moser 1962:185).

In his second essay Moser devoted more attention than before to the influence that the academic study of folklore has had in stimulating folklorism. He worked with the term *Rücklauf* (literally "flowing-back" or "feed-back") which German-speaking folklorists had coined as a label for the incorporation of "scientific or pseudo-scientific insights" into the tradition bearers' conscious knowledge (Moser 1964:10). Journalists, writers of almanacs, and amateur folklorists were considered the principal promoters of *Rücklauf,* and Moser attributed their efforts as mostly owing to pedagogical impulses. His prime example was an Advent custom that had been created in 1954 in a Bavarian village. Local organizers and sympathetic journalists began to press for moving the origin back, basing their claims on scholarly writings about similar customs elsewhere, until ties to pre-Christian customs were evident to everyone. One particular scholarly approach, here specifically the turn-of-the-century fascination with pagan fertility rites, was chosen for mass consumption (1964:21).

Given his own penchant toward careful historical analysis, Moser's reaction to *Rücklauf* and its fondness for the wilder varieties of searches for origin was particularly virulent and mocking. Caught himself in the early attempts to renovate the discipline, he may have been unable to recognize the appeal of precisely those vague but rhetorically powerful hypotheses concerning expressive culture. It would take years for German folklorists to regard such *Rücklauf* tendencies in broader, societal terms instead of through the narrow gaze of a defensive discipline.[42]

Moser's historical orientation also led him to distinguish between "folklorism of our time" and folklorism of the past, the latter clearly separating social classes. The upper stratum (clergy and rulers) with their pedagogical instincts had an urge to regulate. The lower strata discovered material interests that cleverly made use of the upper stratum's desire for a soul of the folk (Moser 1964:25–31). In modern times, however, folklorism was "primarily commercially determined and deeply anchored in the tourism and entertainment industries, both increasingly important branches of the economy" (Moser 1962:199). Moser urged his colleagues to include folklorism as a viable subject in the discipline: "It will be necessary to recognize folklorism as a timeless phenomenon and to account for it as an important factor in the formation of traditions.... Researchers of tradition will not be able to neglect this course of development if *Volkskunde* wishes to get away from romantic conceptions and ideals and to reach a more realistic understanding of the past as well as the present" (Moser 1964:45).

But reactions to Moser's plea were slow in coming. The tardy awakening to the question of cultural commodification gradually shifted the perspective away from the dichotomy of "genuine folklore versus folklorism" to a more integrated view of expressive culture.

Most researchers of tradition initially closed their ears to Moser's call for the study of folklorism, and when they did address it, it was to tie *Rücklauf* to the effect of applied *Volkskunde* (Kriss 1970; Schwedt 1966). Brückner recognized the broader issues at stake and argued for mechanisms other than *Rücklauf* to be considered: "The academic discipline cannot claim to have been solely responsible for discovering the broad spectrum of artistic folk cultural expression. 'Applied' arts, nationalism, economics and totalitarianism have contributed their share to the idea of cultural preservation and the mania of its promotion" (Brückner 1965: 212). Brückner thus implicitly criticized the administrative and political dimensions of applied *Volkskunde* and wondered to what extent "the folk liked their institutional presentation" (1965:213).

For many, applied *Volkskunde* was a thorn in the side of the academic study of expressive culture, and discussing folklorism as arising in that setting was one means to respond to Moser. Another response was to chime into the lament against folklorism and to condemn its pervasive presence in the mass media. "Folklorists will continually have to demand that journalists and reporters get scholarly information about the customs they report on, or else they should stick to mere descriptions instead of attempting interpretations" (Kiesselbach 1970:190–91).

However, many folklorists decided to avoid the subject entirely. Hans Trümpy's first formulation of the Swiss case is representative. "The existence of voluntary associations . . . makes it easier for the Swiss *Volkskunde* Society to nurture an academic discipline without preservationist tendencies" (1969:46). Folklorism was thus seen entirely within the domain of applied *Volkskunde,* as practiced in countless associations; academics could then ignore folklorism and devote themselves to the study of the genuine.

Yet there must have been a strong (unpublished) critique among German folklorists; otherwise, Bausinger would not have felt compelled to give a conference paper entitled "Concerning the Critique of Folklorism-Critique" (1966b).[43] Of course, Bausinger's *Folk Culture in a World of Technology* (1985 [1961]; trans. 1990) already had devoted separate sections to regression, revival, preservation, and historicization. However, in the set of theses he formulated concerning folklorism's critics he not only shook the complacency of some of his colleagues toward folklore in modernity, but he sketched the theoretical issues that would have to be tackled if *Volkskunde* was to do justice to the phenomenon. "The critique in *Volkskunde* of folklorism is more frequent than the explicit discussion of the phenomenon would indicate. There is also a silent critique—the attitude of those who pass by folklorism with silent scorn. My anti-critique is directed against all these silent critics and against all that is implied in the *a priori* rejection of such a phenomenon" (Bausinger 1966b:61). His eight theses, abbreviated, were as follows:

1. Folklorism is applied *Volkskunde* from yesterday.

2. First- and second-hand traditions merge in many respects; excluding one realm in research leads to a falsification of results.[44]

3. The focus on economic factors leads to an overestimation of commercialization. It obstructs our understanding of the *essence* and the function of the phenomenon.

4. The functions of folklorism have to be individually studied; attention must be paid to the needs of the individual as well as to the functions of the social order.

5. Folklorism-critique is often one-sided and fails to recognize shifts in function and perspective.

6. Folklorism is the product of role-expectations and its critique is to a large extent a critique of the democratization of previously exclusively upper-class attitudes.

7. Those who contrast folklorism with "genuine folk culture" draw the latter into a closed circle in which it inevitably mutates towards folklorism.

8. Critique of folklorism is built on the same premises from which folklorism grows: folklorism and folklorism-critique are in many ways identical. (Bausinger 1966b:62–72)

The immediate reaction to Bausinger's paper by other folklorists consisted of a wealth of historical examples,[45] but no one responded to the sharp social criticism in his formulation. He had accused folklorists of undemocratic attitudes in that their insistence on studying "genuine" folklore implied that they knew the boundaries of such a folk culture and that they implicitly wished to preserve their field of study within these limits. This approach could not help but force the genuine to become part of folklorism, and rather than broadening the scope of folklore studies, such studies narrowed it.

In an effort to expand the discussion internationally, Bausinger sent a questionnaire to various folklore institutes in Europe.[46] The questionnaire sought to document primary forms and bearers of folklorism, the position of academic folklorists, the role of tourism and the media, political dimensions, specific social groups and regions, and the historical development of folklorism (Bausinger 1969a). The result revealed some basic consensus about the secondary nature of folklorism, but they also showed drastically different valuations of the phenomenon. The Yugoslav contributor lauded the sudden use of folklore materials for a growing tourist industry (Antonijevic 1969), while the Hungarian voiced skepticism about the same prospects (Dömötör 1969). The Portuguese portrayed the phenomenon as something suitable for study for anthropologists, while folklorists should confine themselves to pure peasant culture (Dias 1969), and the American seized the opportunity to describe his battle against fakelore (Dorson 1969). The Swiss regarded it as a domain to be left unattended by the profession, in part because it was seen as a present-day phenomenon despite claims to its historical continuity (Trümpy 1969:40–46). Only the Pole followed Bausinger in describing the options taken by scholars as "either a complete lack of interest" or as "voicing an attitude that only defends originality"; he, too, felt that folklorism was "a sociocultural phenomenon that is awaiting its treatment by science" (Burszta 1969:20).

The descriptive nature of the survey and the inability to get to the heart of the phenomenon provoked Konrad Köstlin to disapprove of the course that the folklorism discussion had taken thus far. Köstlin proceeded against the trope provided by the legendary figure of Rabbi Ben Akiba, to whom the expression "there is nothing new under the sun" is attributed (Köstlin 1969:237). Köstlin regretted the widespread use of the term folklorism, in part because it simply represented a label for "anything representing an alteration of 'old folk culture.'" That label could not dupe anyone into believing that a suitable theoretical framework for studying the phenomenon existed. The term itself was not a theory, and yet folklorists, who suffered from the common perception of their field as being weak in theory, treated it as one (1969:234–39). Folklorists' reactions to the phenomenon, said Köstlin, had been to prove its longevity and to thereby reassert the traditionality of folklorism. Scholars thus managed to keep on talking about the same subject matter, using folklorism only to provide an additional set of materials. What folklorists missed, however, was "a crucial alternative, namely the question whether in today's society there is a different allocation of goods" (1969:236).

Köstlin's argument was ahead of its time. While Moser had already grappled with the role of industrialization in the process of creating secondhand folklore, it was Köstlin who spelled out what impact such new processes of production had. "Technology allows for an unlimited reproduction of folk cultural goods. . . . The technique of reproducing takes reproduced items out of the realm of any traditionality" (1969:254).

Köstlin's use of Walter Benjamin's modernist essay on this topic (1963), which has become a classic in postmodern cultural studies, indicates his willingness to move the discussion into a broader, theoretical framework.

In the same essay Köstlin links folklorism to the debate concerning the genuine versus the spurious. Two years earlier, an article expanding folksong research into the realm of popular song had sparked lively commentary in the pages of *Zeitschrift für Volkskunde*.[47] Karl Dahlhaus insightfully remarked that genuineness "is a reflexive term; its nature is to be deceptive about its nature" (1967:57). But Köstlin warned of the simple equating of folklorism with the spurious, and he pushed for distinctions between historical forms of folklorism and the new mode by which cultural goods are received and communicated. If folklorism critics resented that they had lost the class-based privilege to distinguish the fake from the real (see no. 6 of Bausinger's thesis above), for Köstlin it was a distraction to study the mechanisms in which older folklorisms differed from newer ones, or to continue demarcating the real from the fake. Köstlin pleaded for the discipline to drop the term folklorism entirely; instead, it should accept the mission of the field without further diversion.

> *Volkskunde* draws its essential boundaries as a discipline from the relationship between humans and things; as such it has a legitimate task and chance. If . . . it is humans who ultimately stand at the center of folkloristic research, then the question can no longer be what happens with these differently mediated goods [that is, whether we study them or not]. Instead one has to ask what happens to humans who find themselves face to face with these goods, and who are at their mercy. [Semantically] to continue calling goods "goods" does not come easy, and is a euphemism: the relationship of the folklorist to his object will not always remain a loving one. (1969:255)

In suggesting a greater emphasis on the human element in the relationship between "humans and things," Bausinger, too, sensed that scholars' infatuation with "things" had kept them from recognizing the human constraints, pain, or suffering inflicted by folklore. Bausinger's subsequent works showed a shift toward Köstlin's direction. Like Köstlin, he recognized folklorism as a direct challenge to the basic canon of the field; the core concepts of *Volkskunde* had to be reexamined if folklorism was to be integrated rather than marginalized theoretically. Bausinger's 1971 textbook on the history and scope of the discipline bears testimony to this paradigm change, including a long discussion of folklorism and related concepts. Referring to Adorno's concept of "culture industry" (Adorno

1991)—in English, generally recast as cultural commodification—Bausinger redefined folklorism: "[Folklorism] *seems* to preserve genuine culture; folklorism denies a connection between culture and industry even though it owes its existence to this very connection" (Bausinger 1971: 209). The last survey text for *Volkskunde* thus far to be produced in Tübingen works not only with new core concepts, but it also integrates folklorism (Bausinger, Jeggle, Korff, and Scharfe 1978). It may have been the implicit acceptance of the term by the dominant school of folkloristics at the time that kept folklorism in the discipline.

Köstlin himself tried to abandon the term. In one essay he assessed folkloristic thought on *relics*, whose function he saw in their ability to invoke a "simultaneity of the non-simultaneous" (1977b), a dynamic he felt had been touched on but not understood in the folklorism discussion. In reviewing the notion of relic, Köstlin did not simply plan to substitute an older discussion for a new one; rather, he showed the semantic linkages between the favored terms of different eras, hence pointing to the language usage examined here. Thus, all concepts, whether the "*antiquities* of romanticism, the *survivals* of evolutionism, the *remnants* of history, [or] the *relics* of culture area research," were informed by particular values (1977b:6, my italics). Of the nineteenth-century discovery and collection of relics, Köstlin writes: "Antiquities and traditions were—admittedly— means or remedies; they served a political goal, the recovery of the nation. The positive valuation of relics changed once progress turned against the past. Progressiveness assigned survivals only an heuristic value, and [such] things assumed a position counter to the present: remnants were proof of a barbaric past" (1977b:5).

In combining questions of social and political scope Köstlin reacts strongly to what he perceives as naively descriptive and strongly evaluative notions. Maintaining cultural artifacts belonging to a different era could not simply be characterized as dysfunctional. Rather, there were functions or needs at work here—for instance, in the continued or revived celebration of agrarian rituals or the decorative use of old tools—that called for the interpretive work of folklorists. Such thoughts led Köstlin to caution against the overly hasty burial of an older canon with its emphasis on custom and ceremony—the "Sunday-like" phenomena—in favor of an exclusive focus on everyday culture, simply to dance to the tune of fashionable "*Ideologiekritik.*" The questions of values and valuation thus increasingly reached the foreground of the folklorismus discussion, an issue that was crucial in the renovation of the canon, but one that could most graphically be demonstrated in purportedly "folklorismic" manifestations.

In a 1978 conference contribution Köstlin again advised against using "folklorism" as a concept as long as it simply served to relieve scholars of the burden involved in understanding "folklorismic" phenomena. Drawing from Anglo-American concepts such as nativism and cultural revitalization, Köstlin strove to present folk culture as a cultural category essentially akin to folklorism—an excerpt of a cultural and historical whole.[48] The emergence of a science of the folk appears, then, much like folklorism of the present, as a form of therapy, an attempt by a particular class and era to heal itself of a perceived alienation. Every age and every class, in Köstlin's view, will design its escapist themes. In the process, the search and the therapy suggested for attaining it become institutionalized.

> Psychotherapy and folklorism are today already institutions of escape, of the alternative. Both promise ways to find the self. But here begins the contradiction, the difference. Psychoanalysis explains to us that the prison of our ego lies in our past; folklorism promises salvation through the past [and] plays with the past as a better alternative to the present. . . . Psychotherapy demands the precise analysis of not only the past but also the present situation. Folklorism takes its point of departure from vague needs, but continues to suggest very precise offerings/bargains. (1982:138)

Köstlin characterizes the theme of escaping—longing, flight, search, liberation from conventions—as being something of its own tradition, "a part of the canon of being human." Its present form differs by being popularized to the point of being so established and so self-understood that it is not even clear "whether the necessity for such flight results from any suffering from [within] society [itself]" (1982:139–40). Folklorism, then, is a kind of game. The many options of folkloristic therapy for perceived alienation from everyday life constitute "an escapism which serves the end of finding the way back home. This home may be experienced as an alternative, but ultimately it is still the everyday, family, work" (1982:141).

Perceived in this fashion, the "game" of folklorism can be regarded as a stabilizing force in society. As such, Köstlin insists on the seriousness of this game that he sees as one of the big themes in any culture. "One strategy of folklorism is the stabilizing of self-understoodness, of self-consciousness, a therapy again. One's own 'contribution' is demonstrated, and this often in reaction to feelings of inferiority in regions which were, in more than one sense, colonized" (1982:144). Köstlin thus indicates the acute link between highly individualistic longings for selfhood and folkloristic scholarship, and that between cultural identities and budding nationalism.

Köstlin's attempt to describe folklorism as something innate to human nature rings somewhat true, particularly when he writes of the "original sin 'alienation'" (Köstlin 1985:61)—a phrase evoking Rousseau's "wound of reflection." The notion of "paradise lost" as the result of acts of self-reflectiveness would indeed appear to constitute nothing new under the sun. The novelty arises from the different means through which redemption from alienation is sought.

In her assessment of folklorism twenty years after Moser's work, Ulrike Bodemann concludes that "a reevaluation of folklorism is crystallizing [as] a specific form of cultural reaction" (Bodemann 1983:103). Ulrike Bodemann's model attempts to integrate "the polyfunctionality as well as the historical depth of folklorism," offering a framework to accommodate anything from economic manifestations, to the fusion of religious and economic folklorism, or to politically motivated invention or revival.[49] To Bodemann, it was the general societal conditions that generated folklorism in the first place which were of interest (Bodemann 1983:107).

Köstlin has been one of the few scholars who have been willing to place the folklorism issue in broader, sociohistorical terms. This constant, self-reflective questioning of the discipline's (and with it the scholar's) existence is hard to integrate into a working paradigm.[50] But Martin Scharfe, while borrowing some of Köstlin's terminology, argued that folklorism "had turned into a sedative" for folklorists who happily labeled aberrant phenomena folklorism and thus robbed the concept of its power (1986: 348). Scharfe sensed a dearth of moral engagement or social responsibility among folklorists, for he felt that "scientific explanations" of folklorism could come close to spelling out the acceptance of questionable if not dangerous phenomena (1986:347).

Folklorism, while not itself a theory, expanded the horizon of a *Volkskunde* that had remained confined to a bracketed, yet constructed vision of its subject matter. From an initial dismissal of folklorism as the spurious and manipulated, historical research had forced folklorists to recognize the parallels between scholarly reconstructions of folk cultural goods and societal efforts to construct aesthetic representations of folkness.

> If one talks . . . of historical waves of folklorism, referring to late middle ages, early 19th century and the present, then all the conceptual differentiations made between [folklorism] phenomena of the 20th century disappear in favor of general concepts of cultural change, of innovation and regression, of cultural fixation or of "renovation of selected traditions". . . . Then folklorism would be structurally equivalent to reformations, restorations and renaissances because of their conscious recourse [to older, better expressions]. *The construction of a purportedly*

> *old folk culture as natural and hence genuine in contrast to new folklor-*
> *isms as put-on, made, manipulated and hence at least suspect and poly-*
> *valent would be less a qualitative differentiation than one of historical*
> *consciousness.* (Brückner 1986:372–73; my emphasis)

Folklorism could, then, be subsumed in a broader notion of historicism; the threesome—"historicism, traditionalism, [and] folklorism"—could be evidence of the "museumizing" tendencies of present-day culture (Assion 1986).[51] "Folklorism is first of all a catch phrase," Bausinger noted, "much like modernization" (1988:324). Yet as much as various "theories of modernization" form a basis for further exploration more than they deliver ultimate answers, "theories of folklorism" established a framework that only begins to allow for closer examinations.

> The term folklorism should not be taken out of circulation. Together with its theoretical implications, this term provided a lever with which to better understand the culture of the present and cultural epochs of the past. This theoretical perspective is a progression from the . . . [earlier scholarly] attitude which froze in lamed reverence whenever a costume part, a folk song or an Easter egg was sighted. It is also a progression from the cheap distancing which avoided all "secondary" forms of folk culture as "fake" . . . and which failed to recognize that folklorism . . . was "a part of the lifestyle of the present" and therefore a very broad ranging phenomenon. (Bausinger 1988:325)

While case studies of folklorism, from tourism (Kapeller 1991) to museums and from music (Baumann 1976) to folk art (Greverus, Schütz, and Stubenvoll 1984), remain common, the effort to lay bare the dichotomy on which the term rests has grown more pronounced, the skepticism toward searches for the authentic more acerbic. Gone from the scholarly realm is the illusion of an authentic folklore.[52]

"Folklorism is not an analytic but a descriptive concept with a critical dimension; it has mostly heuristic value," reads the conclusion of an encyclopedia entry on the term (Bausinger 1984:1408). As a heuristic concept, folklorism moved the field of *Volkskunde* into issues concerning political economy, politics of culture, and folklore in the marketplace well before American scholars began to examine such issues. At the heart of this shift was not only the recognition of the false dichotomies invoked by authenticity; rather, it was the issue of aesthetic categorization in the dynamic between social classes and the impact such categorizing and privileging had on the ideological charter of the field. "Folklorism is not a picturesque, marginal phenomenon, but a form of cultural hegemony and appropriation of the periphery by the industrial centers, of the less-developed countryside by the metropolis. Through [folklorism], the industrially progressive parts of humanity taps those other worlds which they need for recreation" (Daxelmüller 1991:236).

Martin Scharfe's astringent piece "*Volkskunde* in the Nineties," penned in a distanced, "quo-vadis?" tone, clearly reflects the full incorporation of the critique of the discipline engendered by the folklorism discourse. "*Volkskunde* as a science has always been but a function of the main problems of a particular era, inasmuch as [the field] came about and lasted as a historical and compensatory organization" (Scharfe 1990:65). Like folklorism, the study of folklore to Scharfe, then, was only therapeutic and deeply oriented toward the past. *Volkskunde* arose from the societal woes of modernity, and its major effort was directed toward ignoring the modern way of life. Seeing *Volkskunde* as a compensatory enterprise involving "projections" of what folklorists claim to be "realities" makes Scharfe's pessimistic prognosis for the discipline declare that it "will discover the modern lifestyle . . . only when [this style] no longer exists" (1990:65).

German folklore scholarship has always been more historically focused than its American counterpart. Yet Scharfe's pessimism seems misplaced. The most recent themes at the biannual German folklore congresses— symbols (1995), violence in culture (1993), the industrial human (1991), memory and forgetting (1989), culture contact/culture conflict (1987)— demonstrate a deep concern, involving many disciplines, with issues currently confronting German society. Coming to terms with folklorism, and hence the place of authenticity in folkloristic paradigm formation, brought forth an initially hesitant but ultimately thorough self-reflexive analysis of *Volkskunde*'s institutional history and theoretical praxis.

Chapter Seven

From Fakelore to the Politics of Culture

The Changing Contours of American Folkloristics

The 1990s have seen American scholars and practitioners of folkloristics turn toward critical assessments of their recent disciplinary history (Briggs and Shuman 1993), new formulations of key disciplinary terms (Feintuch 1995), and reflections on folkloristic knowledge and practices in society (Cantwell 1993, Hufford 1994). This self-analytic vigor and determination to redraw and legitimize a disciplinary subject in the face of shifting intellectual landscapes attest to the intellectual vibrancy of an institutionally marginal endeavor. The effort to reposition folklore's place builds on the insights drawn from three successive initiatives launched since the late 1950s. Each of these initiatives—Richard Mercer Dorson's campaign against fakelore, the shift toward a performance-centered focus, and the study of the politics of cultural representation—grappled with authenticity's hold on the disciplinary subject. Yet only the last one penetrated to the reflexive awareness of authenticity's elusive and contingent nature, which was the breakthrough needed to explode some of the discipline's self-imposed limitations.

Unlike German folklorists who struggle with considerable guilt vis-à-vis their discipline's authentication practices during the Third Reich, Americans face a more subtle legacy regarding their "crimes of writing" (see Stewart 1991b). The politics of authenticity in the American socio-political landscape—for instance, in the realm of ethnicity—have relied less on scholarly legitimation, and disciplinary debates have found less public resonance, which is typical of a society that, again in contrast to

Germany, expects little counsel from the ivory towers of academia. Some academics, in turn, as the first pages of this chapter will show, went to great pains to preserve folkloristic scholarship untainted from popularized works, and once again authenticity (both of subject matter and of scholarly stance) was pressed into service, this time to ascertain institutional integrity for the discipline.

The moral commitment compelling folklorists to devote their energies to the field did not vanish, but those who chose to place it in the foreground have been less involved in the disciplinary debates discussed in this chapter.[1] There is, however, a distinct moral underpinning that permeates the goals of those who began to seek "new perspectives in folklore" (Paredes and Bauman 1972). It is a moral calling to penetrate to the ethnically distinct aesthetic of folklore in performance. Authenticity lingered in these efforts to legitimize and celebrate diversity, and only the next surge of scholarly interests, which combined historical scrutiny and critique of ideology, forced scholars to disentangle the strands of intertwined authenticity claims in subject matter, performance, and study.

FOLKLORE AND FAKELORE: AUTHENTICITY'S ROLE IN LEGITIMIZING A DISCIPLINE

Since the turn of the century, folklore had been studied in both literature and anthropology departments. While the "dialogue of dissent" (Zumwalt 1988) hampered the smooth growth of the American Folklore Society as an independent organization, both anthropological and literary folklorists nonetheless produced much important work during that era. After World War II, however, intellectual specialization, coupled with more rigorous institutional administration, marginalized interdisciplinary ventures. If folklore was to gain a separate place in American academe, at least according to the young Richard Dorson, the time to accomplish the task had arrived.

For a variety of reasons Dorson saw himself as uniquely predestined to carry the banner of a newly focused and exclusively academically legitimized folkloristics. His tenacious and argumentative nature, and his complete devotion to building the discipline at Indiana University and—through dozens of trained young scholars—throughout the United States, necessitate a consideration of his role in the development of American folklore.

He held a 1943 Harvard Ph.D. in what was "a new field," the history of American civilizations (Dorson 1969:56).[2] Having discovered international folklore scholarship from this particular vantage point, he considered himself a new type of folklorist.

> I stumbled into folklore from a training in American cultural and intellectual history, and . . . no other folklorist at that time had entered our common field through that particular door. Stith Thompson came to folklore through English literature, Archer Taylor through Germanics, Ralph Steele Boggs through Spanish. Consequently the folklore scholars of the '40's were comparative, or literary, or ballad, or anthropological folklorists. But they were not American folklorists; that is, although Americans, they were not Americanists. (1969:57)

The combination of historical training, Americanist interest, and discovery of folklore fostered in Dorson a Romantic nationalist tendency, expressed in many of his works designed to distill American or regional character out of narrative (Dorson 1959, 1964; see Wilson 1989). What he exposed, under the semantically expanding gloss "fakelore," as "ideological manipulation of folklore for the purposes of *Realpolitik*" (Dorson 1983:15) and perceived as separate from academic inquiry permeated his own handling of folklore. While "for Dorson, collecting and analyzing folklore carried . . . a profound commitment to an understanding of available cultural alternatives in the contemporary world," this commitment was coupled with an equally strong persuasion that articulating "the moral usefulness of a pluralistic society" could be best accomplished through the academic enterprise (Abrahams 1989a:27–28).[3] The legacy of John Dewey's pragmatism, which fostered the notion of moral usefulness, remained far less clearly articulated in Dorson's work than in the work of those he chose to combat, even though it was precisely such a commitment that linked him to the likes of Benjamin Botkin and others who were involved in activist folklore programs.

Dorson introduced "fakelore" in a 1950 article in the *American Mercury*, where he "mounted an attack on the growing popularization, commercialization, and resulting distortion of folk materials" (Dorson 1976:5). His initial target was Paul Bunyan stories, which he portrayed as not based on oral tradition but as literary fabrications designed to boost the image of the lumber industry. Dorson then attacked Benjamin A. Botkin's highly successful *A Treasury of American Folklore* and the regionally focused volumes that followed it. Using the *Treasuries* as an example of fakelore, Dorson suggested distinguishing between rewritten materials and properly documented oral folklore collected in the field from real people. The rewritten misled the gullible public, reinforced "existing stereotypes," and promised "some measure of fame and fortune for doing less work" than allotted to those who bothered with "pedantic annotations" (Dorson 1976:4).

Dorson defined fakelore as "spurious and synthetic writings" that posed as the genuine article. In using "synthetic," he added a term invoking the evils of artificial, industrial production to the vocabulary of authenticity (1969:60). Dorson's rhetoric aligned the dichotomy between fake and folk with the facile writings by journalists and others outside the academy set in contrast to the products of a legitimate, academic guild (1976:4).

Botkin was far too busy to enter the debate in the combative terms that Dorson relished, but, if he had, he might have pointed to methods, assets, and goals characteristic of Dorson's own collections of American legends. Dorson represented Botkin's work as "light bedside reading," appealing "to superficial American nationalism," and he deplored the lack of material collected in the field (1969:57), but much of his own research began with printed sources. Complete fidelity to tape-recorded narrative was a skill still practiced according to highly individualistic literary criteria. Dorson prided himself on the readability of his prose, which again tended to compromise the fieldworker's accuracy while emphasizing the writer's skills. Almost all of Dorson's collections sought to recover the essence of American character(s), which indicates that only a fine line exists between this goal and the "superficial nationalism" he accused Botkin of.

Dorson and Botkin endorsed a similar, pluralistic politics, but Botkin, resigning from a university appointment, chose to act on it through his involvement in the Federal Writers Project (FWP). Dorson barely paused to acknowledge Botkin's commitments, characterizing the FWP as "a praiseworthy project but *untrustworthy* in its methods and materials" (Dorson 1969:58; my emphasis),[4] a familiar term from the vocabulary of authenticity. To claim "untrustworthiness" is to argue for clear boundaries between methodologies when there are instead differences in the context of collection and the project's aim. To Dorson, only academically legitimized methods could be trusted; the FWP's reliance on lay collectors "tainted" the entire enterprise.

In hindsight, it is clear that both popular and academic interest in folklore arose from the same cultural circumstances. The Great Depression and Roosevelt's New Deal programs—of which the FWP was but a minor part—brought folk and native culture to the foreground in terms of story, design, and art, capturing the imaginations of some Americans during the

1930s (Bronner 1986:97). Popular publications and projects were as much a legacy of this era as was the interest in the academic pursuit of American civilization and culture.

Botkin, in fact, had considerable concern for methodology, folklore's social mission, and folklore's abuses. To him, the notion of clearly bounded fakelore would have been too simplistic, for he clearly saw the intertwining of sociopolitical interest and literary production. Botkin described his "approach [as] broadly literary and social rather than strictly folkloristic"; he pointed to the *Journal of American Folklore* as a good source for the study of American folklore (Botkin 1944:xxv, xxiv). On the other hand, he distinguished between folklore "as we find it" and folklore "as we believe it ought to be":

> Folklore as we find it perpetuates human ignorance, perversity, and depravity along with human wisdom and goodness. Historically we cannot deny or condone this baser side of folklore—and yet we may understand and condemn it as we condemn other manifestations of human error. Folklore, like life itself, in Santayana's phrase, is animal in its origins and spiritual in its possible fruit. Much of the animalism, of course, does not appear here except by implications because of the taboos surrounding print. What does come through, however, often in violent contradiction of our modern social standards, is the essential viciousness of many of our folk heroes, stories, and expressions, especially in their treatment of minorities. (1944:xxv–xxvi)

The issues of method and corresponding authenticity that Dorson later would attack him for were clearly far from Botkin's mind; he was concerned instead with folklore's social meaning. Botkin was aware of the dangers inherent in the simplistic endorsement of nativism, and he expressed his reservations against "the movement that seeks to make folklore the basis of an entire social or art tradition" (1944:xxvi),[5] even though a certain nostalgia was forgivable. Botkin thus perceived a duality in the human character that generated both spiteful and wise folklore. There was thus a sociopolitical need to address the spiteful tradition, as there was always the potential that in the name of "folksy" nostalgia racist and chauvinist agendas could emerge.

Botkin's thoughts on ideological ramifications as well as the similarities between academic and popular work with folkloric materials ran along lines reminiscent of the later German folklorism discourse. Dorson, by contrast, preferred to visualize battle lines between clearly defined camps, and Botkin served his purpose, even though it required overlooking parts of Botkin's own arguments.[6]

During the Cold War period Dorson expanded his attack on commercial fakelore—which he associated in his occasional antimodernist mode
with the American capitalist market—to the ideological manipulation of
folklore abroad, targeting in particular the communist creation of workers' lore. He used his arguments to attempt to forestall a legislative cut of
federal funding for folklore research, presenting the properly trained folklorist as an important servant of democracy, capable of producing genuine
knowledge and insight on the traditional ideas of the anonymous millions
(Dorson 1962). Sociologist William Fox correctly noted that Dorson's
self-righteousness was somewhat misplaced: "[He] failed to stress sufficiently that ideological and political agendas may underlie quests for and
uses of 'knowledge and insight' even in the least authoritarian, most
democratic societies" (Fox 1980:245). In hindsight, it appears that in his
quest to make a case for folklore as a rigorous, academic discipline worthy
of government funding, Dorson overstated the case of fakelore and underrepresented the actual academic virtues of his discipline.

Dorson's attempts to convince notable academics in other fields of folklore's intellectual worthiness proved just as difficult. Accused of ignoring
folklore or even of producing fakelore themselves, historians and literary
scholars unsurprisingly proved unreceptive. After a particularly dishar-
monious conference at the Newberry Library, Dorson interpreted the
problems in interdisciplinary communication as evidence of folklore's
own disciplinary standing. "If folklore were truly an independent discipline, as I contended, how could it be mastered at one sitting? The reverse
situation would never be contemplated, that a historian would pick up
anthropology, or a philosopher annex sociology, by reading a book or
attending a lecture" (Dorson 1976:15).[7] Dorson's account of the Newberry conference sheds light on his binary division of academics into those
who can handle folklore materials and those who cannot:

> [Some] scholars skilled in their own subjects . . . changed from academics
> to popularizers when they tried their hand at folklore. . . . Blair, a trail-
> blazer into the neglected realm of American humor, committed a chil-
> dren's book of pure fakelore . . . , Jordan, one of the few American his-
> torians who also taught folklore, . . . , wrote adulterated children's
> fakelore books. These scholars would never dream of tampering with the
> texts of *Huckleberry Finn* or the Declaration of Independence, but when
> it came to folklore they abandoned scholarship to recreate arch and fan-
> ciful tales as genuine embodiments of the popular genius. (1976:17)

Paradoxical phrases such as "pure fakelore" point to the dead ends of the
folklore-fakelore dichotomy. Dorson had used the dichotomy to point to

folklore's inherent authenticity and fakelore's inherent inauthenticity, yet by applying standards of purity or genuineness to the purportedly fake, Dorson rendered authenticity a matter of judgment rather than an inherent quality. The arbitrariness and ambiguity of the authenticity criterion were thus inadvertently made manifest by Dorson himself.

It is unfair to equate Dorson's struggle on behalf of authentic folklore entirely with a ploy to gain disciplinary ground and funding.[8] The successive arenas through which Dorson took his crusade against fakelore illustrate a widening notion of what could be included under the term, though the link he saw between authentic folklore and its proper home in academia remained constant.[9]

Dorson's rhetoric remained almost unchallenged in print, at least by fellow folklorists.[10] His formulation rendered manifest the latent authentic versus fake dichotomy in folklore studies. Properly trained folklorists were the only ones capable of recognizing, documenting, and analyzing folkloric material; the untrained, however, could taint such authentic matter.

However, the dichotomy between genuine and spurious folk materials would crumble as the static, text-oriented approach yielded to a process- and performance-oriented folkloristics. Absolute standards of authenticity could not withstand the scrutiny that eventually led to an appreciation for the created and invented as well as the conscious and strategic deployment of expressive culture.

THE PERFORMANCE REVOLUTION: BREAKTHROUGH INTO OLD YEARNINGS

It is easier to appropriate texts or artifacts than to conceive of folklore as a culturally embedded process. The "itemized" perspective allows a weaving of text or artifact into scholarly arguments and exhibits; revival and staging within the context of one's own artistic production or social movement were further options. With few exceptions,[11] folklorists around the globe treated their subject matter as "textual." The notion of "the folk" as an anonymous mass harboring and passing on tradition permitted such disembodied notions of expressive culture, as did the social distance between those studied—the peasantry—and the researchers. Many armchair scholars used manuscript sources along with local intelligentsias (clergy, teachers, or doctors) who associated with the "bearers of tradition" in their professional lives. Enquiry was organized within the parameters of scholarly study, and just as natural scientists isolated their "specimens" for laboratory scrutiny, scholars interested in folklore peeled materials out of their context for analysis and interpretation.

The entrenched, unreflective nature of such scholarly practices provoked a reaction, registered with a mixture of pride and bemusement by Dorson:

> A growing movement among energetic younger folklorists in the United States may be given the umbrella-name "contextual." While as yet they do not form a cohesive school, they do share doctoral training in folklore at the universities of Indiana and Pennsylvania in the 1960s; a leaning toward the social sciences, particularly anthropology, linguistics, and the cultural aspects of psychology and sociology; a strong preoccupation with the environment in which the folklore text is embedded; and an emphasis on theory. They object strenuously to the text being extrapolated from its context in language, behavior, communication, expression, and performance, overlapping terms they continually employ. (Dorson 1972:45)

The turn from a textual to a process-oriented focus was presaged. In the United States, class boundaries between informants and scholarly fieldworkers were less pronounced than in Europe, and many scholar-collectors relished contact with "the folk." Analytic trends, such as structural analysis intertwined with the rise of linguistics, focused on underlying narrative constructions. Field discoveries also forced researchers to consider how texts were generated, as in the work on Yugoslav epic poets by Milman Parry and Albert Lord, recorded in an effort to learn more about the genesis of Homeric poetry (Foley 1988:19–56). Both Lord and Parry remained more interested in Homer than in the singers of tales they found in the Balkans, but their recognition of oral-formulaic composition, their discussion of the apprenticing of young poets, as well as the individual predilections and styles of different poets fostered an interest in the dynamics underlying expressive culture and deemphasized, or even negated, the notion of fixed or permanent folklore texts.

This development of inquiry challenged prevailing notions of authenticity. Dorson could still claim that unadulterated texts collected in the field, and then transcribed and printed, constituted authentic testimonies. Authored texts, even when inspired by folkloric themes but composed by "literates," were fake for him. If it was not text, social class, or anonymous composition that made something genuine folklore, but the process and context in which the text came into being, then authenticity, too, had to reside elsewhere.

Genre Deconstructed

The examination of the concept of genre, the reformulation of the definition of folklore, and, most extensively, the ethnography of speaking with
its turn toward a performance-centered folkloristics contributed to the
search for such a new locus. The controversial *Toward New Perspectives
in Folklore* (Paredes and Bauman 1972) brought together aspects of all
these lines of argumentation. Authenticity, however, remained at issue.

Attempts to delineate boundaries between different forms of narrative are part and parcel of folkloristic yearnings for scientific methodology. The Grimm Brothers' differentiation of *Märchen* and *Sage*,
Antti Aarne's tale-types (Aarne and Thompson 1961), and Andre Jolles's
"simple forms" (1956), each sought to classify verbal art forms. Yet an
interest in how expressive culture was *used* ignited doubts concerning the
clear boundaries of folklore genres. Roger Abrahams, in his work on African American toasts (1964), was one of the first folklorists to incorporate Kenneth Burke's conceptualization of rhetoric as action (Burke 1950).
Building on observations of verbal arts in use, Abrahams formulated his
own set of "conversational" genres such as proverbs, beliefs, or mnemonic
devices (1968).

The move to a dramatic conceptualization of folklore in social life contributed to Abrahams's panoramic vision of genres as a complex web of
potential stages of performer and audience interaction (1976).[12] With his
twin interest in aesthetic choices and the social context of folklore performances, Abrahams made evident that clearly bounded genres were at best
a construct but at worst a hindrance to social understanding. A conceptualization taking into account the relation between performer and audience was thus vital to grasp how "performers employ [pieces] to affect, to
move, the audience" (1976:207). The interdependence of human actors
and interactions and ever-changing, situationally and personally adapted ·
texts was brought out clearly.

Abrahams eventually argued for an "enactment-centered" theory of
folklore (1977), based in part on his own rhetorical-literary heritage, in
part on Victor Turner's dramaturgical perspectives on ritual. Abrahams
foreshadowed the individual and actor-centered experiential orientation
of the late 1980s. Invoking collectivity, his vocabulary barely skirted authenticity yearnings that would manifest themselves more clearly by others, instead foreshadowing the interest in the experiential, even the sen-
sory.[13] "My drawing on enactment, then, is my attempt to find a term
which includes . . . any cultural event in which community members come

together to participate, employ the *deepest and most complex multivocal and polyvalent signs and symbols* of their repertoire of expression and thus enter into a potentially significant experience" (1977:80; my italics).

Dan Ben-Amos, in turn, challenged the genre concept from the vantage point of intellectual history. He contrasted the categorical nature of genres as they emerged in theoretical, Western-defined paradigms with the actual artistic communicative strategies that a scholar might encounter in the field. The scientific blinders of scholars prevented insight into the divergent means of organizing what Ben-Amos termed a cultural system of "ethnic genres." Ben-Amos's critique detects a tendency by scholars to essentialize:

> In our *zeal* for scientific methodology, we abandoned the cultural reality and strove to formulate theoretical analytical systems. We attempted to construct logical concepts. . . . In the process, however, we transformed genres from cultural categories of communication into scientific concepts. We approached them as if they were . . . *autonomous entities* which consisted of *exclusive inherent qualities of their own;* as if they were . . . *absolute forms.* (1976:215–16; my italics)

Ben-Amos thus doubly undermined the genre concept: he argued for distance from static, essentialized notions of genres, and he demanded that folklore be regarded as a communicative process rather than a string of items.[14]

A NEW DEFINITION — A NEW "FOLK"

When Ben-Amos proposed a new definition of folklore as "artistic communication in small groups," he justified his omitting the term "tradition," and with it oral transmission from his formulation. He characterized tradition as an intellectual construct and a convention without absolute existence, a socially instrumental rhetorical device. Longevity, as a frequently invoked aspect of tradition was, in Ben-Amos's view, fairly irrelevant if folklore was defined in context (Ben-Amos 1971:13).

Ben-Amos also linked oral transmission to the notion of "purity" in folklore texts:

> Because of the advent of modern means of communication, folklorists who insist upon this criterion [of purity] actually saw off the branch they are sitting on.[15] They inevitably concentrate upon isolated forms and ignore the real social and literary interchange between cultures and artistic media and channels of communication. In reality, oral texts cross into

the domain of written literature and the plastic and musical arts; conversely, the oral circulation of songs and tales has been affected by
print. . . . The notion of folklore as a process may provide a way out of
this dilemma. (p. 14)

This new definition came at the same time as a new perspective on the
"folk" was developing. Although American folklorists had never been as
hampered as Europeans by a peasant-based concept of the folk, as long as
folklorists searched for folkloric "items" the idea that folklore resided in
marginal groups threatened by mass culture prevailed.[16] Alan Dundes
made the radical suggestion in 1965 that "the term 'folk' can refer to *any
group of people whatsoever* who share at least one common factor"
(1965:2).[17] While overly broad, this formulation facilitated a switch from
seeing only static or dwindling folk groups to one of understanding that
individuals could be members not only of existing multiple groups, but of
groups that were newly emerging. Thus, Richard Bauman arrived at his
insight that the social base of folklore resided in differential (rather than
shared) identity in part through a critique of Dundes's definition (1972a:
31–32). Differential identity allows for a consideration of folklore and
conflict, a departure from the discipline's preference for emphasizing aesthetically pleasing aspects. Yet the interest in dysfunctional aspects of "artistic communication in small groups" was explored initially at best by a
minority of scholars.[18]

The harmonious view of expressive culture contributed to generating a
vocabulary of authenticity: "harmony" itself belongs to that vocabulary.
But it has been difficult to depart from the beautiful, as can be seen with
the development of performance. The first major accomplishment of such
communication-based folkloristics was the description of text-generation.
This brought forth a simultaneous celebration of the beauty of the process
and a lament of the loss of performative languages. The sense of loss again
fits the mold of authenticity-seekers and comes out most clearly in efforts
to find ways of representing performed text in print.[19]

The Poetics of the Moment—The Politics of the Past

The dissolution of genre boundaries, the shift to observing action and enactment, and the acknowledging of the universality of expressive culture,
each could have signified an end to the authenticity quest. If any individual could be a member of numerous, shifting folk groups, then authenticity could no longer be the rare property of isolated groups. *If expressive culture lived in the fleeting moment of enactment, then authenticity
should have been recognized as experiential, rather than static and lasting.*

Yet such insights remained unverbalized. On the one hand, the contextual paradigm was, as a revolt against the historical focus of many text-oriented folklorists, extremely present-oriented. An interest in folkloristic history, and with that an interest in the history of constructed authenticities, did not arise until later.[20] On the other hand, some performance-centered scholars also generated new visions of authenticity. Cases in point are Dell Hymes and the ethnography of speaking, and from a more mechanistic point of view Dennis Tedlock's efforts at rendering the spoken word into print.[21]

Hymes's ethnography of speaking was at heart an effort to recover the verbal art of Pacific Northwest native cultures. This effort was restorative, and authenticity intermeshed with the goal. With the twin emphases on recovering what could be found from languages that were almost extinct and laying bare poetics from an emic point of view, Hymes reinvoked the Herderian tradition.

With reference to Hebrew poetry, Herder had written, "Every language suffers by being thus compared with another. Nothing is more exclusively national and individual than the modes of gratifying the ear, and the characteristic habitudes of the organs of speech" (Herder 1833 [1782]:35). Two hundred years later, Hymes wrote that if Native American literatures were to be heard, read, and appreciated alongside the "great traditions" of world literature, scholars could not eschew the arduous route of linguistic and ethnopoetic analysis. "If we refuse to consider and interpret the surprising facts of device, design, and performance inherent in the words of the texts, the Indians who made the texts, and those who preserved what they made, will have worked in vain" (1981:5).

What has been gained in the two hundred years since Herder is an understanding that cultural relativity presents itself differently from one realm to the next. The verbal art that encodes and expresses such identity, and the exegesis applied to verbal art, occur within culture-specific contexts. To grasp the power of native texts, a native or emic context has to be laid bare—a context that comprises language as much as it does the sensual and social responses within which a performed text is experienced. An ethnopoetic analysis in Hymes's vein reveals the other culture's realm of the self-understood—the once implicit must be made explicit for cross-cultural appreciation and respect:

> Performer and audience shared an implicit knowledge of language and ways of speaking languages. For us, there is no alternative to explicit analysis. As with the grammar of these languages, so with the verbal art underlying relationships, taken for granted by their users, must be

brought to light by conscious effort. Once brought to light, they can en-
able us to understand the creativity and cogency of the discourse in
which they occur. (1981:6)

What distinguishes Hymes's ideological convictions most from Herder's is Hymes's effort to free not his own suppressed and belittled language and people, but rather the language of people threatened with extinction by white colonizers. Hymes wants to alleviate the guilt incurred
by Western cultures in their mistaken feelings of superiority and their
ruthless eradication of those cultures that differed from them. His credo,
set against the backdrop of colonial destruction, was to restore in its authentic dimension that part of Native American cultural identity that may
endure and endow life with significance in a much-changed America:

> Little more than a century ago there were many such Indian people,
> raised in the traditional culture, and those who displaced them did al-
> most nothing to understand and preserve the products of their intelli-
> gence and artistry. Indeed, many worked to destroy them. What we can
> know of the culture of many of the original people of Oregon owes al-
> most nothing to white Oregonians. . . . Oregon must some day acknowl-
> edge that its first, perhaps greatest claim to a place in the history of world
> literature is owed to collaborative work between Indians it ignored and
> scholars who had to cross the continent. . . . It is from work to *restore* to
> Indian people and their neighbors that part of the *original* cultural heri-
> tage of Oregon *which can be recaptured.* . . . It is possible to discover an
> implicit structure and content in them, and a systematic presentational
> form. (1975:357; my emphases)

Restoring and recapturing bespeaks a social engagement in the Boasian
tradition of American anthropology. Anthropology has always been
aware of its latent role in securing a place for those cultural Others who
were threatened with the loss of their culture, religion, identity, and even
their lives as Western economic and cultural expansion proceeded. That
Hymes saw his intensely intellectual labor as an effort at applied folklore
is consistent with his commitment to a social science that serves a constituency (Hymes 1974:54):

> Much of our effort with regard to tradition of our own country's past is
> *to keep their accomplishments alive as part of our country's wealth.*
> Much "applied folklore" is *genuinely part of the traditions* with which
> it deals, a part of their adaptation to new conditions of performance. So
> also close study of old texts may not be merely antiquarian, but the
> means by which *old meanings can take on new life,* perhaps partly in

print instead of the voice, perhaps partly in another language, but with continuity (like Homer and Ecclesiastes) nonetheless. (1975:355; my italics)

There is, then, a place and purpose to preservation, but it is of the meaning in the context of performance, couched in metaphors from the authenticity vocabulary, such as "keeping alive" or "a country's wealth" (as in the treasure metaphor used by nineteenth-century scholars). The continuity and cultural ownership of verbal art matters most; continuity and ownership support a claim or need for authentic heritage that Hymes regards as the democratic right and bargaining power of all peoples (1974:48–54).

But Hymes, like no one else, evokes performance as a recognizable expression of verbal art at its most powerful and authentic. The process of creating folklore is the core of his influential paper "Breakthrough into Performance": "The concern is with performance as . . . something creative, realized, achieved, even transcendent of the ordinary course of events" (1981:81). Such transcendence is achieved as the speaker or actor takes on the responsibility for performance. An ethnography of speaking ought to make it "possible to distinguish performance according to the key in which it occurs; some performances are *desultory,* or *perfunctory,* or rote, while others are *authoritative, authentic*" (1981:81; my emphases).

Here is the crucial difference. A Herderian paradigm located authenticity in the text, allowing those who read it to feel or at least yearn for the authenticity it held. The performance paradigm, by contrast, locates this power solely in the actor, who in performance reaches that momentary pinnacle where artistry and meaning weld together, gripping the performer and a knowledgeable audience for the duration of the performance.

Hymes seeks to reorient where truth in tradition can be found, and truth in a veiled fashion is equated with authenticity. Hymes is aware that "concern for authentic performance has long figured in folkloristic research," but he is equally adamant that such concern has not been "explicitly investigated or adequately taken in account" (1981:86). Performance analysis is for him the means to empirically document authenticity, for performance "is a mode of existence and realization that is partly *constitutive* of what the tradition is" (p. 86; his italics). The nineteenth-century project of tracing and reconstructing texts devoid of their social and performative context is rendered meaningless: "Only the systematic study of performances can disclose the *true structure*" (p. 86; my italics).

Truth and falsehood do, then, figure in Hymes's vocabulary. He regards his efforts to understand verbal art as an approach to truth viable both for the scholar and for those studied, and he has chosen a structurally informed path to do so.

> Where structure is equated with plot and content categories, such a perspective may suffice, rather, never discover its limitations. Such a perspective, I suggest, tends to falsify traditions, analyzing them solely for the light they may shed on something of interest to us, the history of tales or of peoples, or even the uniform working of the mind of man. All these things are important, but they do not include something essential to the peoples who shaped the traditions, the shaping of performances in which tradition was made manifest, through which it was communicated and made part of human lives. (1981:133)

Hymes's notion of authenticity is linked to the discourse on sincerity and authenticity offered by Lionel Trilling (1974). In presenting an interview, Hymes divides the recorded narrative into a reported segment, followed by a segment translated from Wishram, and finally by a full breakthrough into performance in Wishram. To Hymes, this breakthrough could be explained not only by the extremely reluctant informant's subjective assuming of the role of speaker, but also by his "momentary forgetting of the immediate audience," bringing about a *"sincerity* of the identification with the role of speaker" (1981:91; my italics). Sincerity of intent, assumption of responsibility and knowledge of tradition are all elements that characterize performance.

But paradoxes remain. Restoration hangs in a void, as a change, if not a complete disappearance, has occurred in the cultural context within which "the-to-be-restored" existed. Insisting on authenticity in performance must be juxtaposed to the certain knowledge that much Pacific Northwest narrative will not be performed anymore since no speakers of these languages remain. Hymes's recognition that continuity will in many cases be guaranteed only in a different medium, such as print, is a bittersweet mixture of hope and admission of guilt. The complexity of Hymes's restoration appears to be an implicit punishment for Westerners who caused the loss of peoples' expressive culture to begin with.[22]

From Performance to Print

Dennis Tedlock's proposals for the translation of native style constituted a methodological extension of Hymes's work (Tedlock 1972). Tedlock, too, sought a way of honoring native poetics and, akin to Hymes, awarding it a place in world literature. Once a scholar has recognized the dynamics of orality (as opposed to literacy), the seemingly unavoidable, warped vision of orally rendered literature in the eyes of both early Western collectors and analysts appears intolerable.[23] Tedlock amassed a wealth of citations illustrating Western arrogance, a most poignant example of which came from Oliver La Farge who had applauded an English retelling of Native American tales by stating that the stories "have simply been put into a familiar idiom, with restraint and good taste, and in some cases purged of the insistent repetitions and cluttering details that primitive people often stuff into their stories for ulterior purposes" (cited after Tedlock 1972:114). In the very next sentence, Tedlock announced that a "discriminating reader . . . wishing for greater authenticity . . . may turn at last to the vast scholarly collections. . . ." Discriminating readers recognize the literary value of native verbal arts despite all ethnocentric biases. But despite a century of anthropological collecting of native texts, something has gone wrong along the way from the oral performance to the printed page.

Tedlock's case is based on Zuni narratives. His call for (to him) authentic translations of style is preceded by an acerbic assessment of Frank Cushing's and later Boasian scholars' Zuni narrative collections. Tedlock barely acknowledges technological recording constraints and different intellectual paradigms. Aligning himself with the ethnography of speaking and ethnopoetics movement, he points out what he has found to be the actual nature of verbal art among the Zuni and the stylistic and paralinguistic elements that need to be rendered in translation to do justice to Zuni aesthetics. He seems hardly aware that what appears as "actual nature" to him will be as time-bound as was the framework under which Cushing labored.

The goal of both Hymes and Tedlock is the demonstration of Native American narrative's stature as verbal art; likewise, they want to show that with culturally different means, standards of beauty, meaning, and emotion are achieved comparable to those of celebrated Western literature.

> The treatment of oral narrative as dramatic poetry, then, clearly promises many analytic rewards. It should also be obvious that there are immediate aesthetic rewards. The apparent lack of literary value in many past translations is not a reflection but a *distortion of the originals,* caused by the dictation process, an emphasis on content, a *pervasive deafness* to oral qualities, and a fixed notion of the boundary between poetry and prose. (Tedlock 1972:132; my italics)

Tedlock's critique of past treatments of native literatures, coupled with new techniques to record narrative as it was performed, constituted but a new way to capture authenticity. His fundamentally dichotomous way of thinking can be seen in lingering notions of "originals" in his argument, as does his conviction that his proposal offers a means to avoid distortion and render the original more truthfully. Authenticity was never lost; it is just that Westerners' auditory faculties had to be trained to uncover it rather than distort it.

Tedlock continued to interweave the now customary and reflexive consideration of a particular fieldwork event with analytic insights gained from comparing two storytelling events. Despite his emphasis on the singularity and unique structuring of the event, he opens the essay with absolute ideals of authenticity that a researcher yearns for.

> For the first time in a year's devotion to the ethnography of Zuni storytelling, I suddenly found myself in near-perfect conditions for the witnessing of Zuni storytelling *as it really should be*, rather than in near-perfect conditions for the making of studio-recordings. . . . So there it was. *Spontaneous* storytelling was about to take place. Not a storytelling session scheduled in advance by a mythographer, not a session with an audience invited to be present so as to *simulate a spontaneous session*,[24] and not in a place arranged so as to be apart from . . . all the other random auditory disasters[25] of a household conducting business as usual, but a *session initiated by the natives, for the natives, at the proper time of the native day and year, and in the very center of the native household*. (1983:286–87; my italics)

More than 150 years after the Brothers Grimm praised the "spontaneity" of Mrs. Viehmann's storytelling, the idea of unencumbered narration still evokes a thrill in the researcher. The "real thing" is happening despite his presence and without him attempting to simulate it.

Most researchers fail to recognize that their own reflexivity and professional inability to let go of their purpose excludes them from the spontaneity that the authentic experience promises. Some like Tedlock, presume their very presence spoils the authenticity of the event, in the mistaken belief that the "real thing" occurs only in the homogeneous group context. There is a notion of "purity" or "ideal" research circumstance. The fact that in this particular session Tedlock misses both recording equipment and notebook are registered as an additional imperfection beyond the one provided by his very presence. Tedlock's case illustrates the peculiar duality brought forth by the competing authenticities of performance and fieldwork situations. Tedlock is vaguely upset at not even having a note-

book with him, but he then concedes that for the less inhibited procurement of data, training the memory was superior. This assessment he instantly reduces by admitting that it "still amounts to carrying around a
mental notebook; such a notebook may not be visible to others, but it does
make one more distant from the situation at hand" (1983:286). To make
this ideal storytelling event nonetheless useful for research purposes, Tedlock thinks of a number of analytic questions that can be answered precisely because he is lacking all equipment except for his watch.

Thus, one outcome of the performance revolution was descriptive.
Translating the insight that folklore was generated and enacted in communicative processes into analytic parameters resulted in scholarly text
production. Despite the new, in Geertz's terminology, "thicker" description that Richard Bauman's central essay on verbal art permitted (Bauman
1984), the ghost of authenticity lingered. Efforts by Hymes and Tedlock,
with their implicit insistence on recovering or attaining more genuine performances, stalled the transformational potential of the new paradigm. If
Bauman in his introduction to *Toward New Perspectives* had called for a
switch from the consideration of folklore as "items" to "folklore" as
'event'—the doings of folklore" (1972b:xi), the very nature of capturing
such "doings" on the printed page diverted attention from actors and
events. This is not to underrate the recognition of Tedlock, or later Elizabeth Fine (1984), that scholarly transcription techniques were literate in
derivation and stood in the way of doing justice to the aesthetics of aural
performance. But generating techniques for superior, contextually sensitive transcription nonetheless fed the old need to capture authenticity still
more precisely.

The Text / Context "Controversy"

The concern with recovering the most authentic element of culture, albeit
contextually and process-defined, created a loss of momentum. Those
skeptical of the new approach initiated a debate in favor of the traditional
textual study of folklore. Indeed, D. K. Wilgus's intentionally provocative
presidential address to the AFS, "The Text Is the Thing" (1972), "could
have stirred up a controversy that should have taken place but never did"
(Ben-Amos 1979:48–49).

The gauntlet was taken up by Steven Jones who mounted an attack
under the unflattering title "Slouching Towards Ethnography" (1979a).
Wilgus had argued that folklorists were attracted by the materials rather
than the processes of folklore, and they "certainly [did] not need to justify the study of any production of man" (1972:245). Jones went further

by invoking the old split between literary and anthropological folklorists (Zumwalt 1988).[26] He claimed that the new approach attempted to
turn folkloristics into ethnography, or worse, into a jargon-laden "behav-
ioral science," and thus "denigrate[d] the *inherent value* of the products"
(1979a:43; my italics). By presuming such absolute, decontextualized
value, Jones implicitly adopted the Romantic authenticity legacy.

Jones also insisted on the relevance of tradition to the definition of folklore. Ben-Amos, in redefining folklore, had purposely avoided the term,
and in his rejoinder to Jones he expressed concern that "traditionality"
not be overemphasized. "Traditionality is a temporal dimension of the
past, *either real, imagined, or projected* into expressions, beliefs or behaviors" (Ben-Amos 1979:51; my italics). Jones, however, presumed that the
folk shared the folklorist's preference for texts. "It is not the context that
man remembers; it is the text. The folklore text is the best representation
of that particular quality of folklore that enables it to flourish in the temporal sphere of human existence" (1979a:45).[27]

Jones was even more absolute in his claims for the centrality of tradition to the whole raison d'être of folklore as a discipline:

> For tradition is what tests *the esthetic and philosophical weight of hu-
> man expression,* and it is rightfully those expressions that have survived
> that crucial trial of time and transmission . . . that we as folklorists
> should study. . . . I have tried to suggest [that] [the contextualists'] ap-
> proach does not even come the closest to examining and explaining *the
> essence* of folklore. . . . There, in the traditionally *repeated* [his italics]
> text lies *the folklorist's heart of darkness, that crucial distillation of hu-
> man expression that holds the answers to man's eternal questions about
> his world and his self.* (1979b:53; with the noted exception, all italics
> are mine).

A clearer formulation of the folklorist's quest for authenticity would be
hard to find. "Essence," "heart of darkness," and "man's eternal questions" constitute impassioned vocabulary and metaphor fitting for the late
twentieth century, yet the words are ripe with allusions to the tempting
mysteries of authenticity that so many folklorists have always craved to
uncover.

Just as the German folklorism discourse initially was fairly sparse in
print, the "text/context controversy" was limited. But as in the German
case, "tradition" as a concept moved into the foreground and received
increasing critical scrutiny. As American folklorists turned to study large-
scale events, such as ethnic and music festivals, they also encountered the

rhetoric of traditionality. Together with the context- and process-oriented study of folklore, tradition's status as an absolute "essence" was questioned, catapulting into view the most introspective question that folklorists had yet faced—the politics of culture.

THE POLITICS OF CULTURE AND THE POLITICS OF ACADEME: INTERTWINED HISTORIES UNPACKED

American scholars in the 1970s began working more in urban and ethnic settings, arenas that challenged disciplinary notions of communal closedness and continuity. The realities of ethnic cultures in multicultural contexts challenged the unreflective use of "tradition," and by the mid-1980s "authenticity" had been challenged as well. If ethnics strategically deployed folklore and traditionality, to what extent had folklorists contributed to the political use of the very concepts for which they claimed analytic absoluteness? Thus, the study of ethnicity, the deconstruction of tradition, and the politics of folkloristics have generated extensive literatures during the last two decades.

Ethnicity

The concept of ethnicity already existed in the 1940s. But it was only in the 1970s that ethnicity burst forth in all realms of American culture, from cookery to literature, to music, and, most dramatically and lastingly, to cultural politics. The debates over "multiculturalism," ranging from concerns now referred to as "politically correct" to serious issues such as ethnic and gender quotas in the workplace, grew from the discovery of ethnicity and the activism surrounding it.

The relevance of ethnic groups to folklorists had been foreshadowed by William Wells Newell in the later nineteenth century. He suggested "collection of fast-vanishing remains of Folk-lore in America" as a primary goal for authors contributing to the then-new *Journal of American Folklore*. "Relics of Old English Folk-lore" was the first item on his list. The English by that time constituted a small minority among the floods of new immigrants (Newell 1888a:3).

To folklorists, immigrants were a potential vessel of genuine folk materials from the old country, coupled with the familiar folkloristic urge to save and document the authentic before the forces of modernity eradicated it, this survivalist interest left its mark. "The emphasis in Dorson . . . is an 'old' lore which reflects the immigrant's heritage and constitutes the 'pure' state of 'traditional' ethnic behavior. Influences from the new environment are considered 'intrusions,' as if they were unwelcome into the idealistic traditional pattern of the immigrant past" (Stern 1977:10). Stephen Stern associated the survivalist paradigm with "the devolutionary premise in folklore theory" (Dundes 1969), the pervasive anxiety that the genuine stuff of folklore was always on the brink of extinction.

The fear of imminent loss was being slowly undermined by research on the acculturation of ethnic groups. To the studies of "survival" came increasing evidence by the 1970s of "revival" as the ethnic groups' folklore changed (Dégh 1968/69).[28] Revival and survival are terms easily aligned with the notions of spurious and genuine; their use illustrates how students of ethnic lore struggled to master the gap between available theoretical formulations and the dynamics of ethnic processes in American culture.

Thus, a study of Italian-American funerals captures changes in actions and meaning within funerary rites, but rather than accepting the reasons for the changes that the author herself discovers, she nonetheless "seems to attribute greater significance to [continuity]" and hence adheres to "some idealistic model of what constitutes an 'authentic' Italian-American funeral" (Stern 1977:17). Similarly, a study of Romanian-Americans presents an elaborate framework for acculturative stages in expressive culture, but the "framework . . . does not allow for positive evaluation of 'new' folklore expressions" (Stern 1977:19).

The acceptance of ethnic innovation may have been hampered by ethnicity studies concentrating on narrative genres, for the study of narrative carried a large theoretical and methodological burden in establishing authenticity. Studying ethnic display events forced a realization that there were "active, creative uses of folklore as conscious manipulatory techniques for expressing factionalized attitudes" (Stern 1977:23). When Linda Dégh, trained in European methods, encountered the paradoxical combination of strawberry farmers celebrating a grape harvest, she finally deviated from her earlier insistence on separating pure folklore from "pseudo-folklore" productions and concluded that the separation of the genuine from the spurious was to distinguish between inexorably intertwined manifestations (1977–78).[29]

Ethnicity studies forced folklorists to question their dichotomous practices, articulated most fruitfully by Abrahams and Susan Kalčik, who spelled out why Dorson's exclusion of fakelore hampered effective study and participation in the multicultural politics of the 1970s. "It has become evident that this distinction between real and ersatz traditions is losing much of its ideological usefulness" (Abrahams and Kalčik 1978:224). The continuum between expressive culture and popular culture should be explored, with one admonition:

> Eschew the kinds of value judgements involved in distinguishing between the real and the fake and rather become concerned with a description of the change in performer-audience relationships and in setting and how these changes affect the form and content of the performances. By doing this, we will in effect describe the changeover from the folk to the popular, but this change does not need carry with it any feeling of debasement, for the popular dramatization of ethnic diversity carries with it the re-establishment of the sense of legitimacy of being ethnically different. (p. 231)

Folklorists thus drew attention to the enactment perspective called for by Abrahams (1977) as well as to the psychological and sociopolitical use of "ethnic folklore as a resource for the strategic manipulation of ethnic identity" (Stern 1977:32). By considering what is now commonly called agency, and turning to "new and more self-conscious expressions of traditions and on new self-publicizing modes of performance," folklorists would no longer have to "fear contamination" (Abrahams and Kalčik 1978:235).

In allowing motivation, intent, and even political purpose to be part of the inquiry, folklorists were starting to overcome old associations with folkloric authenticity—the "unconsciousness," already invoked by the Grimms, on the part of tradition-bearers. Large-scale, urban display events forced a close look at the motivations for pursuing particular forms. Frameworks for celebration became the focus of analysis, and the processes of revival and invention themselves captured scholarly interest (Abrahams 1981, Cadaval 1991, Manning 1984, Toelken 1991).

A second challenge was the applied work of folklorists themselves. The politics of ethnicity reinforced the dynamics that brought forth annual extravaganzas like the Smithsonian Folklife Festival and that would in 1976 contribute to the passage of the American Folklife Preservation Act (Green 1988).[30] While some folklorists had a mission to further the preservation and celebration of folklore and folklife, guided in part by their own love for the material and the people, and in part by the survivalist paradigm dominating ethnicity studies, others drew from historical examinations of applied folklore projects and their real versus fake differentiations.[31] Public sector folklorists of the late twentieth century by no means hold a uniform view on the issue of authenticity. In addition, some of the legal guidelines governing the appropriation of public funds to public folklore projects required a narrower approach in defining what warrants public sponsorship, informed by notions of "authentic folklore" that resonated with the lawmakers of the day.[32]

Some, in arguing for a reflexive use of the term tradition, point to the dangers of "the rhetoric of authenticity and antiquity" (Staub 1988:176). Authenticity might be used as a "qualifying criterion" for public programming, a problematic development, "because its images are part of the dominant cultural world view" (Staub 1988:175–76). Staub invokes a potent legacy—the perception that the study and furthering of folklore is antihegemonic. By bringing the marginalized or undervalued aesthetics of ethnics, workers, or other minorities to public attention, the forces of an equalizing, capital-driven, dominant (white) American culture are challenged.[33]

Increasing numbers of public folklorists strive to overcome the status of being arbiters of culture and taste; nonetheless, they accept the challenge of acting as brokers of ethnic folklore, aware of their role not simply as organizers of successful community events but as actors in the complex arena of multicultural politics (Auerbach 1991). If public folklorists do not make it their business to question the tacit dichotomous implications of guiding theoretical principles, no one will (Staub 1988:177).

Ethnicity and authenticity have grown to be uneasy partners in areas other than folkloristics, as Henry Louis Gates's assessment of "ethnic literature" has made plain. The existence of "ethnic" works written by those "impersonating" the ethnicity of others leads him to question whether books can be "categorized according to race, gender, ethnicity and so on": "The assumption that the works [such authors] create transparently convey the authentic, unmediated experience of social identities—though officially renounced—has crept quietly in through the back door. Like any dispensation, it raises some works and buries others" (Gates 1991:26).

Literary productions are cultural productions, and Gates proves wrong the assumption that it is "just a matter of the outsider boning up while the genuine article just writes what he or she knows." What to "the ideologues of authenticity" will be a "distasteful truth" nonetheless needs to be stated: "Like it or not, all writers are 'cultural impersonators'" (p. 29). Ethnic writing, like the production of ethnic spectacle, creates something new, even in its efforts to "authentically" represent. Authenticity thus proves to be contextually emergent, lacking the lasting essence that human beings have wished to attach to it.[34]

Tradition

"In folklore studies in America *tradition* has been a term to think with, not to think about." This was Dan Ben-Amos's provocative beginning for an effort to come to terms with a concept central to folklore, even if unquestioned (Ben-Amos 1984:97).[35] It was fitting that Ben-Amos probe the "content" of tradition since he had been a main "contextualist" striving to define the subject matter without the term.

It was not simply a reflexive twist in the discipline or the impact of the ethnicity studies discussed above, but rather a number of works written by sociologists, historians, and anthropologists that appropriated and even subverted the concept of tradition in the early 1980s in ways that caught some folklorists unawares. The sociologist Edward Shils, for example, wrote an entire book, cast as the definitive statement on tradition and reviewing centuries of scholarship about the term, without mentioning a single work by a folklorist (Shils 1981).

Far more influential, however, was a volume by the British social historians Eric Hobsbawm and Terence Ranger, *The Invention of Tradition* (1983). Their point of departure was not the longevity of tradition, but the intentional creations of auras of traditionality and the processes by which such inventions gained acceptance.

Hobsbawm's stance has been criticized for maintaining a dichotomy between unreflected "custom" and invariably constructed "tradition." The formulations of other British social historians, in particular Stuart Hall's concept of "residual culture" (1981) and Raymond Williams's notion of "selective tradition" (cited after Ben-Amos 1984:115), have been critically highlighted instead.[36] But at the time of its appearance, *The Invention of Tradition* not only generated outrage, but struck a receptive chord, particularly among those who had been researching ethnicity.

As paradoxical as the pairing of invention and time-honoring tradition appeared, the label fit the rhetoric and practice that folklorists encountered in fieldwork.[37] The notion of a "new tradition" was insulting only to the purist scholar working with a concept of traditionality that spanned generations. As Ben-Amos observed, it was the element of a *conscious* or willed tradition-formation that prepared the ground for dropping the term entirely—as in his own definition—or in altering its perception. Dell Hymes had suggested the all-important turn from a static to a process-oriented definition:

> Let us root the notion [of tradition] not in time, but in social life. Let us postulate that the traditional is a functional prerequisite of social life. Let

us consider the notion, not simply as naming objects, traditions, but also, and more fundamentally, as naming a process. It seems in fact the case that every person and group, makes some effort to "traditionalize" aspects of its experience. To "traditionalize" would seem to be a universal need. Groups and persons differ, then, not in presence or absence of the traditional—there are none which do not "traditionalize"—but in the degree, and the form, of success in satisfying the universal need. (Hymes 1975:353)

The rhetorical perspective so crucial to the performance school influenced the change that rendered "tradition" a need-based construction. In introducing the verb "to traditionalize," Hymes named "the process of attributing the quality of the traditional to selected experiences and personalities on the basis of correspondence with cultural or personal values and goals" (Ben-Amos 1984:116).

Anthropologists working on ethnic identity and (ethno-) nationalism had most reason to highlight the constructed nature of "tradition." Performance-oriented folklorists had been interested in the rhetorical use of proverbs or other conversational forms of folklore; scholars studying ethnic displays encountered the foregrounding, revival, or invention of foodways, costume, and dance; and some anthropologists encountered the construction and strategic deployment of entire "complexes of tradition" in the effort to legitimize ethnic or national identity.

Thus, Jocelyn Linnekin in her study of Hawaiian identity observed that "the selection of what constitutes tradition is always made up in the present; the content of the past is modified and redefined according to modern significance" (1983:241).[38] Linnekin was interested in the "reflexive consciousness of tradition" fostered by an "internal differentiation of society into urban and rural, educated and uneducated" (1983:249). Richard Handler observed the same kind of reflexive consciousness in the Quebecois nationalist movement, where selective traditional representations— he termed them "cultural objectifications"—were a central tool in the construction and display of a separate national identity (Handler 1988: 11, 13).

Handler's and Linnekin's separate case studies led them to formulate a challenge of both the notion of tradition and the scholarly practice of separating the genuine from the fake. Criticizing what they termed the "naturalistic metaphor" on which Western notions of "tradition" were built, they moved tradition, as Hymes had done, into a socially constructed, process framework. "The reconstruction of tradition is a facet of all social life, which is not natural but symbolically constituted." This reconstruction made it "impossible to separate spurious and genuine tradition, both empirically and theoretically," and even the intent and act of preserving genuine tradition invariably brought about change. Authenticity, then, was a quality that was never objective but "always defined in the present" (Handler and Linnekin 1984:276, 181, 286). From here, Handler forayed into the epistemological foundations of authenticity (1986); he then turned, together with William Saxton, to the ethnography of "enactments" of authenticity (1988). Both works were provocative, and they began, as much as they were acknowledged, to influence folklorists in academe and the public sector alike.[39]

By the late 1980s the invention of culture (Hanson 1989, Kuper 1988, Wagner 1981) or tradition and, in conjunction with the intensifying interdisciplinary study of nationalism, the "imagined" (Anderson 1983) had become central concerns of scholarship. In the process, the idea of absolute authenticity should have been revised, too, but except for increasing numbers of conference panels and a few printed exceptions (Linnekin 1991), authenticity has remained hidden, perhaps because the term itself never had the central, canonical status of "culture" or "tradition." Yet the increasingly rigorous study of the history of folkloristics directed scholars' attention to their own roles in devising analytic absolutes, including the absolute of authenticity.

History of the Discipline

Questioning "tradition" entailed an interrogation of disciplinary practices at the deepest level: an examination of the "tradition" of the discipline itself. Questions about various nationalisms and folklore's contribution to them were brought to the center of the discussion. Unlike Handler's informants and anthropological colleagues who had "expressed occasional surprise, if not dismay, at [his] decision to ground this study of nationalism in an analysis of such phenomena as folklore revivals and, more generally, the politics of culture" (1988:13), folklorists now more than likely would argue that nationalism owes its very force to the aesthetic powers of selected and foregrounded traditions. Yet, until recently, folklorists had become so used to locating the beginnings of their discipline in the period of Romantic nationalism that outside voices were needed to make the relationship between discipline and politics an urgent focus of study.[40]

Only slightly later than their German colleagues, Americans began to unravel the sociopolitical involvement of folklorists and the materials that they isolated for study. However, the analytic eye was trained largely on sites outside the United States, in part because the beginnings of the discipline were associated with Europe, in part because Dorson associated ideological manipulation of folklore with nationalisms elsewhere (1966, 1972:15–20).

The nationalistic adaptations of Herder (Kamenetsky 1973, Wilson 1973) and the case of Finland (Wilson 1976) were among the first instances presented to an American readership of the intertwining of disciplinary history and national aspirations.[41] Most of the essays in Felix Oinas's seminal collection on folklore, politics, and nationalism addressed cases from then-communist countries—the Soviet Union, Eastern European nations, Albania, Turkey, and China (Oinas 1978). Such studies chronicled the use of folklore to further nationalist and communist causes, depicting the folklorist as ideologue or as pawn in the hands of ideologues. Only Reuss's examination of the persecution of left-wing folksong promoters by right-wing politicians in the United States (1971, 1978 [1975]) dared to deal with the politics of folklore at home.

As in ethnicity studies and the discourse on tradition, several authors in the 1980s examined the intertwining of disciplinary history—both applied and academic—and politics. Michael Herzfeld's study of the relationship between burgeoning folklore studies and nation-building in Greece indicated that competing ideologies' "selection of ethnological materials" were at work, not just one "deviant" ideology, as many earlier studies had claimed (1982:vii–ix). Scholars who worked with survivalist concepts and notions of cultural continuity to promote a particular version of a national myth were not simply opportunists. "The development of an indigenous Greek folklore discipline was not a boastful mixture of cynical forgery and political opportunism. On the contrary, it was a sustained, often painful attempt to discern order in chaos, on the part of the people whose national identity was often threatened by the very nations which had appointed themselves as its guardians" (Herzfeld 1982:144). Greek scholars were shown to be engaged, to the best of their knowledge and persuasion, in constructing "cultural continuity in defense of their national identity . . . they assembled what they considered to be the relevant cultural materials and used them to state their case" (1982:4).

Irked by the tone of condescension in discussions of both political manipulation and fakelore, Dundes joined the two discourses in an examination of nationalism, folkloristics, and their relationship to fakelore. "Folklorists have long realized the connection between nationalism and folklore, but what has not been perceived is the possible relationship be-

tween feelings of national inferiority and the tendency to produce fakelore. If folklore is rooted in nationalism, I believe fakelore may be said to
be rooted in feelings of national or cultural inferiority" (1985:13). Along
with the Grimm tales and the Finnish Kalevala, Dundes chose to make his
point using Paul Bunyan tales, one of Dorson's major fakelore targets.
Dundes urged folklorists to "accept the fact that fakelore may be an integral element of culture just as folklore is," and consequently it needed to
be studied "using the tools of folkloristics" (1985:15–16).

David Whisnant, who as a historian was perhaps less inhibited in tack-
ling the political entanglement of the American folklore legacy, studied the
intricate politics of culture in the southern Appalachians, the region that
was regarded as the epitome of a genuine folk culture by ballad and crafts
scholars. Whisnant looked at the production of "cultural Otherness" in
the encounter between upper-class New Englanders and southern rural
populations. This constellation, at least in terms of class hegemony, was
comparable to the early nineteenth-century situation in Germany. Using
the notion of "cultural intervention," Whisnant documented the activities
of two "folk schools" and the peculiar encounter of the intervening folklorist's "romantically conceived culture" concept with the rural students
who were to be saved from the evils of industrialization and modernization (1983:13).

Most enlightening was Whisnant's presentation of the history of the
folk festival on White Top mountain.[42] He depicted the conflicting approaches of "lay" interests in staging and furthering folk music, and
he examined those serious collectors and academics who saw the recording industry as "a grave cultural problem" that "undermin[ed] the rural
and agricultural base of the traditional music" and "vulgariz[ed] an ancient musical treasure" (1983:184). Whisnant made plain the interventionist tendencies of both commercial and academic interests, each group
haunted by a different notion of the gains to be had from preserving cultural "purity."

The promoters of the White Top Festival, in their intent to portray a
particular white notion of folkness for upper-class consumption, were racist and exclusive; they kept the very people whose music was being celebrated from participating as audience members. This festival demonstrated what many late twentieth-century festivals could not avoid being:
"[Not] the presentation of a preexisting reality, but . . . a manipulation of
it, . . . the *creation* of a 'reality' tautologically certified as authentic by the
self-assured promoters who presented it" (Whisnant 1983:247). The historical example recalled by Whisnant served folklorists well. It scrutinized

the ideology behind the illusory distinction between authentic representation and intentionally created cultural spectacle that has been fostered
by folklife preservation policies since the mid-1970s.

Echoes of Whisnant's credo are increasingly audible in folklore, American studies, and history case studies:

> Cultural intervention is a complex process which has taken many forms
> and whose results are subject to a variety of interpretations. We will be-
> gin to understand these episodes and processes in our cultural history
> only when we look at them in detail *as* intervention, and not as benign
> incidents which produced a collection of slave songs, or a revival of
> handweaving, or a colorful festival. In short, we must begin to under-
> stand the politics of culture—especially the role of formal institutions
> and forceful individuals in defining and shaping perspectives, values,
> tastes and agendas for cultural change. (Whisnant 1983:15)

Whisnant and Handler have been credited with introducing the concept of a "politics of culture" into American folklorists. Their insights,
combined with the critical assessment of Hobsbawm and Ranger's "invention of tradition," and the selective adaptation of ideas from other British
historians and sociologists (Burke 1981, 1984; Hall 1981; Thompson
1963; Williams 1958, 1977), have brought a critical awareness of the political component and the subjective intentionality invariably involved in
folkloristic work (Abrahams 1993, Kirshenblatt-Gimblett 1988b).[43]

Ethnicity, the conceptualization of tradition, and the history of the discipline all turn in one way or another around dearly held beliefs in authenticity. Yet the concept of authenticity itself remained but a subtext in these
discussions, which points to a reluctance to accept the centrality of authenticity in theories and practice.

However, by the mid-1980s authenticity finally reached the surface.
The breadth of areas of investigation affected by the authenticity question
became evident in the publication of some of the cases presented at the
1985 AFS meeting; these cases ranged from tourist production (Evans-
Pritchard 1987, Kirshenblatt-Gimblett 1988a) to what Susan Stewart
wistfully calls *Crimes of Writing* (Stewart 1991b). Subsequent conferences
continued to feature discussion panels on case studies of "authenticity
production" as well as of authenticity contestation.

The critical self-examination and historiographic assessment of folklore's problems and assets culminated in a multipanel examination at the
American Folklore Society meetings in 1992, where some of the aging
"Young Turks" joined forces with new generations of introspective folklorists. The published proceedings start as follows: "Folklore as a disci-

pline is concerned with the study of traditional, vernacular, and local cultural productions. Created as a silent Other of modernity, it inherited modernism's binary oppositions between aesthetics and ethics, objectivity and subjectivity, authenticity and the inauthentic, dominant and minority, and global and local" (Shuman and Briggs 1993:109). Not surprisingly, the constructed nature of authenticity appears in many of these papers and was a key concern in Briggs's Folklore Fellow's address to the AFS that year (Briggs 1993).

Having carried out their own archaeology of knowledge, deconstructing the very patterns that constituted authoritative knowledge within their discipline, American folklorists can begin to reconceptualize their subject in the 1990s. Of paramount importance is the growing reflexive awareness of how folkloristic theories enter the cultural fabric and how disciplinary practices of authentication are appropriated by individuals and social groups. Recognizing the *lack* of a divide between scholarly arcana and the public sphere, folkloristic practice can cease to be a prison of ever-newly invented shades of authentication. Rather than remaining a separate, intellectually shielded, and "pure" field of inquiry, folkloristic work can be recognized as one among many flows of discourse on culture within society. As such, folkloristic work is by necessity both cultural and political. What performance scholars, then, have isolated as a key element in aesthetic performances also holds true for folkloristic practitioners—responsibility in the face of an audience.

Those in the public sphere have often welcomed the commitment entailed in such responsibility. They have always been among the most articulate voices in the discourse on the politics of culture. But unlike the American postwar era when the shrill calls for scientific procedure drowned out or demeaned the public work accomplished throughout the depression and war years, public folklorists of the present are an intellectual presence within the American Folklore Society, justifiably unwilling to be relegated to a separate track, and offering their own critiques of academic assessments of their work.[44] Those confining themselves to academia have often failed to recognize their own role in the cultural productions they purportedly studied. Nick Spitzer, a folklorist in the public realm, has perhaps found the most poignant way to articulate the interweaving of intellectual work and society, transcending the divisive issues of different kinds of folkloristic professional practice and different types of commitment:

> I sometimes think that all people are folklorists of sorts (perhaps one reason the term is widely, loosely, and sometimes maddeningly applied

by nonprofessionals) in the sense that we all consciously or unconsciously assess our relationships to cultural tradition through the metaphors we inherit or create. . . . In this view, perhaps cultural *conversation* is a stronger universal metaphor for our public practice than cultural *conservation*. In representing ourselves to communities through talk, we learn their meanings and they ours. We negotiate mutual representations in museums or in the media, on the festival stage or in the text. . . . Folklorists can be catalysts with metaphors, methods, theories, and acts that help to achieve a cultural equity that enriches us all (Spitzer 1992:98–99).

Chapter Eight

Epilogue

The dynamic that underlies our efforts is one between ourselves and those we study. Behind the discourse on what constitutes the disciplinary subject reside relationships between the self and the subject, the self and the profession, and the self with the self. Those who pursue folkloric material step into the legacy of inquiries that from the very outset have held the promise of encounters with authenticity, in whatever version discussed in this study. For some, this promise is the major source of attraction, for others it is an early disease long overcome by scholarly healing through the rigor of inquiry. What the preceding pages have shown is that shades of authenticity linger in the most scientific approaches.

> *Most of us who have worked in the field have had searing experience of this* us vs. them *dilemma. Is it ourselves we are studying? Is it somebody else? Is it the interrelationship between the two that we are studying? . . . That powerful growing together of us and other seems to me typical of folklore past and present, and I think will remain typical of folklore in the future.—Alan Jabbour (1983:242–44)*

On the margins of discourses on the subject there are fragments of personal testimonials that attest to the needs and desires of personal identity, professional ego, and sociopolitical commitment which suffuse the

> *"Folkloristic independent fieldwork": to me this still means "encounter with the folk." . . . He—who is endowed with the necessary previous knowledge, who shows sufficient reverence, who feels [such reverence] himself—may hope that while engaged in fieldwork, he will gain repeated*

> *glimpses in this or that intimate sphere of "folklife" with its strong expressivity. [Such glimpses] are usually closed off from "groups" of researchers and inaccessible to the "tourist," but to him who "encounters" from a distance and lovingly, who is often "ritually accepted," to such a guest [these glimpses] are offered as presents.*—Leopold Kretzenbacher (1986:1–3; quotation marks are his own)

relationship between "the folk and I." They appear in this Epilogue, interspersed and purposely set off rather than integrated, to indicate the multivocality of purpose that practitioners in this field have expressed.

> *I have to have knowledge of savage life, and it matters less to me where I find it, than it does in what measure I find it. Zuni therefore, while I confess it to be a patch of thorns in the side of a civilized being, is attractive to me because of the satisfaction it gives to my craving after knowledge of savage lore and life. . . . I owe a lasting debt of gratitude to the people of Zuni. They have been forging for me, during the past two years of doubt as to my genuine being, the keys which enable me to open their vast and ancient treasure house of Ethnologic information.*—Frank Hamilton Cushing (cited after Hinsley 1983:54 and 1989:179)

Histories of disciplines allow us to recognize that knowledge is made, not found, and that knowledge, once made, is put to use beyond the small community of knowledge-making specialists. In any field addressing "culture" this means, of necessity, that versions of a field's knowledge themselves become part of culture, filtered through individual and group interests, in turn to become part of disciplinary investigation (Beck, Giddens and Lash 1994:vi–vii). This process may be inherent to all inquiry, but it is defining for disciplines that address culture. Cultural knowledge-making contributes to the instability and transformative nature of that which is studied.

> *He who wants to research and learn during travels, should go on his own. Only the solitary hiker lives with the people, only he who comes by himself will be spoken to everywhere. . . . But not just the foreign people open themselves more easily to the lonely. We, too, when we hike by ourselves [are able] to concentrate within ourselves and work [productively]. . . . I like to*

> *compare this funny-serious work with the funny-serious profession of a cavalry trumpeter. The man has to be a virtuoso in riding as well as in blowing. There are folklorists who blow excellently, but they cannot tolerate riding: those are the armchair scholars. There are others who learned blowing poorly, and lose both tone and tact during galloping: those are the tourists. Only the lonely, well-practiced hiker who carries his own luggage on his back and his school bag on top of it, finds the quick glance and the never tiring excitement for restless observation.—Wilhelm Heinrich Riehl (1869:5–6)*

Edifices of categorization and scientific methods signaling rigor of inquiry are efforts to preserve and prolong knowledge; at the same time, these efforts work toward a truth not contingent on the context from which it grows. Such is the legacy of enlightened reason that seeks to build absolute knowledge from particularistic insights. The search for authenticities, with its promise of transcendence, lingers and links back to the divine knowledge that the Enlightenment attempted to depart from; the search also provides a discourse that legitimates the particularism of such scholarly edifices. Scholarly edifices are a means to distract attention from the scholars' immediate responsibility toward and involvement with their interlocutors, offering a shield against the recognition that, socially and economically, cultural knowledge is intertwined with the present.

> *It may be surprising if I claim that folklorists—those who professionally concern themselves with the folk—have an emotionally unresolved, an irrational relationship to the folk. . . . The love for the folk is the unconditional premise of all folkloristics, [the] irrational basis of the rational event folklore-science, [the] ideological basis of our logic. . . . The theme of the love for the folk, the presumed and drummed in love, is always also the theme of aggression against the folk. . . . How do folklorists deal with this love-hate relationship?—Martin Scharfe (1992:69)*

The deconstructive lens, with its focus on the language and ideology of the knowledge-makers, brings about a reflexivity that makes it difficult to continue claiming a disciplinary subject without continually acknowledging one's complicity in its construction. Yet this dilemma generates the necessary momentum for reflection on what the overarching goals of knowledge-making should be. The answers are not in content of knowledge alone but in the question of with whom, or for whom, are we making the knowledge. Authenticity quests easily slip into justifications of knowledge for knowledge's sake, an assertion of science's quasi religious hold on the modern imagination. Surely, at some point, we say, all this knowledge should be of some use. But a perspective that considers the production of cultural knowledge as a collaborative enterprise between the analysts and those who are studied will likely find meaning and fulfillment of a more secular sort.

> *But our work is rooted in recognition that beauty, form, and meaningful expression may arise wherever people have a chance, even if a chance, to share what they enjoy or must endure. We prize that recognition above fashions or prestige. And we see it as the way to understand a fundamental aspect of human nature and human life. . . . The roots of the discipline are in commitment to folklore, the materials, as they are in commitment to concepts and methods. We need critical concepts and analytic methods, but, ideally, concepts and methods can not only give knowledge of folklore, they can also help us to experience it.—Dell Hymes (1975:346, 357)*

Scholarship is fraught with the perennial danger of losing its focus through the particularistic needs of the culture of inquiry itself. Institutions of higher learning and public and private organizations devoted to the dissemination and implementation of insight have a tendency to ossify and, under economic and political pressure, to retrench into structures of knowledge that appear safe and necessary for societal equilibrium.

> *It is therefore important that we remind ourselves that "experience" itself is a deeply coded word in our own culture; that is, the very conditions of modernity, especially as pursued in the United States, value experience for its own sake. Not only do we hunger and thirst for significant doings, but when we find them, simply by recognizing them as significant, by thinking and writing about them, we may elevate such occurrences to a status that makes considered examination difficult. . . . Somehow, the appearance of spontaneity has been identified by us with our notions of the authentic self. But the value we place so strongly on authenticity in turn places a very heavy burden on us: in our heart of hearts, for how many of our acts can we really claim true spontaneity? Moreover, such questions of authenticity affect our perceptions of others, both as participants in a culture that privileges self and originality and as ethnographers constantly testing the behavior of our*

> *informants so as to judge whether or not we are being fooled.—Roger*
> *Abrahams (1986:48, 65)*

Field research, the process of collecting material for study, is a temporary escape from the legitimizing structures of learning and cultural bro-
kerage. If only in isolated moments, it articulates a recognition of the time-
bound and person-bound nature of knowledge-making.

> *Cynics will recoil, but the most important result of field research is that it*
> *proves human beings can meet upon the earth and, despite their apparent*
> *differences, find unity in affection.—Henry Glassie (1993:4–5)*

Malinowski found that searching the deepest essence in ethnographic
work brought confrontation with his own problems. "What is essential in
ourselves?" (cited in Stocking 1986:26–27), he wrote, showing just to
what extent the search for the authentic in the Trobriand Islands was a
search for the authentic in himself and in humankind—the universal
inside the revealing of the particular. For some, perhaps for all at one
time or another, this confrontation is too difficult to endure. Instead
of a posture of sincerity toward self and other, there is the attempt to
entirely avoid Rousseau's wound of reflection, transcending knowledge-
making about the Other to becoming part of the Other. At the other end
of the spectrum of "going native" is elaborate role play, seeking to observe and extract the most genuine by adopting the role considered most

> *[The] collector enters as long as possible an interaction with the folk, shar-*
> *ing happiness and sorrow with them, so that the people begin to believe in*
> *him as one of their own. Then the time of the harvest has come. . . . Be a*
> *Jew to the Jews and a Greek to the Greeks. . . . To him who is deeply caught*
> *in the delusions of folk belief [you should] appear as even more deeply in-*
> *volved.—Ulrich Jahn (writing in the 1890s; cited in Göttsch 1991:7–8)*

appropriate to succeed. In the arena of fieldwork, the fundamental concerns of eighteenth-century thinkers outlined in this study find a constant

replay. The difference between the postures of sincerity and role play is small. One emphasizes the experiential, the other the more externalized, material aspects of collecting—each with their own agendas and vocabularies of authentication. But both equally require a stretching of the researcher's self; both are carried out with great intentionality; both seek authenticity, for the self, for scholarship or for both; and each holds some scorn for the other.

> *What is the origin of academia's ambivalent attitude of respecting performance when done by "the folk" but not when done by a folklorist? My feeling is that it is tied to the emergence of the discipline as "scientific," and the perceived need to establish "objective distance" in the cultural laboratory. . . . Performing ultimately led me to study myself. . . . Becoming a folklorist has made me a more responsible and self-conscious performer. No longer do I throw around words like "authenticity" and "tradition."—Carol Silverman (1989:35)*

The ethnographer's magic has been thoroughly demythologized to make way for scrupulous historiography of the fieldwork process and of the subsequent cultures of ethnographic writing (Stocking 1983, Clifford and Marcus 1986). But beyond such necessary introspection and the concomitant sense of loss, detachment, or irony, the need remains for each individual to make sense of life and self.

> *There is an absolutely new perspective which does not look for the foreign in far away lands anymore, but in the very own deep-down and below. Romanticism knew about this night side of the world and anchored this dimension of foreignness in folkloristic research, without, however, offering methodological scaffolding. Thus folklore studies have harbored this dark treasure but could not . . . recover it scientifically. . . . The conception of the folk . . . moved the denied inner foreignness to the outside.—Utz Jeggle (1986:12–14)*

This study has suggested that Norman Mailer's "ineluctable ore of the authentic" is an escape, not an answer or a goal for cultural scholarship. I do not mean to invalidate personal searches for religious-spiritual or existential meaning, including the authenticities often inscribed in them. But

> *It is not that we as women fieldworkers—with professional careers and,*
> *often, nonconventional ways of structuring family responsibilities—do not*
> *understand the traditions we see; it is that we often understand too much.*
> *It is like looking into a mirror, a wavy carnival mirror, and seeing the life*
> *that might have been. There is a shock of recognition that calls forth deep-*
> *seated emotions—often unresolved—from our own life situations.*
> *Through self-exploration and questions and answers with our fieldwork*
> *subjects, we can identify and work on those emotions and, at the end of the*
> *process, reach coherence and discovery.—Margaret Yocom (1990:34, 37)*

on the basis of examining two hundred years of scholarly discourse, I would argue that cultural scholarship all too easily slides into turning a personal search into a disciplinary goal and legitimation. The result can hold both foolish and dangerous promises—from finding a linkage to the divine through tracing language's origin to arbitrating ethnic and racial purity—and it overestimates the humble place that scholars and educators are granted within increasingly complex, globalizing societies.

> *I am doing very well, I find my way back into myself and begin to dif-*
> *ferentiate what is authentically me and what is alien to me.—Johann*
> *Wolfgang von Goethe (1962 [1787]:445)*

In an address at the German Folklore Society meetings in 1991 Konrad Köstlin somewhat facetiously termed the cultural scholar's responsibility and accountability toward society as those of the storyteller. The metaphor may particularly resonate with folklorists, but it illustrates the interplay between scholars, the stories they spin for one another and for wider publics, and the audiences from whom and for whom they generate their work. Stories may invoke the past or project a future, but they are crafted for the present—protestations of scholarly remoteness from society's immediate concerns notwithstanding. Storytellers live on the margins, alternately scorned and venerated, appreciated and eventually forgotten, much as is true of scholars.

> *It was my first visit since my book about them was published, and my note-*
> *book filled with comparisons between what I had written and what I now*

> *saw, I complained to myself that I had cleansed the countryside: "It's brown, dirty, scruffy, poor. I was not wrong about the people. P is heroic. But he's more the hero because of the tattered context I left undescribed. I'd extended my bright view to the scene as though they—the people—illuminated it." Often my notes worry around this confusion: my scholarly interests keep intruding, getting in the way of friendships deepened beyond the needs of gathering information, and I resent them. Yet those very interests carried me over an ocean and twined my life with theirs, and I need them. I have not invented them to suit my ideas. Rather, they have helped me to invent myself by living daily many of the values I have come to honor and obey.—Henry Glassie (1982:613–14)*

In the age of reflexive modernity and global transculturation, ideas and insights are as much part of the marketplace as are more material consumer goods, although perhaps more cheaply acquired, and the business of being a responsible storyteller has correspondingly gained in complexity. Movie mogul Samuel Goldwyn's happy dictum—"Authenticity remains essential: once you can fake it you've got it made" (cited after Gates 1991:30)—reverberates far beyond the technologies and markets that have helped to render copied originality such a global obsession. Information, and with it morsels of scholarly insight, is disseminated through a myriad of communicative channels, the old accessible alongside and refracted into and by the new. Scholarly authority—contested even within an enormously differentiated landscape of cultural disciplines—may last within society no longer than Andy Warhol's prediction that, in the future, everyone would have their fifteen minutes of fame.

> *[What] you have to do in this line of work is to stop looking for that wonderfully gnarled old woman sitting in front of her foxfire in a just-right-squeaking rocking chair and accept the possibility that your neighbor's teenage son home on vacation from Groton may be a perfect informant.—Edward D. Ives (1980:33)*

It should not be surprising that some of the stories that have managed to cut through this complexity and gain popular appeal are those that hold a promise of authenticity for particular groups, be their present identity formulated around ethnicity, nation, race, or gender. My own storytelling is of less popular appeal. It advocates laying to rest the uses of authenticity within scholarship, and it constitutes my effort to undermine the social and political power of discourses on authenticity.

> *Club folksong fans used the terms "authenticity," "antiquity," "survival," "arrival," and "tradition" as keywords in defining tastes and goals. We felt that artists within folk societies held rights to their material superior to those of interpreters and merchandisers. . . . A few academicians have long branded attention to civic cause and moral issue as debasing the coin of pure scholarship. Others have faulted public efforts as neglecting emerging lore, treasuring fossils, and disregarding contemporary media's stamp on folklife. . . . No magic wand exists to dissipate polarities.—* Archie Green (1989:26–27)

Cultural scholarship evolved alongside and intertwined with nationalism, and folklore studies contributed enormously to the politics of nationhood through its particular discourses of authenticity. We still harvest the fruits of this combination: wars carried out in the name of national and ethnic difference, and devastating campaigns of ethnic cleansing. During the years that this study was researched and written, political parties and electoral campaigns in various regions of the world endorsed a politics or platform of authenticity, which to anyone having lived through the twentieth century should signal the frightening potential of essentialist dogma into which even the most ardent rhetoric of liberation can become transformed.

> *For me, learning to play the smallpipes was a way of repositioning myself, a way of being closer to undefinable essences, a way of experiencing some of what I wanted to know, a way of getting beyond detachment and into the realms of feeling, emotion, and experience from a vantage point many ethnographers have avoided.—Burt Feintuch (1995:303)*

Reflexive historiography of how and why cultural knowledge gets constructed, then, is far from an exercise in intellectual navel gazing. Rather than giving in to the temptation of constructing new, elusive authenticities, cultural scholarship aware of the deceptive nature of authenticity concepts may turn its attention toward learning to tell the story of why humans search for authenticity and why this search is fraught with such agony. A vast gulf separates the negotiation of pluralist diversity and the legitimation of multicultural difference. Authenticity validates the latter; acknowledging the constructed and deceptive nature of authenticity leads to cultural scholarship committed to life on a planet characterized by inescapable transculturation.

Notes
Bibliography
Index

Notes

1. Over the past seven years I have collected stacks of advertisements, catalogs, and columns on the arts, politics, and travel documenting this profusion of authenticities. Among the less ephemeral sources alluded to here are Marsh (1995) and Seiler (1991) for musical authenticity and a National Public Radio (NPR) program on foreign tourists in Harlem (NPR 1996).

2. In Milan an exhibit called *Veramente Falso* (truly fake) was shown in 1991; Salerno opened *Il Museo Del Falso* (the museum of the fake) in 1992. *Fake? The Art of Deception* (Jones 1990, Jones 1992) was thus far the most ambitious exhibit of this nature, staged at the British Museum in London. Myers and Harris (1989) also reflect the interest in forgery on the part of a circle of connoisseurs usually preoccupied with authentication.

3. On questioning the art-historical canon, see Belting (1987); on authenticity in the art-culture system, see Clifford (1988:244), Karp and Lavine (1991), Korff and Roth (1990), Price (1989), and Zacharias (1990).

4. On the "authentic music" movement in the classical music performance traditions, see Kivy (1995); on issues of (anti-) essentializing in popular music, see Lipsitz (1994). Adorno's critical theory still shows traces of a commitment to authenticity (1975, 1984).

5. Olender's *The Languages of Paradise* (1992) provides a useful companion to the early chapters of this book.

6. Among American folklorists, the twenty-one definitions of folklore listed in Leach and Fried (1949) are legendary. Dundes's textbook substituted an enumeration of expressive genres for a concise definition (1965:3). Ben-Amos defined folklore as "artistic communication in small groups" (1971), which served one camp within the field well, but remained too narrow for those interested in larger communicative matrices. Toelken in the 1996 revision of his introductory text finally demonstrates the profound interdisciplinarity of approaches to the subject: "Indeed, the famous story of the blind men describing the elephant provides a valid analogy for the field of folklore: The historian may see in folklore the common person's version of a sequence of grand events already charted; the anthropologist sees the oral expression of social systems, cultural meaning, and sa-

231

cred relationships; the literary scholar looks for genres of oral literature, the psychologist for universal imprints, the art historian for primitive art, the linguist for folk speech and worldview, and so on. The field of folklore as we know it today has been formed and defined by the very variety of its approaches" (1996:1).

7. Lears (1981) and Orvell (1989) have laid further groundwork since then, and in the 1990s a flood of works dealing with authenticity and allied afflictions burst forth.

8. Giddens disagrees with Lash's differentiation of cognitive and aesthetic reflexivity (Beck, Giddens, and Lash 1994:197). I would argue that for the purposes of understanding transculturation, Lash's perspective is conceptually useful, which is also evident in his coauthored work with John Urry (Lash and Urry 1994).

9. See Haring (1990) for an earlier effort in narrative analysis to problematize dichotomous pairs, including authenticity and its opposite.

10. Among the more widely received works are Greenblatt (1991, responding in part to Todorov [1984]) and Pratt (1992).

11. Consider such examples as Whisnant (1983); Fienup-Riordan (1988); Hanson (1989); and Sollors (1989).

12. On the ramifications of relic authenticity requirements in medieval practice, see Geary (1986).

13. Consider for example Grant (1993), a work containing further bibliographical leads.

14. John Vlach enumerates a similar, longer list of terms specifically for the domain of folk art (Vlach 1986).

15. Newmeyer (1986) delineates the case for an autonomous, value-free linguistics, while the authors in Joseph and Taylor (1990) convincingly argue the contrary.

16. The "history of ideas" approach has been used in folkloristics with greatest effect by Dan Ben-Amos, starting with his revolutionary redefinition of folklore (1971) and continuing through his reflections on the idea of "genre" (1976) and his surveys of "tradition" (1984) and "context" (1993).

17. For a lucid consideration of the pitfalls of Rousseau's philosophy and its political application in France, see Blum (1986).

18. The impact of the "exotic" on Western thought, art, and cultural practice forms a backdrop in much of the present-day discussion on issues of authenticity in cultural studies. Among the recent works on this topic are Bitterli (1976, trans. 1989), Kohl (1986), and Pollig (1987).

19. The German word for this rendering is *Befindlichkeit,* for which a decent translation eludes me.

20. Among the most important works are Cohen (1988) and MacCannell (1989), escalating to theorizing commodified travel destinations, Kirshenblatt-Gimblett (1995c); Hughes (1995:799–800) arrives at an idea of existential authenticity recoverable from consumable authenticities; on self-reflexivity in heritage, see Gable and Handler (1996) and Handler and Saxton (1988); for surveys, see Bendix (1994) and Kirshenblatt-Gimblett (1989).

21. Marshall Berman in his two major works (1972, 1988) travels a broader

intellectual and artistic terrain than Trilling, with a similar focus but perhaps a more utopian lens.

22. For a discussion on the connection between Sartre and Heidegger, see Fell (1979). For a study of how Sartre used the concept of play to get beyond what he considered Heidegger's moralistic notion of authenticity, see Gisi (1979).

23. The English translation of *Eigentlichkeit* as "authenticity" is thus broader than what is denoted by the coinage in German.

24. Influential Christian theologians such as Rudolf Bultmann or Martin Buber certainly held Heidegger in high esteem and sought to apply his philosophy of authenticity in their efforts to create a Christian ethos appropriate for the twentieth century (Boni 1982; Hepburn 1967).

25. This quotation from Heidegger's "Die Selbstbehauptung der deutschen Universität" is cited after Bracher (1970:268).

26. Robert Minder, a literary critic, examined Heidegger's vocabulary with the assumption that a careful analysis of vocabulary and phrasing can cut through the linguistic shroud of mystery. He argues that Heidegger's insistence on a "radical all-Germanness" in his writing places him in the company, not of the great German poets and thinkers, but of Nazi literature (1968:234).

27. Bourdieu's essay on Heidegger stands clearly in the French deconstructionist tradition of Derrida (1976) and Foucault (1972).

28. "Origin" is one word within this vocabulary that could yield telling points of convergence and difference between folkloristics and metaphysics. Adorno, who wrote extensively on art and music, considered the question of origin the "false question" to ask. Origin searchers of metaphysical, essentialist, or historical persuasion miss the central characteristic of art he suggested. "Art is a product of becoming" (Adorno 1984:447). Adorno's views foreshadow insights developed in American performance analyses.

29. Personal communication, May 29, 1995.

30. I am aligning myself here with Handler's resistance to argue for "one objectively bounded or isolable entity or body of discourse" within the study of nationalist ideology (1988:26).

31. Kirshenblatt-Gimblett's address as president of the American Folklore Society in 1992, detailing her view of folklore's crisis, appeared in various excerpts in Kirshenblatt-Gimblett (1995a, 1995b, and 1995c). For a broader theorizing of science, its nature, and its place in risk society, see Beck (1986:254–99).

CHAPTER I. POETRY, HISTORY, AND DEMOCRACY:
LOCATING AUTHENTICITY

1. Cocchiara (1981:44–114) bundles together reason (rather than religion and/or superstition), science and truth, encounters with the Other, and an emergent historical consciousness in his history of the field.

2. During the Prussian Enlightenment, confrontation between religion and

reason was partly overcome with the notion of "rational Protestantism." Thus, some branches of theology contributed to the Enlightenment (Möller 1986).

3. Dates are provided only in the early chapters of this book for some of the major figures, particularly German ones, discussed for the benefit of American readers.

4. Hartmann (1988:9–10) seeks to correct the "founding father" strategy in German folklore historiography. In assessments by some American folklorists, overly clear-cut linkages between Herder and Romantic nationalism have led to a somewhat reductionist view of both German literary and philosophical discourse and sociopolitical movements (e.g., Kamenetzky 1973; Wilson 1973).

5. Wolf Lepenies has discussed the German predilection for setting poetry against literature or writing and the fruitful ways in which this opposition contributed to the formation of thinking about social questions—and, ultimately, about social sciences (Lepenies 1988:203–19).

6. Vico's *Scienza Nuova* epitomizes the effort to conduct holistic science (in which human and man-made as much as natural and nature-made domains find room) rather than specialized, compartmentalized science. Vico was not the only advocate of this outlook, and his significance may not have been apparent to his contemporaries (see Trümpy 1982). On Vico, see Berlin (1976) and Cocchiara (1981:95–117).

7. Dictionary definitions of "sentimentality" are relatively narrow and fail to capture the consuming nature and seriousness of that era's discourse on sentiments.

8. Wegmann goes so far as to claim that *Empfindsamkeit* "would not have been successful, had it not shared multiple affinities with Enlightenment discourse" (1988:18).

9. A term occasionally used synonymously, which properly translates as "the sublime," was *das Erhabene* (Pries 1989).

10. This period has received scant literary-historical attention. In the canonical sense the poetry of the time has never been considered "great" (Brandes 1974). However, interest is developing in the communicative media used during the early modern period; thus, the many literary and moralistic journals in which the likes of Gottsched published have emerged as important works to consider. Estermann's multivolume annotated bibliography of literary journals and magazines from the fifteenth to the mid-nineteenth centuries displays both the astonishing breadth of those publications and their tremendous sociopolitical and literary output (1978).

11. This line of thought also was crucial in Jean-Jacques Rousseau's treatise on the origin of language; ultimately, it caused him to favor a virtuous stage of "savagery" that was entirely without language. A study of authenticity could focus on Rousseau's conflicting statements alone, but his voice will remain marginal to the present discussion (see Ferrara 1993). For an excellent work on Rousseau's rhetoric, see Blum (1986); on Rousseau's notion of political authenticity, "the condition in which citizens are transparent to each other," see Hunt (1984:44–46); also consider de Zengotita (1989:76–86). The "literature as lie" concept is older than Rousseau, going back to Plato (see Bauman 1984:9).

12. The works appeared ten years after Gottsched's own "attempt at a critical art of poetry" (1730), and both works rephrased Gottsched's title.

13. Bodmer revised and reprinted "Discourses of the Painters" in 1746 and published them as *Der Mahler der Sitten* (The Painter of Morés). The massive changes that Bodmer undertook indicate how much the ideas advanced in the 1720s by him and his circle had become acceptable, but also how Bodmer had moved from an Enlightenment position to become a proponent of *Empfindsamkeit.*

14. The "Discourses" illustrate the groping for terms that characterize sincerity and authenticity, an effort that Trilling (1974) makes for the same period using French and English sources.

15. The term used in German today is *Binnenexotik;* "binnen" refers to "inland," or "not across an ocean," and the term nicely captures the discovery that the exotic was not necessarily at the far end of the globe, to be reached only after a great journey.

16. Möser produced two important sets of essays, "Attempt at Some Paintings of Our Time," written between 1743 and 1763 (note the similarity to the Bodmer/Breitinger journal), and "Patriotic Fantasies," published beginning in 1766 (reprinted in Möser 1944). Müller produced a cultural history of the Swiss, a work that used oral literature and archival materials. It became an important element in the early search for new Swiss statehood (1786–1808).

17. Berman (1970) offers a reading of Rousseau's work in conjunction with the goals of the French Revolution. Blum (1986) constitutes a more critical assessment of the "sincerity" in Rousseau's own efforts at reaching such authenticity.

18. On the emergence of a cultural statistics in conjunction with governmental efforts to understand and rule cultural diversity, see Linke (1990) and Könenkamp (1988b).

19. Köstlin (1977a) argues that the folk-as-peasant category existed under feudal conditions, but it was constructed conceptually only when the reality of this social class began to break apart. For a concise summary of Herder's relationship to folkloristics and a listing of his central works, see Poltermann (1990).

20. See Hartmann (1988), Handler (1986), and, more comprehensively, Cocchiara (1981:77–134).

21. See Willson (1964:48–71) and Feldman and Richardson (1972:349–64). The impact of the Indian image on literary production and of Sanskrit study on mythological and philological scholarship cannot be followed in detail here. It is interesting to note that in the United States, too, the fascination with India eventually finds a complement in the theorizing of the (native) "common man" (see chapter 3).

22. Sturm und Drang cannot be reduced to its interest in the simplicity and genuineness of the folk, but this aspect is the most important one to my investigation. Voices from within this movement—Herder's, for instance—also crucially shaped an emergent differentiation of self, soul, and psyche, exploring alternate states of being of the mind (see Kaufmann 1995).

23. Historians prefer to see Herder as a pre-Romantic. A sociologically more astute periodization of history places him within the emerging philosophy of the

bourgeoisie, seeking to solidify the ideological basis of civil society. I am indebted to Doris Kaufmann for this observation.

24. For contextualizations of Herder, see Berlin (1976), Cocchiara (1981, part 2), and Pross (1987). Heizmann (1981) examines the poetic aesthetics of the young Herder relative to notions of history and anthropology in the eighteenth century. Grawe (1967) assesses Herder from the perspective of modern cultural anthropology, placing his work in the category of philosophical anthropology and arguing that his humanistic idealism continues to be the philosophical foundation of the anthropological enterprise. Becker (1987) focuses on Herder's literary and historical impact.

25. German *Volkskunde* was not, however, solely influenced by Herder. Rather, the discipline grew out of the dual influence of philology (where Herder's influence was felt more acutely) and social statistics (Linke 1990).

26. Herder's extensive work is varied and not always clear or consistent. Charles Taylor argues that Herder's language philosophy, with its emphasis on expressive power, shaped the interest of generations of scholars in twentieth-century language and communication. The "expressivist critique" facilitated by Herder continues to be direly needed: "As a civilization, we live with a compromise. In our scientific understanding, we tend to be men of the Enlightenment, and we accept the predominance of Enlightenment—one might say, utilitarian—values in setting the parameters of public policy. . . . But people experience things in expressive terms: something is 'more me'; or I feel fulfilled by this, not by that; or that prospect really 'speaks to me'" (Taylor 1985:147).

27. The identity of the recipient of the letters is not evident from the latest critical edition of the text (Pross 1984:821–44). The letter format was a literary convention of the time (Flemming 1988:713). The 1906 volume, in which the "letters on Ossian" appeared, contained poetry by Goethe, a piece by Justus Möser, and Herder's reflections on Shakespeare. Pross considers Herder's juxtaposition of Ossian and Shakespeare particularly relevant, in that "the study of Shakespeare takes on the shape of an attempt [to characterize] the philosophical history of the modern artist and his relationship to original poetry" (1984:821). A number of other fragments in this volume further establish Herder's preoccupation with original poetry. Herder also appears to have been troubled by the notion of having "a voice" or even an acclaimed voice in cultural and literary discourse. His early *Fragmente* on literature and language were published anonymously, and he was greatly upset when his identity became known (Haym 1860). Thanks to Harold Mah for sharing his research on Herder's identity troubles.

28. My translations are largely based on Franz's edition (Herder 1906), although I also checked the wording in Pross's 1984 edition, which, in turn, is based on the classic Supphan edition (Herder 1877–1913); in some instances the two editions differ substantially.

29. Herder must have been aware that the aesthetic shift he was endorsing foreshadowed changes in the politics of social class, although he expressed this recognition only in a veiled way: "Because I know that this letter will not get into the hands of one of the lords of our time who wrinkles his nose at antiquated

rhyme or expression, because I know that you search everywhere with me for more nature than art, I do not have any reservations about sending you a sad and longing love song from a collection of poorly done craftsmen's songs" (1906 [1773]:21).

30. The inadvertent invocation of gender in this quotation opens up authenticity's gendered nature, which latently simmers in this search and warrants separate inquiry.

31. The collector Friedrich David Gräter found texts of Swiss cowherding songs in a medical journal, where they had "awakened the interest of pathologists" because of "the marvellous, homesickness-inducing power of these songs" (Lohre 1902:115).

32. On the Romantic movement's turn toward a national rather than universal authenticity, see Cocchiara (1981, esp. part 3). Wilke (1978:129–205) covers the differentiation of the nationalist and the individualist routes in the Romantic pursuit as they emerged from journals.

CHAPTER 2. FROM EXPERIENCE TO REPRESENTATION:
THE ONSET OF A SCIENTIFIC SEARCH FOR AUTHENTICITY

1. An earlier version of this chapter appeared as "Diverging Paths in the Scientific Search for Authenticity," *Journal of Folklore Research* (1993).

2. Thanks are due to Richard Bauman for once asking whether I knew anything about Carl Lachmann. I started digging and found quite a bit, indeed.

3. Folk art debates illustrate this poignantly, for folk art intersects with the strongly "authorial" notion of authenticity present in the discourse on "high cultural art." For an open confrontation with these legacies, see Vlach and Bronner (1986).

4. Péter Niedermüller observes a similar strategy for a later period in Hungary: "This conceptual organization automatically eliminated the alien urban society from the category of 'folk' which served as the basis for the nation" (1989:50).

5. For the United States, the arbitrariness of this differentiating process is convincingly demonstrated by Levine (1988).

6. In both the United States and Germany the "discovery" or deconstruction of the nationalist legacy of folkloristics occurred hand in hand with the discovery of "fakelore" and folklorismus (Bendix 1988).

7. On Alexander von Humboldt's impact on European visions of South America, see Pratt (1992:111–43).

8. See Leitzmann (1908) for the Humboldt-Schlegel correspondence.

9. My admiration for the Grimms grew as I reacquainted myself with the wealth of work that they carried out in an age when the production of writing and the access to books and manuscripts were so limited. Their correspondence indicates how willingly they shared knowledge and friendship, despite often less than agreeable living circumstances. For a concise summary of the Grimms' works, see Denecke (1990).

10. The claim that the Grimms were the "fathers" or originators of *Volks-*

kunde has been amply disputed. Standard texts (Brednich ed. 1988) discuss the complex web of voices and sociopolitical circumstances that contributed to the emergence of the discipline.

11. The Grimms had contributed to the *Wunderhorn* and sent the first manuscript of their tales to Brentano. Only after Brentano failed to act on it did they proceed on their own. For a punctilious assessment of the first edition of the *KHM*, see Heinz Rölleke's revised edition (Grimm and Grimm 1986). Assiduous editorial efforts such as Rölleke's *also* point to a keen desire to uncover an authentic spirit— namely, that of the Grimms. The whole debate over the Grimms' editorial practice, fueled especially by John Ellis's work (1983), constitutes a long-continued battle over "truthfulness" in scholarship and achievement of the "correct" textual authenticity in the representation of folklore materials (Briggs 1993).

12. Johann Peter Hebel's almanac stories, collectively published as *Schatzkästlein des Rheinischen Volksfreundes* (little treasure chest of the Rhineland's friend) 1980 (1811), set a precedent for titling collections of such mixed natures with the term "treasure chest."

13. Clifford Geertz's observation on nationalist success in twentieth-century Third World countries is pertinent: "It is not that nothing has happened, that a new era has not been entered. Rather, that era having been entered, it is necessary now to live in it rather than merely imagine it, and that is inevitably a deflating experience" (1973:235).

14. The organic trope has characterized the conceptualization of history since the post-Enlightenment revolt against rationalist approaches (White 1973:68– 80). White acknowledges that this rhetorical strategy has found adherents ever since the appearance of "organicist historicism" such as Herder's; the strategy also is evident in White's treatment of the tropes of "The Wild Man" and "The Noble Savage" (White 1978:150–95).

15. Many recent sensationalist "discoveries" of the Grimm's editorial practices probably would have puzzled the Grimms themselves (see, in particular, Ellis 1983). Our age certainly needed to demythologize the way in which the story of the Grimms over the last 150 years had come to portray them as collectors in the field. Yet our "discoveries" illustrate mistakes and a lack of historical sensibility in measuring the Grimms' effort by the standards in fieldwork and ethics of our times, as much as they document what, for the Grimms themselves, was a necessary step in rendering oral materials into aesthetically pleasing and edifying literary materials. On this point, see also Kamenetsky (1992:110).

16. Drawing from the Grimms' later thoughts on storytelling and its relationship to continuity of tradition, Kamenetsky summarizes their appreciation of storytellers: "Good storytellers were close to nature and tradition and were gifted by the power of intuition and a spontaneous expression while possessing a certain simplicity of mind and power of vision. Sharing the naïvete of ancient bards, they were unconscious of themselves as artists. They needed a strong intuition to get as closely as possible to the core of tales, but they also needed a creative mind to activate the dynamics of language" (1992:109).

Kamenetsky's legitimate effort on occasion to contextualize and restore the Grimms' accomplishments abandons the intellectual evolutions and changes of the brothers in favor of essentializing their stance.

17. For a discussion of the Grimms' ideology of an emerging bourgeoisie, see Zipes (1988:19–23).

18. Hermann Bausinger described the transformation of the Romantic charter evident in the *KHM:* "The construction of the unchanging-natural cannot be maintained completely. In place of nature appears the search for lost nature. An analysis of the folktale style of the Grimms shows how the naïve tone is replaced by a sentimentalistic one within which the world of the folktale is something elevated and special. . . . The Grimm style . . . gives to the individual alienated from 'nature' both evidence of naïve nature and harmony with his sentimentalistic longing" (1960:283).

19. India's role in German Romanticism (Willson 1964) forms the "exotic" counterpart of the "native" interests at work in the discourse treated here.

20. The main reference work on German journals and magazines from the late seventeenth century to the mid-nineteenth century is Estermann (1978); see also Wilke (1978).

21. The Grimms' decision to stand up to unconstitutional actions of the new Duke of Hesse cost them their employment (Kamenetsky 1992:21–25). Their colleagues, while expressing admiration for the Grimms' political courage, failed to produce new employment for them. Among their contemporaries and folklore forebears, Ludwig Uhland far more clearly bridged the competing interests of poetry, scholarship, and patriotic conviction, as well as popularization (Bausinger 1988).

22. Herder's essay (1978 [1770]) was also a response to Rousseau's statement on the same question, which in turn had shaped French Revolutionary discourse.

23. Grimm cited this excerpt in Latin. I cite the translation from The Loeb Classical Library, vol. 1, Ammenius Marcellinus (1963 [1935]:179–81). Thanks to Beatrice Locher for tracking down this translation.

24. Blanket statements about individual versus communal genius are hard to maintain. Although Herder did emphasize the power of *Naturpoesie* and its ability to communicate a *Volksgeist,* he also celebrated individual genius, such as Ossian, Shakespeare, or Homer—albeit for their very ability to give perfect expression to the *Volksgeist.* See Heizmann (1981:2–103).

25. For a history of contemporaneous discourse on the high cultural versus the popular in England, see Shiach (1989); for the United States, see Levine (1988).

26. There were tensions in this friendship as well, especially after the Grimms lost their positions (Wyss 1979). However, the published letters are vivid proof of a lasting relationship despite scholarly differences.

27. His editions were accompanied by an extensive, barely penetrable apparatus of notes that explained his choices and omissions. One assessment of Lachmann's approach notes: "He hid his methodological steps in a very terse . . . so called text-critical apparatus. Intolerantly he turned every objection [by others]

into a moral question, and often devalued other opinions [by calling them] amateurism. . . . Rather than placing the Middle High German text as an aesthetic product into the middle of the presentation, [he] reduced it to a minefield of text critical problems" (Schweikle 1988:175–76). Specialized professional language, of course, is a primary means to establish disciplinary authority as well as to exclude those unwilling to learn the code from participation.

28. Wyss terms Grimm's approach "wild philology" and Lachmann's a "domesticated philology . . . that confines itself to the production of aesthetic totalities which are from the beginning cut off from the realities of life" (1979:282).

29. Text editors worked with the concept of *Leseart,* or "way of reading," which in the context of this quotation refers to the way in which the *Parcival* text could be reconstructed from the textual tradition available in Heidelberg.

30. The letters are in large part enumerations of newly discovered rules, with both sides assisting each other with new evidence and corrections.

31. Jacob Grimm, in a eulogy for Lachmann, praised him as a genius whose editorial purism was guided as much by aesthetic questions as by moral ones (Grimm 1879:157). It appears that Lachmann acted on subjective, albeit possibly unconscious, criteria in his construction of an authentic body of medieval literature. Weigel has stated that no one except for Lachmann was able to enact his method (Weigel 1989:229)—a judgment also made about Stith Thompson's motif delineations in folkloristics as well as Claude Lévi-Strauss's structural analysis.

32. A variety of accounts of the academic institutionalization of German language and literature studies in the German-speaking realm are available. See, for example, Fohrmann and Vosskamp (1991), Rosenberg (1989), and Weimar (1989).

33. Hermann Bausinger states that the Grimms' historical apparatus actually served to dehistoricize the past: "One of the paradoxes of the [Romantic] dehistoricizing is the fact that enormous efforts were undertaken in order to leave the historical behind altogether. In the works of Jacob and Wilhelm Grimm this becomes clear: Proof from many centuries is coordinated and continually leads back to a realm which has more mythic than historical qualities; the goal of the research is always the "origin," . . . which is certainly both more and less than a concrete beginning" (1960:279).

CHAPTER 3. AMERICAN ROMANTICISM AND THE EMERGENCE OF FOLKLORE STUDIES

1. For historical assessments and opinions on the influence of Continental scholarship on reshaping the American landscape of higher learning, see Clark (1989), Diehl (1978), and Graff (1987).

2. The unpublished Emerson papers reveal considerable intellectual investment in the antislavery movement (Gougeon 1990), an aspect that earlier Emerson biographers had considered far from a more fatalistically and inwardly oriented

Emerson (esp. Whicher 1953), a perspective also challenged by a 1995 biography of Emerson (Richardson 1995). Emerson may have reached his abolitionist stance on the basis of his belief in individualism and the virtue, and especially the "perfectibility," within every individual self; there remains little doubt, though, that Emerson considered non-Caucasians far from civilized perfection. See also Bercovitch (1978:200–201).

3. These were the central preoccupations of eighteenth-century aesthetic and literary philosophy, fueling both English and German Romanticism. M. H. Abrams's *The Mirror and the Lamp* (1953) excludes the American continuation of this discourse on whether poetry should be an imitation of nature, and hence of God, or radiate like a light from its own inner spirituality. Abrams mentions Emerson only in a footnote, where he implies that Emerson's capabilities of differentiation were considerably inferior to Thomas Carlyle's (1953:376, n. 74).

4. American literate circles responded ultimately to the poetic and spiritual challenge inherent in the newly translated Hindu mythologies. In Germany, the initial Romantic enthusiasm for the Indic materials collided with "the new philological and historical schools" (Feldman and Richardson 1972:349). The turn from a spiritual to a scholarly response is perhaps best exemplified in Friedrich Schlegel. He undertook to learn Sanskrit in order to corroborate the Romantic postulate that India was the true origin of all language and religion, yet his philological scrutiny, in effect, dismantled Romantic visions (Willson 1964:220). In the American case, the emphasis lay first in the incorporation of this discovery into the individual self. In the German case, the Indo-European discoveries became rather an external, scholarly preoccupation, with a drive toward representation, not emulation.

5. Harold Bloom's *The Anxiety of Influence* (1973) develops this philosophical-psychological preoccupation in the discourse on poetic inspiration. Bloom's work is strongly influenced, not only by Freud, but by Nietzsche; Nietzsche, in turn, was one of the few Europeans who saw in Emerson a kindred spirit (see Moran 1967). For further discussion of the continuities of such anxieties in literary theory, see Lentricchia (1980:83–84, 318–46).

6. White America is arguably built on ever-new utopias (not just Transcendentalism)—the hope to build a new ideal community within which the highest social and religious ideals can be realized (see Moment and Kraushaar, 1980). The failure of human beings to realize what they yearn for, in turn, generates ever-new attempts to improve and achieve the ideal community (Bercovitch 1978).

7. The emphasis was pronouncedly on the male gender. This is in interesting contrast to the frequent association of purity with the female gender in the authenticity discourse at large; in the American case, it also shows in the construction of blacks as feminine in character (see Frederickson 1971:114–15).

8. Ironically, this steadfast path to success renders the common man highly *un*common. More than a decade would pass before social activists like Theodore Parker would point to the lack of logic in this individualist construction: "Turning

inward to affect the outward requires recognition of the Other; self completion is inherently social" (personal communication from Ron Radano, 1993; see Parker 1969 [1911]).

9. It is likely that, like John Ruskin, Greenough was influenced by Thomas Carlyle's "theory of work as a source of human identity" (Evans 1988:251).

10. Plainness and simpleness, frugality and austerity were also emphasized by the religious charters of many Protestant groups in the early American colonies. They also emphasized individual devotion and commitment rather than hierarchical church organization. Frederick Jackson Turner's frontier hypothesis is perhaps the best-known effort to essentialize the American spirit, but Richard M. Dorson's vision of American folklore shows similar contours.

11. In 1828 Cooper had written "under the guise of a travelling foreigner"— and hence, using the same framing device so vital to the success of seventeenth-century French cultural critics—about the apparent lack of great art, but the abundance of "beautiful, graceful, and convenient ploughs," and "in this single fact may be traced the history and character of the people, and the germ of their future greatness" (Matthiessen 1941:145, n. 2).

12. The professionalization of American academe was strongly influenced by the German model. Some American students in Germany felt alienated by the German style—the "insolence" and "immorality" of students—as well as by the "image of scholarship as a trade." They also were disturbed by the "infidelity" of engaging in biblical scholarship that tended toward atheism (Diehl 1978:90–100). Some of these sentiments can be attributed to culture shock, which then as now is weathered differently by every exchange student. Still, some Americans were deeply impressed and inspired by the German specialist-scholars whose sole duty appeared to be the pursuit of knowledge, whose teaching was confined to their speciality, and who were not bothered with maintaining discipline and good study habits among students, as was the case for American college professors (Graff 1987:55–80; Hart 1989 [1874]).

13. Child, who studied in Göttingen and Berlin, discredits Diehl's conclusion that American scholars studying in Europe were only capable of copying the German academic *vocation* but not the *vision* engendered by German humanistic inquiry. Although Child mocked certain kinds of German scholars in letters to his friends (Diehl 1978:142), he nonetheless emulated the scholarship of the Grimms, whose picture he kept on the mantelpiece in his Cambridge residence.

14. His only statement was an encyclopedia article (Child 1874), which he apparently did not like to see cited (Wilgus 1959:6). Michael Bell has challenged this assessment, shedding light on both Child's article and Gummere's disregard of it (1988).

15. I am indebted to Roger Abrahams and Michael Bell for steering me toward Lowell, giving me access to his transcript of the lecture manuscript, and for providing me with crucial materials for this segment of the book. For another reading of Lowell, see Bell (1995).

16. The institute had been endowed with the funds of John Lowell, Jr., as a

center for literate entertainment and learning in the Boston area, administered by members of the Lowell family (Hale 1899:112).

17. The topics were (1) Definitions; (2) Piers Ploughman's Vision; (3) the Metrical Romances; (4) the Ballads; (5) Chaucer; (6) Spenser; (7) Milton; (8) S. Butler; (9) Pope; (10) Poetic Diction; (11) Wordsworth; (12) the Function of the Poet (Hale 1899:112–16).

18. Lowell himself wrote to a friend that the crowd had listened attentively, despite the fact that the subject had been "somewhat abstract" (Scudder 1901: 370–75), and various contemporaries registered this intellectual event with surprise and enthusiasm (Duberman 1966:140–41).

19. Aside from his own prolific production of poetry and prose, Lowell in 1854 edited Keats, Dryden, and Wordsworth for a series called *British Poets*, edited by Child (Howe and Cottrell 1952:6).

20. Duberman (1966) and Scudder (1901) record the testimonies of auditors like Longfellow or Charles Sumner, both of whom felt much moved by Lowell's "admirable performance" and who saw the lecture on the ballad as the best of Lowell's offerings (see Bell 1995:144–45).

21. Child warmed to Lowell as a result of the lectures, which he had thought hasty but delightful, and "quite the best thing he had ever heard from the 'perverse' Lowell" (Duberman 1966:140).

22. Lowell was likely far more inspired by Sir Walter Scott's *Minstrelsy of the Scottish Border,* or Bishop Percy's *Reliques of Ancient English Poetry,* whereas Child would bring the scholar's skepticism toward Scott's and Percy's editorial methods (Wilgus 1959:3–4).

23. The most recent assessment of Percy's "scandalous" treatment of the famous manuscript is Stewart's (1991b:110–15). Both Stewart and Shiach (1989) treat the procedures of authenticating ballads in eighteenth-century Great Britain in connection with social class and the search for national literatures.

24. This is not to claim that they lived withdrawn lives; all of these men participated in the public sphere in various ways, which is amply evident in their biographies.

25. See Solomon (1972) for an account of the ethnic "state of mind" of New England's Brahmins and their changing tolerance for the new cultural traditions brought by immigrants.

26. Fredrickson summarizes Romantic racialism as "The romantic racialist view of the Negro and his role in American society, popular and even influential by 1864, occupies a curious and anomalous position in the history of American racial thinking. It was benevolent in intent and, generally speaking, not linked to an unequivocal theory of white supremacy. . . . As characteristically put forth by whites, however, it often revealed a mixture of cant, condescension, and sentimentality, not unlike the popular nineteenth-century view of womanly virtue, which it so closely resembled" (1971:125).

27. The following argument has profited greatly from Ron Radano's "Denoting Difference" (1996).

28. Eric Lott has interpreted blackface minstrelsy as an expression of sexually potent fear, desire, and theft (1992).

29. German thought and research may have greatly influenced American academic development, but Sir Walter Scott left a far greater impression on a more popular level in both northern and southern states. Aside from his ballad collection and the romantic, nostalgic tone with which he introduced it, he set his novels in a pure, honorable, and vividly imagined medieval time. His fiction inspired members of southern plantation society to stage enactments of neomedieval tournaments. As Roger Abrahams observed, "These last events, involving as they did elaborate costuming and role playing on the theme of courtly love (as understood through its representation in the novels of Sir Walter Scott) and the taking on of heroic names, enacted the theme that preoccupied them: facing the loss of honor and gentility" (1992:51).

30. This short treatment on the question of race in American authenticity quests cannot even begin to unravel the different legacies encountered in the southern United States. Roger Abrahams's work on corn-shucking festivities contains valuable data on southern white experiences of black performances and the ambiguous desires bound up in white observance (1992).

CHAPTER 4. LATENT AUTHENTICITY QUESTS IN FOLKLORE
DEFINITIONS AND THEORIES IN TURN-OF-THE-CENTURY GERMANY

1. See Bausinger (1965), Emmerich (1971), Gerndt ed. (1987, trans. Dow and Lixfeld 1994), Lixfeld (1991 and 1994).

2. Chapter 6 incorporates elements of the Nazi discourse as well as the reflexive historiography published from the 1960s to the 1990s.

3. In this segment the differentiation between *Volkskunde* and folklore will occasionally be made because the word "folklore" began to carry a negative connotation in German scholarly discourse during this period, while it attracted increased use on the part of laypersons. However, inasmuch as possible, I will continue to use folkloristics, folklore studies, and expressive culture as terms for the field and the subject matter.

4. The umbrella organization dissolved in the Nazi period, but the common scholarly discourse has continually improved. Until the voice of public sector folklorists grew louder in the 1970s and 1980s, the "separateness" of the scholarly discussion from the regional associations' prime interests was maintained. The German folklore congress is attended by scholars from all three countries, and scholars often teach in their colleagues' countries—a pragmatic choice given the paucity of folklore chairs.

5. See Ben-Amos (1976) for a survey on the genre concept in folkloristics.

6. For an assessment of Weinhold's growth as the scholar, his correspondence with Jacob Grimm, and his latent nationalistic tendencies that seemed to subside only when he landed a professorship in Berlin, see Eberhart (1991).

7. I suspect that besides education, the social class and political stature of any

given lay specialist influenced whether his voice was heard as competent or as one "spoiling" the true mission of folkloristics.

8. The process of "imagining a community" that Benedict Anderson has seen as key in the building of nation-states was rendered far more concrete in the imagining in the activities of such voluntary groupings. The top-down model proposed by Anderson would require considerable adjustment in this regard, as ideas on national essence traveled up the social ladder as well, not only down (see Bendix 1992). Work on this area of social history is only in its early stages. Griebel (1991a and 1991b) has offered a regionally confined analysis of the protection of folk costume in Bavaria; some studies are under way on one of the most lasting protectionist institutions, the *Heimatschutz* (Göttsch 1994).

9. The turn-of-the-century discourse on genuine music and song left a particularly stringent mark on folkloristic work, evident in a young scholar's apologetic tone for making the "blasphemous" suggestion that "all songs can be folk songs" (Moser 1989:57).

10. In Hoffmann-Krayer's differentiation, ethnology and *Volkskunde* were not concerned with "the faraway" as opposed to "the close-by," as in Weinhold; rather, ethnology produced objective descriptions of foreign "nations" (in the sense of cultures or tribes) in their entirety, while *Volkskunde* studied the "social" aspects of modern civilized peoples. The availability of a written historical record facilitated historical, comparative research (1897:10–11). Burckhardt-Seebass points out that his sociological orientation avoided the romantic concept of folk-based nation or race (1988:50).

11. See his essay "About a Museum for Comparative *Volkskunde*" originally published in 1910 and revised in 1926 (Hoffmann-Krayer 1946:205–22).

12. *Heimatschutz* literally translates as "protection of the homeland"; the term is still used by local and regional associations. Their current goal is mostly the preservation of buildings, with an emerging link to environmental issues.

13. Burckhardt-Seebass is the late-twentieth-century successor to Hoffmann-Krayer's Basel folklore chair and is administratively and socially confronted with this particular legacy, one that also is evident in the work of Hoffmann-Krayer's student and fellow editor of the *Handwörterbuch des deutschen Aberglaubens,* Hanns Bächtold (1916). Academic folklore positions in Switzerland, Germany, and Austria have applied facets to them, since part of the job demands participation in or supervision of regional folklife preservation projects. Courses for preservation specialists may need to be offered, or scholars may be consulted in the development of public school curricula on *Heimatschutz.* This is not true in all universities, but in states where regional governments influence academic appointments (that is, where universities are public and subordinate to state governments) a folklore professor's ability to appeal to applied constituencies is vital. I am indebted to Silke Göttsch for this point.

14. This emerging interdependence is far too complex to be discussed in full here, and thus far little historiographic work has been conducted on it, with the exception of the Nazi period. Dilemmas of this sort were universally faced by

German-speaking folklorists of the period. Some scholars, such as Weinhold, were adamant in emphasizing their exclusively scientific calling—a position easier to embrace for scholars working on folk narrative and the like; an interest in material culture with its ties to museum work, on the other hand, made the intersection of scholarly and public domains more acute.

15. Lepenies places Riehl in the broader struggle "Between Literature and Science" in England, France, and Germany, characterizing "Riehl's optimism" as deceptive: "Fundamentally the discipline was already antiquated at the moment of its birth. It bore too many of the traits of old-fashioned science to become a true key-discipline in the nineteenth century" (1988:201). What renders a field a "true key-discipline" and to whom, both remain unexplained by Lepenies.

16. Riehl developed these thoughts more fully in his *Wanderbuch* (1869). He proved to be ahead of his time in recognizing the impact on European ethnography of European expansion and the colonial encounter with the Other when he stated: "If America had not been discovered we would today not know half as well what things look like in the middle of Germany" (1958 [1859]:30). For a concise characterization of the intellectual heritage Riehl represented and built on, see Sievers (1988:33–36).

17. Weinhold abstained, rather to his chagrin, from fieldwork during his years in Graz because he had trouble understanding the dialect (Eberhart 1991:27).

18. Once considered the leading folklorist of the early twentieth century, Adolf Spamer has become a bone of contention among German folklorists, as the Nazi period has been ever more closely scrutinized. Spamer's statements from the 1920s and the early 1930s, in particular his assessments of the emergence of the discipline and his contributions to the question of the scientific nature of the field, are at issue here. His willing or unwilling entanglement with Nazi institutions and the demise to which that association led him has been chronicled by his (formerly) East German students, from whom Lixfeld (1991) has drawn.

19. The generally held shorthand version of Hoffmann-Krayer's definition of the folk as *vulgus in populo* is not accurate.

20. The lack of empirical support for this position will strike anyone who has ever observed children negotiate (and hence attempt to assimilate to each other) which game to play and how.

21. In his second rebuttal, Strack claimed that his objection was primarily to the term *vulgus*—disregarding Hoffmann-Krayer's careful differentiation: "This term which bears the stamp of intellectual arrogance—should from my point of view not be used simply for reasons of reverence toward the *folk researcher*" (Strack 1958 [1903]:75–76, my emphasis; one would expect reverence toward the "folk" before reverence toward the "researcher.").

22. Reinhard Schmook assumes that Naumann drew his characterization of "primitive communal culture" from Lucien Lévy-Bruhl, whose work had just been translated into German (Schmook 1991:74). Naumann's repeated comparisons between the European native peasantry and "southern primitives" as well as Indians also points to this influence.

23. Naumann expanded on this example in his 1922 text (1922:56–57), just as he further developed other aspects of the 1921 essay in the fuller version.

24. To bolster his claim, Naumann, cites, without attribution, Hoffmann-Krayer's phrase "the folk reproduces, it does not produce," to which Hoffmann-Krayer in the marginalia of his own copy (held at the University of Basel) responded vigorously, feeling justifiably misquoted.

25. John Meier summarizes this discourse (1906 [1898]:1–13). Schepping provides a more up-to-date summary (1988:405–9).

26. Klaus Geiger, one of Meier's students, documented the rising interest in and imitation of folksong in Switzerland in the eighteenth and early nineteenth centuries (1912).

27. The "devolutionary premise" in folkloristic history has been clearly documented by Dundes. But while many of the examples that Dundes cites address the assumption that folklore devolves in the process of civilization, Naumann presupposes evolutionary or civilizatory progress to be the exclusive prerogative of high culture, or, as Dundes puts it, of "aristocratic origin," and hence folklore to be an inferior "good" to begin with (see Dundes 1969:6).

28. He kept his academic position, but he concluded his career in the German Democratic Republic.

29. Hoffmann-Krayer's "clairvoyance" should not be overestimated. Thus, he uncritically adopted Mannhardt's vegetation rite theories and applied them to historical evidence of Swiss folk customs (1946:160–204).

30. The three major efforts that were all begun in the early nineteenth century were the folksong archives in Freiburg, the *Handwörterbuch des deutschen Aberglaubens,* and the Atlas of German Folk Culture. An encyclopedia of the folktale was begun immediately before World War II, but then lay dormant until the 1970s.

CHAPTER 5. DEFINING A FIELD, DEFINING AMERICA

1. A first set of case studies on American folklore history appeared in the *Journal of the Folklore Institute* in 1973. Especially noteworthy among the intellectual biographies to appear since the mid-1980s are Hirsch (1987), Kodish (1986), and Zumwalt (1992).

2. For a critical historical assessment of the cultural interventionism of the folk school movement, see Whisnant (1983).

3. Newell presented his more poignant formulations on this issue at the International Folk-Lore Congress in London. Newell, in his case study of folktale dissemination, argued that materials passed from the civilized to the primitive, and not vice versa (Newell 1892a; Bell 1973:15–16), thus arguing like John Meier and others in Germany (in particular with the issue of "art song in oral tradition," Meier 1906). One is tempted to see in Newell's stance against "Britain," as represented by Andrew Lang, another vestige of American academic linkages to Germany.

4. It should be kept in mind that this story of recouping the native authentic

happened within the larger context of American policies toward land use and the treatment of native tribes occupying these lands; forcing dislocation of tribes from their lands, warring against those who refused, setting up reservations, founding schools with the intent of assimilating (and thus eradicating) native cultures, all are among the political and economic realities against which proposals such as Newell's took shape.

5. The belief in positivism can be gleaned from an address read by Powell at the annual meeting of 1891: "Major Powell said that the various sciences had now been differentiated into a great number of departments, each cultivated by an army of investigators. The only hope for successful philosophy of the future was that a system might be gradually erected by the united efforts of all thinkers and investigators, as the final generalization of their labors" (Newell 1892b:2).

6. Dwyer-Shick (1979:393) lists publications by Wayland D. Hand on how local and regional folklore societies were connected to the growth of folklore research.

7. In this regard, the way that Knortz, a German-American collector operating largely outside academe, has been rediscovered for American folkloristics is telling. McNeil describes him as "ahead of his time . . . one of the first folklorists to give extensive scholarly attention to the traditions of American ethnics, . . . an avid field worker who relied largely on his own collectanea . . . [who] frequently gave not only the text but the context as well when setting the material he recorded into print" (McNeil 1988:1). The kernel of modern scholarly standards of academically oriented fieldwork are highlighted, whereas the complexities of his bicultural life and ambition seem to be only diluting filters, detracting from the scholarly promise.

8. On the echoes of the Herderian *Volksgeist* in Boas's work, see Stocking ed. (1996).

9. Umberto Eco has cynically referred to such efforts as "hyperreality" (1986). The variant of living history has been sympathetically discussed by Anderson (1984); a critical review can be found in Handler (1990b); a theoretical engagement with this phenomenon is presented in Handler and Saxton (1988) and Gable and Handler (1996).

10. In his introduction to the *Handbook of American Indian Languages* Boas is very explicit on this point (Boas 1966 [1911]:46–47).

11. I have consulted the microfilm version of the Franz Boas Professional Correspondence from 1858–1942 (hereinafter BPC) available at the library of the department of anthropology, University of Pennsylvania. Thanks to Yanna Lambrinidou for helping with the task of sifting through segments of this material.

12. BPC, reel 5, November 27, 1903.

13. BPC, reel 5, September 18, 1903.

14. BPC, reel 5, December 9, 1903.

15. BPC reel 43, March 5, 1940.

16. BPC, reel 43, August 7, 1940, from Ella Deloria.

17. BPC, May 9, 1903, to Archer M. Huntington.

18. BPC, Microfilm 76, Reel 34.

19. BPC, Microfilm 76, Reel 34.

20. It is interesting that efforts to revive the art of telling tales have increased in the United States during the last few decades. One of the latest installments in this process is the telling of literary tales, such as *The Velveteen Rabbit,* by movie stars on an educational medium, public radio, with a currently major star, Mel Gibson, as host.

21. In Europe, Carl Wilhelm von Sydow was the most astute critic concerning that same issue. Voicing doubts about the viability of the historic-geographic school, he advocated that the role of the active tradition-bearer needed to be accounted for strongly in the creation and spread of tradition (von Sydow 1948).

22. This relationship was of central interest to John Meier in Germany, and Barry worked with Meier's term "zersingen," which Barry interpreted positively (1939:101–3).

23. Kodish does not miss the irony that Gordon's work, so keenly preoccupied with studying the authentic, was largely overlooked by historians of the discipline, because in his journalistic endeavors Gordon hardly fit the image of the "authentic scholar."

24. I assume that this distinction is connected to skill (collecting music requires additional notational ability) and with the fact that folksong truly became appropriated by new media such as radio and commercial recordings.

25. Roger Abrahams, personal communication, July 14, 1994. Wilgus (1959: 158) corroborates this title.

26. The link between the ethnographer's poetic response to cultural realities and his/her ethnographic research has been newly invigorated by the Society for Humanistic Anthropology, which has published research alongside what to Sapir would be sincere expressions of the researcher's innermost life—poetry and belletristic prose.

27. Darnell explains the essay's ambiguity in part with Sapir's recourse to aesthetic argument, in part with the fact that Sapir was working toward a "psychologizing" of Boasian anthropology, seeking to work the individual personality into the notion of cultural wholes (Darnell 1990:148–49; 168–70). Some passages do read like psychological elaborations of Boas's Baffin Island insight on "tradition" cited earlier.

28. Roger Abrahams, personal communication, July 14, 1994. Maud Karpeles, who clearly assisted Sharp in his collection and who later wrote a work on folksong, deferred to Sharp, apparently considering herself not a collector or thinker in her own right. On this point, see also Kodish 1987.

29. Sharp's "American harvest" seems to be a British counterpart to Child's work with the English and Scottish Ballads in its ability to outdo the natives on their own territory.

30. For a critical historical description and analysis of the rise and fall of this

festival, as well as of the other cultural interventionist programs in the southern mountains touched upon here, refer to Whisnant (1983). For the case of Nova Scotia, arguably larger in scale, see McKay (1994).

CHAPTER 6. DEPARTURES AND REVISIONS: TOWARD A
VOLKSKUNDE WITHOUT CANON

1. Parts of this chapter were presented at the annual meeting of the American Anthropological Association in San Francisco, 1992; my thanks go to Ellen Badone who invited me to participate. The chapter incorporates revised excerpts of my earlier discussion of folklorismus (Bendix 1988).

2. Dow and Lixfeld (1994) represents an expanded translation of the conference proceedings.

3. This often but not always self-critical movement has been made more complex with the unification of Germany. Folklore's role in the former GDR needs to be assessed, as do the colonial ramifications of unification.

4. For more on implicated individuals and institutions, see Dow and Lixfeld (1991 and 1994); Gerndt ed. (1987); Holzapfel (1991); Jeggle (1988:59–65); Lixfeld (1991 and 1994); Schmook (1991).

5. For a survey, see Mieder (1982:435–36); also consider Kamenetsky (1972a and 1972b).

6. Some of the debates recorded in Gerndt ed. (1987), as well as the contribution by Dow and Lixfeld (1991), reveal many personal vendettas and much hurt.

7. Matthias Zender, aided in part by Günter Wiegelmann, completed the evaluation of the prewar questionnaires; although Zender raised methodological questions concerning the *Atlas*, the Nazi interest in the project was simply forgotten. The *Enzyklopädie des Märchens*, when it began operation again, did acknowledge the limitations of Mackensen's work and distanced itself from it, proclaiming a new start for the entire enterprise.

8. Helmut Eberhart's work on the Austrian Viktor von Geramb's rich correspondence illustrates this point very well (1992). The debate surrounding the far more greatly implicated John Meier, in which Dow and Lixfeld (1991) and Holzapfel (1991) take opposing positions, brings home how difficult it is to make judgments when only decontextualized fragments of historical documents can be found. The language and policy of Nazi folklore institutions, publications, and private correspondences go beyond the bounds of this study, but a great deal of work has been done or is under way (Brückner and Beitl, 1983, Gerndt 1987, Lixfeld 1994).

9. Trümpy refers to a rebuttal to Oppenheimer that Max Weber delivered: "The real question in the racial problem would be: Are there any *relevant* differences of historical, political, cultural, historically developmental nature that are demonstrably inherited and inheritable, and what are these differences? In most fields, this question can today [1912] not even be posed, and certainly not answered" (quoted after Trümpy 1987:171).

10. In some places one wonders to what extent Dünninger was convinced by what he wrote. When he stated, "The hard reality which becomes a political duty to everyone that experiences it, has, however, not been recognized in its complete danger in *Volkskunde*" (1937:16), he may have been expressing his own ambivalence as much as commenting on the situation of the day. Amazingly, the National Socialist reception of Dünninger's book was negative; one of the party's main folklore administrators claimed Dünninger did not sufficiently stress the negative influences of non-German historical strands that affected the purity of German *Volksgeist* (discussed in Bausinger 1985:175). Dünninger's publication list shows that he was practically inactive during World War II; the bulk of his work appeared after the war, and two massive Festschrifts for his sixty-fifth and eightieth birthdays (Harmening et al. 1970; Harmening and Wimmer 1986) indicate the esteem in which he was held by others as well as by his students at Würzburg.

11. Geramb "felt at least an affinity with National Socialism, which was, in his own understanding, absolutely sufficient. He recognized too late that the NSDAP accepted only those who followed its dictates completely" (Eberhart 1992:693).

12. See Becker for a consideration of Herder's reception in the past two centuries. He argues that Herder's style and the loose structural organization of his opus "lacks a definite commitment," which permits an extremely broad set of interpretations and adaptations (Becker 1987:217–25).

13. This statement is not intended as an apology; rather, it is a reaffirmation of the call for continuous careful scrutiny of our vocabulary and its potential users, including ourselves.

14. The ideology of such resistance-folklorists often barely differed from the fascist version; it was the practice that caused friction (Emmerich 1971:117–22).

15. This issue was raised with reference to the personal ambitions of Geramb by Helmut Eberhart; see the transcribed discussion in Gerndt ed. (1988:62).

16. Another discipline compromised by Nazi interests was, not surprisingly, prehistory, since here, too, the interest in documenting beginnings could easily be subverted by arguments of destiny inscribed in origins; the active role of anthropology, with institutes bearing names such as "Anthropology and Science of Race," has also been historiographically documented (Prinz and Weingart 1990). Moser (1988 [1954]) considers such cross-disciplinary issues as well. *Völkerkunde*'s role in the Third Reich has been assessed by Fischer (1990).

17. On the genesis of the myth of Germanic continuity during the Nazi period, see Emmerich (1971:132–61).

18. Schmidt's argument again demonstrates that *Volkskunde* was committed to a conservative politics, and an avowed leftist author such as Brecht therefore "tainted" the field. The theoretical and methodological clashes between German folklorists thus often had clear political subtexts, with socialist and conservative agendas battling for disciplinary or institutional supremacy.

19. The English translation of this study added a chapter on "Relics—and what can become of them" from Bausinger's textbook (1971), which expands on

the issues of folklorismus and commodity culture only hinted at in this earlier work.

20. For the events of the late 1960s from the perspective of institutes and students, see Fachschaft EKW (1986:349–58).

21. Wolfgang Brückner, chair of the Würzburg *Volkskunde* department and still one of the leading voices in German folkloristics, edited the circulars, pamphlets, and recorded discussions in a mimeographed volume (1971). The line between personal and intellectual assault was at times rather rudely ignored—evidence of the emotional involvement that the process of deconstruction entailed.

22. One participant in this conference half-jokingly suggested publishing the entire proceedings in Latin to avoid the popularizing distortions unavoidable when a "science of the folk" reached the folk. The title was specifically rendered in Latin to avoid the term *Volk* (Bausinger et al. 1966:5–6).

23. Ernst Klusen quoted Max Kommerell: "A doubter would say: Herder not only invented the name [folksong], Herder also invented the thing. But to know the relationship between finding and inventing in the realm of German song, that would be an important insight to be gained" (in Klusen 1969:7). Bausinger's survey of verbal arts already puts quotation marks around folk poetry in the title, stating that "all this makes it clear that 'folk poetry' is here not a fact of oral tradition, but a creative fiction which brought folk and art together" (1968:14).

24. The similarities to later nationalistic practices of invention are noteworthy. Köstlin's argument parallels and predates the ideas exemplified in Hobsbawm and Ranger (1983). His use of costume and custom as culturally manipulated practices to achieve community also provides a counterpoint to Anderson's *Imagined Communities* derived from literate/literary practices (1983).

25. Greverus has repeatedly tackled projects that provided an opportunity to examine the interplay between fragments of older notions and practices with regard to culture and present-day sentiments and actions. See, for instance, her volume on *Heimat* and cultural nostalgia (1979), or her reports on working as a consultant for cultural preservation (Greverus and Schilling 1982).

26. Burke contributed his views on how history and ethnology shaped the "discovery" of popular cultures as a field of study (1981, 1984) and how difficult it would be to keep the interest in its study from initiating a process of objectification. "In our time the discovery of popular culture has itself become popularized. Even farmers find traditional peasant culture exotic" (1984:12).

27. Wolfgang Brücker (1984) had a particularly strong reaction against Muchembled; Wolfgang Kaschuba shares some of these reservations (1988).

28. Even such a hard-earned insight easily can be lost when new ideological uses of *Volk* appear. The unification efforts in the former GDR using the slogan "We are one *Volk*" quickly provoked an essay pointing to the ideological embeddedness of the term; an "innocent" use of the term was impossible to restore (Bausinger 1991c).

29. Kaschuba emerged from the Bausinger school and now directs European Ethnology at Humboldt University in Berlin.

30. The volume of essays edited by van Dülmen and Schindler (1984) shows the overlap between historians and folklorists.

31. One of the major Swiss postwar folklorists, Arnold Niederer, shared this perception inasmuch as he advocated *Volkskunde* as a field concerned with the underprivileged (Niederer 1975).

32. Mohammed Rassem's postwar dissertation foreshadowed the historiographic and ideology-critical framework of the late 1960s: "One cannot satisfactorily define a science by naming its object [here, the folk]; everything depends on the conceptions with which [a science] approaches [its object]" (1979 [1951]:9). Perhaps because Rassem, as he acknowledges in hindsight, worked on the history of folklore studies ignorant of a number of existing works in the history of science, he was able to recognize the intimate relationship between politics and expressive culture. Rassem is rarely cited, but his imprint on the work of Köstlin is clear (e.g., Köstlin 1977a).

33. This Bausinger article "On the algebra of continuity" anticipates much that Hobsbawm and Ranger would develop (1983), whereby Bausinger's "innovative" and "renovative" scenarios (1969c:18–21) surpass the relatively narrow conception laid out in Hobsbawm's introduction (Hobsbawm 1983).

34. The revolutionary Tübingen students who voiced their frustration in 1969 (many of whom, such as Utz Jeggle or Martin Scharfe, have graduated to prestigious professorships) reflect on the nature of their critical discourse in Fachschaft EKW (1986:349–58).

35. Half-timbered houses are associated with the beauty of folklife, and Jeggle's jibe is directed toward the folklorist who contributes to the restoration and preservation of "things" without concern for the real problems of those living in older dwellings.

36. This Swiss scholar and his work took on symbolic proportions in the postwar German reorientation. Switzerland remained neutral during World War II, and Weiss's scholarship seemed uncompromised by Nazi ideology. During the Nazi years the Swiss mobilized a "spiritual national defense" in part through folkloric displays (Bendix 1992), and the ties to German scholarship receded, with folkloristic research strongly focusing on the alpine regions—which held the place of geographic and cultural bulwark in the Swiss mentality.

37. For a critique of Weiss's functionalist framework, see Metzen (1970). Although he leaves almost nothing of Weiss's work standing, Metzen does credit Weiss for having considered his own work a sketch, and he himself would have rejected the "biblical status" that his work was accorded in postwar scholarship (Metzen 1970:173).

38. The German folklore society (*Deutsche Gesellschaft für Volkskunde*) holds congresses biannually.

39. For a vehement critique of this text, see Möhler (1981).

40. Moser was not the first person to use the term. Hultkranz lists French ethnologist A. Marinus's use of "neo-folklorisme" during the 1930s and 1940s as

a new theoretical orientation toward expressive culture (Hultkranz 1961:188–89). German folklorists refer to Heintz (1958) as the term's source.

41. Social historian Norbert Schindler's assessment of Hans Moser as a folkloristic historian goes a long way in explaining why Moser broached the issue of folklorism: "Moser has always understood the 'critique of tradition' as an integral part of his empirical work, never as an abstract-theoretical matter. His basic premise was that the liberation from the legacies of the past and the new orientation of *Volkskunde* after 1945 could only ensue if it was possible to familiarize [the discipline] with historically precise methods. . . . Many of his essays on the histories of customs served such a demythologizing of tradition" (Schindler 1985:85).

42. See, for instance, Greverus and Haindl's collection "Efforts to Escape from Civilization" (1983), which embraces an ethnographic approach to understand the remnants of countercultural experiments in various European settings. Although the work contains no reference to the folklorism-*Rücklauf* issues, even the title demonstrates a recognition of the broader philosophical traditions that engendered particular choices in alternate lifestyles.

43. A translation of this essay appeared in Dow and Lixfeld (1986:113–23); the following excerpts are my own translations.

44. Brückner's formulation in the same volume echoes this point: "It is only seemingly a contradiction that such [demonstrations and shows of the *Heimat*] reflect the reality of customary life only conditionally, but nonetheless represent a piece of reality in present day folk culture. Only the theoretical confrontation of authentic and manipulated folk culture leads to such perceptions" (1966:77).

45. The historical documentation continues and has resulted in a number of valuable case studies. See esp. Griebel (1991a, 1991b, 1991c); Brednich (1988); or Braun (1986), who integrates Hobsbawm and Ranger's work into the German historical assessment of folk cultural invention.

46. Six of fifteen questionnaires were returned and printed in *Zeitschrift für Volkskunde*. See Bausinger (1969a).

47. This discussion may have contributed to Ernst Klusen's book-length study, "Folksong: Find and Invention" (1969), that attempted a history of the role of song in life and in intellectual discourse and politics. Klusen tried to suggest a definition of folksong that was free of its cumbersome ideological baggage. Songs are sung in groups, he maintains, and are "not a pure, adorable phenomenon distorted by mythological misconceptions, but simply a basic item within the lives of groups." In words reminiscent of later American performance notions, Klusen states that only face-to-face group situations create the context within which songs are performed, and that song texts and music have no life of their own outside such contexts (1969:189).

48. A decade earlier, Tamas Hofer also used the term "revitalization movement" to characterize the emergence of folklore studies (1968:311–15).

49. The most frequently cited case of economic folklorism is Jeggle and Korff (1974a and 1974b); see also Korff (1980) and the work being done in tourism, for example, Kapeller (1991). On the fusion of religious and economic interests, Korff

(1970:95–97) remains, to my knowledge, one of the few who have raised this issue. On politically motivated revival, see, for example, Brückner (1965, 1966), Griebel (1991a), Köstlin (1988).

50. In a personal correspondence from February 2, 1992, Köstlin wrote: "I believe (and this would be my credo) that scholarly work is always informed by subjective states. The reception of scholarly texts cannot be understood in some kind of larger intellectual framework, without [knowing] the states of humans (*Befindlichkeit der Menschen*). Therefore I think that one has to accentuate more pronouncedly how much pre- or extra-scientific thinking enters into an approach termed scholarly, and that one ought to state where this lies hidden."

51. Peter Assion contributed to the focus in German scholarship of the late 1980s and early 1990s that examined museums as loci of cultural production (see Korff and Roth, 1990; Zacharias 1990).

52. The 1992 conference, "Authentic Folksong in the Alps," organized by the academy for music and art, *Mozarteum,* and by the Institute for Musical *Volkskunde* in Innsbruck, points, however, to the stronghold of authenticity in "pockets" of scholarship. The Austrian Folk Song project, despite an articulate critique (Johannes Moser 1989), remains convinced of its ability to distinguish between the real thing and the fake, and some of its representatives have even made tabloid headlines for their insistence on battling against the popularization and mass distribution of real folk music (Gerlinde Hain, personal communication, Salzburg, June 15, 1992).

CHAPTER 7. FROM FAKELORE TO THE POLITICS OF CULTURE:
THE CHANGING CONTOURS OF AMERICAN FOLKLORISTICS

1. Henry Glassie, who perhaps has most clearly articulated a moral credo in his works, draws his philosophical lineage from English communalists such as Ruskin or Morris rather than from Dewey (Glassie 1983).

2. For a gloss on the emergence of inquiry into the American experience, both popularly and in academe, see Bronner (1986:97–101).

3. Abrahams compares Dorson and MacEdward Leach, one of the founders of the University of Pennsylvania's folklore program, and finds them ideologically compatible, although they embraced strategically incompatible routes (1989a: 29–30). Indeed, Dorson so thoroughly loathed Leach's endorsement and support for folklorists outside academe that he occasionally referred to Leach not by name but simply as AFS's "Secretary-Treasurer" housed with the faction of folklorists at the University of Pennsylvania (Dorson 1976:8). In an earlier piece (1969:62), however, Dorson names the participants in the "bitter shouting matches" at AFS conventions.

4. For a sympathetic assessment of Botkin's work and life, see Jackson (1976).

5. He may have been alluding to the festivals and folk school movements analyzed much later by David Whisnant (1983).

6. Dorson's verbiage may have been intended more for institutional purposes:

"In any history of the American folklore scene, Ben Botkin deserves a respected place. . . . When as a callow graduate student in 1939 I first met Ben in Washington, D.C., he showed me every kindness, and he has always generously assisted younger folklorists" (Dorson 1969:63–64).

7. Dorson's efforts to delineate the disciplinary uniqueness of folklore remained vague, but he was unwilling to settle for "interdisciplinarity" as folkloristics' strong suit. See his discussion of the "Skills of the Folklorist" (1972:4–5). The "uniqueness" of folkloristics came out more strongly in his elaboration of past and present "theories," whereby a closer examination of these theories shows them to be anything but exclusively folkloristic.

8. Two special journal issues, both edited by Robert Georges (1989a and 1989b), comprehensively assess Dorson's life and work.

9. Henry Rosovsky, an academic dean at Indiana University during the 1950s, remembers Dorson's repeated efforts to talk him into granting a separate undergraduate major for folklore; although Rosovsky turned him down, the lobbying was noticed (personal communication, March 1993).

10. Fox (1980) is one of the few exceptions, and even he does not take issue with the dichotomy.

11. The so-called "narrative biology" school emerging in turn-of-the-century Russian scholarship considered community, the teller, and her/his tales as a whole (see Dégh 1972:57–58).

12. In hindsight, Abrahams regards his "The Complex Relations of Simple Forms" (1976 [1969]) as something "formulated for classroom purposes simply to reveal the range of expressive forms" (personal communication, summer 1993). Yet the piece is the clearest formulation of the socially situated, fluid, and fuzzy nature of expressive behavior. The emergence of the dramatic or performance perspective in folklore and other social sciences also was greatly indebted to the work of Erving Goffmann (see Geertz 1983:23–30). Abrahams's later homage to Goffman raises concerns about his exclusive focus on the drama metaphor at the expense of other dimensions of play and celebration (Abrahams 1984).

13. Abrahams drew some of his inspiration from McDermott (1976), known for his editions of William James's work. Abrahams's focus on experience received its clearest articulation in Turner and Bruner (1986). Recourse here to the philosophies of Dewey, Dilthey, and Schütz points to recognition of a philosophically grounded understanding of the interrelationship among self, culture, and experiential authenticity. The theater director *cum* anthropologist Richard Schechner has offered the clearest formulation and description of what might be termed individual authenticity in enactment (Schechner 1985:35–116).

14. Among the first efforts to document a system of genres from the ethnic rather than the scholarly perspective were works by the Herskovitses (1958) and Gossen (1972); Ben-Amos's essay also mentions Ruth Finnegan's work with the Limba. Bascom (1965) differentiated analytic and native categories, but he sought to strengthen the validity of analytic terminology.

15. This formulation constitutes a complete parallel to Bausinger's (1966b); see chapter 6.

16. Abrahams (1972) began a critique of the latent peasant-based concept in conjunction with Ben-Amos's new definition.

17. Dundes developed this definition further in his essay "Who Are the Folk?" (1978 [1977]).

18. Not surprisingly, it has largely been scholars who worked on minority groups (e.g., Americo Paredes and his student José Limón working with Chicano materials, or Rayna Green representing Native American voices) who have pointed to hegemonic discrepancies expressed or challenged through folklore. Bruce Jackson working with prisoners and motorcycle gangs, or Lydia Fish in addressing the folklore of Vietnam veterans, each have drawn attention to the folklore of groups regarded as "difficult" by the majority culture. The collection *"And other neighborly names . . ."* (Bauman and Abrahams 1981) remained for some time the only work elaborating on "differential identity." John Roberts (1993) astutely outlined the problem of containing diversity within single scholarly categories of African American "folkness."

19. Bauman was far less prone to seek the authentic and most engaged in trying to generate an analytic vocabulary, and to arrive at insights into the *social* ramifications of performance (1984 [1977], 1986).

20. Roger Abrahams felt uneasy with both the ahistorical nature of Ben-Amos's new definition and his definition of the emergent ethnography of communication. Abrahams felt that omitting "tradition" from the definitional discussion was "neglecting to recognize that the folk themselves regarded tradition as an important feature of their performances" and that the definition should somehow accommodate this fact (personal communication, summer, 1993).

21. One reader of this book was startled that Hymes and Tedlock were "claimed" as major figures in a historiography of folklore's disciplinary trajectory. Both scholars were trained in anthropology, but their respective work has focused heavily on verbal arts. Each of them had considerable influence on folklore, while, in turn, they were drawing ideas from folklorists' work. In addition, Hymes has held the presidency of the American Folklore Society and taught courses in the Department of Folklore and Folklife at the University of Pennsylvania.

22. Widespread acceptance of performance-centered analyses throughout the 1980s indicates, however, that a framework developed with materials generated by "vanishing cultures" can be fruitfully applied to cultures that are thriving. The works in this area are too numerous to cite. See Bauman and Briggs (1990) and the new introduction to Bauman and Sherzer (1989) as bibliographical guideposts.

23. The flurry of research on orality and literacy since the mid-1970s has pointed to the intricate interweaving of oral and literate media and has aided in dispelling the long-standing dichotomy in folkloristics—that is, that oral equals authentic, while printed stands for spurious (see Ong 1982; Stewart 1991a). The complexity of authenticity standards with regard to writing as opposed to oral tradition was already evident in the work of Carl Lachmann (see chapter 2).

24. This phrase invokes a practice debated since—or even before—Kenneth Goldstein suggested the notion of the "induced natural context" (Goldstein 1964).

25. The notion of "auditory disasters" points to yet another realm of unex-

amined authenticity standards crucial to the world of recording, a realm that cannot be elaborated on beyond this note. Recording technology has generated ever-more stringent desires for purity of sound, and this "auditory discrimination" has affected ethnographers working with elaborate recording equipment. In music recording this particular "hierarchy of sound" is held at bay, with an even fiercer discourse on authenticity generated by considerations of the authenticity of instruments and the contexts of performance (see Kivy 1995). Both lines of argument entail a good measure of musical ideology and auditory taste, neither of which lend themselves to analytic distance (see, for instance, Baugh 1988, Seiler 1991).

26. Wilgus, by contrast, mentioned the paradoxically reversed positions on folklore of anthropologists and literary scholars, with the move toward process growing more strongly out of the literary camp, while anthropologists still treated verbal art in a more textual fashion (1972:252).

27. I am not aware of any data that would support such a claim, and Jones supplies none; I would suggest instead that to many individuals a particular context helps render a given "text" memorable or forgettable.

28. For detailed assessments of such studies, see Stern (1977) and, in updated form, the introduction to Stern and Cicala (1991).

29. At the same time, Stern pointed to the unproductive nature of dichotomies: "Folklorists have armed themselves with a battery of terminology to differentiate their 'legitimate' area of inquiry from those of others, such as mass media and popular culture, and have drawn such dichotomies as 'folklore' versus 'fakelore' (or 'pseudo-folklore'), 'authentic' versus 'inauthentic,' and 'tradition' versus 'quasi-tradition'" (Stern 1977:25).

30. Robert Cantwell's account of the festival's emergence and nature evocatively details the cultural and political circumstances leading to the festival's institutionalization (1993). In the specifics of music appropriation and revival across various segments of American culture, Roger Abrahams's manuscript on the social history of American folksong complements Cantwell's perspective.

31. In 1978 a sophisticated seminar among a variety of practitioners and academics discussed issues of cultural intervention implied in folklife festivals, drawing on historical introspection (Whisnant 1979). The major handbook for folk festival organizers avoids all responsibility for reflexive awareness by stating at the outset that "there is no intent here to pass judgements upon different types of events" (Wilson and Udall 1982:3).

32. For a governmentally sanctioned discussion of issues in cultural conservation, see Loomis (1983). The volume edited by Mary Hufford (1994) brings together a reflexive, fresh assessment that implicitly distances itself from Loomis.

33. The most prominent legacy in this regard is John Lomax's. His son, Alan Lomax, is credited with saying, "There comes a time when those of us who swill at the trough must bite the hand that feeds us" (personal communication from Roger Abrahams, summer 1993). The view has been advocated for new generations by Archie Green (1983, 1989); for a restated text by a younger scholar, see Baron (1992). While I sympathize with the political commitment in this view, the

paradox inheres in using the governmental funding apparatus devised by hegemonic majority culture programs to promote minority voices. It is difficult to maintain the democratic intent of folklife programming since the funding apparatus will always generate mechanisms of judgment (worthy or not worthy of funding) that discriminate on the basis of taste and ideology, thus again reinstating judgmental criteria over folk materials.

34. Werner Sollors's *The Invention of Ethnicity* collection draws together ethnic writers and academics questioning the attainability of ethnic essence and celebrating its very constructedness (1989). The volume unfortunately disregards most of the earlier work done by folklorists, and to an extent it puts forward similar insights from a different disciplinary angle.

35. Among the standard twenty-one definitions of folklore (Leach and Fried 1949: 398–403), only six did not use tradition as a defining element.

36. Barbara Kirshenblatt-Gimblett's (1988b) much-cited critique, for instance, dwells extensively on both Hall (1981) and Williams (1988). British historian Peter Burke's contributions were possibly more influential in the German discourse (Burke 1981, 1984), but they also contributed to the historical introspection to be discussed.

37. Innovation previously had been addressed under the pairing "tradition and creativity" without foregrounding the problematic of a disembodied concept of tradition. Charles Briggs, by contrast, had begun to deal with the intersection of the Anglo art market and its (top-down) attempts to shape and revive notions of traditionality and aesthetics among New Mexico wood carvers; Briggs clearly was intrigued by the processes of change and invention, and he was not hampered by disciplinary notions of absolute tradition (Briggs 1978: 36–52).

38. In many ways Linnekin's formulations constituted a theoretical expansion on Wallace's classic statement on revitalization movements (1956) and Linton's earlier assessment of nativistic movements (1943).

39. This anthropological perspective on issues of cultural preservation and living history is analytic and reflexive; hence, it can stand in stark opposition to the enthusiastic commitment that often characterizes practitioners of such movements (e.g., Anderson 1984). It should also be noted, however, that many folklorists working in the public sector had encountered forms of framed, reflexive, or invented tradition for years, long before the issue entered printed academic discourse. Various program booklets for folklife celebrations or reports to the National Endowment for the Arts—until the mid-1990s a major source of funding for public folklife sponsorship—bear witness to this point (personal communication from Roger Abrahams, summer 1995). More than anyone else, folklorists in the public sector responded to the whole "invention of tradition" discourse with a sense of "what else is new," and few of them responded in print. Staub (1988) is one of the notable exceptions. The lack of effective communication, particularly in this area, between public sector folklorists and those in the academy fueled Kirshenblatt-Gimblett's impassioned argument in "Mistaken Dichotomies" (1988b).

40. The first major field guide pragmatically suggested taking recourse to na-

tionalist sentiment among subjects to elicit data: "Nationalism may also assist in the establishment of rapport. . . . The intense cultural nationalism of small countries is especially conducive to such an approach" (Goldstein 1964:53).

41. Honko's treatment of the *Kalevala*, focusing on authenticity, offers an interesting, "native" balance to Wilson (1976) and Dundes (1985). Bluestein's work appeared during the same period (1972), but since it addressed literary theory more than sociopolitical or nationalistic programs, it echoed more quietly in the discussion of folklore and nationalism.

42. Whisnant spent considerable effort in alerting folklorists to the political dimensions of producing folk music festivals by pointing to historical examples (Whisnant 1979); perhaps the resistance he encountered in such settings partly inspired *All that is native and fine* (1983).

43. The book-length treatment of Morag Shiach, built on the work of Williams, deserves wider readership in American folkloristics. Shiach's statement that "the desire for an autonomous and authentic cultural sphere leads to a tendency in many cultural critics to repress or mythify history" sums up a variety of the issues underlying the history of folkloristics as well as the writing of this history (Shiach 1989:11).

44. The proceedings of the first major public folklore conference (Feintuch 1988) and a reader of salient essays (Baron and Spitzer 1992) attest to the vibrancy in public folklore theorizing and commitment; public folklorists also were vocally present in the groundbreaking conference on "exhibiting cultures" (Karp and Lavine 1991). Not all folklorists would share my view here; for instance, an acerbic exchange took place in the pages of the American Folklore Society newsletter during the early 1990s, in which at least one leading academic folklorist argued for the formation of two separate professional societies since he felt that the needs of public folklorists could not and should not have to be addressed by those in the academy.

Bibliography

Aarne, Antti, and Stith Thompson. 1961. *The Types of the Folk-Tale; a Classification and Bibliography.* Folklore Fellows Communication, 184. Helsinki.

Abrahams, Roger D. 1964. *Deep Down in the Jungle.* Hatboro, Pa.: Folklore Associates.

Abrahams, Roger D. 1968. A Rhetoric of Everyday Life: Traditional Conversational Genres. *Southern Folklore Quarterly* 32:44–59.

Abrahams, Roger D. 1972. Personal Power and Social Restraint. In Paredes and Bauman, eds., *Toward New Perspectives in Folklore*, pp. 16–30.

Abrahams, Roger D. 1976 (1969). The Complex Relations of Simple Forms. In Dan Ben-Amos, ed., *Folklore Genres,* pp. 193–214. Austin: University of Texas Press.

Abrahams, Roger D. 1977. Toward an Enactment-Centered Theory of Folklore and Folklife. In William R. Bascom, ed., *Frontiers of Folklore,* pp. 79–120. Washington, D.C.: AAAS.

Abrahams, Roger D. 1981. Shouting Match at the Border: The Folklore of Display Events. In Bauman and Abrahams, eds., *"And other neighborly names . . . ,"* pp. 303–21.

Abrahams, Roger D. 1984. Goffman Reconsidered: Pros and Players. *Raritan Review* 3:76–94.

Abrahams, Roger D. 1986. Ordinary and Extraordinary Experience. In Turner and Bruner, eds., *The Anthropology of Experience,* pp. 45–72.

Abrahams, Roger D. 1989a. Representative Man: Richard Dorson, Americanist. *Journal of Folklore Research* 26:27–34.

Abrahams, Roger D. 1989b. The American Folklore Society Centennial, 1888–89 to 1988–89. *Folk Music Journal* 5:608–19.

Abrahams, Roger D. 1992. *Singing the Master: The Emergence of African-American Culture in the Plantation South.* New York: Penguin.

Abrahams, Roger D. 1993. Phantoms of Romantic Nationalism in Folkloristics. *Journal of American Folklore* 106:3–37.

Abrahams, Roger D. n.d., manuscript. The Folksong-Smithsonian Book of American Folksong.

Abrahams, Roger D., and Susan Kalčik. 1978. Folklore and Cultural Pluralism.

In Richard M. Dorson, ed., *Folklore in the Modern World*, pp. 223–36. The Hague: Mouton.

Abrams, M. H. 1953. *The Mirror and the Lamp: Romantic Theory and the Critical Tradition.* New York: Oxford University Press.

Ackerman, Robert. 1991. *The Myth and Ritual School.* New York: Garland.

Adorno, Theodor W. 1975 (1958). *Philosophie der neuen Musik.* Frankfurt: Suhrkamp.

Adorno, Theodor W. 1973. *The Jargon of Authenticity.* Trans. Kurt Tarnowski and Frederic Will. Evanston, Ill.: Northwestern University Press. (Original German ed. 1964.)

Adorno, Theodor W. 1984. *Aesthetic Theory.* Trans. C. Lenhardt. London: Routledge and Kegan Paul. (Original German ed., 1970.)

Adorno, Theodor W. 1991. *The Culture Industry.* Ed. J. M. Bernstein. London: Routledge.

Allen, William Francis, Charles Pickard Ware, and Lucy McKim Garrison. 1992 (1867). *Slave Songs of the United States.* Baltimore: Genealogical Publishing.

Ames, Michael M. 1992. *Cannibal Tours and Glass Boxes: The Anthropology of Museums.* Vancouver: University of British Columbia Press.

Anderson, Benedict. 1983. *Imagined Communities.* London: Verso.

Anderson, Jay. 1984. *Time Machines: The World of Living History.* Nashville: American Association for State and Local History.

Angus, Ian, and Sut Jhally. 1989. *Cultural Politics in Contemporary America.* New York: Routledge.

Antonijević, Dragoslav. 1969. Folklorismus in Jugoslawien. *Zeitschrift für Volkskunde* 65:29–39.

Appadurai, Arjun, ed. 1986. *The Social Life of Things: Commodities in Cultural Perspective.* Cambridge: Cambridge University Press.

Arnim, Achim von. 1963 (1818). Nachschrift an den Leser. In *Des Knaben Wunderhorn,* vol. 3, pp. 258–65. Munich: dtv.

Arnim, Achim von, and Clemens Brentano. 1979 (1806). *Des Knaben Wunderhorn: Studienausgabe.* Ed. H. Rölleke. Stuttgart: Kohlhammer.

Assion, Peter. 1986. Historismus, Traditionalismus, Folklorismus: Zur musealisierenden Tendenz der Gegenwartskultur. In U. Jeggle, G. Korff, M. Scharfe, and B. J. Warneken, eds., *Volkskultur in der Moderne,* pp. 351–62. Hamburg: Rowohlt.

Auerbach, Susan. 1991. The Brokering of Ethnic Folklore: Issues of Selection and Presentation at a Multicultural Festival. In Stern and Cicala, eds., *Creative Ethnicity,* pp. 223–38.

Bächtold, Hanns. 1916. Volkskunde. *Heimatschutz. Zeitschrift der Schweizerischen Vereinigung für Heimatschutz* 11 (6):81–94.

Baron, Robert. 1992. Postwar Public Folklore and the Professionalization of Folklore Studies. In Baron and Spitzer, eds., *Public Folklore,* pp. 307–38.

Baron, Robert, and Nicholas R. Spitzer, eds. 1992. *Public Folklore.* Washington, D.C.: Smithsonian Institution Press.

Barry, Phillips. 1939. *Folk Music in America.* American Folk Song Publications no. 4. Works Progress Administration, Federal Theater Project. New York: National Service Bureau.

Barry, Phillips. 1961. The Part of the Folk Singer in the Making of Folk Balladry. In M. Leach and T. P. Coffin, eds., *The Critics and the Ballad*, pp. 59–67. Carbondale: Southern Illinois Press.

Bascom, William R. 1965. The Forms of Folklore: Prose Narrative. *Journal of American Folklore* 78:3–20.

Baudrillard, Jean. 1994. *Simulacra and Simulation*. Trans. Sheila Faria Glaser. Ann Arbor: University of Michigan Press.

Baugh, Bruce. 1988. Authenticity Revisited. *Journal of Aesthetics and Criticism* 46 (4):477–87.

Bauman, Richard. 1972a. Differential Identity and the Social Base of Folklore. In Paredes and Bauman, eds., *Toward New Perspectives in Folklore*, pp. 31–41.

Bauman, Richard. 1972b. Introduction. In Paredes and Bauman, eds., *Toward New Perspectives in Folklore*, pp. xi–xv.

Bauman, Richard. 1984 (1977). *Verbal Art as Performance*. Prospect Heights, Ill.: Waveland Press.

Bauman, Richard. 1986. Performance and Honor in 13th-Century Iceland. *Journal of American Folklore* 99:131–50.

Bauman, Richard, and Roger D. Abrahams, eds. 1981. *"And other neighborly names . . .": Social Process and Cultural Image in Texas Folklore*. Austin: University of Texas Press.

Bauman, Richard, and Charles Briggs. 1990. Poetics and Performance as Critical Perspectives on Language and Social Life. *Annual Review of Anthropology* 19:59–88.

Bauman, Richard, and Joel Sherzer. 1989. *Explorations in the Ethnography of Speaking*. New York: Cambridge University Press.

Baumann, Max Peter. 1976. *Musikfolklore und Musikfolklorismus*. Winterthur: Amadeus.

Bausinger, Hermann. 1960. "Historisierende" Tendenzen im deutschen Märchen seit der Romantik. *Wirkendes Wort* 5:279–86.

Bausinger, Hermann. 1962. Volkskultur und industrielle Gesellschaft. *Beiträge zur deutschen Volks- und Altertumskunde* 6:5–20.

Bausinger, Hermann. 1965. Volksideologie und Volksforschung: Zur nationalsozialistischen Volkskunde. *Zeitschrift für Volkskunde* 61:177–204.

Bausinger, Hermann. 1966a. Folklore und gesunkenes Kulturgut. *Deutsches Jahrbuch für Volkskunde* 12:15–25.

Bausinger, Hermann. 1966b. Zur Kritik der Folklorismuskritik. In Bausinger, ed., *Populus Revisus*, pp. 61–72.

Bausinger, Hermann. 1966c. Eduard Hoffmann-Krayer—Leistung und Wirkung. *Zeitschrift für deutsche Philologie* 85:431–47.

Bausinger, Hermann. 1968. *Formen der "Volkspoesie."* Grundlagen der Germanistik, vol. 6. Berlin: Erich Schmidt.

Bausinger, Hermann. 1969a. Folklorismus in Europa: Eine Umfrage. *Zeitschrift für Volkskunde* 65:1–8.

Bausinger, Hermann. 1969b. Kritik der Tradition: Anmerkungen zur Situation der Volkskunde. *Zeitschrift für Volkskunde* 65:232–50.

Bausinger, Hermann. 1969c. Zur Algebra der Kontinuität. In Bausinger and Brückner, eds., *Kontinuität?*, pp. 9–30.

Bausinger, Hermann. 1971. *Volkskunde*. Darmstadt: Carl Habel.

Bausinger, Hermann. 1973. Dialekt oder Sprachbarriere? In Bausinger, ed., *Dialekt als Sprachbarriere: Ergebnisse einer Tagung zur alemännischen Dialektforschung*, pp. 8–27. Tübingen: Tübinger Vereinigung für Volkskunde.

Bausinger, Hermann. 1980. *Formen der "Volkspoesie."* Berlin: Erich Schmidt. (2d, rev. ed.; original ed. 1968).

Bausinger, Hermann. 1984. Folklorismus. In K. Ranke et al., eds., *Enzyklopädie des Märchens*, vol. 4, pp. 1405–10. Berlin: Walter de Gruyter.

Bausinger, Hermann. 1985. Traditionale Welten. *Zeitschrift für Volkskunde* 81: 173–91.

Bausinger, Hermann. 1986 (1961). *Volkskultur in der technischen Welt*. Frankfurt: Campus.

Bausinger, Hermann. 1987. Volkskunde and Volkstumsarbeit im Nationalsozialismus. In Gerndt, ed., *Volkskunde und Nationalsozialismus*, pp. 131–41.

Bausinger, Hermann. 1988. Da capo: Folklorismus. In Lehmann and Kuntz, eds., *Sichtweisen der Volkskunde*, pp. 321–29.

Bausinger, Hermann. 1990. *Folk Culture in a World of Technology*. Trans. Elke Dettmer. Bloomington: Indiana University Press. (Translation of Bausinger 1986 (1961).)

Bausinger, Hermann. 1991a. *Der blinde Hund*. Tübingen: Schwäbisches Tagblatt.

Bausinger, Hermann. 1991b (1982). Zum Begriff des Folklorismus. In Bausinger, *Der blinde Hund*, pp. 92–103.

Bausinger, Hermann. 1991c. Volk und Sprache. *Zeitschrift für Volkskunde* 87: 169–80.

Bausinger, Hermann, ed. 1966. *Populus Revisus: Beiträge zur Erforschung der Gegenwart* (= *Volksleben* vol. 14). Tübingen: Tübinger Vereinigung für Volkskunde.

Bausinger, Hermann, and Wolfgang Brückner, eds. 1969. *Kontinuität? Geschichtlichkeit und Dauer als Volkskundliches Problem*. Berlin: Erich Schmidt.

Bausinger, Hermann, Utz Jeggle, Gottfried Korff, and Martin Scharfe. 1978. *Grundzüge der Volkskunde*. Darmstadt: Wissenschaftliche Buchhandlung.

Beck, Ulrich. 1986. *Risikogesellschaft: Auf dem Weg in eine andere Moderne*. Frankfurt: Suhrkamp.

Beck, Ulrich. 1992. *Risk Society: Towards a New Modernity*. Trans. M. Ritter. London: Sage Publications. (Translation of Beck 1986.)

Beck, Ulrich, Anthony Giddens, and Scott Lash. 1994. *Reflexive Modernization: Politics, Tradition and Aesthetics in the Modern Social Order*. Stanford, Calif.: Stanford University Press.

Becker, Bernhard. 1987. *Herder-Rezeption in Deutschland: Eine ideologiekritische Untersuchung*. St. Ingbert: Werner J. Röhrig.

Behler, Ernst. 1983. *Die Zeitschriften der Brüder Schlegel: Ein Beitrag zur*

Geschichte der deutschen Romantik. Darmstadt: Wissenschaftliche Buchhandlung.

Bell, Michael J. 1973. William Wells Newell and the Foundation of American Folklore Scholarship. *Journal of the Folklore Institute* 10:7–21.

Bell, Michael J. 1988. "No Borders to the Ballad Maker's Art": Francis James Child and the Politics of the People. *Western Folklore* 47:285–307.

Bell, Michael J. 1995. "The Only True Folksongs We Have in English": James Russell Lowell and the Politics of the Nation. *Journal of American Folklore* 108: 131–55.

Belting, Hans. 1987. *The End of the History of Art?* Trans. C. S. Wood. Chicago: University of Chicago Press. (Original German ed. 1984.)

Ben-Amos, Dan. 1971. Toward a Definition of Folklore in Context. *Journal of American Folklore* 84:3–15.

Ben-Amos, Dan. 1973. A History of American Folklore Studies: Why Do We Need It? *Journal of the Folklore Institute* 10:113–24.

Ben-Amos, Dan. 1976. Analytic Categories and Ethnic Genres. In Ben-Amos, ed., *Folklore Genres*, pp. 215–42. Austin: University of Texas Press.

Ben-Amos, Dan. 1979. The Ceremony of Innocence. *Western Folklore* 38:47–52.

Ben-Amos, Dan. 1984. The Seven Strands of Tradition: Varieties in Its Meaning in American Folklore Studies. *Journal of Folklore Research* 21:97–131.

Ben-Amos, Dan. 1993. "Context" in Context. *Western Folklore* 52:209–26.

Bender, Wolfgang. 1973. *J. J. Bodmer and J. J. Breitinger.* Realien zur Literatur, vol. 113. Stuttgart: Metzler.

Bendix, Regina. 1985. *Progress and Nostalgia.* Berkeley: University of California Press.

Bendix, Regina. 1988. Folklorism: The Challenge of a Concept. *International Folklore Review* 6:5–15.

Bendix, Regina. 1989a. Tourism and Cultural Displays: Inventing Traditions for Whom? *Journal of American Folklore* 102:131–46.

Bendix, Regina. 1989b. *Backstage Domains: Performing* William Tell *in Two Swiss Communities.* Bern: Peter Lang.

Bendix, Regina. 1992. National Sentiment in the Enactment and Discourse of Swiss Patriotic Ritual. *American Ethnologist* 19 (4):768–90.

Bendix, Regina. 1994. Zur Problematik des Echtheitserlebnisses in Tourismus und Tourismustheorie. In B. Pöttler and U. Kammerhofer-Aggermann, eds., *Tourismus und Regionalkultur*, pp. 57–84. Vienna: Selbstverlag des Vereins für Volkskunde.

Bendix, Regina. 1995. *Amerikanische Folkloristik: Eine Einführung.* Berlin: Dietrich Reimer.

Benedict, Ruth. 1940. *Race: Science and Politics.* New York: Modern Age Books.

Beneš, Bohuslav. 1981. Folklorismus in der Tschechoslowakei. *Narodna Umjetnost* (Zagreb). Sonderheft Folklore and Oral Communication, pp. 115–24.

Benjamin, Walter. 1963. *Das Kunstwerk im Zeitalter seiner technischen Reproduzierbarkeit.* Frankfurt: Suhrkamp.

Benjamin, Walter. 1969. *Über Literatur.* Frankfurt: Suhrkamp.

Bercovitch, Sacvan. 1978. *The American Jeremiad.* Madison: University of Wisconsin Press.

Bergen, Fanny D. 1891. Topics for Collection of Folk-Lore. *Journal of American Folklore* 4:151–54.

Berlin, Isaiah. 1976. *Vico and Herder: Two Studies in the History of Ideas.* New York: Viking Press.

Berman, Marshall. 1972. *The Politics of Authenticity.* New York: Atheneum.

Berman, Marshall. 1988 (1982). *All That Is Solid Melts Into Air: The Experience of Modernity.* New York: Penguin.

Bitterli, Urs. 1976. *Die "Wilden" und die "Zivilisierten": Grundzüge einer Geistes- und Kulturgeschichte der europäisch-überseeischen Begegnung.* Munich: Beck.

Bitterli, Urs. 1989. *Cultures in Conflict: Encounters between European and Non-European Cultures, 1492–1800.* Trans. Ritchie Robertson. Stanford, Calif.: Stanford University Press.

Black, Nancy B., and Bette S. Weidman. 1976. *White on Red: Images of the American Indian.* Port Washington, N.Y.: Kennikat Press.

Bloom, Harold. 1973. *The Anxiety of Influence: A Theory of Poetry.* London: Oxford University Press.

Bluestein, Gene. 1972. *The Voice of the Folk: Folklore and American Literary Theory.* Amherst: University of Massachusetts Press.

Blum, Carol. 1986. *Rousseau and the Republic of Virtue: The Language and Politics of the French Revolution.* Ithaca, N.Y.: Cornell University Press.

Boas, Franz. 1916. *Tsimshian Mythology.* 31. Annual Report of the Bureau of American Ethnology, 1909–1910. Washington, D.C.: U.S. Government Printing Office.

Boas, Franz. 1940. *Race, Language, and Culture.* New York.

Boas, Franz. 1966 (1911). Introduction. *Handbook of American Indian Languages.* Reprint, ed. Preston Holder. Lincoln: University of Nebraska Press.

Boas, Franz. 1973 (1932). *Bella Bella Tales.* New York: Kraus.

Boas, George. 1969. *Vox Populi: Essays in the History of an Idea.* Baltimore: Johns Hopkins University Press.

Bockhorn, Olaf. 1987. Pflege, Tracht und Ideologie—Eine Klarstellung. In K. Beitl and O. Bockhorn, eds., *Kleidung—Mode—Tracht: Buchreihe der Österreichischen Zeitschrift für Volkskunde,* vol. 7, pp. 281–83. Vienna: Selbstverlag des Vereins für Volkskunde.

Bodemann, Ulrike. 1983. Folklorismus—Ein Modellentwurf. *Rheinisch-Westfälische Zeitschrift für Volkskunde* 28:101–10.

Bodmer, Johann Jakob. 1740. *Critische Abhandlung von dem Wunderbaren in der Poesie und dessen Verbindung mit dem Wahrscheinlichen.* Reprint. Stuttgart: Metzler, 1966.

Bodmer, J. J., and J. J. Breitinger. 1721–23. *Die Discourse der Mahlern.* Facsimile reprint. Hildesheim: Georg Olms, 1969.

Bodmer, J. J., and J. J. Breitinger, eds. 1748. *Proben der alten schwäbischen Poesie des Dreyzehnten Jahrhunderts aus der Manessischen Sammlung.* Reprint. Hildesheim: Gerstenberg, 1973.

Bodmer, J. J., and J. J. Breitinger. 1746. *Der Mahler der Sitten.* Facsimile reprint. Hildesheim: Georg Olms. 1972.

Boggs, Ralph Steele. 1940. Folklore in University Curricula in the United States. *Southern Folklore Quarterly* 4:93–109.

Bollmus, Reinhard. 1970. *Das Amt Rosenberg und seine Gegner.* Stuttgart: Deutsche Verlags-Anstalt.

Bollmus, Reinhard. 1987. Zwei Volkskunden im Dritten Reich. In Gerndt, ed., *Volkskunde und Nationalsozialismus,* pp. 49–60.

Bolte, Johannes, and Jiři Polivka. 1913–31. *Anmerkungen zu den Kinder- und Hausmärchen der Brüder Grimm.* 5 vols. Berlin: Dieterich.

Boni, Pat. 1982. King Lear and the Real: Religious and Philosophical Dimensions of Authenticity. Ph.D. Dissertation, Temple University.

Boorstein, Daniel J. 1962. *The Image or What Happened to the American Dream.* New York: Atheneum.

Botkin, Benjamin A. 1944. *A Treasury of American Folklore.* New York: Crown.

Bourdieu, Pierre. 1991. *The Political Ontology of Martin Heidegger.* Trans. Peter Collier. Stanford, Calif.: Stanford University Press.

Bracher, Karl Dietrich. 1970. *The German Dictatorship.* Trans. Jean Steinberg. New York: Holt, Rinehart and Winston.

Brandes, Helga. 1974. *Die "Gesellschaft der Maler" und ihr literarischer Beitrag zur Aufklärung.* Studien zur Publizistik, vol. 21. Bremen: Schünemann Universitätsverlag.

Braun, Rudolf. 1965. *Sozialer und kultureller Wandel in einem ländlichen Industriegebiet.* Stuttgart: Eugen Rentsch.

Braun, Rudolf. 1986. "The Invention of Tradition": Wilhelm II. und die Renaissance der höfischen Tänze. *Schweizerisches Archiv für Volkskunde* 82: 227–49.

Brednich, Rolf Wilhelm. 1988. Volkswelt als Kulisse: Folklorismusphänomene im 18. Jahrhundert. In N.A. Bringeus et al., eds., *Volkskultur im Wandel: Festschrift für Günter Wiegelmann,* vol. 2, pp. 741–56. Beiträge zur Volkskultur in Nordwestdeutschland, vol. 60. Münster.

Brednich, Rolf Wilhelm, ed. 1988. *Grundriss der Volkskunde.* Berlin: Dietrich Reimer.

Breitinger, Johann Jakob. 1740. *Critische Dichtkunst.* Reprint 1966.

Bressler, Sandra Gross. 1995. Culture and Politics: A Legislative Chronicle of the American Folklife Preservation Act. Ph.D. Dissertation, University of Pennsylvania.

Briggs, Charles. 1978. *The Woodcarvers of Cordova, New Mexico: The Social Dimension of an Artistic Revival.* Knoxville: University of Tennessee Press.

Briggs, Charles. 1993. Metadiscursive Practices and Scholarly Authority in Folkloristics. *Journal of American Folklore* 106:387–434.

Briggs, Charles, and Amy Shuman. 1993. Theorizing Folklife: Toward New Perspectives on the Politics of Culture. *Western Folklore* (special issue) 52, nos. 2, 3, and 4.

Bronner, Simon. 1986. *American Folklore Studies: An Intellectual History.* Lawrence: Presses of the University of Kansas.

Bronner, Simon. 1992. Martha Warren Beckwith, America's First Chair of Folklore. *Folklore Historian* 9:5–49.

Brückner, Wolfgang. 1965. Heimat und Demokratie: Gedanken zum politischen Folklorismus in Westdeutschland. *Zeitschrift für Volkskunde* 61:205–13.

Brückner, Wolfgang. 1966. Vereinswesen und Folklorismus. In Bausinger, ed., *Populus Revisus,* pp. 77–98.

Brückner, Wolfgang. 1976. Ruf nach dem Kanon. *Bayrische Blätter für Volkskunde* 3:3–17.

Brückner, Wolfgang. 1984. Popular Kultur: Konstrukt, Interpretament, Realität. *Ethnologia Europaea* 14:14–24.

Brückner, Wolfgang. 1986. Trachtenfolklorismus. In U. Jeggle, G. Korff, M. Scharfe and B. J. Warneken, eds. *Volkskultur in der Moderne,* pp. 363–82. Hamburg: Rowohlt.

Brückner, Wolfgang, ed. 1971. Falkensteiner Protokolle. Frankfurt a.M.: limited duplicated materials.

Brückner, Wolfgang, and Klaus Beitl, eds. 1983. *Volkskunde als akademische Disziplin.* Österreichische Akademie der Wissenschaften, vol. 414. Vienna: Verlag der Österreichischen Akademie der Wissenschaften.

Brunner, Heinz-Rudi. 1974. *Volksfeste zwischen Rhein, Main und Neckar.* Studien zum Folklorismus in der Gegenwart. Frankfurt: a.M.: Herbert Lang.

Buchanan, Annabel Morris. 1937. The Function of a Folk Festival. *Southern Folklore Quarterly* 1:29–34.

Bullock, Marcus Paul. 1990. Reading Comes to Grief: Style and the Philosophy of History in Martin Heidegger and Walter Benjamin. *Germanic Review* 65 (4): 138–49.

Bunzl, Matti. 1996. Franz Boas and the Humboldtian Tradition: From *Volksgeist* and *Nationalcharakter* to an Anthropological Concept of Culture. In Stocking, ed., Volksgeist *as Method and Ethic,* pp. 17–78.

Burckhardt-Seebass, Christine. 1988. Echt—gepflegt—organisiert? Hoffmann-Krayers Gedanken zur Volkskultur. In S. Göttsch and K. Sievers, eds., *Forschungsfeld Museum,* pp. 49–60. Kiel: Kommissionsverlag Walter G. Mühlau.

Burke, Kenneth. 1950. *A Rhetoric of Motives.* New York: Prentice-Hall.

Burke, Peter. 1981. The "Discovery" of Popular Culture. In S. Raphael, ed., *People's History and Socialist History,* pp. 216–26. London: Routledge and Kegan Paul.

Burke, Peter. 1984. Popular Culture between History and Ethnology. *Ethnologia Europaea* 14:5–13.

Burszta, Jozef. 1969. Folklorismus in Polen. *Zeitschrift für Volkskunde* 65:9–20.

Buzard, James M. 1988. Forster's Trespasses: Tourism and Cultural Politics. *Twentieth-Century Literature* 34:155–79.

Bibliography

269

Cadaval, Olivia. 1991. Making a Place Home: The Latino Festival. In Stern and Cicala, eds., *Creative Ethnicity*, pp. 204–22.

Camp, Charles, ed. 1989. *Time and Temperament: A Centennial Publication of the American Folklore Society.* Washington, D.C.: American Folklore Society.

Cannizo, Jeanne. 1983. George Hunt and the Invention of Kwakiutl Culture. *Canadian Review of Sociology and Anthropology* 20:44–58.

Cantwell, Robert. 1993. *Ethnomimesis: Folklore and the Representation of Culture.* Chapel Hill: University of North Carolina Press.

Carnap, Rudolf. 1931. Überwindung der Metaphysik durch logische Analyse der Sprache. *Erkenntnis* 2:219–41.

Carstens, H. 1890. An die Freunde der Volkskunde! *Am Ur-Quell. Monatsschrift für Volkskunde* 1:1–3.

Charmé, Stuart Zane. 1991. *Vulgarity and Authenticity: Dimensions of Otherness in the World of Jean-Paul Sartre.* Amherst: University of Massachusetts Press.

Child, Francis James. 1874. Ballad Poetry. In F. A. P. Barnard, ed., *Johnson's New Universal Encyclopedia*, pp. 365–68. New York: A. J. Johnson and Sons.

Child, Francis James, ed. 1965 (1884–98). *The English and Scottish Popular Ballads.* 5 vols. New York: Dover.

Clark, William. 1989. On the Dialectical Origins of the Research Seminar. *History of Science* 27 (2):111–54.

Clifford, James. 1985. Histories of the Tribal and the Modern. *Art in America*, April, pp. 164–215.

Clifford, James. 1988. *The Predicament of Culture.* Cambridge, Mass.: Harvard University Press.

Clifford, James, and George Marcus, eds. 1986. *Writing Culture.* Berkeley: University of California Press.

Cocchiara, Giuseppe. 1981. *The History of Folklore in Europe.* Trans. John N. McDaniel. Philadelphia: Institute for the Study of Human Issues.

Cohen, Erik. 1988. Authenticity and Commoditization in Tourism. *Annals of Tourism Research* 15:371–86.

Cohen, Jonathan. 1988. "If Rabbi Akiba were alive today . . ." or The Authenticity Argument. *American Jewish Congress* 37:136–42.

Cole, Douglas. 1983. "The Value of a Person Lies in His *Herzensbildung*": Franz Boas' Baffin Island Letter-Diary, 1883–1884. In Stocking, ed., *Observers Observed*, pp. 13–52.

Cole, Douglas. 1985. *Captured Heritage: The Scramble for Northwest Coast Artifacts.* Vancouver: Douglas and McIntyre.

Cosma, Anton. 1987. The Modern Career of a Concept: Authenticity. *Romanian Review* 41:50–58.

Crüger, Johannes. 1965 (1884). *Joh. Christoph Gottsched und die Schweizer Joh. J. Bodmer und Joh. J. Breitinger.* Darmstadt: Wissenschaftliche Buchgesellschaft.

Cushing, Frank H. 1970 (1882–83). *My Adventures in Zuni.* Palo Alto, Calif.: American West.

Dahlhaus, Carl. 1967. Zur Dialektik von "echt" und "unecht." *Zeitschrift für Volkskunde* 63:56–57.

Darnell, Regna. 1973. American Anthropology and the Development of Folklore Scholarship—1890–1920. *Journal of the Folklore Institute* 10, no. 1/2: 23–39.

Darnell, Regna. 1988. *Daniel Garrison Brinton: The "Fearless Critic" of Philadelphia.* University of Pennsylvania Publications in Anthropology no. 3. Philadelphia: Department of Anthropology.

Darnell, Regna. 1990. *Edward Sapir: Linguist, Anthropologist, Humanist.* Berkeley: University of California Press.

Daxelmüller, Christoph. 1991. "Heimat": Volkskundliche Anmerkungen zu einem umstrittenen Begriff. *Bayrische Blätter für Volkskunde* 4:223–41.

de Caro, Francis. 1986. Vanishing the Red Man: Cultural Guilt and Legend Formation. *International Folklore Review* 4:74–80.

Dégh, Linda. 1968/69. Survival and Revival of European Folk Cultures in America. *Ethnologia Europaea* 2–3:97–108.

Dégh, Linda. 1972. Folk Narrative. In Richard M. Dorson, ed., *Folklore and Folklife,* pp. 53–83. Chicago: University of Chicago Press.

Dégh, Linda. 1977/78. Grape-Harvest Festival of Strawberry Farmers: Folklore or Fake. *Ethnologia Europaea* 10:114–31.

Dégh, Linda. 1980. Is the Study of Tale Performance Suspect of Aggressive Nationalism? *and* Reply: Folk and *Volk. Journal of American Folklore* 93:324–27, 331–34.

Denecke, Ludwig. 1990. Grimm, Jacob Ludwig Carl and Grimm, Wilhelm Carl. In K. Ranke et al., eds., *Enzyklopädie des Märchens,* vol. 6, pp. 171–95. Berlin: Walter de Gruyter.

Denecke, Ludwig, and Charlotte Oberfeld. 1989. Die Bedeutung der "Volkspoesie" bei Jacob und Wilhelm Grimm. In C. Oberfeld et al., eds., *Brüder Grimm Volkslieder,* vol. 2. Marburg: N. G. Elwert.

Derrida, Jacques. 1976. *Of Grammatology.* Trans. G. C. Spivak. Baltimore: Johns Hopkins University Press.

Dias, Jorge. 1969. Folklorismus in Polen. *Zeitschrift für Volkskunde* 65:47–55.

Diehl, Carl. 1978. *Americans and German Scholarship, 1770–1870.* New Haven, Conn.: Yale University Press.

Dieterich, Albert. 1958 (1902). Über Wesen und Ziele der Volkskunde. In Lutz, ed., *Volkskunde,* pp. 78–88.

Dömötör, Tekla. 1969. Folklorismus in Ungarn. *Zeitschrift für Volkskunde* 65:21–28.

Dorson, Richard M. 1955. The Eclipse of Solar Mythology. *Journal of American Folklore* 68:393–416.

Dorson, Richard M. 1959. *American Folklore.* Chicago: University of Chicago Press.

Dorson, Richard M. 1962. Folklore and the NDEA. *Journal of American Folklore* 75:160–64.

Dorson, Richard M. 1964. *Buying the Wind.* Chicago: University of Chicago Press.

Dorson, Richard M. 1966. The Question of Folklore in a New Nation. *Journal of the Folklore Institute* 6:277–98.

Dorson, Richard M. 1969. Fakelore. *Zeitschrift für Volkskunde* 65:56–64.

Dorson, Richard M. 1972. Introduction. In Dorson, ed., *Folklore and Folklife,* pp. 1–50. Chicago: University of Chicago Press.

Dorson, Richard M. 1976. Folklore, Academe and the Marketplace. In Dorson, *Folklore and Fakelore,* pp. 1–29. Cambridge, Mass.: Harvard University Press.

Dorson, Richard M. 1982. The State of Folkloristics from an American Perspective. *Journal of the Folklore Institute* 19:71–105.

Dorson, Richard M. 1983. Teaching Folklore to Graduate Students: The Introductory Proseminar. In Dorson, ed., *Handbook of American Folklore,* pp. 463–69. Bloomington: Indiana University Press.

Dow, James, and Hannjost Lixfeld, eds. 1986. *German Volkskunde: A Decade of Theoretical Confrontation, Debate, and Reorientation 1967–1977.* Bloomington: Indiana University Press.

Dow, James, and Hannjost Lixfeld, eds. 1991. National Socialistic Folklore and Overcoming the Past in the Federal Republic of Germany. *Asian Folklore Studies* 50:117–53.

Dow, James, and Hannjost Lixfeld, eds. 1994. *The Nazification of an Academic Discipline: Folklore and the Third Reich.* Bloomington: Indiana University Press.

Duberman, Martin. 1966. *James Russell Lowell.* Boston: Beacon Press.

Duerr, Hans Peter, ed. 1987. *Authentizität und Betrug in der Ethnologie.* Frankfurt: Suhrkamp.

Dülmen, Richard van, and Norbert Schindler, eds. 1984. *Volkskultur: Zur Wiederentdeckung des vergessenen Alltags.* Frankfurt: Fischer.

Dundes, Alan. 1965. *The Study of Folklore.* Englewood Cliffs, N.J.: Prentice-Hall.

Dundes, Alan. 1969. The Devolutionary Premise in Folklore Theory. *Journal of the Folklore Institute* 6:5–19.

Dundes, Alan. 1978 (1977). Who Are the Folk? In Dundes, *Analytic Essays in Folklore,* pp. 1–21. Meerut (India): Folklore Institute.

Dundes, Alan. 1985. Nationalistic Inferiority Complexes and the Fabrication of Folklore. *Journal of Folklore Research* 22:5–18.

Dünninger, Josef. 1937. *Volkskultur und geschichtliche Welt: Gesetz und Wege des deutschen Volkstums.* Berlin: Essener Verlagsanstalt.

Dwyer-Shick, Susan. 1976. Folklore and Government Support (Review Essay). *Journal of American Folklore* 89:476–86.

Dwyer-Shick, Susan. 1979. The American Folklore Society and Folklore Research in America, 1888–1940. Ph.D. Dissertation, Department of Folklore and Folklife, University of Pennsylvania.

Eberhart, Helmut. 1991. Karl Weinhold in Graz. In Kai Detlev Sievers, ed., *Bei-*

träge zur Wissenschaftsgeschichte der Volkskunde im 19. und 20. Jahrhundert: Studien zur Volkskunde und Kulturgeschichte Schleswig-Holsteins, vol. 26, pp. 23–40. Neumünster: Karl Wachholtz.

Eberhart, Helmut. 1992. Viktor von Geramb und seine Bedeutung für die Österreichische Volkskunde. In O. Pickl and R. Hausmann, eds., *800 Jahre Steiermark und Österreich 1192–1992*, pp. 681–702. Graz: Historische Landeskommission für Steiermark.

Eco, Umberto. 1986. *Travels in Hyperreality*. Trans. William Weaver. Orlando, Fla.: Harcourt Brace Jovanovich.

Ellis, John M. 1983. *One Fairy Story Too Many: The Brothers Grimm and Their Tales*. Chicago: University of Chicago Press.

Ellison, Julie. 1984. *Emerson's Romantic Style*. Princeton, N.J.: Princeton University Press.

Emerson, Ralph Waldo. 1971. *The Collected Works of Ralph Waldo Emerson*. Vol. 1. Cambridge, Mass: Belknap Press of Harvard University.

Emmerich, Wolfgang. 1971. *Zur Kritik der Volkstumsideologie*. Frankfurt a.M.: Suhrkamp.

Ergang, Robert R. 1966. *Herder and the Foundations of German Nationalism*. New York: Octagon Books.

Estermann, Alfred, ed. 1978. *Die Deutschen Literatur-Zeitschriften: Bibliographien—Programme—Autoren*. Nendeln: KTO Press.

Evans, Timothy H. 1988. Folklore as Utopia: English Medievalists and the Ideology of Revivalism. *Western Folklore* 47:245–68.

Evans-Pritchard, Deirdre. 1987. The Portal Case: Authenticity, Tourism, Tradition, and the Law. *Journal of American Folklore* 100:287–96.

Fachschaft EKW. 1986. Legenden und Wirklichkeit: Institutsgeschichte aus studentischer Sicht. In Utz Jeggle et al., eds., *Tübinger Beiträge zur Volkskultur*, vol. 69, pp. 348–73. Tübingen: Tübinger Vereinigung für Volkskunde.

Feintuch, Burt. 1995. Learning Music in Northumberland: Experience in Musical Ethnography. *Journal of American Folklore* 108:298–306.

Feintuch, Burt, ed. 1988. *The Conservation of Culture*. Lexington: University Press of Kentucky.

Feintuch, Burt, ed. 1995. Common Ground: Keywords for the Study of Expressive Culture. *Journal of American Folklore* (special issue) 108:391–528.

Feldman, Burton, and Robert D. Richardson. 1972. *The Rise of Modern Mythology, 1680–1860*. Bloomington: Indiana University Press.

Fell, Joseph P. 1979. *Heidegger and Sartre: An Essay on Being and Place*. New York: Columbia University Press.

Ferrara, Alessandro. 1993. *Modernity and Authenticity: A Study of the Social and Ethical Thought of Jean-Jacques Rousseau*. Albany: State University of New York Press.

Fienup-Riordan, Ann. 1988. Robert Redford, Apanuugpak, and the Invention of Tradition. *American Ethnologist* 15:442–55.

Fine, Elizabeth. 1984. *The Folklore Text: From Performance to Print*. Bloomington: Indiana University Press.

Fischer, Hans. 1990. *Völkerkunde und Nationalsozialismus: Affinität und Behauptung einer wissenschaftlichen Disziplin.* Berlin: Dietrich Reimer.

Flemming, Walter. 1988. Auszug aus einem Briefwechsel über Ossian. In W. Jens, ed., *Kindlers Neues Literaturlexikon,* pp. 713–14. Munich: Kindler.

Fohrmann, Jürgen, and Wilhelm Vosskamp, eds. 1991. *Wissenschaft und Nation.* Munich: Fink.

Foley, John Miles. 1988. *The Theory of Oral Composition.* Bloomington: Indiana University Press.

Foucault, Michel. 1972. *The Archeology of Knowledge and the Discourse on Language.* Trans. A. M. Sheridan Smith. New York: Harper and Row.

Fox, William. 1980. Folklore and Fakelore. *Journal of the Folklore Institute* 17: 244–61.

Frazer, James George. 1911–15. *The Golden Bough: A Study in Comparative Religion.* 3d ed. London.

Frederickson, George M. 1971. *The Black Image in the White Mind.* New York: Harper and Row.

Freudenthal, Herbert. 1934. *Mein Kampf* als politische Volkskunde der deutschen Gegenwart auf rassischer Grundlage. *Zeitschrift für Volkskunde,* n.s., 6:122–35.

Freudenthal, Herbert. 1935. *Deutsche Wissenschaft im Kampf um das Volk.* Berlin-Leipzig. (Cited in Trümpy 1987, p. 172)

Freudenthal, Herbert. 1964. Nomen est Omen. *Beiträge zur Deutschen Volks- und Altertumskunde* 8:7–20.

Gable, Eric, and Richard Handler. 1996. After Authenticity at an American Heritage Site. *American Anthropologist* 98:568–578.

Gauger, Wilhelm. 1987. Die Ossianische Verlegenheit. In Duerr, ed., *Authentizität und Betrug in der Ethnologie,* pp. 333–56.

Gates, Henry Louis, Jr. 1991. "Authenticity," or the Lesson of Little Tree. *New York Times,* Nov. 24.

Geary, Patrick. 1986. Sacred Commodities: The Circulation of Medieval Relics. In Appadurai, ed., *The Social Life of Things,* pp. 169–91.

Geertz, Clifford. 1973. *The Interpretation of Cultures.* New York: Basic Books.

Geertz, Clifford. 1983. Blurred Genres: The Refiguration of Social Thought. In Geertz, *Local Knowledge,* pp. 19–35. New York: Basic Books.

Geertz, Clifford. 1986. Making Experiences, Authoring Selves. In Turner and Bruner, eds., *The Anthropology of Experience,* pp. 373–80.

Geiger, Klaus, Utz Jeggle, and Gottfried, Korff, eds. 1970. *Abschied vom Volksleben.* Untersuchungen des LUI, vol. 27. Tübingen: Tübinger Vereinigung für Volkskunde.

Geiger, Paul. 1912. *Volksliedinteresse und Volksliedforschung in der Schweiz.* Bern: Francke.

Georges, Robert, ed. 1989a. Richard M. Dorson's Views and Works: An Assessment. *Journal of Folklore Research* (special issue) 26, no. 1.

Georges, Robert, ed. 1989b. Richard Dorson. *Western Folklore* (special issue) 48, no. 4.

Georges, Robert, and Michael O. Jones. 1980. *People Studying People*. Berkeley: University of California Press.

Geramb, Viktor von. 1958 (1924). Die Volkskunde als Wissenschaft. In Lutz, ed., *Volkskunde* pp. 108–26.

Geramb, Viktor von. 1937. Urverbundenheit. *Hessische Blätter für Volkskunde* 36:1–31.

Gerndt, Helge. 1986. *Kultur als Forschungsfeld*. Münchner Beiträge zur Volkskunde, vol. 5. Munich: Münchner Vereinigung für Volkskunde.

Gerndt, Helge. 1988. Einleitung. In Gerndt, ed., *Fach und Begriff "Volkskunde" in der Diskussion*, pp. 1-21.

Gerndt, Helge. 1995. Deutsche Volkskunde and Nationalsozialismus: Was haben wir aus der Geschichte gelernt? *Schweizerisches Archiv für Volkskunde* 91: 53–76.

Gerndt, Helge, ed. 1987. *Volkskunde und Nationalsozialismus*. Münchner Beiträge zur Volkskunde, vol. 7. Munich: Münchner Vereinigung für Volkskunde.

Gerndt, Helge, ed. 1988. *Fach und Begriff "Volkskunde" in der Diskussion*. Darmstadt: Wissenschaftliche Buchgesellschaft.

Gisi, Martin. 1979. *Der Begriff Spiel im Denken J.-P. Sartres*. Monographien zur Philosophischen Forschung, vol. 176. Königstein: Forum Academicum.

Glassie, Henry. 1982. *Passing the Time in Ballymenone*. Philadelphia: University of Pennsylvania Press.

Glassie, Henry. 1983. The Moral Lore of Folklore. *Folklore Forum* 16:123–52.

Glassie, Henry. 1993. *Turkish Traditional Art Today*. Bloomington: Indiana University Press.

Goethe, Johann Wolfgang. 1962. *Reisen. Goethes Werke in 10 Bänden*. Vol. 9. Ed. P. Boerner. Zurich: Artemis.

Goldstein, Kenneth S. 1964. *A Guide for Fieldworkers in Folklore*. Hatboro, Pa.: Folklore Associates.

Gossen, Gary. 1972. Chamula Genres of Verbal Behavior. In Paredes and Bauman, eds., *Toward New Perspectives in Folklore*, pp. 145–67.

Göttsch, Silke. 1991. Feldforschung und Märchendokumentation. *Zeitschrift für Volkskunde* 87:1–18.

Göttsch, Silke. 1994. Frühe Tourismuskritik in der Heimatschutzbewegung. In B. Pöttler und U. Kammerhofer-Aggermann, eds., *Tourismus und Regionalkultur*, pp. 25–40. Vienna: Selbstverlag des Vereins für Volkskunde.

Gottsched, Johann Christoph. 1730. *Versuch einer critischen Dichtkunst vor die Deutschen*. Leipzig: Breitkopf.

Gougeon, Len. 1990. *Virtue's Hero: Emerson, Antislavery, and Reform*. Athens: University of Georgia Press.

Graff, Gerald. 1987. *Professing Literature: An Institutional History*. Chicago: University of Chicago Press.

Grant, Robert M. 1993. *Heresy and Criticism: The Search for Authenticity in Early Christian Literature*. Louisville, Ky.: Westminster/John Knox Press.

Grawe, Christian. 1967. *Herders Kulturanthropologie: Die Philosophie der Ge-*

schichte der Menschheit im Lichte der Modernen Kulturanthropologie. Bonn: Bouvier.

Green, Archie. 1983. Interpreting Folklore Ideologically. In Richard M. Dorson, ed., *Handbook of American Folklore*, pp. 351–58. Bloomington: Indiana University Press.

Green, Archie. 1988. P.L. 94-201—A View from the Lobby. In Feintuch, ed., *The Conservation of Culture*, pp. 269–79.

Green, Archie. 1989. The Folklorist as Cultural Critic. In Camp, ed., *Time and Temperament*, pp. 26–27.

Greenblatt, Stephen. 1991. *Marvelous Possessions: The Wonder of the New World.* Chicago: University of Chicago Press.

Greverus, Ina-Maria. 1978. *Kultur und Alltagswelt.* Munich: C. H. Beck.

Greverus, Ina-Maria. 1979. *Auf der Suche nach Heimat.* Munich: C. H. Beck.

Greverus, Ina-Maria, and Heinz Schilling, eds. 1982. *Heimat Bergen-Enkheim*, vol. 12. Frankfurt: Institut für Kulturanthropologie.

Greverus, Ina-Maria, and Erika Haindl, eds. 1983. *Versuche der Zivilisation zu entkommen.* Munich: C. H. Beck.

Greverus, Ina-Maria, Otfried Schütz, and Willi Stubenvoll, eds. 1984. *Naif: Alltagsästhetik oder ästhetisierter Alltag*, vol. 19. Frankfurt: Institut für Kulturanthropologie und Europäische Ethnologie.

Griebel, Armin. 1991a. Trachtenvereine und Politfolklore: Zur Situation in Nürnberg 1919 bis 1933. *Jahrbuch für Volkskunde* 14:79–100.

Griebel, Armin. 1991b. *Tracht und Folklorismus in Franken.* Volkskunde und Kulturgeschichte, vol. 48. Würzburg: Richard Mayr.

Griebel, Armin. 1991c. *Amtliche Berichte zur Tracht in Franken.* Volkskunde und Kulturgeschichte, vol. 49. Würzburg: Richard Mayr.

Grimm, Jacob. 1867. *Jacob Grimms Briefe, 1829–1859.* Vienna: Carl Gerolds Sohn.

Grimm, Jacob. 1876 (1835). *Deutsche Mythologie.* Ed. E. Meyer. 4th ed. Berlin: Dümmlers Verlagsbuchhandlung.

Grimm, Jacob. 1879. *Reden und Abhandlungen.* 2d ed. Berlin: Dümmlers Verlagsbuchhandlung.

Grimm, Wilhelm. 1889 (1829). *Die Deutsche Heldensage.* 3d ed. Gütersloh: Bertelsmann.

Grimm, Jacob, and Wilhelm Grimm. 1976 (1819). *Kinder- und Hausmärchen.* Munich: Winkler.

Grimm, Jacob, and Wilhelm Grimm. 1980 (1857). *Kinder- und Hausmärchen.* Ed. H. Rölleke. Stuttgart: Reclam.

Grimm, Jacob, and Wilhelm Grimm. 1981 (1816). *The German Legends of the Brothers Grimm.* Ed. and trans. Donald Ward. Philadelphia: Institute for the Study of Human Issues.

Grimm, Jacob, and Wilhelm Grimm. 1986. *Kinder- und Hausmärchen: Gesammelt durch die Brüder Grimm.* Vergrösserter Nachdruck der zweibändigen Erstausgabe von 1812 und 1815 nach dem Handexemplar des Brüder Grimm-Museums Kassel mit sämtlichen handschriftlichen Korrekturen und Nachträgen der Brüder Grimm sowie einem Ergänzungsheft, Transkriptionen und Kommentaren. Ed. H. Rölleke and U. Marquart. 3 vols. Göttingen: Vandenhoeck and Ruprecht.

Grosser Herder. 1952. *Der Grosse Herder.* Freiburg: Herder.

Grunewald, Eckhard. 1988. *Friedrich Heinrich von der Hagen 1780–1856: Ein Beitrag zur Frühgeschichte der Germanistik.* Berlin: Walter de Gruyter.

Gummere, Francis B. 1961 (1897). The Ballad and Communal Poetry. In M. Leach and T. P. Coffin, eds., *The Critics and the Ballad,* pp. 20–29. Carbondale: Southern Illinois University Press.

Haberlandt, Michael. 1895. Zu Beginn! *Zeitschrift für österreichische Volkskunde* 1:1–3.

Habermas, Jürgen. 1971. *Knowledge and Human Interest.* Trans. J. Shapiro. Boston: Beacon Press. (Original German ed., 1962.)

Habermas, Jürgen. 1989. *The Structural Transformation of the Public Sphere.* Trans. Thomas Burger. Cambridge, Mass.: MIT Press. (Original German ed., 1962.)

Hahn, J. G. von. 1876. *Sagwissenschaftliche Studien.* Jena: Friedrich Maukes.

Hale, Edward Everett. 1899. *James Russell Lowell and His Friends.* Boston: Houghton Mifflin.

Hall, Stuart. 1981. Notes on Deconstructing "The Popular." In Samuel Raphael, ed., *People's History and Socialist History,* pp. 227–40. London: Routledge and Kegan Paul.

Handler, Richard. 1986. Authenticity. *Anthropology Today* 2 (1): 2–4.

Handler, Richard. 1987. Overpowered by Realism: Living History and the Simulation of the Past. *Journal of American Folklore* 100:337–41.

Handler, Richard. 1988. *Nationalism and the Politics of Culture in Quebec.* Madison: University of Wisconsin Press.

Handler, Richard. 1989. Anti-Romantic Romanticism: Edward Sapir and the Critique of American Individualism. *American Quarterly* 62:1–14.

Handler, Richard. 1990a. Boasian Anthropology and the Critique of American Culture. *American Quarterly* 42:252–73.

Handler, Richard. 1990b. Consuming Culture (Genuine and Spurious) as Style (Review Essay). *Cultural Anthropology* 5:346–57.

Handler, Richard, and Jocelyn Linnekin. 1984. Tradition: Genuine or Spurious. *Journal of American Folklore* 97:273–90.

Handler, Richard, and William Saxton. 1988. Dyssimulation: Reflexivity, Narrative, and the Quest for Authenticity in "Living History." *Cultural Anthropology* 3:242–60.

Hanson, Allan. 1989. The Making of the Maori: Culture Invention and Its Logic. *American Anthropologist* 91:890–902.

Haring, Lee. 1990. Variability and Authenticity. In V. Calame-Griaul, ed., *D'Un Conte a l'autre: La variabilité dans la culture orale,* pp. 415–16. Paris: Editions du CNRS.

Harmening, Dieter, et al., eds. 1970. *Volkskultur und Geschichte: Festgabe für Josef Dünninger zum 65. Geburtstag.* Berlin: Erich Schmidt.

Harmening, Dieter, and Erich Wimmer, eds. 1986. *Volkskultur und Heimat: Festschrift für Josef Dünninger zum 85. Geburtstag.* Würzburg: Königshausen und Neumann.

Hart, James Morgan. 1989 (1874). German Universities: A Narrative of Personal Experience. In G. Graff and M. Warner, eds., *The Origins of Literary Studies in America: A Documentary Anthology,* pp. 17–24. New York: Routledge.

Hartmann, Andreas. 1988. Die Anfänge der Volkskunde. In Brednich, ed., *Grundriss der Volkskunde,* pp. 9–30.

Haym, Rudolf. 1860. *Herder nach seinem Leben und seinen Werken.* Berlin: Rudolph Gaertner.

Hebel, Johann Peter. 1980 (1811). *Schatzkästlein des Rheinischen Hausfreundes.* Tübingen: Wunderlich.

Heidegger, Martin. 1962. *Being and Time.* Trans. J. Macquarrie and E. Robinson. New York: Harper and Bros. (Original German ed., 1927.)

Heidegger, Martin. 1971. The Origin of the Work of Art. In *Poetry, Language, Thought,* trans. Albert Hofstadter, pp. 17–87. New York: Harper and Row.

Heilfurth, Gerhard. 1988 (1962). Volkskunde jenseits der Ideologien. In Gerndt, ed., *Fach und Begriff "Volkskunde" in der Diskussion,* pp. 179–205. (Originally published in *Hessische Blätter für Volkskunde* 54:9–28.)

Heintz, Peter. 1958. Sozialer Wandel. In R. König, ed., *Soziologie: Fischer Lexikon,* pp. 268–74. Frankfurt a.M: Fischer.

Heizmann, Bertold. 1981. *Ursprünglichkeit und Reflexion: Die poetische Aesthetik des jungen Herder im Zusammenhang der Geschichtsphilosophie und Anthropologie des 18. Jahrhunderts.* Bern: Peter Lang.

Hepburn, Ronald W. 1967. Bultmann, Rudolf. In P. Edwards, ed., *The Encyclopedia of Philosophy,* pp. 424–26. New York: Macmillan.

Herder, Johann Gottfried. 1807 (1774). *Stimmen der Völker in Liedern.* Ed. v. Müller. Tübingen.

Herder, Johann Gottfried. 1782. *Vom Geist der Ebräischen Poesie: Eine Anleitung.* Leipzig: Joh. Philipp Haugs Wittwe. Reprinted in B. Suphan, ed., *Herders sämtliche Werke,* vol. 11 (1879), pp. 213–475. Berlin: Weidmannsche Buchhandlung.

Herder, Johann Gottfried. 1833. *The Spirit of Hebrew Poetry.* Trans. James Marsh. Burlington, Vt.: E. Smith.

Herder, Johann Gottfried. 1877–1913. *Herders sämtliche Werke.* Ed. B. Suphan. 33 Vols. Berlin: Weidmannsche Buchhandlung.

Herder, Johann Gottfried. 1906 (1773). *Über Ossian und die Lieder alter Völker.* In R. Franz, ed., *Ausgewählte Prosa,* pp. 1–28. Bielefeld: Velhagen & Klassing.

Herder, Johann Gottfried. 1987 (1770). *Abhandlung über den Ursprung der Sprache.* Ed. W. Pross. Hanser Literatur-Kommentare, vol. 12. Munich: Carl Hanser.

Herskovits, M. J. 1951. Folklore: Social Science or Humanistic Discipline? (Editorial). *Journal of American Folklore* 64:129.

278 Bibliography

Herskovits, M. J., and Frances S. Herskovitz. 1958. *Dahomean Narrative: A Cross-Cultural Comparison.* Evanston, Ill.: Northwestern University Press.
Herzfeld, Michael. 1982. *Ours Once More: Folklore, Ideology, and the Making of Modern Greece.* Austin: University of Texas Press.
Higginson, Thomas Wentworth. 1870. *Army Life in a Black Regiment.* Boston.
Hinsley, Curtis. 1983. Ethnographic Charisma and Scientific Routine. In Stocking, ed., *Observers Observed,* pp. 53–69.
Hinsley, Curtis. 1989. Zunis and Brahmins: Cultural Ambivalence in the Gilded Age. In George W. Stocking, Jr., ed., *Romantic Motives: Essays on Anthropological Sensibility,* History of Anthropology, vol. 6, pp. 169–207. Madison: University of Wisconsin Press.
Hirsch, Jerrold. 1987. Folklore in the Making: B. A. Botkin. *Journal of American Folklore* 100:3–38.
Hitt, Jack. 1994. Would You Baptize an Extraterrestrial? *New York Times Magazine,* May 29, pp. 36–39.
Hobsbawm, Eric. 1983. Introduction. In Hobsbawm and Ranger, eds., *The Invention of Tradition,* pp. 1–14.
Hobsbawm, Eric, and Terence Ranger, eds. 1983. *The Invention of Tradition.* Cambridge: Cambridge University Press.
Hodder, Alan D. 1989. *Emerson's Rhetoric of Revelation: Nature, the Reader, and the Apocalypse Within.* University Park: Pennsylvania State University Press.
Hofer, Tamas. 1968. Comparative Notes on the Professional Profile of Two Disciplines. *Current Anthropology* 9:311–15.
Hoffmann-Krayer, Eduard. 1897. Zur Einführung. *Schweizerisches Archiv für Volkskunde* 1:1–12.
Hoffmann-Krayer, Eduard. 1931. Das Trachtenfest in Genf. *Schweizer Volkskunde* 21:65–67.
Hoffmann-Krayer, Eduard. 1946. *Kleine Schriften zur Volkskunde von Eduard Hoffmann-Krayer.* Ed. P. Geiger. Schriften der Schweizerischen Gesellschaft für Volkskunde, vol. 30. Basel: G. Krebs.
Hoffmann-Krayer, Eduard. 1946 (1902). Die Volkskunde als Wissenschaft. In Hoffmann-Krayer, *Kleine Schriften zur Volkskunde von Eduard Hoffmann-Krayer,* ed. P. Geiger, pp. 1–23.
Hoffmann-Krayer, Eduard. 1958 (1903). Naturgesetz im Volksleben? In Lutz, ed., *Volkskunde,* pp. 67–72.
Holzapfel, Otto. 1991. The German Folk Song Archive Freiburg i.Br. in the Third Reich. *Musicological Research* 11:189–200.
Honko, Lauri. 1987. Die Authentizität des Kalevala. In Duerr, ed., *Authentizität und Betrug in der Ethnologie,* pp. 357–92.
Hörander, Edith, and Hans Lunzer, eds. 1982. *Folklorismus.* Neusiedel: Verein Volkskultur um den Neusiedlersee.
Howe, DeWolfe, and G. W. Cottrell, Jr., eds. 1952. *The Scholar's Friend: Letters of Francis James Child and James Russell Lowell.* Cambridge, Mass.: Harvard University Press.

Hufford, Mary, ed. 1994. *Conserving Culture: A New Discourse on Heritage*. Urbana: University of Illinois Press.

Hughes, George. 1995. Authenticity in Tourism. *Annals of Tourism Research* 22: 781–803.

Hult, David F. 1988. Reading It Right: The Ideology of Text Editing. *Romanic Review* 79:74–88.

Hultkranz, Ake. 1961. *General Ethnological Concepts: International Dictionary of Regional European Ethnology and Folklore*. Copenhagen.

Hunt, Lynn. 1984. *Politics, Culture, and Class in the French Revolution*. Berkeley: University of California Press.

Hurston, Zora Neale. 1978 (1935). *Mules and Men*. Bloomington: Indiana University Press.

Hustvedt, Sigurd Bernhard. 1930. *Ballad Books and Ballad Men*. Cambridge, Mass.: Harvard University Press.

Hymes, Dell. 1975. Folklore's Nature and the Sun's Myth. *Journal of American Folklore* 88:345–69.

Hymes. Dell. 1981. *"In vain I tried to tell you": Essays in Native American Poetics*. Philadelphia: University of Pennsylvania Press.

Hymes, Dell. 1981 (1975). Breakthrough into Performance. In Hymes, *"In vain I tried to tell you,"* pp. 79–141.

Hymes, Dell, ed. 1974. *Reinventing Anthropology*. New York: Vintage Books.

Ives, Edward D. 1980. *The Tape-Recorded Interview*. 2d ed. Knoxville: University of Tennessee Press.

Jabbour, Alan. 1983. American Folklore Studies: The Tradition and the Future. *Folklore Forum* 16:235–47.

Jackson, Bruce. 1976. Benjamin A. Botkin (Obituary). *Journal of American Folklore* 89:3–7.

Jackson, Bruce. 1987. *Fieldwork*. Urbana: University of Illinois Press.

James, Thelma. 1961 (1933). The English and Scottish Popular Ballads of Francis J. Child. In M. Leach and T. P. Coffin, eds., *The Critics and the Ballad*, pp. 12–19. Carbondale: Southern Illinois University Press.

Jeggle, Utz. 1970. Wertbedingungen der Volkskunde. In Geiger, Jeggle, and Korff, eds., *Abschied vom Volksleben*, pp. 11–26.

Jeggle, Utz. 1984. Zur Geschichte der Feldforschung in der Volkskunde. In Jeggle, ed., *Feldforschung*, pp. 11–46.

Jeggle, Utz. 1986. Das Fremde und das Eigene. In A. Kuntz-Stahl, ed., *Ort und Feld*, pp. 5–30. Hamburg: Institut für Volkskunde der Universität Hamburg.

Jeggle, Utz. 1988. Volkskunde im 20. Jahrhundert. In Brednich, ed., *Grundriss der Volkskunde*, pp. 51–71.

Jeggle, Utz, ed. 1984. *Feldforschung: Qualitative Methoden in der Kulturanalyse*. Untersuchungen des Ludwig-Uhland Instituts, vol. 62. Tübingen: Tübinger Vereinigung für Volkskunde.

Jeggle, Utz, and Gottfried Korff. 1974a. Zur Entwicklung des Zillertaler Regionalcharakters. *Zeitschrift für Volkskunde* 70:39–57.

Jeggle, Utz, and Gottfried Korff. 1974b. Homo Zillertaliensis; oder, Wie ein Menschenschlag entsteht. *Der Bürger im Staat* 24:182–88.

Jolles, André. 1956 (1930). Einfache Formen. Ed. A. Schossig. 2d ed. Halle: Max Niemeyer.

Jones, Mark, ed. 1990. *Fake? The Art of Deception.* Berkeley: University of California Press.

Jones, Mark, ed. 1992. *Why Fakes Matter: Essays on Problems of Authenticity.* London: British Museum Press.

Jones, Steven. 1979a. Slouching Towards Ethnography: The Text/Context Controversy Reconsidered. *Western Folklore* 38:42–47.

Jones, Steven. 1979b. Dogmatism in the Contextual Revolution. *Western Folklore* 38:52–55.

Joseph, John E., and Talbot J. Taylor, eds. 1990. *Ideologies of Language.* London: Routledge.

Kaindl, Raimund Friedrich. 1903. *Die Volkskunde: Ihre Bedeutung, ihre Ziele und ihre Methode.* Leipzig: Franz Deuticke.

Kamenetsky, Christa. 1972a. Folklore as a Political Tool in Nazi Germany. *Journal of American Folklore* 85:221–35.

Kamenetsky, Christa. 1972b. Political Distortion of Philosophical Concepts: A Case-History—Nazism and the Romantic Movement. *Metaphilosophy* 3:198–218.

Kamenetsky, Christa. 1973. The German Folklore Revival in the Eighteenth Century: Herder's Theory of *Naturpoesie. Journal of Popular Culture* 6 (4):836–48.

Kamenetsky, Christa. 1977. Folktale and Ideology in the Third Reich. *Journal of American Folklore* 90:168–78.

Kamenetsky, Christa. 1980. The Uses and Misuses of Folklore Terminology *and* A Final Reply. *Journal of American Folklore* 93:327–30, 334–35.

Kamenetsky, Christa. 1992. *The Brothers Grimm and Their Critics.* Athens: Ohio University Press.

Kapchan, Deborah. 1993. Hybridization and the Marketplace. *Western Folklore* 52:303–26.

Kapeller, Kriemhild. 1991. Tourismus und Volkskultur: Folklorismus—Zur Warenästhetik der Volkskultur. Dissertationen der Karl-Franzens-Universität Graz, vol. 81. Graz: dbv-Verlag.

Karp, Ivan, and Steven D. Lavine. 1991. *Exhibiting Cultures: The Poetics and Politics of Museum Display.* Washington, D.C.: Smithsonian Institution Press.

Karpeles, Maud. 1973. *An Introduction to English Folk Song.* London: Oxford University Press.

Kaschuba, Wolfgang. 1988. *Volkskultur zwischen feudaler und bürgerlicher Gesellschaft: Zur Geschichte eines Begriffs und seiner gesellschaftlichen Wirklichkeit.* Frankfurt: Campus.

Kaufmann, Doris. 1995. *Aufklärung, bürgerliche Selbsterfahrung und die "Erfindung" der Psychiatrie in Deutschland, 1770–1850.* Göttingen: Vandenhoeck und Ruprecht.

Kiesselbach, Dorothee. 1970. Volkskultur im Program der Massenmedien. In Harmening et al., eds., *Volkskultur und Geschichte*, pp. 190–99.

King, Magda. 1964. *Heidegger's Philosophy*. New York: Macmillan.

Kirshenblatt-Gimblett, Barbara. 1988a. Authenticity and Authority in the Representation of Culture. In Ina-Maria Greverus et al., eds., *Kulturkontakt— Kulturkonflikt*, vol. 28, pp. 59–70. Frankfurt: Institut für Kulturanthropologie und Europäische Ethnologie.

Kirshenblatt-Gimblett, Barbara. 1988b. Mistaken Dichotomies. *Journal of American Folklore* 101:140–55.

Kirshenblatt-Gimblett, Barbara. 1989. Tourism. In *Encyclopedia of Communications*, vol. 4, pp. 249–53. Oxford: Oxford University Press.

Kirshenblatt-Gimblett, Barbara. 1995a. Ausblick: Die Krise der Folkloristik. In Bendix, *Amerikanische Folkloristik*, pp. 201–22.

Kirshenblatt-Gimblett, Barbara. 1995b. From the Paperwork Empire to the Paperless Office: Testing the Limits of the "Science of Tradition." In Regina Bendix and Rosemary L. Zumwalt, eds., *Folklore Interpreted: Essays in Honor of Alan Dundes*, pp. 69–92. New York: Garland.

Kirshenblatt-Gimblett, Barbara. 1996c. Theorizing Heritage. *Ethnomusicology* 39:367–80.

Kittredge, George Lyman. 1932. Introduction. In Kittredge and Helen Child Sargent, eds., *English and Scottish Popular Ballads*, pp. xi–xxxi. Boston: Houghton Mifflin.

Kittredge, George Lyman. 1957. Francis James Child. In Child, ed., *The English and Scottish Popular Ballads*, pp. xxiii–xxxi.

Kivy, Peter. 1995. *Authenticities: Philosophical Reflections on Musical Performance*. Ithaca, N.Y.: Cornell University Press.

Klusen, Ernst. 1969. *Volkslied: Fund und Erfindung*. Cologne: Musikverlag Hans Gerig.

Knortz, Karl. 1988 (1905). Zur amerikanischen Volkskunde. Trans. H. B. Van Iten and James R. Dow. *Folklore Historian* 5:14–43.

Koch, Georg. 1935. *Die bäuerliche Seele: Eine Einführung in die religiöse Volkskunde*. Berlin.

Kodish, Debora. 1986. *Good Friends and Bad Enemies: Robert Winslow Gordon and the Study of American Folksong*. Urbana: University of Illinois Press.

Kodish, Debora. 1987. Absent Gender, Silent Encounter. *Journal of American Folklore* 100:573–78.

Kohl, Karl-Heinz. 1986. *Entzauberter Blick: Das Bild vom Guten Wilden*. Frankfurt: Suhrkamp.

Könenkamp, Wolf-Dieter. 1988a. Natur und Nationalcharakter: Die Entwicklung der Ethnographie und die frühe Volkskunde. *Ethnologia Europaea* 18:25–52.

Könenkamp, Wolf-Dieter. 1988b. Volkskunde und Statistik: Eine wissenschaftsgeschichtliche Korrektur. *Zeitschrift für Volkskunde* 84:1–26.

Korff, Gottfried. 1970. *Heiligenverehrung in der Gegenwart*. Untersuchungen des LUI, vol. 29. Tübingen: Tübinger Vereinigung für Volkskunde.

Korff, Gottfried. 1980. Folklorismus und Regionalismus. In Konrad Köstlin and Hermann Bausinger, eds., *Heimat und Identität*, pp. 39–52. Neumünster: Karl Wachholz.

Korff, Gottfried, and Martin Roth. 1990. Einleitung. In Korff and Roth, eds., *Das historische Museum: Labor, Schaubühne, Identitätsfabrik*, pp. 9–37. Frankfurt: Campus.

Kosellek, Reinhart. 1959. *Kritik und Krise*. Freiburg: Karl Alber.

Köstlin, Konrad. 1969. Folklorismus und Ben-Akiba. *Rheinisches Jahrbuch für Volkskunde* 20:234–56.

Köstlin, Konrad. 1977a. Feudale Identität und dogmatisierte Volkskultur. *Zeitschrift für Volkskunde* 73:216–33.

Köstlin, Konrad. 1977b (1973). *Relikte: Die Gleichzeitigkeit des Ungleichzeitigen*. Ethnologia Bavarica 6. Würzburg: Bayrische Blätter für Volkskunde.

Köstlin, Konrad. 1982. Folklorismus als Therapie? Volkskultur als Therapie? In Hörander and Lunzer, eds., *Folklorismus*, pp. 129–48.

Köstlin, Konrad. 1984. Die Wiederkehr der Volkskultur. *Ethnologia Europaea* 14:25–31.

Köstlin, Konrad. 1985. Freilichtmuseums-Folklore. In H. Ottenjann, ed., *Kulturgeschichte und Sozialgeschichte im Freilichtmuseum*, pp. 55–67. Cloppenburg: Museumsdorf Cloppenburg.

Köstlin, Konrad. 1988. Zur frühen Geschichte staatlicher Trachtenpflege in Bayern. In Lehmann and Kuntz, eds., *Sichtweisen der Volkskunde*, pp. 301–19.

Köstlin, Konrad. 1990. Die "Historische Methode" der Volkskunde und der "Prozess der Zivilisation" des Norbert Elias. In Dieter Harmening and Erich Wimmer, eds., *Volkskultur—Geschichte—Region*. pp. 58–76. Würzburg: Königshausen und Neumann.

Köstlin, Konrad. 1995. Lust aufs Ganze: Die gedeutete Moderne oder die Moderne als Deutung—Volkskulturforschung in der Moderne. *Österreichische Zeitschrift für Volkskunde* 49:255–75.

Kramer, Dieter. 1986 (1970). Who Benefits from Folklore? In Dow and Lixfeld, eds., *German Volkskunde*, pp. 41–53.

Kretzenbacher, Leopold. 1986. *Ethnologia Europaea: Studienwanderungen und Erlebnisse auf volkskundlicher Feldforschung im Alleingang*. Beiträge zur Kenntnis Südosteuropas und des Nahen Orientes, vol. 39. Munich: Dr. Rudolf Trofenik.

Kriss, Rudolf. 1970. Brauchtum, Folklorismus und Fremdenverkehr im Berchtesgadenerland. In Harmening et al., eds., *Volkskultur und Geschichte*, pp. 200–209.

Kroeber, Alfred. 1917. The Superorganic. *American Anthropologist* 19:163–213.

Krohn, Kaarle L. 1971. *Folklore Methodology*. Translated by R. L. Welsch. Austin: University of Texas Press.

Kroskrity, P. V., B. B. Schieffelin, and K. A. Woolard, eds. 1992. *Pragmatics* (Special issue on language ideologies) 2:235–453.

Kuhn, Thomas. 1970. *The Structure of Scientific Revolutions*. 2d ed. Chicago: University of Chicago Press.

Kuper, Adam. 1988. *The Invention of Primitive Society: Transformations of an Illusion.* London: Routledge.

Lachmann, Karl. 1960 (1841). *Der Nibelunge Noth und die Klage.* Berlin: Walter de Gruyter.

Lash, Scott. 1994. Reflexivity and Its Doubles: Structure, Aesthetics, Community. In Beck, Giddens, and Lash, *Reflexive Modernization,* pp. 110–73.

Lash, Scott, and John Urry. 1994. *Economies of Signs and Space.* London: Sage Publications.

Leach, Maria, and Jerome Fried, eds. 1949. *Funk and Wagnalls Standard Dictionary of Folklore, Mythology, and Legend.* New York: Funk and Wagnalls.

Lears, Jackson T. J. 1981. *No Place of Grace: Antimodernism and the Transformation of American Culture, 1880–1920.* New York: Pantheon.

Lee, Molly. 1991. Appropriating the Primitive: Turn-of-the-Century Collection and Display of Native Alaskan Art. *Arctic Anthropology* 28 (1):6–15.

Lehmann, Albrecht, and Andreas Kuntz, eds. 1988. *Sichtweisen der Volkskunde: Zur Geschichte und Forschungspraxis einer Disziplin.* Berlin: Dietrich Reimer.

Leitzmann, Albert, ed. 1908. *Briefwechsel zwischen Wilhelm von Humboldt und August Wilhelm Schlegel.* Jena: Verlag der Frommannschen Buchhandlung.

Leitzmann, Albert, ed. 1927. *Briefwechsel der Brüder Jacob und Wilhelm Grimm mit Karl Lachmann.* 2 vols. Jena: Verlag der Frommannschen Buchhandlung.

Lentricchia, Frank. 1980. *After the New Criticism.* London: Athlone Press.

Lepenies, Wolf. 1988. *Between Literature and Science: The Rise of Sociology.* Trans. R. J. Hollingdale. Cambridge: Cambridge University Press.

Levine, Lawrence W. 1988. *Highbrow, Lowbrow: The Emergence of Cultural Hierarchy in America.* Cambridge, Mass.: Harvard University Press.

Linke, Uli. 1990. Folklore, Anthropology, and the Government of Social Life. *Comparative Studies of Society and History* 32:117–48.

Linnekin, Jocelyn. 1983. Defining Tradition: Variations on the Hawaiian Identity. *American Ethnologist* 10:241–52.

Linnekin, Jocelyn. 1991. Cultural Intervention and the Dilemma of Authenticity. *American Anthropologist* 93:446–49.

Linton, Ralph. 1943. Nativistic Movements. *American Anthropologist* 45:230–40.

Lipsitz, George. 1994. *Dangerous Crossroads: Popular Music, Postmodernism and the Poetics of Place.* London: Verso.

Liss, Julia E. 1996. German Culture and German Science in the *Bildung* of Franz Boas. In Stocking, ed., Volksgeist *as Method and Ethic,* pp. 155–84.

Lixfeld, Hannjost. 1991. Adolf Spamers Rolle als Wegbereiter einer nationalsozialistischen Volkskundewissenschaft. In Sievers, ed., *Beiträge zur Wissenschaftsgeschichte der Volkskunde im 19. und 20. Jahrhundert,* pp. 91–120.

Lixfeld, Hannjost. 1994. *Folklore and Fascism: The Reich Institute for German Volkskunde.* Trans. James Dow. Bloomington: Indiana University Press.

Lohre, Heinrich. 1902. *Von Percy zum Wunderhorn: Beiträge zur Geschichte der Volksliedforschung in Deutschland*. Palaestra, vol. 22. Berlin: Mayer & Müller.

Lomax, Alan. 1993. *The Land Where the Blues Began*. New York: Pantheon.

Lomax, John A. 1947. *Adventures of a Ballad Hunter*. New York: Macmillan.

Loomis, Ormond H. 1983. *Cultural Conservation: The Protection of Cultural Heritage in the United States*. Washington, D.C.: Library of Congress.

Lott, Eric. 1992. Love and Theft: The Racial Unconscious of Blackface Minstrelsy. *Representations* 38:23–50.

Lowell, James Russell. 1897. *The Ballads: From His Lectures on the English Poets*. Transcribed by Robert Carter. Cleveland: The Rowfant Club (orally delivered, 1855).

Lutz, Gerhard, ed. 1958. *Volkskunde: Ein Handbuch zur Geschichte ihrer Probleme*. Berlin: Erich Schmidt.

MacCannell, Dean. 1989 (1976). *The Tourist: A New Theory of the Leisure Class*. New York: Schocken Books.

McDermott, John J. 1976. *The Culture of Experience: Philosophical Essays in the American Grain*. New York: New York University Press.

McGrane, Bernard. 1989. *Beyond Anthropology: Society and the Other*. New York: Columbia University Press.

McKay, Ian. 1994. *The Quest of the Folk: Antimodernism and Cultural Selection in Twentieth-Century Nova Scotia*. Montreal: McGill-Queens University Press.

McMurtry, Jo. 1985. *English Language, English Literature*. Hamden: Archon Books.

McNeil, William K. 1980. A History of American Folklore Scholarship Before 1908. Ph.D. Dissertation, Department of Folklore, Indiana University.

McNeil, William K. 1988. Preface. *Folklore Historian* 5:1.

Mackensen, Lutz, ed. 1930/33–1934/40. *Handbuch des deutschen Märchens*. Berlin: Walter de Gruyter.

Mackenzie, D. 1921. Transcendentalism. In J. Hastings, ed., *Encyclopedia of Religion and Ethics*, vol. 12, pp. 419–25. New York: Charles Scribner's Sons.

Malinowski, Bronislaw. 1961 (1922). *Argonauts of the Western Pacific*. New York: E. P. Dutton.

Mannhardt, Wilhelm. 1905 (1875–77). *Wald- und Feldkulte*. 2 vols. Berlin.

Manning, Frank. 1984. Carnival in Canada: The Politics of Celebration. In B. Sutton-Smith and D. Kelly-Byrne, eds., *The Masks of Play*, pp. 24–33. New York: Leisure Press.

Marsh, Dave. 1995. Punk Rock 101 Unplugged. *City Pages* (Alternative News and Arts Weekly of the Twin Cities), April 12, pp. 8–13.

Mason, Otis T. 1891. The Natural History of Folk-Lore. *Journal of American Folklore* 4:97–105.

Matthiessen, F. O. 1941. *American Renaissance: Art and Expression in the Age of Emerson and Whitman*. New York: Oxford University Press.

Maus, Heinz. 1946. Zur Situation der deutschen Volkskunde. *Die Umschau* 1: 349–59.

ography 285

Mead, Margaret. 1952. Foreword. In M. Zborowski and E. Herzog, *Life Is with People: The Culture of the Shtetl,* pp. 11–21. New York: Schocken Books.
Meier, John. 1906 (1898). *Kunstlied und Volkslied in Deutschland.* Halle: Max Niemeyer.
Meier, John, ed. 1938. *Deutsches Volkstum.* Berlin: Walter de Gruyter.
Metraux, Rhoda. 1959. Foreword. In Margaret Mead, *An Anthropologist at Work: Writings of Ruth Benedict,* pp. iii–vii. Westport, Conn.: Greenwood Press.
Metzen, Thomas. 1970. Anmerkungen zur "Volkskunde der Schweiz" von Richard Weiss. In Geiger, Jeggle, and Korff, eds., *Abschied vom Volksleben,* pp. 173–90.
Mieder, Wolfgang. 1982. Proverbs in Nazi Germany: The Promulgation of Anti-Semitism and Stereotypes through Folklore. *Journal of American Folklore* 95:435–64.
Mieder, Wolfgang. 1985. *Disenchantments.* Hanover, N.H.: University Press of New England.
Mieder, Wolfgang. 1987. *Tradition and Innovation in Folk Literature.* Hanover, N.H.: University Press of New England.
Mille, Richard de. 1990 (1980). *The Don Juan Papers: Further Castañeda Controversies.* Belmont, Calif.: Wadsworth.
Miller, Frank. 1990. *Folklore for Stalin: Russian Folklore and Pseudofolklore of the Stalin Era.* Armonk, N.Y.: M. E. Sharpe.
Minder, Robert. 1968. Heidegger und Hebel oder die Sprache von Messkirch. In Minder, *Dichter in der Gesellschaft,* pp. 234–94. Frankfurt: Suhrkamp.
Mogk, Eugen. 1958 (1907). Wesen und Aufgabe der Volkskunde. In Lutz, ed., *Volkskunde,* pp. 89–101.
Möhler, Gerda. 1981. Review of *Grundzüge der Volkskunde. Bayrische Blätter für Volkskunde* 8:269–80.
Möller, Horst. 1986. *Vernunft und Kritik: Deutsche Aufklärung im 17. und 18. Jahrhundert.* Frankfurt a.M.: Suhrkamp.
Moment, Gairdner B., and Otto F. Kraushaar, eds. 1980. *Utopias: The American Experience.* Metuchen, N.J.: Scarecrow Press.
Moran, Michael. 1967. Emerson, Ralph Waldo. In P. Edwards, ed., *The Encyclopedia of Philosophy,* vol. 2, pp. 477–79. New York: Macmillan.
Moser, Dietz-Rüdiger. 1977. Authentizität. In K. Ranke et al., eds., *Enzyklopädie des Märchens,* vol. 1, pp. 1076–80. Berlin: Walter de Gruyter.
Moser, Hans. 1988 (1954). Gedanken zur heutigen Volkskunde (revised). In Gerndt, ed., *Fach und Begriff "Volkskunde" in der Diskussion,"* pp. 92–157. (Originally in *Bayerisches Jahrbuch für Volkskunde* [Regensburg, no. vol.], pp. 208–34.)
Moser, Hans. 1962. Vom Folklorismus in unserer Zeit. *Zeitschrift für Volkskunde* 58:177–209.
Moser, Hans. 1964. Der Folklorismus als Forschungsproblem der Volkskunde. *Hessische Blätter für Volkskunde* 55:9–57.

Moser, Hugo. 1956. Volk, Volksgeist, Volkskultur: Die Auffassungen J. G. Herders in heutiger Sicht. *Zeitschrift für Volkskunde* 53:127–40.

Moser, Johannes. 1989. Ansätze zu einer neueren Volksliedforschung. *Jahrbuch für Volksliedforschung* 34:56–69.

Möser, Justus. 1944. *Sämtliche Werke*. 14 vols. Ed. W. Kohlschmidt. Berlin: Stalling.

Mosse, George L. 1975. *The Nationalization of the Masses*. New York: Howard Fertig.

Mueller-Vollmer, Kurt. 1986. The Digested and the Indigestible: Abandonment as a Category in the History of German Criticism. *Stanford Literature Review* 3:31–46.

Myers, Robin, and Michael Harris, eds. 1989. *Fakes and Frauds: Varieties of Deception in Print and Manuscript*. Detroit: Omnigraphics.

National Public Radio. 1996. Harlem Churches Find Room for Foreign Tourists. *All Things Considered,* Aug. 26, segment 14, transcript 2317.

Naumann, Hans. 1921. Deutsche Volkskunde. *Deutscher Pfeiler,* July, pp. 1–11.

Naumann, Hans. 1922. *Grundzüge der deutschen Volkskunde*. Leipzig: Quelle und Meyer.

Newell, Venetia J. 1987. The Adaptation of Folklore and Tradition (Folklorismus). *Folklore* 98:131–51.

Newell, William Wells. 1883. *Games and Songs of American Children*. New York: Harper and Bros.

Newell, William Wells. 1888a. On the Field and Work of a Journal of American Folklore. *Journal of American Folklore* 1:3–7.

Newell, William Wells. 1888b. Notes and Queries. *Journal of American Folklore* 1:79–81.

Newell, William Wells. 1889. Editorial. *Journal of American Folklore* 2:1–2.

Newell, William Wells. 1890a. First Annual Meeting of the American Folk-Lore Society. *Journal of American Folklore* 3:1–16.

Newell, William Wells. 1890b. Additional Collection Essential to Correct Theory in Folk-Lore and Mythology. *Journal of American Folklore* 3:23–32.

Newell, William Wells. 1892a. Lady Featherflight. In J. Jacobs and A. Nutt, eds., *International Folk-Lore Congress: Papers and Transactions*. London.

Newell, William Wells. 1892b. Third Annual Meeting of the American Folk-Lore Society. *Journal of American Folklore* 5:1–8.

Newmeyer, Frederick J. 1986. *The Politics of Linguistics*. Chicago: University of Chicago Press.

Niederer, Arnold. 1975. Kultur im Erdgeschoss: Der Alltag aus der Sicht des Volkskundlers. *Schweizer Monatshefte* 55:461–67.

Niederer, Arnold. 1983. Le Folklore Manipulé. *Schweizerisches Archiv für Volkskunde* 79:175–86.

Niedermüller, Péter. 1989. National Culture: Symbols and Reality. *Ethnologia Europaea* 29:47–56.

Norton, Sara, and M. A. DeWolfe Howe, eds. 1913. *Letters of Charles Eliot Norton with Biographical Comment*. 2 vols. Boston: Houghton Mifflin.

Oinas, Felix, ed. 1978. *Folklore, Nationalism and Politics.* Columbus, Ohio: Slavica.

Olender, Maurice. 1992. *The Languages of Paradise: Race, Religion, and Philology in the Nineteenth Century.* Trans. A. Goldhammer. Cambridge, Mass.: Harvard University Press.

Ong. Walter J. 1982. *Orality and Literacy.* Cambridge: Cambridge University Press.

Ortner, Sherry. 1974. Is Female to Male as Nature is to Culture? In M. Rosaldo and L. Lamphere, eds., *Woman, Culture, and Society,* pp. 67–87. Stanford: Stanford University Press.

Orvell, Miles. 1989. *The Real Thing: Imitation and Authenticity in American Culture, 1880–1940.* Chapel Hill: University of North Carolina Press.

Paredes, Américo, and Richard Bauman, eds. 1972. *Toward New Perspectives in Folklore.* Austin: University of Texas Press.

Parker, Theodore. 1969 (1911). *The Rights of Man in America.* Ed. F. Sanborn. New York: Negro University Press.

Parsons, Elsie Clews. 1925. *A Pueblo Indian Journal, 1920–1921.* American Anthropological Association Memoirs, no. 32.

Patri, Umesh. 1987. *Hindu Scriptures and American Transcendentalists.* Delhi: Intellectual Publishing House.

Peuckert, Will-Erich, and Otto Lauffer. 1951. *Volkskunde: Quellen und Forschungen seit 1930.* Bern: A. Francke.

Pfeiffer, Franz. 1856. Prospectus. *Germania: Vierteljahresschrift für Deutsche Altertumskunde* 1:1–3.

Pollig, Hermann, ed. 1987. *Exotische Welten—Europäische Phantasien.* Stuttgart-Bad-Cannstadt: Edition Cantz.

Poltermann, Andreas. 1990. Herder, Johann Gottfried. In K. Ranke et al., eds., *Enzyklopädie des Märchens,* vol. 6, pp. 832–34. Berlin: Walter de Gruyter.

Pommel, Josef. 1899. Was wir wollen. *Das deutsche Volkslied: Zeitschrift für seine Kenntnis und Pflege* 1:1–3.

Pörksen, Uwe. 1989. *Plastikwörter: Die Sprache einer internationalen Diktatur.* Stuttgart: Klett.

Pratt, Mary Louise. 1992. *Imperial Eyes: Travel Writing and Transculturation.* New York: Routledge.

Price, Sally. 1989. *Primitive Art in Civilized Places.* Chicago: University of Chicago Press.

Pries, Christine, ed. 1989. *Das Erhabene: Zwischen Grenzerfahrung und Grössenwahn.* Weinheim: VCH Acta Humaniora.

Prinz, Wolfgang, and Peter Weingart, eds. 1990. *Die sogenannten Geistesenwissenschaften: Innenansichten.* Frankfurt: Suhrkamp.

Pross, Wolfgang. 1984. Anmerkungen. In Pross, ed., *Herder und der Sturm und Drang, 1764–1774,* pp. 693–936. Munich: Carl Hanser.

Pross, Wolfgang. 1987. Herder und die Anthropologie der Aufklärung. In Pross, ed., *Johann Gottfried Herder, Werke,* vol. 2, pp. 1128–1229. Munich: Carl Hanser.

Rabinow, Paul. 1977. *Reflections on Fieldwork in Morocco.* Berkeley: University of California Press.

Radano, Ronald M. 1996. Denoting Difference: The Writing of the Slave Spirituals. *Critical Inquiry* 22:506–44.

Rassem, Mohammed. 1979 (1951). *Die Volkstumswissenschaft und der Etatismus.* Dissertation Universität Basel. 2d printing with new appendix. Mittenwald: Mäander Kunstverlag.

Readings, Bill. 1996. *The University in Ruins.* Cambridge, Mass.: Harvard University Press.

Reuss, Richard A. 1971. American Folklore and Left-Wing Politics: 1927–56. Ph.D. dissertation, Indiana University.

Reuss, Richard A. 1978 (1975). American Folksong and Left-Wing Politics: 1935–56. In Oinas, ed. *Folklore, Nationalism and Politics,* pp. 9–31.

Richardson, Robert D., Jr. 1995. *Emerson: The Mind on Fire.* Berkeley: University of California Press.

Riegl, Alois. 1895. Das Volksmässige und die Gegenwart. *Zeitschrift für österreichische Volkskunde* 1:4–7.

Riehl, Wilhelm Heinrich. 1855. *Die Naturgeschichte des Volkes als Grundlage einer deutschen Social-Politik.* Stuttgart: Cotta.

Riehl, Wilhelm Heinrich. 1958 (1859). Die Volkskunde als Wissenschaft. In Lutz, ed., *Volkskunde,* pp. 23–37.

Riehl, Wilhelm Heinrich. 1869. *Wanderbuch.* Stuttgart: Cotta.

Rihtman-Augustin, Dunja. 1988. Folklore: Models and Symbols. *Narodna Umjetnost* (Zagreb). Special issue 9, pp. 9–22.

Roberts, John W. 1993. African-American Diversity and the Study of Folklore. *Western Folklore* 52:157–71.

Rohner, Pius Martin. 1984. Die Entwicklung eines schweizerischen Sprachbewusstseins bei Johann Jakob Bodmer. Ph.D. Dissertation, Zurich.

Rölleke, Heinz. 1979. Zur Entstehungsgeschichte des Wunderhorns. In Arnim and Brentano, *Des Knaben Wunderhorn,* pp. 17–75.

Rosenberg, Rainer. 1989. *Literaturwissenschaftliche Germanistik: Zur Geschichte ihrer Probleme und Begriffe.* Berlin: Academie–Verlag.

Rushdie, Salman. 1990. *Haroun and the Sea of Stories.* London: Granta Books.

Safi, Louay M. 1994. *The Challenge of Modernity: The Quest for Authenticity in the Arab World.* New York: University Press of America.

Sapir, Edward. 1951 (1924). Culture, Genuine and Spurious. In D. Mandelbaum, ed., *Selected Writings of Edward Sapir,* pp. 308–31. Berkeley: University of California Press.

Scharfe, Martin. 1970. Kritik des Kanons. In Geiger, Jeggle, and Korff, eds., *Abschied vom Volksleben,* pp. 74–84.

Scharfe, Martin. 1986. Einführung. "Ungleichzeitigkeiten." In U. Jeggle, G. Korff, M. Scharfe, and B. J. Warneken, eds., *Volkskultur in der Moderne,* pp. 347–50. Hamburg: Rowohlt.

Scharfe, Martin. 1990. Hessisches Abendmahl. *Hessische Blätter für Volks- und Kulturforschung* 26:9–46.

Scharfe, Martin. 1992. Volkskunde in den Neunzigern. *Hessische Blätter für Volkskunde* 28:65–76.

Schechner, Richard. 1985. *Between Theater and Anthropology.* Philadelphia: University of Pennsylvania Press.

Schenda, Rudolf. 1977. *Volk ohne Buch. Studien zur Sozialgeschichte der populären Lesestoffe, 1770–1910.* Frankfurt: dtv.

Schepping, Wilhelm. 1988. Lied- und Musikforschung. In Brednich, ed., *Grundriss der Volkskunde,* pp. 399–422.

Schindler, Norbert. 1985. Brauchforschung zwischen Volkskunde und Geschichte. *Bayrische Blätter für Volkskunde* 12:81–95.

Schmidt, Aurel. 1992. *Wege nach unterwegs: Das Ende des Reisens.* Zurich: Benziger.

Schmook, Reinhard. 1991. Zu den Quellen der volkskundlichen Sichtweise Hans Naumanns. In Sievers, ed., *Beiträge zur Wissenschaftsgeschichte der Volkskunde im 19. und 20. Jahrhundert,* pp. 73–90.

Schöck, Gustav. 1970. Sammeln und Retten: Zwei Prinzipien volkskundlicher Empirie. In Geiger, Jeggle, and Korff, eds., *Abschied vom Volksleben,* pp. 85–104.

Schwedt, Eduard. 1966. Brauchpflege und angewandte Volkskunde. *Beiträge zur deutschen Volks- und Altertumskunde* 10:85–92.

Schweikle, Günther. 1988. Ludwig Uhland als Germanist. In Hermann Bausinger, ed., *Ludwig Uhland: Dichter, Gelehrter, Politiker,* pp. 149–81. Tübingen: Attempo.

Scudder, Horace Elisha. 1901. *James Russell Lowell: A Biography.* 2 vols. Boston: Houghton Mifflin.

Seiler, Christian. 1991. Sie spielen auch den Blues. *Die Weltwoche,* March 12, pp. 41–43.

Shiach, Morag. 1989. *Discourse on Popular Culture: Class, Gender and History in Cultural Analysis, 1730 to the Present.* Stanford, Calif.: Stanford University Press.

Shils, Edward. 1981. *Tradition.* Chicago: University of Chicago Press.

Sievers, Kai Detlev. 1988. Fragestellungen der Volkskunde im 19. Jahrhundert. In Brednich, ed., *Grundriss der Volkskunde,* pp. 31–50.

Sievers, Kai Detlev, ed. 1991. *Beiträge zur Wissenschaftsgeschichte der Volkskunde im 19. und 20. Jahrhundert.* Studien zur Volkskunde und Kulturegeschichte Schleswig-Holsteins, vol. 26. Neumünster: Karl Wachholtz.

Silverman, Carol. 1989. The Folklorist as Performer. In Camp, ed., *Time and Temprament,* pp. 34–35.

Sollors, Werner, ed. 1989. *The Invention of Ethnicity.* Oxford: Oxford University Press.

Solomon, Barbara Miller. 1972. *Ancestors and Immigrants: A Changing New England Tradition.* Chicago: University of Chicago Press.

Spamer, Adolf. 1924. Um die Prinzipien der Volkskunde. *Hessische Blätter für Volkskunde* 23:67–108.

Spamer, Adolf. 1958 (1928). Vom Problem des Volksgeistes zur Volkskunde als Wissenschaft. In Lutz, ed., *Volkskunde*, pp. 15–22.

Spamer, Adolf. 1933a. *Deutsche Volkskunde als Lebenswissenschaft vom deutschen Volkstum*. Leipzig: B. G. Teubner.

Spamer, Adolf. 1933b. *Die Volkskunde als Wissenschaft*. Stuttgart: W. Kohlhammer.

Spamer, Adolf, ed. 1934. *Die Deutsche Volkskunde*. Berlin: Herbert Stubenrauch.

Spitzer, Nicholas R. 1992. Cultural Conversation: Metaphors and Methods in Public Folklore. In Baron and Spitzer, eds., *Public Folklore*, pp. 77–103.

Staub, Shalom. 1988. Folklore and Authenticity: A Myopic Marriage in the Public Sector. In Feintuch, ed., *The Conservation of Culture*, pp. 166–79.

Stein, Mary Beth. 1987. Coming to Terms with the Past: The Depiction of Volkskunde in the Third Reich since 1945. *Journal of Folklore Research* 24: 157–85.

Stern, Stephen. 1977. Ethnic Folklore and the Folklore of Ethnicity. *Western Folklore* 36:7–32.

Stern, Stephen, and John Allan Cicala, eds. 1991. *Creative Ethnicity*. Logan: Utah State University Press.

Sternemann, Reinhard. 1984. *Franz Bopp und die vergleichende indoeuropäische Sprachwissenschaft*. Innsbrucker Beiträge zur Sprachwissenschaft 33. Innsbruck: Institut für Sprachwissenschaft.

Stewart, Susan. 1984. *On Longing: Narratives of the Miniature, the Gigantic, the Souvenir, the Collection*. Baltimore: Johns Hopkins University Press.

Stewart, Susan. 1991a. Notes on Distressed Genres. *Journal of American Folklore* 104:5–31.

Stewart, Susan. 1991b. *Crimes of Writing*. New York: Oxford University Press.

Stocking, George W., Jr. 1968. *Race, Culture, and Evolution: Essays in the History of Anthropology*. New York: Free Press.

Stocking, George W., Jr. 1974. Introduction. In Stocking, ed., *The Shaping of American Anthropology 1883–1911: A Franz Boas Reader*, pp. 1–20. New York: Basic Books.

Stocking, George W., Jr. 1983. History of Anthropology: Whence/Whither. In Stocking, ed., *Observers Observed: Essays on Ethnographic Fieldwork*, pp. 3–12.

Stocking, George W., Jr. 1986. Anthropology and the Science of the Irrational: Malinowski's Encounter with Freudian Psychoanalysis. In Stocking, ed., *Malinowski, Rivers, Benedict and Others: Essays on Culture and Personality*. History of Anthropology, vol. 4, pp. 13–49. Madison: University of Wisconsin Press.

Stocking, George W., Jr. 1992. The Ethnographic Sensibility of the 1920s. In Stocking, *The Ethnographer's Magic and Other Essays in the History of Anthropology*, pp. 276–341. Madison: University of Wisconsin Press.

Stocking, George W., Jr., ed. 1983. *Observers Observed: Essays on Ethnographic Fieldwork*. History of Anthropology, vol. 1. Madison: University of Wisconsin Press.

Stocking, George W., Jr., ed. 1985. *Objects and Others: Essays on Museums and Material Culture*. History of Anthropology, vol. 3. Madison: University of Wisconsin Press.

Stocking, George W., Jr., ed. 1996. Volksgeist *as Method and Ethic: Essays on Boasian Ethnography and the German Anthropological Tradition*. History of Anthropology, vol. 8. Madison: University of Wisconsin Press.

Strack, Adolf. 1958 (1902). E. Hoffmann-Krayer, *Die Volkskunde als Wissenschaft* (review). In Lutz, ed., *Volkskunde*, pp. 61–66.

Strack, Adolf. 1958 (1903). Der Einzelne und das Volk. In Lutz, ed., *Volkskunde*, pp. 73–78.

Sydow, Carl Wilhelm von. 1948. *Selected Papers on Folklore*. Copenhagen: Rosenkilde and Bagger.

Taylor, Charles. 1985. *Human Agency and Language: Philosophical Papers I*. New York: Cambridge University Press.

Taylor, Charles. 1989. *Sources of the Self: The Making of the Modern Identity*. Cambridge, Mass.: Harvard University Press.

Taylor, Charles. 1991. *The Ethics of Authenticity*. Cambridge, Mass.: Harvard University Press.

Tedlock, Dennis. 1972. On the Translation of Style in Oral Narrative. In Paredes and Bauman, eds., *Toward New Perspectives in Folklore*, pp. 114–33.

Tedlock, Dennis. 1983. *The Spoken Word and the Work of Interpretation*. Philadelphia: University of Pennsylvania Press.

Thompson, E. P. 1963. *The Making of the English Working Class*. New York: Pantheon.

Thoreau, Henry David. 1985 (1854). *A Week, Walden, Maine Woods, Cape Cod*. Selected by Robert F. Sayre. New York: Library Classics of the United States.

Thoresen, Timothy H. H. 1973. Folkloristics in A. L. Kroeber's Early Theory of Culture. *Journal of the Folklore Institute* 10:41–55.

Todorov, Tzvetan. 1984. *The Conquest of America: The Question of the Other*. Trans. Richard Howard. New York: Harper and Row.

Toelken, Barre. 1991. Ethnic Selection and Intensification in the Native American Powwow. In Stern and Cicala, eds., *Creative Ethnicity*, pp. 137–56.

Toelken, Barre. 1996. *The Dynamics of Folklore*. Rev. and expanded ed. Logan: University of Utah Press.

Tönnies, Ferdinand. 1957 (1887). *Community and Society*. Trans. Charles P. Loomis. New York: Harper and Row.

Tocqueville, Alexis de. 1945 (1835) *Democracy in America*. (Henry Reeve text.) 2 vols. New York: Knopf.

Trilling, Lionel. 1974 (1971). *Sincerity and Authenticity*. London: Oxford University Press.

Troy, Timothy. 1990. Ktaadn: Thoreau the Anthropologist. *Dialectical Anthropology* 15:74–81.

Trümpy, Hans. 1964. Aus Eduard Hoffmann-Krayers Briefwechsel. *Schweizerisches Archiv für Volskunde* 60:113–32.

Trümpy, Hans. 1969. Folklorismus in der Schweiz. *Zeitschrift für Volkskunde* 65 :
40–46.

Trümpy, Hans. 1982. Die Entdeckung des Volkes. In *Vorromantik in der Schweiz*.
6. Kolloquium der Schweizerischen Geisteswissenschaftlichen Gesellschaft,
pp. 279–93. Fribourg: n.p.

Trümpy, Hans. 1983. Folklorism from the Swiss Point of View. *International
Folklore Review* 3 : 16–20.

Trümpy, Hans. 1987. "Volkscharakter" und "Rasse": Zwei fatale Schlagworte
der NS-Volkskunde. In Gerndt, ed., *Volkskunde und Nationalsozialismus*,
pp. 169–77.

Turner, Victor, and Edward Bruner, eds. 1986. *The Anthropology of Experience*.
Urbana: University of Illinois Press.

UNESCO. 1976. The Effects of Tourism on Socio-Cultural Values. *Annals of
Tourism Research* 4 : 74–105.

Vlach, John Michael. 1986. "Properly Speaking": The Need for Plain Talk about
Folk Art. In Vlach and Bronner, eds., *Folk Art and Art Worlds*, pp. 13–26.

Vlach, John Michael, and Simon Bronner, eds. 1986. *Folk Art and Art Worlds*.
Logan: Utah State University Press.

Wagner, Roy. 1981. *The Invention of Culture*. Chicago: University of Chicago
Press.

Wallace, Anthony F. C. 1956. Revitalization Movements. *American Anthropologist* 58 : 264–81.

Wegmann, Nikolaus. 1988. *Diskurse der Empfindsamkeit: Zur Geschichte eines
Gefühls in der Literatur des 18. Jahrhunderts*. Stuttgart: Metzler.

Weigel, Harald. 1989. *Nur was du nie gesehn wird ewig dauern: Carl Lachmann
und die Entstehung der Wissenschaftlichen Edition*. Freiburg: Rombach.

Weimar, Klaus. 1989. *Geschichte der deutschen Literaturwissenschaft bis zum
Ende des 19. Jahrhunderts*. Munich: Fink.

Weinhold, Karl. 1958 (1890). Was soll die Volkskunde leisten? In Lutz, ed. *Volkskunde*, pp. 38–42. (Originally in *Zeitschrift für Völkerpsychologie und
Sprachwissenschaften* 20 : 1–5).

Weinhold, Karl. 1891. Zur Einleitung. *Zeitschrift des Vereins für Volkskunde* 1 :
1–10.

Weiss, Richard. 1978 (1946). *Volkskunde der Schweiz*. Erlenbach/Zurich: Eugen
Rentsch.

Wetterer, Angelika. 1981. *Publikumsbezug und Wahrheitsanspruch: Der Widerspruch zwischen rhetorischem Ansatz und philosophischem Anspruch bei
Gottsched und den Schweizern*. Studien zur Deutschen Literatur, vol. 68.
Tübingen: Max Niemeyer.

Wetzel, Klaus Michael. 1985. *Autonomie und Authentizität*. Bern: Peter Lang.

Whicher, Stephen E. 1953. *Freedom and Fate: An Inner Life of Ralph Waldo
Emerson*. New York: A. S. Barnes.

Whisnant, David E. 1979. *Folk Festival Issues: Report from a Seminar*. Los Angeles: John Edwards Memorial Foundation, UCLA.

Whisnant, David E. 1983. *All that is native and fine: The Politics of Culture in an Appalachian Region.* Chapel Hill: University of North Carolina Press.

White, Hayden. 1973. *Metahistory: The Historical Imagination in Nineteenth-Century Europe.* Baltimore: Johns Hopkins University Press.

White, Hayden. 1978. *Tropics of Discourse: Essays in Cultural Criticism.* Baltimore: Johns Hopkins University Press.

White, Hayden. 1987. *The Content of the Form.* Baltimore: Johns Hopkins University Press.

White, Newman Ivey. 1952. General Introduction. In *The Frank C. Brown Collection of North Carolina Folklore,* vol. 1, pp. 5–28. Durham, N.C.: Duke University Press.

Wilgus, D. K. 1959. *Anglo-American Folksong Scholarship Since 1898.* New Brunswick, N.J.: Rutgers University Press.

Wilgus, D. K. 1972. The Text Is the Thing. *Journal of American Folklore* 85: 241–52.

Wilke, Jürgen. 1978. *Literarische Zeitschriften des 18. Jahrhunderts (1688–1789).* Stuttgart: Metzler.

Williams, Raymond. 1958. *Culture and Society, 1780–1950.* Harmondsworth, Eng.: Penguin.

Williams, Raymond. 1977. *Marxism and Literature.* Oxford: Oxford University Press.

Willson, A. Leslie. 1964. *A Mythical Image: The Ideal of India in German Romanticism.* Durham, N.C.: Duke University Press.

Wilson, Joe, and Lee Udall. 1982. *Folk Festivals: A Handbook for Organization and Management.* Knoxville: University of Tennessee Press.

Wilson, William A. 1973. Herder, Folklore and Romantic Nationalism. *Journal of Popular Culture* 6: 819–35.

Wilson, William A. 1976. *Folklore, Nationalism and Politics in Modern Finland.* Bloomington: Indiana University Press.

Wilson, William A. 1989. Richard M. Dorson as Romantic-Nationalist. *Journal of Folklore Research* 26: 35–42.

Woolard, Kathryn A., and Bambi B. Schieffelin. 1994. Language Ideology. *Annual Review of Anthropology* 23: 55–82.

Wyss, Ulrich. 1979. *Die Wilde Philologie: Jakob Grimm und der Historismus.* Munich: Beck.

Yocom, Margaret R. 1990. Fieldwork, Gender, and Transformation: The Second Way of Knowing. *Southern Folklore* 47: 33–44.

Zacharias, Wolfgang, ed. 1990. *Zeitphänomen Musealisierung: Das Verschwinden der Gegenwart und die Konstruktion der Erinnerung.* Essen: Klartext.

Zender, Matthias, ed. 1959–1964. *Atlas der deutschen Volkskunde: Auf Grund der von 1929–1935 durchgeführten Sammlungen.* Marburg: N. G. Elwert.

Zengotita, Thomas de. 1989. Speakers of Being: Romantic Refusion and Cultural Anthropology. In George W. Stocking, Jr., ed., *Romantic Motives: Essays on Anthropological Sensibility,* History of Anthropology, vol. 6, pp. 74–123. Madison: University of Wisconsin Press.

Zipes, Jack. 1988. *The Brothers Grimm: From Enchanted Forests to the Modern World*. New York: Routledge.

Zumwalt, Rosemary L. 1988. *American Folklore Scholarship: A Dialogue of Dissent*. Bloomington: Indiana University Press.

Zumwalt, Rosemary L. 1992. *Wealth and Rebellion: Elsie Clews Parsons, Anthropologist and Folklorist*. Urbana: University of Illinois Press.

Index

Abolitionism: and authenticity, 92–93; and Emerson, 240–42*n2*

Abrahams, Roger D., 21, 143, 208–9, 223; on enactment, 196; on Scott, 244*n29;* on "simple forms," 256*n12;* and philosophical traditions, 256*n13;* on folklore definition, 257*n20*

Abschied vom Volksleben, 170, 174–76

Academic folklore: guiding preservation, 105; search for legitimation, 129. *See also* academic/lay dichotomy; folkloristics; *Volkskunde*

Academic/lay dichotomy, 95–96, 98–102, 168; in Hoffmann-Krayer, 103; in America, 128–31. *See also* applied folklore

Adorno, Theodor, 157, 182–83; critique of Heidegger, 19; on origin, 233*n28*

Aesthetics: relation to existential philosophy, 20; communal aesthetics as core of folkloristics, 20; and politics, 20; 236–37*n29;* in verbal art restoration, 203; in English and German Romanticism, 241*n3*

African-American. *See* black culture

Alienation, 8, 97, 124, 151, 172, 184; and Lowell, 78; and Child, 88; linked to *Volkskunde's* ideology, 174; as "original sin," 185

Allen, William F., 91–92

Am Ur-Quell, 99

American Folklore Society, 122–24; and regional societies, 130–31

American higher education, 76–77. *See also* disciplines, university

Anderson, Benedict, 245*n8*

Anthropology: historiography of, 4; role of authenticity in, 17; role in AFS, 123, 142; as social action, 172. *See also Völkerkunde*

Anxiety: late 20th ct., 10; in early scientific methods, 66

Applied folklore: seen as spoiling agent, 96; scholarly participation in, 102–4, 245*n13;* differentiated from science, 116; importance in early American folkloristics, 150; in folklorism discourse, 179; in Hymes' social convictions, 200; theoretical vibrancy of public folkloristics, 217, 259*n39,* 260*n44;* interdependence with academic folklore, 245–46*n14;* and politics of public programming, 258–59*n33. See also* academic/lay dichotomy, genuine/spurious dichotomy

Appropriation: of black expressive forms, 91

Archive of American folksong, 145–46, 149

Arnim, Achim von, 43

Art history, 4

Art song and folksong, 109, 114, 145. *See also Kunstpoesie, Naturpoesie*

Artifactualization: of culture, 5; and Stewart, 48; in Grimms, 54

Atlas project, 162; limitations, 174; Nazi interest in, 250*n7*

Authenticity: and market, 1, 9, 17, 62, 139, 227; in everyday life, 3; and culture concept, 4; and folklore's subject, 5, 15, 50; elusive nature of, 6; rhetoric of, 6; and experience, 7, 13, 54; material represen-